MONOGRAPHS OF
THE INSTITUTE OF EGYPTIAN ART
AND ARCHAEOLOGY, 1

SERIES EDITOR
William J. Murnane

FRAGMENTS OF
A SHATTERED VISAGE:

The Proceedings of the International Symposium of

Ramesses the Great

EDITED BY
Edward Bleiberg
and
Rita Freed

WITH THE TECHNICAL ASSISTANCE OF
Anna Kay Walker

Memphis State
University

Memphis, Tennessee
1991

ISBN 0-9636816-0-5

"I met a traveller from an antique land

Who said: 'Two vast and trunkless legs of stone

Stand in the dust...

Near them, on the sand,

Half sunk, a shatter'd visage lies..."'

P. B. Shelley, *Ozymandyas*

TABLE OF CONTENTS

ACKNOWLEDGEMENTS

Fragments of a Shattered Visage: The Proceedings of the International Symposium on Ramesses the Great is the result of the joint efforts of many people. The symposium itself was held in April, 1987 at the Fogelman Executive Center on the campus of Memphis State University. It was made possible through a grant from the National Endowment for the Humanities, a Federal Agency, through the office of Programs in Museums and Historical Organizations. The Institute of Egyptian Art and Archaeology is very grateful to the National Endowment for the Humanities for its support.

This publication was made possible through funds of the Center of Excellence program of the State of Tennessee. This program is the primary funding source for the Institute of Egyptian Art and Archaeology. The IEAA is a component of the Department of Art at Memphis State University.

Many people gave their time and energy to this project. The editors gratefully acknowledge the help of Anna Kay Walker, Curator of Education for the IEAA, who cheerfully aided in the technical aspects of producing the manuscript. Special thanks goes to Annette Webb, Secretary at the IEAA, who typed the entire manuscript. Thanks also to Paula Wewers, who arranged the plates and to Dr. Alberte Ungar, who helped with French language proofreading. Any errors, are of course, the responsibility of the editors.

EDITOR'S NOTE

The editors have attempted to keep editorial intrusions to a minimum in this volume. For that reason, each author's documentation procedures, both in footnote style and in abbreviations, have been left intact. Whatever is lost in uniformity, it is hoped, will be gained in accuracy.

GRAECO-ROMAN USES AND ABUSES OF RAMESSIDE TRADITIONS[1]

Robert S. Bianchi

For both historians[2] and art historians[3] alike, the arrival of Alexander the Great into Egypt late in the year 332 B.C. marks the end of pharaonic civilization and the beginning of a new, and in some ways different, cultural epoch, one dominated by the Hellenistic background of Egypt's Macedonian ruling class. Such a view, however, implies the immediate rejection of all things pharaonic and the concomitant acceptance of everything Hellenistic by all sectors of the population. And that certainly is a view which cannot be maintained.[4] While it is true that Alexander the Great and the Ptolemies after him were responsible for introducing new elements into the culture of pharaonic Egypt, it is becoming increasingly evident that the modern scholar, and not the Egyptian living during the Graeco-Roman Period, might be the one who cannot factor out the traditional from the novel in the cultural expressions of this particular period. This symposium is, therefore, a convenient forum in which to explore the extent to which the Egyptians of the Graeco-Roman Period knew and understood their Ramesside past and to suggest possible ways by which that awareness might have been transmitted. I should like, therefore, to pass in review four categories of Ramesside monuments known to the Egyptians of the Graeco-Roman Period. Such a review will reveal the rather incomplete state of our present evidence and will, simultaneously, caution one against drawing sweeping generalizations about cultural dislocations and ruptures caused by the Hellenistic, and later Roman, presence in Egypt.

To the first category belong usurpations[5] and appropriations of actual Ramesside monuments by the Egyptians of the Graeco-Roman Period. Such malpractices characterize almost every aspect of ancient Egypt's long history and are not unique to this period. Many of these instances were expeditiously effected for the mere sake of convenience. To this category belongs the reuse of the tomb of Touy, the mother of Ramesses II himself, in the Valley of the Queens, which served as a convenient sepulcher for Egyptian families during the reigns of Ptolemy III Euergetes I and Ptolemy IV Philopator.[6] Occasionally, a

---

1 I wish to thank the administration of the Institute of Egyptian Art and Archaeology at Memphis State University for sponsoring this symposium and Dr. Rita Freed for the kind invitation to participate in it.

2 A. Gardiner, *Egypt of the Pharaohs - An Introduction* (Oxford 1961), 378-383.

3 C. Aldred, *Egyptian Art in the Days of the Pharaohs 3100-320 B.C.* (New York 1980), 240.

4 A.K. Bowman, *Egypt after the Pharaohs 332 B.C. - A.D. 642* (London 1986), 30-32, 124, *passim*; J.G. Griffiths, "Egyptian Nationalism in the Edfu Temple Texts," in J. Ruffle, G.A. Gaballa, and K.A. Kitchen (eds.), *Glimpses of Ancient Egypt: Studies in Honor of H.W. Fairman* (Warminster 1979), 74 ff; N. Lewis, *Life in Egypt under Roman Rule* (Oxford 1983), 198; and A.B. Lloyd, "Nationalist Propaganda in Ptolemaic Egypt," *Zeitschrift für Alte Geschichte* 21 (1982), 33-55.

5 See also the discussion of T.G.H. James in his remarks contained in the closing paper of this volume.

6 Chr. Leblanc, "Une collaboration franco-égyptienne dans la Vallée des Reines, pour l'enregistrement et la protection des tombeaux brûles," in N.-C. Grimal (ed.), *Prospection et sauvegarde des Antiquitiés de l'Egypte--Actes de la Table Ronde organisée à l'occasion*

Ramesside statue might be removed from its original position and be re-erected without altering its inscriptions in a Graeco-Roman sanctuary as the archaeological context of the statue of one Amenmose in the attitude of a standard bearer which was found in Cyrene demonstrates.[7] More common, however, was the practice of usurping Ramesside royal monuments for use by the Ptolemaic kings themselves. The above-named Ptolemies usurped the now-missing Ramesside colossi which they incorporated into their renovations of the Propylon at Karnak North.[8] In the Luxor Temple that same Ptolemy IV made repairs to the Ramesside Colonnade.[9] There is, however, nothing unusual or striking about any of the phenomena just described.

When, on the other hand, one looks more closely at examples such as the Ptolemaic repairs to the First Pylon of the Temple of Mut at Karnak, one asks whether the Egyptians of that period had any deep knowledge of their Ramesside past at all. There, on the western side of the corridor of the First Pylon, the name of Ramesses VI was incorrectly restored as that of Amenhotep III,[10] presumably occasioned by a cursory glance at what was then preserved of the figure of Maat which resulted in the erroneous conclusion about the name so-written. From examples such as this, one might conclude that the Egyptians of the Graeco-Roman Period were only vaguely aware of their Ramesside past and cavalierly adopted, reused, or appropriated such monuments as suited their immediate needs or whims. Such evidence would certainly affirm past scholarly opinion about the Bentresh Stele,[11] the anomalies of which, in this context, accord well with the observations made regarding the Ptolemaic repair in the corridor of the First Pylon of the Temple of Mut at Karnak.

Such assessments, however, are constantly in need of review because of the ever-changing picture of the evidence developed by continued excavations. Members of the Epigraphic Survey of the University of Chicago recently discovered over thirty fragments of a dismantled wall in front of the First Pylon of the Luxor Temple which belonged to a recension, if one will, of the Bentresh Stele edited during Dynasty XXX.[12] It was,

---

du centenaire de l'IFAO, 8-12 Janvier 1981 (Cairo 1981), 36-42; and the presentation of C. Desroches-Noblecourt in this volume.

7 A. Rowe, *New Light on Aegypto-Cyrenaean Relations* (Cairo 1948), 64-68, and pl. XIV, where both the name of the owner and the dating of the statue are incorrect. The owner has now been identified as one Amenmese, owner of Theban Tomb 373, whose *flourit* spans the reigns of Sety I and Ramesses II, as established by C. Chadefaud, *Les Statues porte-enseignes de l'Egypte ancienne (1580-1085) - Signification et insertion dans le culte du ka royal* (Paris 1982), 112-113, no. PE L. 2.

8 P. Barguet and J. Leclant, *Karnak-Nord* IV (1949-1951) (Cairo 1954), 44, 45, and figs. 75 and 77a-b.

9 Cl. Traunecker, "Amon de Louqsor," 61-63; and J. Quaegebeur, "Louqsor sous les Ptolemées," 63, both in *Dossiers/Histoire et Archéologie - Egypte: Louqsor, Temple du ka royal* 101 (January 1986).

10 Unpublished; I wish to thank Charles C. Van Siclen, III, for sharing this observation of his with me.

11 Paris, Musée du Louvre C 284: S. Donadoni, "Per la data della 'Stele di Bentres'," *MDAIK* 15 (1957), 47-50, for a convenient synopsis of the issue. See also the comments by T.G.H. James in his concluding remarks in this volume.

12 L. Bell, "Une nouvelle version de l'inscription de Bekhtan de Ramsès II et la fête d'Opet

apparently, this version upon which the known Ptolemaic edition was based. The Bentresh Stele, then, belongs to the second category of monuments, those belonging to the Ramesside Period and which were, themselves, transmitted to the Graeco-Roman Period in altered form through the agency of an intervening dynasty. To this category, as well, belongs the Ptolemaic practice of incorporating into the cartouches of its monarchs confronted, anthropomorphic signs.[13] This convention occurs first on the sealings of Amenhotep III, is rampant during the Ramesside Period, particularly in the inscriptions of Ramesses II, and then apparently disappears, only to be revived again during Dynasty XXX, from which period the Ptolemies adopt the practice. The close ties between the Ramesside Period and Dynasty XXX can be seen at Iseion[14] and similar sites where the Sebennytic kings began rebuilding Ramesside projects, which were ultimately completed by the kings of the early Ptolemaic Period.[15] An examination, therefore, of the monuments in this second category would seem to reinforce conclusions drawn from a study of those in the first, namely that the Egyptians of the Graeco-Roman Period had but a second-hand knowledge of Ramesside monuments and that that knowledge was filtered through to them by their own use of monuments of Dynasty XXX.[16]

Monuments in the third category seem, however, to suggest a more intimate knowledge of and respect for certain Ramesside traditions. So, for example, one is surprised to learn that the principal route used from the Temple of Horus at Edfu to that of Hathor at Dendera is perpendicular to the temple's main axis. That route, upon which one of the major festivals of the temple was celebrated, is oriented with and incorporates the remains of the pylon of Ramesses III at Edfu, built some six hundred years earlier.[17] Equally unexpected is the attestation of a prophet of the statues of Merenptah by a member of the Memphite clergy of the second century B.C.[18] These monuments imply a first-hand knowledge of aspects of

dans la légende tardive," *Dossiers/ Histoire et Archéologie - Egypte: Louqsor, Temple du ka royal* 101 (January 1986), 24; and E. S. Meltzer, "The Ancient Egyptian Contribution to Fantastic Literature," *BAKKA Magazine* (Fall 1977), 38, *passim*, for a more recent interpretation of this stele; and D. Devaudhelle, "Notes sur la stèle de Bentresh," *RdE* 37 (1987), 149-50.

13 H.G. Fischer, *Egyptian Studies II - The Orientation of Hieroglyphs, Part I: Reversals* (New York 1977), 11.

14 E. Naville, *The Shrine of Saft el Henneh and the Land of Goshen (1885)* (London 1887), 4.

15 G. Steindorff, "Reliefs from the Temple of Sebennytos and Iseion in American Collections," *The Journal of The Walters Art Gallery* VII-VIII (1944-1945), 38-59.

16 The use of the rebus in the group sculpture of Nectanebo II under the falcon (New York, The Metropolitan Museum of Art 34.2.1: Aldred, op. cit., p. 237, and fig. 196; see, too, the comments of Ali Radwan in his contribution to this volume, is likewise indebted to the Ramesside tradition for such visual puns as seen at Abu Simbel in the representation of the figure over the central doorway and in the statue group of Ramesses II as a child under the protection of Haroun (Cairo, The Egyptian Museum JE 64735): R. Freed, *Ramesses the Great - An Exhibition in The City of Memphis* (Memphis 1987), 72 and 130-131, respectively.

17 S. Cauville, *Edfou* (Cairo 1984), 7-8.

18 London, The British Museum 378: E. Otto, "Eine memphitische Priesterfamilie des 2. Jhr. v. Chr.," *ZÄS* 81 (1956), 118 ff., where the name of the owner is misread.

the Ramesside Period as does the painted ceiling from a tomb at Atfieh[19] which evokes the astronomical ceilings of the Ramesside royal tombs, that of Sety I being a good example,[20] rather than the expected type, exemplified by the Zodiac at Dendera[21] which belongs to the tradition used in other private tombs of the period.[22] It is possible, therefore, that examples in this category were based on actual Ramesside monuments as the following clearly shows.

The Museum at Roanne possesses a fragment of a sarcophagus with a very unusual depiction of the goddess Qadesh, who was extremely popular during the Ramesside Period.[23] On stylistic grounds this object has been assigned to the Graeco-Roman Period. Even a cursory glance at the principal figure reveals how maladroitly it is rendered. This stylistic peculiarity might be explained by the fact that, because there are so few images of Qadesh known between the Ramesside and Graeco-Roman Periods,[24] the artist in question had only a vague familiarity with a prototype. Such, however, is not the case. This sarcophagus fragment appears to be based on an actual Ramesside stele now in Paris in

For a more recent discussion of this piece and its owner, Herieus, see D. Wildung, *Die Rolle aegyptischer Könige im Bewusstsein ihrer Nachwelt, Teil I: Posthume Quelle über die Könige der ersten vier Dynastie* (Berlin 1969), 19, note 10; J. Quaegebeur, "Documents concerning the Cult of Arsinoe Philadelphus at Memphis," *JNES* 30 (1971), 253 ff.; and *idem*, "Inventaire des stèles funéraires memphites d'époque ptolémaique," *CdE* 49 (1974), 67, note 16. Refer also to the comments made in their respective papers in this volume by both D. O'Connor and K.A. Kitchen, regarding the architectural activities of Merenptah at Memphis.

19 G. Daressy, "Tombeau ptolémaïque à Atfieh," *ASAE* 2 (1902), 160-180, esp. 175 ff.

20 Theban Tomb 17: K. Lange and M. Hirmer, *Aegypten: Architektur - Plastik - Malerei - in drei Jahrtausenden* (Munich 1975), fig. 217 (top).

21 Paris, Musée du Louvre D 38: L. Kakosy, *Egyiptoms es Antik Csillaghit* (Budapest 1978), pl. 2; for the fascinating post-pharaonic history of this monument, see (Anonymous), "Le Zodiaque de Dendereh sera 'prêtre' par la France à l'Egypte," *Cahiers d'histoire égyptienne* Serie III, fasc. I (November 1950), 432-433; (Anonymus), "(Tierkreis von Dendera)," *Archiv für Orientforschung* 161 (1951), 167; and J.T. Irwin, "The Symbol of the Hieroglyphs in the American Renaissance," *American Quarterly* 26, 2 (1974), 105, for a discussion of this zodiac as employed by H. Melville in his novel *Moby Dick*. It is, nevertheless, of interest to note that elsewhere in the inscriptions of the Temple of Dendera, the list of decans follows Ramesside models; see G. Daressy, "Une ancienne liste des decans égyptiens," *ASAE* 1 (1900), 79-90.

22 *Inter alia*, F.W. von Bissing, "Tombeaux d'époque romain à Akhmin-lettre ouverte au Dr. Etienne Drioton," *ASAE* 50 (1950), 562.

23 Apparently without any inventory number: J. Leibovitch, "Une Imitation d'époque gréco-romain d'une stèle de la déesse Qadech," *ASAE* 41 (1942), 77-81.

24 A. Mariette, *Karnak - Etude topographique et archéologique* (Cairo 1875), Text, p. 65, and Plates, pl. 43. The line drawing here cited, according to the notes penciled into his own copy by Charles Edwin Wilbour which is now in the Wilbour Library of Egyptology, indicates that even less than what Mariette published was still preserved at the time of Wilbour's visit to the Temple of Mut at Karnak in May, 1881, in which this monument, from the time of Taharqa, was then found. Wilbour's notes also indicate that the plate as published in that volume is reversed.

terms of both the composition of the scene and in the replication of the names and titles of the Ramesside individuals on the original.[25] To my knowledge, no one has called the Roanne fragment into question with regard to its authenticity. This piece, therefore, belongs to the fourth category of monuments, those which are demonstrably direct and accurate copies of Ramesside monuments. And many of those Ramesside monuments are themselves quite obscure and appear to have survived to this day by chance.

Of all the monuments in this fourth category, papyri are the most important. Vandier has shown conclusively that the Ramesside *Hymnen an das Diadem der Pharaonen*, preserved in the *Papyrus Chester Beatty* VIII, is known in at least four variants, two still unpublished on the walls of the Graeco-Roman temple at Elkab and one each at Edfu and at Philae.[26] Yoyotte had earlier shown how an inscription of Ptolemy X at Edfu was itself based on an extremely rare passsage in the *Great Harris Papyrus*, wherein the campaigns of Ramesses III against the Peoples of the Sea are recounted.[27] One might, I suppose, suggest that both of these papyri as preserved today were the actual sources of the quotations thereof appearing on the walls of those great Graeco-Roman temples. Such a possibility is, however, remote. It seems more reasonable to posit that there were available to the temple scribes of the Graeco-Roman Period archives which could be consulted as the needs arose. Those needs were not necessarily limited to random selections of what might be termed famous quotations of the past. The examples just cited belong to an enlarged category of such quotations as these additional examples will reveal.

In a pioneering article, Derchain had formulated his theory about the *grammaire du temple* and later employed as a model for his definition correspondences between certain scenes on the pylons of Medinet Habu and Edfu.[28] There he saw strict correspondences and direct relationships between both the depiction of the mountains of *Bakhou* and *Manou* and their accompanying inscriptions, as well as between the scenes and texts of the dispatching of the foe and the hunting of the wild bulls on the walls of the same two temples. He accounted for their differences in terms of the evolution of religious ideas over time.[29] In light of Derchain's contribution, the copying cited by Vandier and Yoyotte is understandable. Those copies are part of the broader picture of the development of

---

25 Paris, Musée du Louvre C 86: Leibovitch, loc. cit. and Freed, op. cit., 56 (top right). That the Egyptians of the Graeco-Roman Period knew Ramesside monuments first-hand as tourists is evident not only from the remarks of Strabo and their graffiti left on such monuments as the Colossus of Memnon at Thebes, but also from investigations of J.G. Milne, "Greek and Roman Tourists in Egypt," *JEA* 3 (1916), 76 ff.; M. Muszynski, "Hécatée d'Abdère, Diodore de Sicule et l'Egypte," *Studia Aegyptiaca* 2 (1976), 89 ff.; M. Rostovtzeff, "Greek Sightseers in Egypt," *JEA* 14 (1928), 13 ff.; and M.P. Speidel, "Two Greek Graffiti in the Tomb of Rameses V," *CdE* 49 (1974), 384 ff.

26 J. Vandier, "Quatre Variants ptolémaiques d'un hymne ramesside," *ZÄS* 93 (1966), 132-143.

27 J. Yoyotte, "Un Souvenir des campagnes de Ramsès III au temple d'Edfou," *Kêmi* 12 (1952), 92-93.

28 P. Derchain, "Remarques sur la décoration des pylones ptolémaïques," *BiOr* 18 (1961), 46-48; and *idem*, "Réflections sur la décoration des pylones," *BSFdE* 46 (1966), 17-24. See also the remarks of D. O'Connor in this volume regarding the association of *Bakhou* and *Manou* with temple pylons.

29 *Ibid.*

Egyptian religion in the Graeco-Roman Period, a development which goes back at least to Ramesside times for its origin.

When regarded in this context, certain peculiarities of the Ptolemaic and later Roman temples can be better understood as the climax of a process of which the Ramesside Period was a part. Both Jaquet[30] and Berlandini[31] refer to an unusual libation basin of the Ramesside Period which is associated with the god Ptah as the one who hears prayers and with numerous "ear stelai" of the New Kingdom. These are related in turn to the phenomenon whereby the pious of low social status might still beseech a deity for assistance while being denied access to certain areas of the sanctuary. Such supplication could be made at enclosure walls or at other areas of the temple. At Karnak, during the Ramesside Period, the area serving the requirements of the cult of Amun-re Who Hears Prayers was protected by a balustrade, and that area was later modified under the reign of Ptolemy VIII Euergetes II.[32] This same Ptolemaic king seems to have incorporated the original Ramesside feature of a balustrade into his own modification of the temple at Kom Ombo.[33] Final form was given to this last expression of popular religion at Kom Ombo during the reign of the Roman Emperor Trajan when the so-called *rélief cultuel* was incorporated into the design of the rear of the temple.[34]

The fact that some Egyptians did abuse and misuse aspects of their Ramesside cultural heritage during the Graeco-Roman Period is now obvious. It would, however, be a gross distortion of the evidence to focus exclusively on those circumstances. A careful examination of the record reveals that other Egyptians of the same period of time were keenly aware of their past, particularly that of the Ramesside era. Those Egyptians had access to monuments and/or documents which, in light of our present knowledge, are known today only from isolated randomly preserved papyri. This circumstance strongly suggests that there may well have been one or more archives available to the members of the priesthoods of Graeco-Roman Egypt in which a cleric could find passsages appropiate

---

30 J. Jaquet, "Un Bassin de libation du Nouvel Empire dédié à Ptah. Première Partie. L'architecture," *MDAIK* 16 (1958), 161-167.

31 J. Berlandini, "La Chapelle de Sethi I: Nouvelles découvertes," *BSFdE* 99 (1984), 28 ff. I wish to thank E. Werner for making available to me a copy of this article which was missing from my library. See, too, the comments by Ali Radwan in his contribution to this symposium regarding ear stelai.

32 P. Barguet, "L'Obélisque de Saint-Jean-de-Lateran dans le temple de Ramsès II à Karnak," *ASAE* 50 (1950), 269-280.

33 A. Gutbub, "Eléments ptolémaiques préfigurant le rélief cultuel de Kom Ombo," in H. Maehler and V.M. Strocka (eds.), *Das ptolemaische Aegypten* (Mainz 1978), 165-176.

34 The comment by Gutbub, *loc. cit.*, to the effect that the appearance of such cultic reliefs may be due to foreign influence, has to be questioned in light of a similar architectural feature briefly published by Ahmed Kadry from the Middle Kingdom in *Alam al Bena* 70 (June 1986), 2-3. Moreover, from the graffiti on the exterior wall of the Ptah Temple at Karnak North, the needs of those denied access to the temple proper were served, as explained by J. Quaegebeur, "Prêtres et cultes Thébains à la lumière de documents égyptiens et grecs," *BSFdE* 70-71 (1974), 49; the suggested wooden chapel there (*loc. cit.*) may very well have been instead a balustrade. The area in the vicinity of the image of Hathor at the rear of her temple at Dendera may also have fulfilled a similar function.

to his immediate requirements. Such prelates ought not to be regarded as pedantic forerunners of T.S. Elliot, who went rummaging through dark and dusty reading rooms in an effort to resurrect an obscure citation from the tenets of a decaying atrophied religion. On the contrary, the evidence now marshalled points undeniably to the existence of a learned priesthood attached to the great temples of Upper Egypt during the Graeco-Roman Period - a select cadre,[35] to be sure, but one which regarded its members as the direct linear descendants of their religious forefathers of earlier ages.[36] These prelates understood their past and used that past, transmitted in part by such archives, as the basis for the continued vibrant development of ancient Egypt's pharaonic religion.

While this forum is not an appropriate venue in which to debate the question of such scriptoria,[37] two examples, belonging to the fourth category as defined above, at least suggest the possibility of their existence and use. The first is a hieratic papyrus in the collections of The Brooklyn Museum,[38] thought to have come from just such a scriptorium datable to the late fourth or early third century B.C.,[39] which contains a prophylactic text of the *Stp-s3*-rite exactly parallel to one found on a statue of Ramesses III now in Cairo.[40] Aspects of that rite are also found among the inscriptions in the temple of Edfu.[41] The second example is that offered by Derchain regarding passages of the conflict between Horus and Seth. Passages of that cycle in the inscriptions, again in the temple at Edfu, incorporate sections of *Papyrus Chester Beatty* I, passages which have also been identified in a second papyrus excavated at Memphis.[42] A model based on these two examples of the fourth category suggests the conclusions to be drawn from such an inquiry are simply that the Graeco-Roman temples of Upper Egypt are more clearly indebted to Ramesside

---

35 S. Sauneron, *The Priests of Ancient Egypt* (New York 1969), 9-27 and 113-170.

36 On this issue, see particularly, D.B. Redford, *Pharaonic King-Lists, Annals, and Day-Books: A Contribution to the Study of the Egyptian Sense of History* (Mississauga 1986), whose lead I follow in eschewing the use of the word "archaizing" in such matters.

37 E.A.E. Reymond, "From the contents of a temple library," *Aegyptiaca Treverensia* 2 (1983), 81-83; idem, *From the Ancient Egyptian Hermetic Writings* (Vienna 1977), which treats the libraries of the Temple of Sobek in the Faiyum; V. Wessetzky, "Gedanken über die Bearbeitung der altägyptishen Bibliothek," *GM* 25 (1977), 89-93; idem, "Die Bücherliste des Temples von Edfu und Imhotep," *GM* 83 (1984), to which add the remarks of Cauville, *op. cit.*, 17-18 and 74.

38 Brooklyn 47.218.138: J.-C. Goyon, "Un Parallèle tardif d'une formule des inscriptions de la statue prophylactique de Ramsès III au Musée du Caire," *JEA* 57 (1971), 154-159.

39 For a discussion of the lot of papyri to which this one belongs, see S. Sauneron, *Le Papyrus Magique illustré de Brooklyn (Brooklyn 47.218.156)* (Brooklyn 1970), vii-ix and 3-5; and M. Bierbrier, *The Tomb-Builders of the Pharaohs* (London 1982), 35, for a similar library from the Ramesside Period.

40 Cairo J.E. 69771: Goyon, *loc. cit.*

41 *Ibid.*, 158-159.

42 P. Derchain, "Sur la Composition du Mythe d'Horus," *RdE* 26 (1974), 13-15; and H.S. Smith, "La Mère d'Apis. Fouilles récentes de l'Egypt Exploration Society à Saqqara-Nord," *BSFdE* 70-71 (1974), 26-27.

traditions than one has recognized, heretofore, and that that indebtedness is due, at least in part, to the crucial role played by scriptoria and their papyri in the transmission of texts.

The threads of the Graeco-Roman Period are, therefore, so deeply woven into the fabric of ancient Egypt that it would be an extreme disservice to the discipline of Egyptology to cut off and discard any swatches thereof from the discussions of pharaonic Egypt, a nation which did not die with the arrival of Alexander the Great. As the late Serge Sauneron once remarked, certain eras of the Graeco-Roman Period *"correspond à une véritable renaissance spirituelle des collèges sacerdotaux,"*[43] and that spirit of intellectual vitality relied upon a profound understanding of Egypt's Ramesside past.

---

43 S. Sauneron, *L'Ecriture figurative dans les textes d'Esneh* (Cairo 1982), 10.

ELEMENTS OF STABILITY AND INSTABILITY IN RAMESSIDE EGYPT: THE SUCCESSION TO THE THRONE

M. L. Bierbrier

The ruler, the son of Re, was positioned at the apex of the social and political structure of ancient Egypt. For the system of government to function smoothly, it was essential for the office of pharaoh to pass quickly and effectively from one generation to the next without more than a momentary pause in the state machinery to carry out the necessary formalities. This course of action seems to have been largely accomplished during the Eighteenth Dynasty when the succession to the throne appears to have been settled without undue fuss, although there were undoubtedly some minor problems such as the accession of Thutmose I to his childless relation Amenhotep I and the usurpation of Hatshepsut. Unfortunately, we do not have enough information about the inner workings of the court in the Eighteenth Dynasty to compare the procedures in detail with later Ramesside practice. It is probable that the heir was usually designated as such during his father's lifetime, but no actual evidence has survived to confirm this assumption, apart from the dubious coregency of Amenhotep II with his father and the even more dubious coregency of Akhenaten with Amenhotep III.[1]

Indeed, references to princes in the reigns of their fathers are extremely scarce compared to those of royal princesses, but that may only be due to the accidents of survival of material. Fortunately, the red herring of the heiress concept, by which it was thought that the new king had to marry his sister to legitimize his rule, has now been shown to be without foundation and can be dismissed from further consideration.[2] Several princes, Ahmose and Siamun sons of Ahmose I, Amenmose son of Thutmose I, Amenemhat son of Thutmose III, and Thutmose son of Amenhotep III, bear the title, *s3 nsw smsw*, "king's eldest son," but that need not necessarily imply that they were the designated heirs, although it may well do so.[3] Certainly, the title of *sem*-priest of Ptah does not indicate an heir, as some have supposed.[4] The best that can be said is that the heir is likely to have been the eldest surviving son of a queen or perhaps the eldest surviving son by any wife if the queen had no heirs. The unexpected succession of Thutmose IV may have been due to the untimely death of the designated heir and not necessarily to a surprise usurpation. There may have been many more unrecorded occurrences of this nature.

The military played an important role in the political structure of the New Kingdom. The Eighteenth Dynasty was born out of military conflict with the Hyksos, and subsequent military success enhanced the prestige of the throne. With the confusion consequent to the Amarna Period and the apparent extinction in the male line of the ruling dynasty, as far as we know, the role of the army would appear to have become crucial in determining the succession to the throne. After the ephemeral Ay, who may have been related to the preceding dynasty, it comes as no surprise when the chief military commander, Horemheb, occupied the throne. He apparently tried to facilitate his new role by marrying a relation of

1 W.J. Murnane, *Ancient Egyptian Coregencies*, (Chicago, 1977), 44-57, 123-68.

2 G. Robins, *GM* 62, (1983), 67-77.

3 B. Schmitz, *Untersuchungen zum Titel S3-Njswt "Königssohn"*, (Bonn, 1976), 288, 290, 292, 295.

4 D. Redford, *JEA* 51, (1965), 114, note 4.

the old dynasty after his succession, since he apparently had a different wife in private life.[5] Horemheb seems to have enjoyed a long and prosperous reign. He certainly prided himself on restoring stability and order to the land which had been racked by civil dissension in the Amarna Period. Under these circumstances, he was obviously bound to try to ensure a peaceful succession to the throne on his demise, especially as his wives apparently failed to provide him with any heirs of his own body. In the event, the succession passed off smoothly as the Crown devolved upon the vizier, Paramesses, the most powerful and influential official in the country, who had no doubt ensured, in advance, that there would be no opposition to his accession. Since he had evidently been a military officer earlier in his career and probably a companion-in-arms of Horemheb, he undoubtedly had the backing of the army in assuming the Crown.[6] Although it does not appear that he had been technically designated as heir, there was certainly a precedent for the vizier to succeed to the throne, as in the case of Amenemhat I.

Unlike his immediate predecessor, Ramesses I had the inestimable advantage of having a son who was moreover adult and active. Although he himself lasted barely more than a year, the succession of his son, Sety I, was apparently without incident. If the vizier Sety of the Year 400 Stela was indeed the future Sety I, then he, like his father before him, had been installed in the most influential office of the land in order to facilitate a peaceful transfer of power when the time came.[7] A question has recently been raised about the position of the mysterious Mehy, who is depicted next to Sety I in various wall-reliefs at Karnak and whose image was later largely expunged by Ramesses II.[8] Might he not have been a possible contender for the throne? Since Sety I himself had a son, it is obvious that he would have destined the future Ramesses II to succeed to the throne, as no pharaoh would have ever dreamed of diverting the succcession away from his own bodily heirs. The reliefs can be seen to represent a favourite courtier or attendant who was easily disposable when Ramesses II wished to invent a place for himself in his father's campaigns, although it is not ruled out that some personal animosity was involved as well.

In fact, Sety I seems to have taken positive action to signal that Prince Ramesses was the designated heir, although much of his action rests, unfortunately, on the word of Ramesses II alone. According to that king, his father bestowed upon him the titles of king's eldest son and rp^ct.[9] This last title makes its first appearance as a clear designation of the crown prince. Ramesses appears with this title and next to his father on reliefs at Karnak and Abydos, but it is not certain that these references are all contemporary with the reign. Ramesses also bears the title, *s3 nsw tpy*, "first king's son," on a stela of his father's reign.[10] However, Sety I went further and installed his son as coregent with his own titulary although not evidently his own year dates.[11] The young Ramesses was, moreover, given

5 G.T. Martin, *The Memphite Tomb of Horemheb, Commander in Chief of Tutankhamun*, (London, 1989), 106.

6 W. Helck, *Zur Verwaltung des Mittleren und Neuen Reichs*, (Leiden, 1958), 308-10, 446-7.

7 W. Helck, *op. cit.*, 310-11, 447.

8 W.J. Murnane, *The Road to Kadesh*, (Chicago, 1985), 163-175.

9 *KRI* II, 327, lines 13-14.

10 *KRI* I, 343; L. Limme, *Stéles Égyptiennes*, (Brussels, 1979), 28-31.

11 K.A. Kitchen, *Pharaoh Triumphant*, (Warminster, 1982), 27-41.

alternative? Our information is too scanty to determine whether or not both Sety I and Ramesses II were only sons. Certainly, there are no references to any brothers who might have presented problems. On the basis of their names, it would seem that both Sety I and Ramesses II were, indeed, the eldest sons of their respective fathers.

Ramesses II seems to have complicated the succession by fathering innumerable sons and living to an interminable age. However, like his father before him, he took great care to designate a crown prince although not to raise him to the rank of coregent. His eldest son, Amenherkhepeshef, alias Amenherwenmef, whose mother was the chief queen Nefertari, was the first heir and seems to have held this office for the first third of the reign. He bore the titles rp^ct, royal scribe, general, and king's eldest son and was depicted next to his father in a relief at Abydos and on statues where he appears alone or with female relations and is clearly and openly marked out as heir apparent.[12] It is perhaps wise to consider now the mysterious figure of Prince Sethherkhepeshef, who features in diplomatic correspondence to the king of the Hittites and who appears on several monuments with the titles of rp^ct, royal scribe, and general.[13] It has been speculated that he was a younger son of the king named as crown prince to replace his deceased older brother, Amenherkhepeshef. However, his name does not appear in the list of the king's first twenty-five sons, although he could conceivably have been born after this list was compiled.[14] It is most unlikely that the king would or, indeed, could bypass his twenty-five sons to promote a junior prince who was apparently functioning around year 21, when the Hittite treaty was concluded. Such an appointment would almost certainly have been a recipe for civil unrest and dynastic instability. In view of other examples in royal names of the interchange between Seth and Amun at this period, such as Prince Sethemwia, alias Amenemwia, it seems logical to view the names, Amenherkhepeshef and Sethherkhepeshef, as variants denoting the one and the same crown prince.

Apparently, unlike previous pharaohs, Ramesses II actively and conspicuously vaunted the position of his heir apparent as well as recording the names and titles of his other sons. The close connection of the dynasty with the military establishment was enhanced by the military titles granted to many of the king's sons, such as general, first charioteer of His Majesty, etc. It is not entirely certain whether some of these titles might have been merely honorific, but some of the princes did, indeed, see military action and may have actually functioned in the roles assigned to them. If so, the links of the princes to the military might, in due course, have contributed to the weakening of the Crown, as other princes might have formed factions powerful enough to challenge the position of the heir designate. No such problem was to face the heir of Ramesses II. The chief obstacle was simply to survive the old man. This Amenherkhepeshef/ Sethherkhepeshef failed to do. The succession then passed to the second son of Ramesses II by Queen Isetnofret, General Ramesses, who bears the title rp^ct on some monuments.[15] He, too, failed to survive his father, and the title of crown prince then passed, apparently, to his full brother, Khaemwese, the king's fourth son. Khaemwese's career is well known as *sem*-priest and later high priest of Ptah, although he also uses the titles, rp^ct ḥry-tp t3wy and rp^ct sty Gb,

---

12 *KRI* II, 509-10, 591, 860, 869.

13 *KRI* II, 914-5; K.A. Kitchen, *op. cit.*, 102.

14 *KRI* II, 859-60, for the list of sons. After the twenty-fifth son, the order is speculative.

15 *KRI* II, 385, 854.

which might tend to indicate that he was briefly heir to the throne. However, some doubt has been cast upon this role by Gomaà.[16]

The undoubted final heir of Ramesses II was his thirteenth son, Merenptah, also by Queen Isetnofret. He appears on reliefs and statues with the titles rp^Ct $ḥry$-tp $t3wy$, general, rp^Ct sty Gb, and kings's eldest son.[17] In his case, there can be no doubt that these titles indicate the heir. It is interesting to note Merenptah's connection with the military. It has been often assumed that Merenptah was now the king's eldest surviving son, but this need not have been the case, as it is equally possible that Merenptah was the eldest surviving son of a queen, and older brothers with less exalted maternal ancestry had been brusquely pushed aside.[18] Merenptah's younger half-brother, Meryatum, son of Queen Nefertari, also used the title rp^Ct but once in combination with $ḥ3ty$-^{C} so not indicating crown prince but a title used by high officials. It is a warning that r^Cpt alone in the title of a prince need not indicate that he was the heir. Meryatum also called himself first son of the king, $s3$ nsw tpy, and he was certainly not the eldest surviving son, although he may have been at that time the eldest surviving son of Queen Nefertari.[19] So, Merenptah may have been the eldest surviving son of Queen Isetnofret but not necessarily the eldest son of the king. Merenptah seems to have assumed quasi-royal power in the last years of his aging father so that his own succession, although delayed, seems to have been unopposed and uneventful.

Merenptah naturally intended that after him the throne should descend to a son, and he certainly had at least one, Sety, whom he clearly designated as his heir. He was accorded the titles of rp^Ct $ḥry$-tp $t3wy$, rp^Ct m st Gb, $ḥrp$ $t3wy$ n $it.f$, general, and king's eldest son and appears next to his father on statues and reliefs.[20] The same procedures which had worked well in the previous reign were put into operation to smooth the succession of Sety II. Yet these were now not enough to secure an untroubled accession, and the dynasty went rapidly to pieces. What went wrong? Obviously, it was not time, since Merenptah reigned long enough to put the succession process into motion and to publicize his choice. This choice was obviously not acceptable to some, since Sety II's claim to rule was challenged by Amenmesses, and the ensuing confusion fatally weakened the dynasty. It is perhaps interesting to speculate that Amenmesses might have been closely related to the dynasty, possibly a son of Merenptah, to launch a sustained challenge to the established heir. Sety II managed to prevail in the end and to secure his kingdom, but not for several years. Naturally, he was most anxious to secure the triumph of his own line, and reliefs in Karnak show that he too had an heir, the rp^Ct $ḥry$-tp $t3wy$, king's eldest son, Sety-Merenptah.[21] However, there was to be no Sety III or Merenptah II. This prince disappears from view, possibly dying before his father, and Sety II was, in fact, succeeded by the mysterious Siptah, whose exact parentage remains unclear. He could have been another son of Sety II or a collateral member of the royal family, but our information is not precise enough to establish his parentage without doubt. Queen Tewosret, the widow of Sety II, followed as the last ruler of the Nineteenth Dynasty, but her reign did not mean that the royal family

---

16 S. Gomaà, *Chaemwese*, (Wiesbaden, 1973), 15-19.

17 *KRI* II, 902-5.

18 R. Stadelmann, *MDAIK* 37, (1981), 463, note 53.

19 *KRI* II, 852, 906-7.

20 *KRI* IV, 49, 56, 59, 67, 82, 90; see also M. Eaton-Krauss, *GM* 50, (1981), 15-21.

21 *KRI* IV, 257-9.

lacked male heirs. The vizier Hori, who was appointed to office under Sety II, was, in fact, a great-grandson of Ramesses II and a grandson of a former Crown Prince Khaemwese.[22] The vizerate had not so long ago been the stepping-stone to the throne itself, but the apparent extinction of the main line of the royal family appears to have elicited no claim from one of the most powerful officials in the land. The throne went elsewhere.

The new pharaoh and founder of the Twentieth Dynasty, Sethnakhte, nowhere indicates his true parentage. If he were an offspring of the Nineteenth Dynasty, one would have expected this fact to have been mentioned by him or by his son, Ramesses III, who consciously and conspicuously aped his great predecessor, Ramesses II. However, no such claims were put forward, probably because they had no basis in fact. The misrule at the end of the Nineteenth Dynasty apparently discredited that line, or so Sethnakhte would have liked us to believe. The description of the chaos at the end of the Nineteenth Dynasty rings slightly hollow when it is noticed that the vizier Hori, a scion of the Nineteenth Dynasty, remained in office through the reign of Sethnakhte and into that of his son, tolerating and tolerated by the new dynasty. It does, indeed, seem odd that one of the chief officials of the previous regime, which was being maligned, was kept in office, especially when his claim to the throne was, perhaps, better than the present occupant. It would obviously be of great interest to know the true story of the advent of the Twentieth Dynasty. Despite his short reign, Sethnakhte was able to ensure the succession of his son without any undue fuss. It has been suggested that Ramesses III could have been a mere child on his accession to the throne, as the inscriptions of his campaigns in his early years might be regarded as rhetorical rather than factual.[23] However, it is extremely unlikely that a mere child would have been able to succeed and successfully hold the throne after a period of turbulence and brief reigns, unless, of course, he, like Siptah, was someone else's puppet. There is no evidence for this. It seems more logical to regard Ramesses III as the adult son of a middle-aged father. As an active young man, he would be in a strong position to strengthen his family's hold on the throne. The fact that this interpretation may not agree with the age estimation of his mummy is, in my opinion, of little consequence, since the various age estimates of other mummies are so at variance with historical facts that one must suspect a failure of some kind in the scientific analysis.

As Ramesses III reigned thirty-two years and had a fairly successful reign, one would have expected him to make some effort to ensure a peaceful succession to the throne. A crown prince is depicted at Medinet Habu with his name left blank, but, as the scenes in which he appears were copied from those of Ramesses II at the Ramesseum, these omissions of the name cannot be regarded as significant. Ramesses III certainly had plenty of sons, and, like Ramesses II, this may have aggravated rather than helped the situation. It has been speculated that Ramesses III deliberately followed his predecessor, Ramesses II, in the naming of his sons and that some of these sons were born prior to his accession to the throne.[24] These two points seem incompatible. The nonentity, Ramesses son of Sethnakhte, would not have been giving his sons grandiose names like Amenherkhepeshef, Khaemwese, etc. Therefore, unless there was a wholesale renaming of children when the Twentieth Dynasty was founded, all of Ramesses III's sons should have been born after the accession of Sethnakhte, at the very least. A tomb survives for the rp^ct $ḥry-tp$ $t3wy$

22 H. De Meulenaere, *Annuaire de l'Institut de Philologie et d'Histoire Orientales et Slaves* 20, (1968–72), 191–6.

23 J.E. Harris and E.F. Wente, *An X-Ray Atlas of the Royal Mummies*, (Chicago, 1980), 263–266.

24 K.A. Kitchen, *JEA* 58, (1972), 186–189.

Amenherkhepeshef, who may have been the eldest son, and also for other sons, two of whom are *s3 nsw tpy*, while Sethherkhepeshef is *s3 nsw smsw*.[25] The former title certainly does not indicate an heir, as the case of Meryatum son of Ramesses II shows. It is possible that the title, king's eldest son, might designate a crown prince, but this is not proved, and the lack of *rp^{c}t* is surprising, if he were the heir. At any rate, the eventual heir was the son, Ramesses, who appears with the titles, general and royal scribe, in the reign of his father and once with that of *rp^{c}t*. Unfortunately, the main source for his position as heir in the latter part of his father's reign, the tomb of Amenemope, was inscribed in his own reign, although there is no reason to doubt the statement concerning his position as designated crown prince.[26] This state of affairs could well explain the Harem Conspiracy as an attempt of one of the princes to divert the succession from the designated heir into his own hands. Its failure indicated the strength of the new dynasty or, at any rate, that of the crown prince who smartly occupied the vacant throne as Ramesses IV.

The question regarding the succession of the monarchs of the rest of the Twentieth Dynasty is complicated by the lack of clear and unequivocal information as to their parentage. The series of short reigns certainly does not indicate a straight father-to-son succession, and it appears more than likely that brothers and uncles may have intervened. The implication seems to be that either a number of pharaohs died without sons to follow them or the country and the royal family would not tolerate the rule of a child at this increasingly unstable time. However, there does not appear to have occurred the internecine fighting within the royal family and high officialdom which seems to have led to the fall of the Nineteenth Dynasty. If there were any intrigue in irregularly obtaining the succession, it was confined to the court, and the accession of each new pharaoh was accomplished with no fuss and accepted by the country at large. Later in the dynasty, the longer reigns imply a more stable situation in the royal family. Indeed, there is a reference to the *rp^{c}t ḥry-tp t3wy*, general, and king's eldest son, Ramesses-Montuherkhepeshef, which indicates that the regular designation of the heir continued when it was possible to do so.[27] The power of the Crown progressively diminished as the dynasty drew to its close, so that the position of heir became as titular as that of pharaoh. The dynasty seems to have died of atrophy rather than lack of physical heirs. The Ramesside era ended not with a bang but a whimper, as far as the royal family was concerned.

---

25 K.A. Kitchen, *JEA* 68, (1982), 118-121.

26 K.A. Kitchen, *op. cit.*, 116-8; *KRI V*, 372-3.

27 K.A. Kitchen, *KRI* VI, 463-5.

RAMESSES - RE WHO CREATES THE GODS

M. Eaton-Krauss

The specialist who would undertake a study of the statuary of Ramesses II is confronted with the initial problem of how to approach the vast quantity of works available for analysis. Sculpture in the round is known in such quantity from the reign of no other king in the entire course of Egyptian history.[1] For the temples of the Ramesside capital, Per-Ramesses alone, the king commissioned more than 50 stone statues, life-size or larger.[2]

The task of compiling even a summary catalogue of the statuary inscribed for Ramesses II is indeed a daunting prospect, in view of the mass of available data. But it is precisely the sheer bulk that provides an unparalleled opportunity to study the fundamental problem of style (chronological and/or regional) and the relationship of style to quality, an issue rarely faced squarely by the art historian who works with material from ancient Egypt.[3]

In his seminal study of ancient Egyptian statuary, J. Vandier made a valiant though ultimately unsuccessful attempt to classify the statues of Ramesses II in three groups.[4] Vandier described his own system as arbitrary and provisional at best; it was intended simply to provide a rudimentary framework for discussing the statuary of the reign. Those statues which impressed Vandier as depicting a youthful ruler he ascribed to a first group. Elegance of contour and finely drawn facial features were characteristic of the statues belonging to this category. In other words, an additional implicit criterion for assignment to the first group was consistent high quality.

Since CG 42142 is one of a very few statues datable with some confidence to the beginning of the reign, it is surprising that Vandier did not include it among the supposed early works. Both textual and iconographic criteria support the dating of the piece among the earliest statues produced following Ramesses' accession.[5] Leaves of the *ished* tree inscribed with the throne name are shown in relief on the statue base, iconography alluding to the assumption of the titulary at the accession (or coronation). The epithets that accompany the throne name in the statue's texts do not include *stp.n-R^c* which became standard in the second regnal year.[6]

---

1 See H. Altenmüller, "Königsplastik", *Lexikon der Ägyptologie* (hereafter: *LÄ*) III, W. Helck - W. Westendorf, eds., Wiesbaden 1980, 574 f. with notes 355-402.

2 So E. Uphill, *The Temples of Per Ramesses*, Warminster 1984, passim.

3 Cf. Altenmüller, op. cit.: "*Der ungewöhnlich hohe Reichtum an plastischen Werken führte allerdings in vielen Fällen zu einer erheblichen Qualitätsminderung, so dass häufig genug...Massenware zu erkennen ist*".

4 *Manuel d'archéologie égyptienne III Les grandes époques. La statuaire*, Paris 1958, 392 ff.

5 *Ramsès le Grand* (exhibition catalogue, Galeries nationales du Grand Palais), Paris 1976, no. 49, 232 ff. (text: R.S. Antelme).

6 For the epithet, see W.J. Murnane, *Ancient Egyptian Coregencies* (*SAOC* 40), Chicago 1977, 63 and passim, with references.

In such statues that depict the king in a semi-prostrate attitude, the ruler does not wear a crown but rather a headcloth (either the *nemes* or the *khat*.[7] Probably aesthetic as well as technical considerations provide the reason why the sculptor eschewed a crown in the context of a semi-prostrate figure.[8] Whereas Egyptian crowns tend to be tall, both *nemes* and *khat* are relatively close-fitting headdresses that follow the contour of the head and do not disturb the horizontal silhouette. If CG 42142 be viewed in its entirety, it becomes clear that such considerations played a decisive role in determining the proportions of the figure itself. No Egyptian possessed such extremely long arms. Similarly, the extended right leg is also relatively long.[9] These proportional peculiarities are not obvious at first glance; only when the statue is subjected to scrutiny, do they become evident. Apparently, the elongation of the limbs is well suited to the attitude portrayed.

Vandier considered Turin 1380 to be the most important piece among the statues depicting the youthful Ramesses.[10] In 1958 when the third volume of the *Manuel* was published, the assignment of the Turin group to Ramesses II was disputed. Vandier freely admitted that there were among his colleagues those who were convinced that Ramesses had usurped the statue from his father. The inscriptions of the statue include the titulary of the king, as well as the names of Queen Nefertari and of the oldest King's-Son Amenherkhepeshef. Careful examination of the texts has shown them to be pristine.[11] If the statue were made under Sety I, then it remained uninscribed until his son's accession.

The royal figure in the Turin group has often been compared to the black granite bust from Tanis CG 616.[12] Consensus claims the pieces are very close in style. Surely both are works of high quality, made of the same material, and both depict the king in the same attitude. The claim that the sculptor "was attentive to the modelling of the torso; even the left breast is delineated beneath the heavy pleating of the tunic"[13] cannot be confirmed in the case of the Tanis bust nor with reference to the Turin statue. The nipples are indeed shown beneath the garment of the Tanis bust (in contrast to Turin 1380) but certainly not as organic elements of the body. Their presence is to be explained by the sculptor's interest in

---

7 Cf., e.g., the representations of two such statues, both evincing the *khat* and depicting Tuthmosis III, in TT 100: N. deG. Davies, *The Tomb of Rekh-mi-Re at Thebes*, New York 1943, pls. 36 and 37. For a comparable actual statue, cf., e.g., the fragment from a statue of Akhenaten, E. Brunner-Traut - H. Brunner, *Die Ägyptische Sammlung der Universität Tübingen*, Mainz 1981, 35 f. with pls. 74-77.

8 In other words, the choice of headgear is appropriate for the composition; contrast the remark in *Ramsès Le Grand*, 236.

9 The extended right leg is restored below the knee, but the proportions are entirely consistent with the length of the limb's preserved portion.

10 Despite the plethora of references in PM II (2nd ed.) 214, good detail photographs of the king's face in this group are rare: see, recently, S. Curto, *L'antico Egitto nel Museo Egizio di Torino*, Turin 1984, 146.

11 J. Yoyotte, *Les trésors des pharaons*, Geneva 1968, 144.

12 For this statue, see the commentary of Terrace in E.L.B. Terrace - H.G. Fischer, *Treasures of the Cairo Museum. From Predynastic to Roman Times*, London 1970, 141 ff. and cf. *Ramsès le Grand*, no. 16, 83 ff. (text: M. Nelson).

13 So Terrace, in *Treasures*, 141, describing CG 616.

detail and patterning, not as a result of his desire to reproduce the interplay of body and drapery. The pleating hardly impresses as belonging to a heavy fabric. It has, in fact, no existence as fabric at all; it is rather simply a pattern applied upon the surface of the undifferentiated torso.[14] In general, a disinterest in modelling is to be observed in the treatment of both bodies. The bent arm and hand with the scepter merge into the chest. In the Tanis bust, the bracelet at the wrist is carefully but flatly rendered. Like the pleating, the bracelet is simply a two-dimensional pattern applied to the surface.

A comparison of the faces of the two statues reveals significant differences that contrast with the similarities of the bodies. Both have slightly bulging eyeballs, but, generally speaking, the eye region of the Turin king is more naturalistically reproduced; the cosmetic strip is lacking and the brows though plastically rendered do not have the abstracted, applied form and appearance of those of the Tanis bust. The lips of the latter are relatively full and somewhat pursed, resulting in a simpering expression alien to the Turin face.

Vandier described the style of the statuary he attributed to a second group as "*epais et lourd*".[15] Many of the sculptures belonging to this group are well over life-size. Figures created on a monumental scale are a hallmark of the reign. Some of them are neither squat nor clumsy. Immediately, the Mit Rahineh colossus springs to mind as one of the most impressive and magnificent works created by the ancient Egyptian sculptor.[16]

The study of the colossi is hampered by the problem of obtaining adequate photographic documentation, because of their very size and since relatively few are now exhibited as the sculptor intended them to be viewed. Discussions of the colossi have focused on their iconography and function, ignoring for the most part their aesthetic qualities. Labib Habachi, for example, made good use of the iconography and inscriptions of several colossi to support his conclusions regarding the deification of Ramesses II.[17] In such a context, an appreciation of the colossi as works of art is perhaps inappropriate. But in the *Propylaean-Kunstgeschichte* where art historical analysis and commentary are to be expected, the colossal statues of Ramesses II are not treated in the first instance as works of art. Instead, the text emphasizes the propagandistic and ideological aspects of the works. For example, in the discussion of the fragmentary colossal bust from the Ramesseum now in the British Museum (BM 19), it is suggested that the natural coloring of the stone was purposefully utilized by the sculptor; "*Die Farbe des Gesteins geht am Hals vom Grau des Körpers zu einem lichten Gelbbraun über, sicherlich ein solarer Anspruch der...Statue.*"[18] The interpretation put forward ignores the fact that traces of the original red-brown painting of the statue's face are still in evidence.[19]

---

14 For this traditional treatment of the relationship of garment to the body it clothes, see the comments of P. Munro, "Körper u. Gewand," *LÄ* III, 664 ff.

15 *Manuel*, 393. Vandier's third group, not considered here, comprised the statuary of Ramesses II that was assignable to neither of the other groups.

16 'Abû el-Hôl': PM III (2nd ed.) 835 f. J. Màlek and H. McKeown recorded the texts of the colossus in 1985, see *JEA* 72, 1986, vi.

17 *Features of the Deification of Ramesses II (Abh. DAI Kairo Ägyptologische* Reihe 5), Mainz 1969.

18 *Propylaean-Kunstgeschichte* 15: *Das alte Ägypten*, C. Vandersleyen, ed., Berlin 1975, 254, with pl. 203 (text: M. Seidel - D. Wildung); cf. PM II (2nd ed.) 436.

19 I.e., the sculptor's supposed intent in choosing the banded stone would not have been

The art historical commentary in the case of BM 19 derives the style of the piece from the statues of Akhenaten; "*Der lächelnde Mund, die vollen Lippen, die geblähten Nasenflügel, die grossen Augen, die Falten am Hals verleihen dem Gesicht trotz seiner Monumentalität eine fast feminine Weichheit,*" in sum, "*das Erbe von Amarna.*"[20] While the description of the features is generally accurate, neither a derivation of the traits from the works of Akhenaten nor the estimation that the overall impression created is soft and feminine is acceptable. Rather, this and other monumental depictions of Ramesses II as well portray a benevolent yet aloof pharaoh. The source is not the Amarna Period, but instead the statuary of Amenhotep III.[21] In this tendency to refer to the works of Amenhotep III, Ramesses II follows the lead of his post-Amarna predecessors, most notably Tutankhamun.[22]

That Ramesses II appropriated statuary made for Amenhotep III is well known. Although works depicting practically all Ramesses' New Kingdom predecessors (with the exceptions of Hatshepsut and Akhenaten) did not escape usurpation, nevertheless, a marked preference for the statues of Amenhotep III is discernible. It would seem that the reign was marked by a conscious effort to emulate the accomplishments of that ruler, as J. Yoyotte has proposed.[23] Representative examples of the usurpations side by side with imitations of statuary depicting Amenhotep III are the colossi of Luxor Temple.[24] The purposeful imitation of statues representing Amenhotep III - imitations not only of their style but also of their spirit - implies Ramesses II's conscious intent to associate himself with the last orthodox ruler before the Amarna Period, like Tutankhamun - admittedly on a more modest scale and to another purpose[25] - before him.

---

obvious to a visitor to the Ramesseum, as C. Leblanc, in *Mélanges Gamal eddin Mokhtar* (*BdÉ* 97), Paris 1985, II, 80, has noted.

20 *Propylaean-Kunstgeschichte*, 254.

21 See F. Yurco, most recently in "Égypte - Louqsor. Temple du ka royal," *Les dossiers: histoire et archéologie* 101, Jan. 1986, 39 f. and C. Strauss-Seeber, in *Temple und Kult* (*Äg. Abh.* 46), W. Helck, ed., Wiesbaden 1987, 24 ff.

22 Here the similarity of works created under Ramesses II to those of the post-Amarna period deserves mention. It has often enough resulted in problems of attribution, a good example being the assignment of the Cranbrook Amun (now in the Kestner Museum, Hannover) to the reign of Tutankhamun (see W.H. Peck, *JEA* 57, 1971, 73 ff.). As a comparison of this statue with depictions of Amun dated or datable to the post-Amarna period shows (e.g., the Karlsruhe Amun [*Osiris, Kreuz und Halbmond* (exhibition catalogue), E. Brunner-Trautx - H. Brunner - J. Zick-Nissen, eds., Mainz 1984, no. 23, 38 ff.] and the quartzite Amun colossus in Karnak Temple [PM II (2nd ed.) 90], respectively) the Cranbrook Amun must be a Ramesside creation (see my study of the Karnak Amun, in preparation).

23 Yoyotte, *Trésors*, 144.

24 See note, 21, above. That the appropriated colossi in the Ramesside court of the temple exemplify 'auto-usurpation' (i.e., Ramesses II reusing/ reinscribing his own statuary) has been suggested in the *resumée* of a paper that was not however, delivered (see C. Barocas, in *Fourth International Congress of Egyptology. Munich 1985, Abstracts of Papers*, S. Schoske, ed., Munich 1985, 9). The thesis remains to date unpublished.

25 The motive for emphasizing Tutankhamun's affiliation with Amenhotep III, passing over the king's Amarna predecessors, was legitimacy (a point argued in my forthcoming study of

Ramesses' reuse of Middle Kingdom statuary is well attested. Possibly the appropriation of Middle Kingdom works is related to an antiquarian interest, reflecting the wish to revive the glories of the classical past. The reign witnessed the culmination of a trend toward historical awareness,[26] a trend whose beginnings can be traced back to the early years of the New Kingdom.

A problematic usurped piece that may date to the Middle Kingdom is CG 555, a group statue depicting a king enthroned between two goddesses (Plates 1, 2).[27] In a recent exhibition catalogue, the slightly under life-size statue was unhesitatingly described as an original work of Ramesses II.[28] Certain features are, however, inconsistent with the dating of the piece according to the inscriptions that unequivocally name Ramesses II as beloved of the divine ladies accompanying the king. The ears, for example, were once larger; as L. Borchardt remarked, they have been reduced in size.[29] The faces of all three figures have been reworked. Various details such as the beard strap (and probably the separately made beard itself) as well as the creases on the figures' necks are obvious additions; so, too, the borders adorning the goddesses' dresses. The original may date to the early Middle Kingdom,[30] but a hindrance for this dating is the preponderance of the back slab.

Curiously enough, no new statue type was introduced during the reign. Instead, a phenomenal production of known genres was undertaken. The example that springs to mind immediately is the standard bearer, the subject of a monograph by C. Chadefaud.[31] H. Satzinger also studied the type and has restated his views on the subject in a review of Chadefaud's book.[32] My opinion concerning the function of these statues differs from those of both Chadefaud and Satzinger. I believe the type was intended to serve as an intercessor.[33] The inscription associated with the depiction of a standard-bearing statue in the tomb of a mid-Dynasty XVIII official (TT75) designates it an intermediary standing ready to hear the petitioner and to pass on his plea to the god in whose cult the ruler served as priest bearing the divine image.[34] The proliferation of royal standard-bearing statues

---

Tutankhamun's reign), while Ramesses II's intent can best be described as aggrandizement (cf. Yoyotte, *Trésors*, 144).

26 See the references cited in *LÄ* V, Wiesbaden 1985, 110.

27 Both detail photographs were made with the kind permission of the Director of the Cairo Museum, Dr. Mohammed Saleh, whose cooperation is here gratefully acknowledged.

28 *Nofret - Die Schöne. Die Frau im Alten Ägypten*, D. Wildung - S. Schoske, eds., Mainz 1984, no. 80, 170.

29 *Statuen und Statuetten von Königen und Privatleuten im Museum von Kairo* II (*Catalogue général*), Berlin 1925, 103.

30 The date of the statue's manufacture is considered in a study of the group in preparation.

31 *Les statues porte-enseignes de l'Égypte ancienne*, Paris 1982.

32 *BiOr* 41, 1984, 375 ff.

33 See *SAK* 4, 1976, 67 ff. In *JARCE* 24, 1987, 13 ff., B. Bryan identified JE 43611, a statue of Thutmosis IV, as the earliest preserved standard-bearing statue of the New Kingdom.

34 See most recently, the commentary of Bryan, *JARCE* 24, 19 f. with note 35.

under Ramesses II[35] reflects the ruler's pretension to a semi-divine status in the religious life of his subjects.

Another genre that would affirm the king's aspiration to divinity is the group statue depicting Ramesses II in association with one or more gods. Such statues are well-documented products of the sculptor's atelier during the reign. Group compositions are known not only from numerous actual specimens but also from relief representations of them. Depictions of dyads showing Ramesses II enthroned or standing beside various gods were discussed by Habachi in an article on the 'jubilees' of the ruler.[36] He published three blocks found at Saqqara that belong to a scene showing seated dyads. The provenance of another block (Brooklyn 54.67) with representations of dyads depicting standing figures is not known. In both cases the figures are shown in raised relief against a cut-down background, a technique that Habachi theorized was intended to emphasize the importance of the figures. It is more likely, however, that the sunken area renders a structural element of the statues, viz. the back slab against which the figures were carved.

Because the inscription on the largest Saqqara block mentions millions of 'jubilees,' Habachi plausibly identified the dyads as statues created on the occasion of the festival which the king celebrated a total of fourteen times.

On the block in Brooklyn, the Syrian goddess Anat is described as "Mistress of Heaven, of Ramesses-Meryamun." A dyad depicting the king enthroned beside Anat who bears the same designation was found at Tanis to which it had been removed from Per-Ramesses.[37] Evidence for the cults of deities designated "God NN of Ramesses" is concentrated at the Delta residence, but additional documents derive from a variety of other sites as well, southward even into Nubia. The dyads are perhaps the most conspicuous evidence for these cults.

In the composition of actual preserved dyads, the royal figure presumes precedence over the deity. A case in point is the colossal red granite dyad in the Ny Carlsberg Glyptothek, AEIN 1483, that Petrie excavated in the enclosure of the Ptah temple at Mit Rahineh.[38] Neither figure is worked fully in the round, but that depicting the ruler appears to be more three-dimensional, an impression created by the projecting and receding silhouette of his costume and regalia that are much more complex than the iconography of the god. Furthermore, the royal figure occupies more than half of the volume of the block. At the broadest point, Ramesses' body is about one-fifth wider than the god's; it extends beyond the vertical axis of the statue drawn through the *ankh*-sign that marks the mid-point of the text running around the base. Indeed, Ptah-Tatenen almost seems to turn slightly to the side to make room for the sovereign.

---

35 Cf. Chadefaud's catalogue, *Statues porte-enseignes*, 24 ff.

36 *ZÄS* 97, 1971, 70 f. with pl. VII and figs. 4-5.

37 Now in the Cairo Museum; cf. P. Montet, *Les nouvelles fouilles de Tanis 1929-1932*, Paris 1933, 107 ff. with pls. LIV-LV.

38 See O. Koefoed-Petersen, *Catalogue des statues et statuettes égyptiennes (Publications de la Glyptothèque Ny Carlsberg* 3), Copenhagen 1950, no. 58, 34 f. with pls. 68-69. I owe the following analysis of the group's composition to C.E. Loeben.

The inscriptions of AEIN 1483 refer in their entirety to the king; the god is identified solely in the epithet that follows the cartouche. The text on the front of the back slab inscribed between the figures is oriented toward Ramesses, as if the god would recite it to assert his association with the king.

The texts that describe the deity in group statues often include the addition "of Ramesses" - but not, it should be noted, in the particular case of the Copenhagen group. Naville, who found a statue depicting "Ptah of Ramesses" at Bubastis, suggested that this and similar designations coupling the name of the deity with that of the king document Ramesses II's claim to "a kind of right of property or possession."[39]

P. Montet authored an alternative theory. He understood the king's name as an abbreviation of Per-Ramesses. According to his view, the deities so named were at home in the Delta residence, regardless of where statues depicting them were to be found.[40]

Uphill devoted a brief appendix in his book on the temples of Per-Ramesses to a consideration of the cults of deities bearing the epithet "of Ramesses," proposing that the statues were created for the king's personal religious requirements;

> ...the by now extraordinarily complex court life demanded a complete set of new cult statues and temples for the king's own particular use, so that he could conveniently worship at one time all the principal deities of Egypt at whichever major city he was in....the traditional deity worship performed by king and people continued as before, so that Amun and Amun of Ramesses existed alongside one another.[41]

D. Wildung's hypothesis concerning the deities described as "God NN of Ramesses" understood the gods as epiphanies of the deified Ramesses himself, *"Erscheinungsformen der Göttlichkeit des Königstums."*[42] Wildung asserted that, *"Ramesses beim Opfer vor z.B. Ptah des Ramesses hat als Bild des Königs vor seinem in Gestalt des Ptah vergöttlichten Selbst zu gelten."*[43] This is certainly neither explicit nor implicit in the associated texts, however.

That Ramesses II claimed exalted status in the dyads cannot be gainsaid, but it is doubtful that the divinities were intended to embody a divine aspect of the king or to serve as his epiphany. Rather, it can be conjectured that Ramesses himself in these statues assumes the role of Re, of the sun god at the head of the pantheon, the demiurge who called the other gods into being. That the king presumed to divine status in statues of this type, as well as in the representations of them, is confirmed by the presence of the sun disc in his iconography, assimilating him to Re, as does the epithet R^c-msj-ntrw. This title is included, for example, in the inscriptions on the back slab of the Copenhagen group. Ramesses incorporated the designation into his titulary as an adjunct to the *Nebty*-name at some time between years 30 and 34, in conjunction with the celebration of the 'jubilee.'[44] Following

39 *Bubastis (1887-1889) (EEF Memoir 8)*, London 1891, 42.

40 *Studies Presented to F. Ll. Griffith*, London 1932, 406 ff.

41 *Temples of Per Ramesses*, 235 f.

42 *OLZ* 68, 1973, 559 f.

43 Other proponents of this interpretation are cited by L. Bell, *Mélanges Mokhtar* I, 51 n. 123.

44 See *LÄ* V, 111, n. 2 and 114 n. 53.

the lead of E. Wente,[45] it may be rendered "Re-who-creates-the gods" and interpreted to refer to the numerous cult statues, among them the dyads, carved at the king's order.

---

45 *JNES* 30, 1971, 317.

Plate 1

Plate 2

23

LATEST EXCAVATIONS IN MEMPHIS:

PROGRESS REPORT

G.A. Gaballa

In the Southwest corner of ancient Memphis, lies Kom el-Fakhry, the site granted to Cairo University for its excavations. Covering an area of about 19.5 acres, the Kom's maximum length is 375 meters (E-W), and the maximum width is 260 meters (N-S). It is bordered on the north by the village of Mit Rahineh, on the south by the main Saqqara-Badrashin Road, on the east by a minor road (leading to the village) and the Great Temple of Ptah, and on the west by another minor road, also leading to Mit Rahineh. On EES survey maps it is located between 1100-1360N and 600-980E.[1]

Previous Work

Considering the enormous importance of Memphis as the oldest and most durable capital of Egypt, it is surprising how relatively little planned and systematic work has been carried out there to unveil its secrets before they disappear forever. Kom el-Fakhry is no exception. The only substantial digging that took place there happened by accident. In 1954 a road was cut near its southern end to connect Badrashin with Saqqara. The project was abandoned as the workers came across stone monuments, which proved later on to be a cemetery from the First Intermediate Period.[2] In 1981 limited excavations immediately to the east of the cemetery were conducted by the local inspector of antiquities, revealing a small Middle Kingdom settlement. A full publication is still awaited.[3]

From 1981 until the present, the Egypt Exploration Society has undertaken the task of a comprehensive and systematic archaeological survey of the ruinfields of Memphis. The results of this ambitious project are proving invaluable.[4]

Present Work

The spot chosen to begin the excavations is located at the north edge of the unfinished road, some 90 meters to the west of the Great Temple of Ptah. In preparation, a grid of five-meter squares was marked and the site levelled. The actual digging commenced on January 17th, and so far it has covered 27 squares. The removal of the top layer of debris revealed mud brick structures which can be tentatively divided into three sections, all covering three north squares, i.e. 15 meters. The eastern section extends about 18 meters, and its rooms contain no less than nine ovens and hearths. Near the northern side is a circular shape (diameter 2.7 m) in which seven large storage jars were embedded. The

---

1 D.G. Jeffreys, *The Survey of Memphis* I, London, 1985, drawings 4, 7, 15; cf. also H.S. Smith and D.G. Jeffreys, "A Survey of Memphis, Egypt," *Antiquity* 60 (1986), 88-95.

2 A brief note on the site is given by Abdel Tawab el-Hitta in *La Révue du Caire* 33/175 (1955), 50-51. A fuller but still insufficient account is given by Dr. Christine Lilyquist in *JARCE* 11 (1974), 27-30, and pls. 1-111; cf. also Jeffreys, *Survey*, drawing 19.

3 Jeffreys, *Survey*, 29, drawing 20.

4 H.S. Smith, D.G. Jeffreys, and J. Malek, *JEA* 69 (1983), 30-42, *JEA* 70 (1984), 23-32, *JEA* 71 (1985), 5-11.

whole section is enclosed on the north and west sides with a wall 65-80 centimeters in thickness. The thickness of the walls of the rooms averages 35-40 centimeters. The constructions fall into two successive levels, and a third level of an earlier date is already showing.

A narrow street(?), 1.5 meters wide, separates the eastern section from the middle one. The latter, which extends for just over 13 meters from east to west, contains three circular granaries but no sign of ovens or hearths.

The third (western) section of buildings also extends for just over 13 meters from east to west and contains a remarkable set of seven granaries with diameters averaging 1.5-2.2 meters. It also contains three ovens, average diameter 0.5-0.6 meters. A small rectangular storeroom, 2.2 meters long and 0.45 meters wide, was also found. On each of its short sides, stood two jars with a dish between them.

Finds

As expected, heaps of pottery keep turning up, a few complete (or almost complete), but the vast majority is in the form of sherds. Preliminary sorting out indicates that we have all styles and shapes: bowls, storage jars, bottles, dishes, cups, pilgrim bottles, flasks, braziers, spinning bowls, crucibles (or fire dogs?)[5], pot stands, etc. Although the majority is not painted, a considerable number of sherds bear the famous Eighteenth Dynasty blue paint with linear and floral motifs. Other jars show three bands around the neck in black and red. Some sherds are obviously Egyptian, but their linear motifs are imitations of foreign (Cypriot?) ones. Two handles of large jars are stamped with cartouches containing the names ᶜAkheperkare (Thotmosis I) and Haremhab, respectively. A number of sherds of foreign make and motif were also discovered. These include sherds from the shoulder of a ewer and from the shoulder and body of a stirrup jar, both dating to Minoan Late Palace Period. (c.1700-1380 B.C.)[6] More sherds are of Cypriot origin and date to the Late Bronze Age (c.1550-1050 B.C.)[7]

Stone tools and implements are plentiful, e.g. mortars, grinding palettes, pounders, weights, loom weights, rubbing stones, sharpeners, a cosemtic jar, parts of vessels, dishes, and a spinning bowl, etc. Also found were chair supports and seats. A considerable number of flint tools were discovered, including knives, scrapers, blades, and sickle blades. Conversely, metals are extremely rare. Apart from a few bronze lumps, only a knife (?) and a javelin head were found.

A number of male and female figurines of terra cotta were unearthed. They are all nude and incomplete with the upper and lower parts of the bodies missing. We also found the head of a bird with rather enlarged eyes and the figure of a horse, but the head is lost.

The few scarabs which we found are either uninscribed or bear decorative motifs or hieroglyphic signs.

---

5 R. Anthes, *Mit Rahineh 1955*, 34-40; *Mit Rahineh 1956, 1957-8*, and pl. 67.

6 F. Matz in I.E.S. Edwards et al. (eds.), *CAH (3rd ed.)* II/1, 55 ff.

7 H.W. Calling in id. *CAH (3rd ed.)* II/2. 188.

A large quantity of animal bones turned up. As they have not been examined yet, we are in no position to determine their different species.

Nature of Site

The main features of the site, i.e. ovens, hearths, granaries, together with the majority of the finds, i.e. mortars, grinding palettes, pounders, not to mention the vast amount of pottery and pottery sherds, all point to the nature of the site as a services rather than a residential area. This impression may be further enhanced by the rarity of personal possessions or ornaments. However, we should be cautious in emphasizing this view as the pottery is of the domestic kind.

Date

In view of the fact that the work is still in progress, it might be premature to suggest a definite date for the site. Nevertheless, the evidence thus far gained from the pottery, Egyptian and foreign, the scarabs, and most of all the stamps on the jar handles, shows that the site was occupied right through the Eighteenth Dynasty, bordering on early Nineteenth.

THE BLESSING OF PTAH

Ogden Goelet, Jr.

Introduction

If I had to choose a quintessential portrait of the reign of Ramesses II and place it into the quintessential Ramesside setting, the Blessing of Ptah (or, more accurately, Ptah-Tatenen)[1] would probably be the first text to come to my mind. It appears at the monument we probably most associate with Ramesses II, his grandiose temple at Abu Simbel. Furthermore, the study of the Blessing, as I shall call it, began with the earliest days of modern Egyptology, when Champollion, the decipherer of the hieroglyphs and father of our discipline, first discovered and copied it at that dramatic site.[2] Nonetheless, it is a very hard text to discuss due to its length. Even among the texts of Ramesses II, who was a rather long-winded fellow, the Blessing is one of the longest, as well as one of the most frequently copied.[3] Accordingly, this paper will concentrate on a few points of particular interest that have not received much attention in recent studies. This discussion is intended as the preliminary stage for a longer study of this inscription in the future. In the interest of space, therefore, I shall confine my remarks to Ptah's speech, which is the Blessing proper, and leave a treatment of Ramesses' reply to a later date.

The Blessing is fascinating to most who read it, a fact reflected in the various titles that have been used to describe it: "The Dialogue of Ptah and Ramesses,"[4] "The Decree of Ptah

---

1 In a brief discussion of this text, H.A. Schlögl, *Der Gott Tatanen (OBO* 29) (Göttingen 1980) 64-66, correctly points out that the god of this text is, properly speaking, not Ptah but Ptah-Tatenen. Especially telling is Schlögl's remark (op. cit. 65) that in the very opening line of the text, Ramesses is described as "the son of Re who emerged from Tatenen, born of Sekhmet the Great," *KRI* II 262, 10.

2 J.F. Champollion, *Monuments de l'Egypte et de la Nubie* I (Paris 1835) pl. 38 "Ipsamboul... grand stèle." The direction of the text is strangely reversed, and the scene at the top is not reproduced. The same error in reproducing the direction of the text was made shortly after by I. Rosellini, *Monumenti dell'Egitto e della Nubia I Monumenti storici* (Pisa 1832) pl. 113; the scene was reproduced separately on pl. 112. For a general bibliography of the Ipsamboul stela, which is the best preserved of the examples dating to the reign of Ramesses II, see *PM* VII 106 and *KRI* II 258.

3 The bibliography for the stela and its variants is extensive; only a selection limited to the larger treatments will be given here. For the most reliable copy of the texts with some bibliography, see *KRI* II 258. A recent study of the Aksha version was published by A. Rosenvasser, "Aksha: la estella de la 'Bendicion de Ptah'," *RIHAO* 4 (1978) 9-61, with extensive commentary. The version of Ramesses III was treated extensively in W.F. Edgerton and J.A. Wilson, *The Historical Records of Ramesses III (SAOC* 12) (Chicago 1936) 119-129, which accompanies the illustrations in *The Epigraphic Survey, Medinet Habu* II (*OIP* 9) (Chicago 1932) pls. 105-106. The most recent translation of Ramesses II's texts into English still remains that of J.H. Breasted, *Ancient Records of Egypt* III (Chicago 1906) 175-182. There is also a translation with a limited commentary by H. Te Velde, "De Zegeningen van Ptah-Tatanen. Een egyptische konigsinscriptie uit de 13 eeuw v. Chr.," *Schrijvend verleden*, K.R. Veenhof, ed., (*MVEOL* 24) (Leiden 1983) 355-360.

4 The text has been treated as a dialogue between Ptah and Ramesses by M. Görg, *Gott-König-Reden in Israel und Ägypten (Beiträge zur Wissenschaft vom Alten und*

for Ramesses II," and the one I have chosen here, "The Blessing of Ptah upon Ramesses II." These titles reflect its complex nature; the Blessing can be legitimately considered a religious document, a royal and divine decree, or even a literary text. Significantly, the Blessing was itself the basis of a nearly identical inscription of Ramesses III, that conscious imitator of his more glorious predecessor. The discussion will focus upon the Nineteenth Dynasty text, but in one instance I will mention some editing done by Ramesses III, since it reveals much about the nature of the original.

The Blessing marks a sharp change in the religious and administrative focus of Ramesses' reign. In this text Amun is reduced to a titulary element, while Ptah seemingly becomes the king's patron deity. Ramesses never explained the reasons for this shift, but it may simply be connected with a decision to spend more time in the northern capital at Memphis and in Pi-Ramesses. Ptah accordingly assumed a greater role in Ramesses' inscriptions beginning with Year 30, particularly in his syncretized form of Ptah-Tatenen. Not coincidentally, this aspect of the deity has a strong connection with the *Heb-Sed* festival, whose repeated celebration was a major fixture of the latter part of his reign.[5] Ptah-Tatenen occurs regularly in the later forms of Ramesses II's titulary in the epithet attached to his Horus name: *nb ḥbw-sd mi it.f Ptḥ-t3ṯnn* "Possessor of *Heb-Sed* festivals like his father Ptah-Tatenen."[6]

The Distribution of the Document

If we were to examine the Blessing as a literary document, this approach would cast much light on its many other aspects. By considering how the Blessing came to be "published," so to speak, we can see the many influences that operated on this text. If we momentarily looked at this inscription as a manuscript destined for publication in a newspaper, the analogy would not be too far from reality. The Blessing clearly drew upon several sources for material, then the resulting text was composed for attractive appearance on a stela and distributed for maximum effect. After we have followed the text through these stages of composition, publication, and distribution, we can examine its literary background.

No text tells us exactly how a royal inscription was written, but as E. Bleiberg[7] has recently proposed in an appropriate article on Egyptian propaganda, a number of royal texts claim that the king himself composed the inscription, which was subsequently proclaimed before the court, the nobility, and often the general populace as well. There are many examples of this *topos*. What concerns us more here is how the Blessing was actually inscribed and placed throughout Egypt and Nubia. Because the various examples are so close to each other, there can be no doubt that a master copy was made and then distributed to those

---

Neuen Testament Sixth Series 5) (Stuttgart 1975) 237-250, where he, nonetheless, calls the text "Der 'Segen des Ptah'."

5 K.A. Kitchen, *Pharaoh Triumphant* (Mississauga 1982) 178-182.

6 For the syncretism and the connection between Ptah-Tatenen and the *Heb-Sed* festival, see H.A. Schlögl, *Der Gott Tatanen* 54-63. The association with Memphis is treated, ibid. 79-82.

7 E. Bleiberg, "Historical Texts as Political Propaganda during the New Kingdom," *BES* 7 (1985/86). On the question of the composition and distribution of royal texts for which several copies exist, see H.W. Helck, "Das Verfassen einer Königsinschrift," in *Fragen an die altägyptische Literatur*, J.A. Assmann, E. Feucht, R. Grieshammer, eds., (Wiesbaden 1977) 241-256, henceforth cited here as *Fragen*.

who actually inscribed it;[8] the same holds true for its companion piece, the Marriage Stela. The special layout of the Karnak version of the text, in particular, reveals that occasionally a text might be carefully designed much as a modern newspaper page is laid out. In this case, a deliberate effort seems to have been made to place the king's cartouches at or near the edge of the inscription's right and left sides, so that his name formed a visible frame for the text.[9] In addition to this, the royal name effectively divides the text into topically separate paragraphs in all versions. Finally, we might add that in the Ipsamboul version of Ramesses II, as well as in Ramesses III's re-edition of the Blessing, the speech of the king begins a new line of text on the stela, a circumstance which could hardly be fortuitous.

The Blessing was intended to be among the most conspicuous texts in the temples where it appears - it was usually placed outside the entranceway; in most cases it is also paralleled by the Marriage Stela, with which it shares much phraseology. Ramesses III also accorded the Blessing the same prominence, placing it on the exterior of the first pylon at Medinet Habu. A major exception, curiously enough, was the best preserved of all versions, the stela at Abu Simbel, which was placed in the great hall of Ramesses II's temple.

The Divine Birth Legend

It has been said that the principle underlying much of the Egyptian king's relationship with his god can be summarized in the Latin phrase *do ut des*, "I give in order that you might give." This relationship writ large is the very composition of the entire inscription - first, Ptah describes his gifts on behalf of Ramesses, and then Ramesses responds by relating his largess on Ptah's behalf. Of all Ptah's benefactions, the first is perhaps the most remarkable (and important) of all - the divine origin of Ramesses. By asserting that the god literally engendered the King in his earthly mother, the inscription places itself in a long tradition best exemplified by the divine birth legend of Hatshepsut and its copy by

---

8 W.F. Edgerton and J.A. Wilson, op. cit. 119-120, propose a complex interrelationship between the Abu Simbel version, a possible original inscribed at Memphis for Ramesses II's jubilee, and the later copy by Ramesses III. They call the Abu Simbel version "obviously secondary" and remark that several errors in the Abu Simbel text show that it may have been copied from a hieroglyphic original, and "One may suppose that a parent hieroglyphic text was copied into hieratic for transmission to Abu Simbel, where the text was put back into hieroglyphic." For an example of a confusion arising out of this procedure, see Note 14 below.

9 There is reason to believe that Ramesses II's Karnak version may itself have been usurped. The cartouches have been erased or damaged in a rather systematic fashion. In this respect it is interesting that the prenomen is seldom completely damaged - the element *stp-n-Rc*, "the one whom Re chose," is often the only part that has been touched. There is a somewhat similar systematic damage to the nomen, since quite often the epithet *mri-Imn*, "beloved of Amun," is the only part which has been defaced. In any case, this general pattern is far from consistent; there are places where the cartouches have been completely erased and even a few instances in which they were left unaltered. One could also raise the possibility of usurpation for other elements of the text as well. The entire "mystery section" (*KRI* II 275, 2 ff., and see below in the discussion of this part of the text) has been lost. This loss, however, could certainly be due to many reasons other than deliberate erasure. Even so, it is intriguing that in many of the places where the text of *MH* and *I* vary greatly, there has been a loss or erasure in the *K* version. Although one would like some more conclusive evidence, it may be that the text was changed and not just usurped by a later king. The manner in which the cartouches have been attacked make it improbable that any one other than a Ramesside pharaoh, in particular, Ramesses III, would have left the cartouches only partially destroyed.

Amenophis III, both of which were undoubtedly known in Ramesses' time, since extensive "restorations" at both Deir el-Bahri and Karnak were done during his reign.[10] Not only does internal evidence from the text of the Blessing show this, but also a block from Medinet Habu, dating to Ramesses II, preserves a fragmentary scene of the birth legend's critical scene with the god seated next to the king's earthly mother on the nuptial bed.[11] Given a clear origin for this important section of the text, Ramesses' version of the legend is an ideal place to begin an examination of the Blessing's literary antecedents. Here, of course, I use the term "literary" in a very broad sense.

Occuring as it does in the very beginning of Ptah's speech, the divine procreation of Ramesses is thereby stressed. One of the most remarkable features of this section of the Blessing is that not only does it employ much of the phraseology of the Eighteenth Dynasty versions of the divine birth legend, but it also apparently roughly follows the same order of events shown in the earlier reliefs. The borrowing is by no means exact; significant changes have been made, first, by Ramesses II and, then, later re-edited by Ramesses III. This is not surprising, since, as H. Brunner has shown, the evidence points strongly to an earlier origin for the entire cycle, perhaps as far back as the Old Kingdom.[12] Reduced to the essentials which concern us the most, the Eighteenth Dynasty story is as follows: the god falls in love with the future king's earthly mother; he transforms himself into the image of her husband, appears before her in the guise of her husband, and procreates the later king, whom he has predestined to rule. The child and the royal *ka* are fashioned together on a potter's wheel by the ram-headed god, Khnum. Amun acknowledges the child as his offspring, dandling the infant upon his knees before an audience of jubilating gods. The infant's future kingship and titulary are proclaimed, then the king's propitious rule and beneficence towards Amun are predicted. In light of this, the god also proclaims a series of blessings upon the child.

In the Blessing of Ptah, the narration is by necessity much abbreviated, yet even so, there are significant changes and omissions that cannot be ascribed to shortness of space alone. The most obvious change is that Ptah has completely supplanted Amun in the Blessing. Except for his appearance in Ramesses' titulary, Amun goes unmentioned in this text. Another major change is that no annunciation of Ramesses' divine nature and future kingship seems to take place prior to birth. The god states:[13]

---

10 For a discussion of the divine birth legend, see Brunner, *Die Geburt des Gottkönigs* (*ÄA* 10) (Wiesbaden 1964), henceforth cited here as *Geburt*, and "Geburtslegende," *LÄ* II 475-476. In addition to these two articles, J. Osing has recently published a study of stylistic aspects of Hatshepsut's divine birth legend, "Die Patenschaft der Götter für Königin Hatschepsut," in *Fragen* 361-383. A Ptolemaic version of the legend has been treated by H. Sternberg, "Die Geburt des göttlichen Kindes als mythisches Motiv in den Texten von Esna," *GM* 61 (1983) 31-48.

11 H. Brunner, *Geburt* 7-8, with pl. 24a ("Szene VI" should be changed to "Szene IV"). Further blocks from Ramesses II's version of the divine birth legend have been found, see S. Gaballa, "New Evidence on the Birth of the Pharaoh," *Or.* 36 (1967) 299-304 and L. Habachi, "La reine Touy, femme de Séthy I," *RdÉ* 21 (1969) 32-39, with pls. I, II.

12 For a complete exposition of Brunner's dating, see *Geburt* 183-187, 197-199; a different view of its relationship with the Old Kingdom has been expressed by S. Morenz in his review of Brunner's book, "Die Geburt des ägyptischen Gottkönigs," *Forschungen und Fortschritte* 40 (1967) 368-370.

13 Here and elsewhere in the discussion, the text shall be cited according to the lines in the Abu Simbel or Ipsamboul (I) version in *KRI*, except here noted. The present

I was your father among the gods. So that your flesh might be (that of) the gods, I made my transformation as Banebdedet. I impregnated you in your noble mother, (because) I knew that you would be a protector and that you would perform benefactions for my *ka*. When you were born at the rising of Re, I raised you up in front of the gods....

In this brief passage, the theme of *do ut des*, which dominates the entire text, is stated, and the king's divine parentage is asserted. It is striking, however, that the father is now Ptah, who, nonetheless, changes himself into the image of *another* deity before procreating Ramesses. The reason for the second transformation is unclear, as is the rarely made connection between Ptah and Banebdedet, a somewhat obscure deity of the nome of Mendes.[14] The verbs *sti*, "to eject, shoot, pour,"[15] in Ramesses II's version and *nk*, "to copulate" (here written *nnk*), in Ramesses III's edition, make it clear that a physical engenderment and not spiritual parentage was intended by this description. On this point the Ramesside texts are even more explicit than those of Dynasty XVIII. The diminished role of the mother in the Ramesside versions also serves to stress the king's divine parentage. One might say that Ramesses is attempting to assert that the legitimacy of his rule is derived primarily from Ptah rather than his earthly family. In the opening line of the text, in fact, the goddess Sakhmet is said to be the king's mother.[16]

The parallels between the Eighteenth and Nineteenth Dynasty versions of the divine birth legend are much stronger in the next section, when the god acknowledges his paternity before an audience of other deities. The god in both instances recognizes the child as his own, first, by a verbal statement, then by having the child dandled before the gods. In the Blessing's words:[17]

---

citation is Blessing I 3, *KRI* II 263.

14 On the deity Banebdedet, whose name means literally, "the Ram (*b3*) the Lord of Mendes," see Bonnet, *Reallexikon der ägyptischen Religionsgeschichte* Berlin 1952) 868-871, *s.v.* "Widder"; H. De Meulenaere, *LÄ* III 44, *s.v.* "Mendes"; and A. Rosenvasser, op. cit. 21-22. In the final analysis, the primary reason for Banebdedet's appearance here is that the ram is the symbol *par excellence* of fertility and procreative power. The connections between Banebdedet and Ptah-Tatenen are unclear and are rarely made; in addition to the references cited in Bonnet, see also the discussion of a Ptolemaic era statue in D. Wildung, *Imhotep und Amenhotep (MÄS* 36) (Berlin 1977) 129-130. Bonnet, op. cit. 869, noted in connection with this passage that Hatshepsut's mother, Ahmes (*Urk.* IV 224, 17), is called *mry b3*, "beloved of the Ram," and "*d3tt* of the Ram," the Ram (*b3*) presumably being the Ram of Mendes. The hieroglyph depicting the animal was in both instances restored under Ramesses II, perhaps not coincidentally. The unusual title *d3tt b3* is discussed by Brunner (*Geburt* 79), who also sees a relationship between the present quotation in the Blessing and Ahmes' title.

15 The sign used in I, ⟨glyph⟩ , is probably an error for ⟨glyph⟩ (Gardiner Sign-List F29), as W.F. Edgerton and J.A. Wilson suggest, op. cit. 121, note 4b. The sign F29 in hieratic can easily be confused for the group ⟨glyph⟩ *nnk*, which in this case had a similar meaning by chance. The verb *sti*, "to eject, shoot, pour," with the phallus as determinative seems to have the sense of "ejaculate" here.

16 Blessing I 1, *KRI* II 262, 10, omitted in Ramesses III's version.

17 Blessing I 4-6, *KRI* II 263-264.

When you were born at the rising of Re, I raised you up in front of the gods, Oh (Ramesses II's name and epithets) the fashioners (*ḫnmw*) and formers (*ptḥw*) were dandling (*rnn*), while your birth-brick (*msḫnt*) rejoiced and shouted, since my image(?) was brought(?) (which was) august, great, and tall. The nobles and the great ones of the temple of Ptah and the Hathors of the temple of Atum were celebrating.

Although the "fashioners" and "formers" - both puns on gods' names - are the ones who actually dandle the child, there can be no doubt that the action is done on Ptah's behalf. The key verb *rnn*, here translated by "dandle," sometimes has the more specific meaning, "to take (a child) upon the knees."[18] The identical word appears in the Blessing and the Eighteenth Dynasty versions of the divine birth tale. *Rnn* is easily confused with two homonyms which mean "to nurse"[19] and "to rejoice,"[20] but in the Blessing the determinative used clearly shows a seated female figure with a child facing away from her and held out from her body.[21] Similarly, the relief accompanying this passage in Amenophis III's version at Luxor shows Hathor standing before Amun and offering him the newborn.[22] The child sits on her outstretched palms and also faces the god, while Amun confronts them and reaches out to touch the future king. Significantly, the same verb occurs in the text of the Marriage Stela and its shortened version, in each case apparently in the phrase:[23] "He (Ramesses II) was dandled for Banebdedet." Unfortunately, this still does not explain why the god of Mendes figures so prominently in this context. Curiously enough, Ramesses III's version does not follow this pattern and substituted the verb *nhm*, "to shout," in this passage, although this is clearly not what the original version of the Blessing intended. Comparing reliefs, determinatives, and vocabulary, it seems certain that roughly the same event is described in both the Eighteenth and Nineteenth Dynasty versions.

This gesture is not confined to the Egyptian culture alone. Several times in Genesis, the knees and the lap appear to be associated with a gesture of adoption or recognition. The barren Rachel gives her servant, Bilhah, to her husband Jacob with these words (Gen. 30:3): "Here is my maid Bilhah; go in to her, that she may bear upon my knees, and even I may have children through her." An allusion to the same method of acknowledging kinship most probably is made near the end of the tale of Joseph (Gen. 50:23): "...the children also of Machir the son of Manasseh were born upon Joseph's knees." A little earlier there is probably a reference to the same gesture in Genesis 48:11-12, when Joseph's near-blind father is shown his grandchildren for the first time:

---

18 Brunner, *Geburt* 111-112; *Wb.* II 436, 4.

19 *Wb.* II 436, 4-10.

20 *Wb.* II 435, 9-10.

21 Blessing I 5, *KRI* II 264, and the Karnak version, line 4, *KRI* 264, 1-2. Several of the references in the *Belegstellen* for the verb *rnn* also show the child being held in this manner and facing in the same direction as the figure holding it. In many such cases, the verb has the meaning of "dandle" rather than "nurse."

22 Brunner, *Geburt* pl. 10.

23 Marriage Stela, Ipsamboul version, line 10, *KRI* II 237, 5.

And Israel said to Joseph, 'I had not thought to see your face; and lo, God has let me see your children also.' Then Joseph removed them from his knees, and he bowed himself with his face to the earth."

In classical literature a passage in the *Odyssey* relates how Autolykos received his grandchild for the first time:[24]

> Well, Autolykos on a trip to Ithaka arrived just after his daughter's child was born. In fact, he had no sooner finished supper than nurse Eurykleia put the baby down in his own lap and said: 'It is for you, now choose a name for him, your child's dear baby....'

Doubtless, many other parallels to this gesture can be cited; what is striking about the Egyptian examples, however, is that a god performs the act.

The deities mentioned in this passage of the Blessing strongly recall gods who occur in literary divine birth stories. In an excerpt from the Westcar Papyrus, dating to the late Middle Kingdom, among the gods assisting the earthly mother in the birth of Re's children, we encounter Meskhent (*Msḫnt*) and Khnum (*Ḫnmw*). The Blessing's mention of "the Hathors" is also striking because the seven Hathors function as the predictors of a newborn's destiny in the New Kingdom "Tale of the Doomed Prince" and the "Tale of the Two Brothers."[25]

After dandling the infant king, the presentation to the sponsoring deity, his acknowledgement of the child, and the jubilation of the witnessing gods, the divine birth story, in both the Eighteenth and Nineteenth Dynasty renditions, concludes with additional blessings and celebrations by the divine audience. Except in a most general way, the two divine birth legends do not have much in common from this point on. One reason for this is that the continuation of Ptah's speech might well be considered as an expansion of the various divine benedictions that appear at the end of the Eighteenth Dynasty legend. In the Ramesside inscriptions, however, Ptah alone makes the Blessings.

The Blessing of Ptah and the Hittite Marriage

There can be no doubt that there is a close connection between the Marriage Stela of Year 34[26] and the Blessing of Year 35. As mentioned previously, the stelae relating these two

---

24 Book XX, 400 ff., trans. by R. Fitzgerald, *The Odyssey* (Anchor Books A333) (New York 1963) 366. In this situation the naming of the child is involved. In the legal code of Crete, however, the expression "at the knee" is connected with adoption, see M.S. Smith, "Greek Adoptive Formulae," *Classical Quarterly* (1967) 302 ff. I would like to thank Mr. Paul O'Rourke for this reference.

25 The concept of predestination plays a significant role in this part of the text. The interrelationship between these sources and the various deities appearing in them is worthy of a lengthy study in itself. Rosenvasser, op. cit. 24-33, has summarized many of the chief points and the allusions which are made in this passage. On this point, see also Brunner, *Geburt* 203-206.

26 On the Marriage Stela, see, principally for the main text, *KRI* II 233-256 and for the *Abrégée, KRI* II 256-257. The most extensive treatments remain those of G. Lefebvre, "Une version abrégée de la *Stèle du Mariage*," *ASAE* 25 (1925) 34-45 and Ch. Kuentz, "La *Stèle du Mariage* de Ramsès II," *ASAE* 25 (1925) 181-238. Some additional

great events were placed in close proximity to each other, often at a temple gateway where they would clearly act as companion pieces.[27] As such, it is not surprising that the Blessing should, in some way, refer to the earlier text. In fact, the last two paragraphs of Ptah's speech are devoted to this great event, which Ramesses rightfully regarded as one of the most important moments of his reign and a sure sign of divine favor.[28] The description of the Hittite marriage seems to fall into two sections, both of which are couched in words of wonder and miracles. Were it not for its position within the Blessing, we could consider these two parts of the inscription merely as additional items in a long string of benefactions upon the king. The allusions to the Peace Treaty of Year 21 and the Hittite Marriage, however, appear at the end of Ptah's speech, so that they become the culmination of all Ptah's blessings. The second, and more obscure, final paragraph seems to relate more to the treaty than to the marriage and, therefore, does not strictly follow the chronological sequence of events. As I will attempt to show shortly, this section apparently was a later interpolation into the original text.

The penultimate section of Ptah's speech begins with words reminiscent of the description of the remarkable weather in the Marriage Stela, when "days of Summer (*šmw*) happened in the Winter (*prt*)."[29] In the Blessing Ptah relates the events as follows:[30]

> I shook (*mnmn*) for you in order that I might foretell (*sr*) for you great and excellent wonders (*bi3wt?*). The sky quivered (*ktkt*), and those who are therein rejoiced at what has happened to you. The mountains, the waters, and the walls which are upon earth shook (*mnmn*), since they saw the decree which I have made for you (namely): 'The land of Hatti shall be serfs of your palace.'

This is followed by a brief description of the arrival of the Hittite princess:[31]

> I have put it into their hearts to bring themselves, bowing to your *ka*, the booty of their chiefs and everything of their gifts to the might of his Majesty, L.P.H., his eldest daughter being at their head....

In the most complete examples of the Marriage Stela from Elephantine and Abu Simbel, the brief speech accompanying the representation of the Hittite king describes his daughter's cortege into Egypt with virtually the identical phrase: "...my eldest daughter at the head of them."[32]

---

bibliography appears in K.A. Kitchen, *Pharaoh Triumphant* 251.

27 On this point, see K.A. Kitchen, *Pharaoh Triumphant* 88.

28 Blessing I 23-28, *KRI* II 275-276.

29 Marriage Stela, Ipsamboul version, line 28, *KRI* II 250, 1-4.

30 Blessing I 23-25, *KRI* II 273-274.

31 Blessing I 25-26, *KRI* II 274.

32 *KRI* II 234, 15.

The vocabulary employed in the opening lines of the paragraph reminds one strongly of a well known passage from "The Shipwrecked Sailor" when the god-like serpent appears:[33] "I heard a thundering(?) sound (*ḥrw n kri*) and I thought, that it was a wave of the sea. Trees were breaking (*gmgm*), and the earth was shaking (*mnmn*)." Similarly, in the Marriage Stela, its shortened version (the "*Abrégée*"), and the Blessing, a momentous occasion is signaled by the shaking earth. Both versions of the Marriage Stela, in fact, use the same two verbs as the Blessing:[34] "The sky trembled (*ktkt*), and the earth shook (*mnmn*), since he has ruled the kingship of Re." In all three texts of Ramesses II, the narration of these events seem to precede the description of the marriage itself, as if they were portents of the wedding. This passage in Ramesses III's rendition of the text, in fact, reminded W. Edgerton and J.A. Wilson of the action of an oracular bark, especially since it employs the verb *sr*, "to predict, foretell, announce."[35]

Although the words chosen for these excerpts from the Marriage Stelae and the Blessing at first seem quite obscure, they actually lend themselves to a straight-forward explanation for their appearance in these inscriptions - they describe an earthquake. L.-A. Christophe pointed out that an earthquake at Abu Simbel during Ramesses' reign would be the simplest explanation for the disintegration of the second colossus from the left.[36] There are several other traces of an earthquake at the site, most likely occurring in the second half of Ramesses II's reign, most likely around Year 31.[37] In the chamber of the Great Temple where the colossal Osiride figures stand, two large fissures are visible, one just under the architrave and the other about half-way up, running across all four surfaces of the fourth pillar on the south side. In order to cover up the damages and support the pillars, walls were erected inside the hall. On the west face of the third pillar, the blank surface of this shoring masonry was used to inscribe the Blessing of Ptah. In all probability, not only did the earthquake supply an opportunity to inscribe the Blessing, this event may well have also been the inspiration for the composition of the text. If this is the case, it is also conceivable that Ramesses might have seen the quake as a good omen from a chthonic god,[38] perhaps even the very announcement of the Hittite marriage. Ramesses III's editing of this paragraph, interestingly enough, retained allusions to a possible earthquake but removed all references to the marriage.

---

33 Pap. Leningrad 1115, lines 56-60, A.M. Blackman, *Middle-Egyptian Stories (BiAe 2)* (Brussels 1932) 43, 5-7.

34 Marriage Stela, Ipsamboul version, line 9, *KRI* II 236, 14-237, 1, and similarly in the *Abrégée*, line 6, *KRI* II 257, 2. On the relation between these passages and the present section of the Blessing, see A. Rosenvasser, *RIHAO* 4 (1978) 43-46.

35 W.F. Edgerton and J.A. Wilson, op. cit. 126, note 35b and Rosenvasser, op. cit. 43-44.

36 L.-A. Christophe, *Abou-Simbel et l'épopée de sa découverte* (Brussels 1965) 206-207, and K.A. Kitchen, *Pharaoh Triumphant* 135-136.

37 K.A. Kitchen, *Pharaoh Triumphant* 135.

38 The many chthonic aspects of this god are summarized by H.A. Schlögl, *LÄ* VI 238-240, s.v. "Tatenen."

The "Mystery Section"

Before Ramesses' reply to Ptah, there is one final paragraph in the god's speech, a passage whose vocabulary lends itself well to the title, "Mystery Section," which I shall use here. The topic of the paragraph immediately preceding Ramesses' speech is once more the marriage and the Egyptian-Hittite peace treaty, one of the rare instances in the text where the subject matter of one section is continued into the following one. There are several features which set this section off from the rest of the text. For one, the prior paragraph about the Hittite marriage and the earthquake concludes with the only example of Ramesses' titulary in Ptah's speech that includes the element, *nb-t3wy*, "Lord of the Two Lands."[39] Otherwise, *nb-t3wy* occurs only in the scenes above the main text, in the main titulary at the beginning of the text proper, and, finally, at the end of the entire inscription. In light of this, it appears as if the original intention was to conclude Ptah's speech at that point. Finally, unlike all other paragraphs in Ramesses II's version, the "Mystery Section" begins with a nominal sentence rather than the usual narrative verb form:[40] *bi3t ʿ3 sst3(t)*, "(It is) a great secret...." Significantly, this is precisely how Ramesses III's edition interpreted the text, apparently feeling that the "Mystery Section" was extraneous to the later king's purposes and omitted it entirely. The subject matter of this section appears to be the new relationship between Hatti and Egypt, which Ramesses undoubtedly thought guaranteed his country peace and prosperity for the rest of his reign, at least. It was Ptah's supreme gift; thus the god's speech and the Blessing proper ended with the "Mystery Section."

---

39 Blessing I 26, *KRI* II 275.

40 Blessing I 26, *KRI* II 275. Compare the similar passage in the Marriage Stela, Elephantine version, line x+5, *KRI* II 254, 3: *ist f.f hnw 3w st3 bi3t sbkt*, "Now then, (it) was a great mysterious benefaction and splendid wonder...."

RAMESSES II - APPEARANCE AND REALITY

T.G.H. James

"Now his Majesty was a youthful lord, active and without equal; his arms were strong, his heart valiant, his power like the god Montju at his time; good of form like the god Atum, at whose beauty men rejoiced; great of victory over all foreign lands, who does not know when he will start to fight; a firm wall around his army, its shield on the day of battle; a bowman without equal; braver than hundreds of thousands all together...." And so the hyperbole continues, for just as much again, and ends with: "his heart is like a hill of copper: King of Upper and Lower Egypt, Userma'atre-Setepenre, Son of Re, Ramesses-meryamun, given life."

Thus extravagantly, the author of the literary record of the great Battle of Qadesh describes the grandeur, nobility, bravery, sagacity, etc., etc. of his lord and master, Ramesses II. Are we to believe it? Is this a fair assessment of the monarch who is commonly called Ramesses the Great, whose reputation persisted in antiquity long after his time, who was called Rhampsinitus, Ozymandias, and possibly - although certainly erroneously - Sesostris, by Greek writers; who became famous for his monuments when ancient Egypt was rediscovered in the early nineteenth century and before his name could be read with certainty; who gave his name to one of the cities named in the Bible as having been built for Pharaoh by the Children of Israel?

It is almost always a mistake to take anyone at his own valuation; and we should be in no doubt that the above valuation was an authorized, accepted description of Ramesses II - gilt-edged by Egyptian standards, but perhaps not particularly valuable by absolute standards. Words are potent and persuasive weapons, and when we read ancient Egyptian texts written for official purposes, we may be sure that we are reading what is intended to be the accepted and acceptable version.

Now, the ancient Egyptians during the New Kingdom - that is, the period during which Ramesses II reigned - set great store by an element in their religion which they called Ma'at. It received particular emphasis during the time when the so-called heretic Pharaoh, Akhenaten, ruled, about one hundred years before Ramesses. Traditionally, Ma'at has been seen as a goddess, the personification of Truth, often represented by a feather, the symbol against which the heart of a dead person might be weighed in his judgement in the realm of the god Osiris, King of the Underworld.

But Ma'at was, clearly, not simply Truth, the opposite of Falsehood. It was particularly the element of good order in the world, what distinguished the proper state of affairs when things were running smoothly and correctly. Ma'at, when it was applied to the rule and behaviour of the Pharaoh, signified good rule and good behaviour, as befitted the monarch of the Egyptian state. It was, therefore, right and proper to describe the rule and behaviour of the Pharaoh in hyperbolic clichés of the kind quoted above.

There was nothing new in this kind of royal presentation. Any king who had pretensions to fame was presented in the best possible light in the inscriptions set up in temples and elsewhere. One of the greatest problems facing the historian of ancient Egypt is to penetrate the lush verbiage which makes up the greatest part of the surviving written record. Whatever was recorded was intended not simply to be a factual record of what may have happened in the lifetime of a king or in a particular campaign in which he was engaged. There was always the intention to enhance the reputation of the monarch, for only by his successes could he be justified as King of Egypt, Lord of the Two Lands, the living god Horus. In this way of recording what happened, there was little room for weakness, scarcely the possibility that this living Horus could fail his country.

Consequently, what seems to us like unwarranted boasting was, in fact, part of the magical presentation of Egyptian royalty. It should not be judged by our own standards of what is fit and proper, but in the context of what was thought to be fit and proper for royalty in ancient Egypt.

In the conventions of behaviour expected of the great men in the land, the ancient Egyptian was urged to be gentle, modest, understanding, considerate. The great sage Ptahhotpe said:

> If you are powerful, achieve respect by knowing, and by mildness of words. Do not order except as is appropriate, for the man who stirs up resentment causes trouble for himself. Do not be over-weaning, in case you are brought low....When you reply to someone in a fury, turn away your face and check yourself....He who walks carefully will have a well-prepared path.

It was always advantageous for a man in high position to claim that he had behaved with justice and moderation, particularly towards those who were in no position to defend themselves against his might and authority. In setting out his worthy achievements, a man would naturally put the best interpretation on his life and works, but always within the limits of the accepted canon of behaviour. He might well have excelled his fellows - and he would not hesitate to say as much - he might claim to have been praised by his king for what he had succeeded in accomplishing. But he would never place himself in competition with his king, the Pharaoh.

The Pharaoh, however, as I have indicated, was special, and it was quite in order for him to boast and exaggerate his achievements while at the same time claiming to have exercised his rule over his people in the most equitable and indulgent manner. Of course, in the kind of vaunting declaration used of Ramesses II in the account of the Battle of Qadesh, we must also recognize that it is Ramesses' behaviour against the foreigner that is being described, and the foreigner always fared adversely in the competition for Pharaonic favours.

Egypt in antiquity was an exceedingly inward-looking nation. It was special because the gods had made it special; no other land had the natural advantages of Egypt - in this respect the ancient claim of superiority had more than a little substance - and it was right and proper that the King of Egypt should be superior to all kings and that all nations should be considered as vassals of Egypt. The common motif of foreign lands shown as bound prisoners being led into the presence of Pharaoh seriously represented an attitude which was deeply rooted in the Egyptians' general view of their own country. This graphic commonplace, used even when the ruling king had no possible pretensions of exercising the universal role of dominance, seems to have been a fiction which sprang from the uniqueness of Egyptian culture. The Egyptian universe was wholly Egyptian-centred; everything was seen in Egyptian terms and judged by Egyptian standards. Even the Egyptian gods were exclusive, and the Egyptian cosmogony was constructed on the basis of life in Egypt. For an Egyptian the after-life was to be passed in a realm based closely on the physical characteristics of the land of Egypt, with an eternal Nile watering an eternal Egyptian landscape, farmed by eternal Egyptians existing eternally in a mirror-image of their mundane life.

The king of such a land was, as by definition, the most important ruler on earth, and even if the truth of such a belief was often challenged, it remained throughout the Pharaonic

Period a fundamental aspect of the Egyptian concept of their own royalty. Each new king assumed the divine mantle of omnipotence, which he was to wear for the duration of his reign. Thereafter, it would pass to his successor, who became, in turn, the living Horus. Continuity in monarchy existed in the succession of humans transformed into living gods, and the glory and fame of a particular king were as transient as human life itself.

Yet glory and fame meant much to the Egyptians, and nothing pleased a man so much as the thought that his name might endure long beyond his lifetime. That is why inscriptions and representations in sculpture and relief were so important: they perpetuated the memory of a man, and particularly that of a king, long after he was dead. Reality, sadly, in its outcome, rarely matched expectation. No Egyptian king should have had any illusion about what might happen to his memory and to his monuments after his death. The land of Egypt was littered with the remains of monuments of past kings, wilfully destroyed or even dismantled for building later structures by successor kings who cared nothing for those who had gone before.

Sometimes, however, a reputation lasted long after the death of a king and settled into the consciousness of successive generations, often changed, frequently garbled, and almost always romanticized. Such was the case with Ramesses II, and it is well worth considering his subsequent reputation and the impact of his memory on later generations, even down to the early nineteenth century when Egypt once more rose in the consciousness of modern man.

The most positive indication of the survival of Ramesses' reputation is given by a long inscription, now preserved in the Louvre Museum in Paris, which purports to give an account of events that took place in the reign of Ramesses II. According to the text, Ramesses, during a tour of inspection of his subject states in Syria, received tribute from many princes, including the ruler of Bakhtan, a country so far away that it has never been identified. Among his gifts to Ramesses was his daughter, who became a favoured wife of the Egyptian king and was given the Egyptian name, Neferure.

Subsequently, a messenger came from Bakhtan with the news that Neferure's younger sister, Bentresh, was seriously ill. Could Ramesses please send a skilled doctor? So the best in the land, Djehuty-em-heb, was chosen and sent to Bakhtan. Unfortunately, he found that his skills were incapable of subduing the evil spirit which afflicted Bentresh; and the prince of Bakhtan sent a further message to Ramesses requesting that a god should be sent to help.

So Ramesses took advice from the gods in Karnak, and he was recommended to send the god, Khons-the-Contriver, who was specially good at driving out evil spirits. After a long journey lasting one year and five months, Khons-the-Contriver arrived in Bakhtan and in no time effected a cure. There was much rejoicing, and for good reason; the whole operation had taken, so far, about five or six years from the time of the arrival of the first messenger.

The prince of Bakhtan, however, was not at all inclined to return Khons-the-Contriver to Egypt immediately, and he delayed his departure for three years and nine months. In due course, the prince was advised in a dream that the god was not pleased at having to stay, and the hint was taken. Khons-the-Contriver was returned to Egypt with much treasure and arrived in Thebes on the nineteenth day of the second winter month in the thirty-third year of Ramesses II. The whole episode lasted ten years.

Now, this romantic and fanciful tale, presented on a stone slab as if it were a true royal record, does contain a germ of fact. The one event in Ramesses' long reign which he commemorated more than any other was his so-called triumph over the Hittites at the Battle of Qadesh. This took place in his fifth year. After years of an uneasy truce, a formal treaty was signed between Egypt and the Hittite nation in Ramesses' twenty-fifth year. In Year 34, after protracted negotiations, a Hittite princess was sent to Egypt to join Ramesses' harem of wives. This event was marked by celebrations, and it was recorded with unusual detail in inscriptions set up in appropriate temples, including Karnak and Abu Simbel. The new queen's Egyptian name was Ma-hor-neferure. You will recall that the foreign princess of Bakhtan was simply called Neferure. It cannot be doubted that the memory of the Hittite marriage was the source for part, at least, of the so-called Bentresh text.

It is, nevertheless, difficult to understand the purpose behind the composition and carving on a very hard stone, in a formal and official manner, of this extraordinary tale, which contains more than a touch, or suggestion, of the *Arabian Nights*. It is particularly difficult to understand, when it is realised that the story was carved in about 200 B.C., more than one thousand years after Ramesses' reign. The most plausible explanation is that it was devised to enhance the reputation of the two gods, Khons-the-Contriver and Khons-Neferhotep, by ascribing to their powers wonderful events that had happened long ago in the reign of a Pharaoh whose name was still remembered.

As far as Ramesses himself is concerned, the significance of the Bentresh story is that it indicates quite clearly that the great Ramesses was still remembered, even though Egyptians of about 200 B.C. might have been at a loss to say why he was remembered, or even who he was. Nevertheless, it seems that his was a name to conjure with. Thus, he enters, often incidentally, into a series of stories, also of very late date, which principally concern his famous son, Khaemwese, who for the last years of his life was Ramesses' crown prince. During his actual existence during the reign of his father, Khaemwese was the High Priest of the god Ptah in Memphis. Ptah is often described as an intellectual deity because his particular kind of theology was abstract and cerebral. His high priest, therefore, might be thought to have required rather more intellectual capacity than might be adequate for high priests of less thought-provoking theologies. Khaemwese seems to have fitted the position splendidly, and his undoubted reputation in his lifetime persisted for at least one thousand years. He emerges as the main character in a series of stories which have happily been preserved for us on papyri written in the third century B.C.

Again, we must suppose that the silence which exists between Khaemwese's lifetime and the writing of the stories is due to the absence of surviving documents. In any case, it is clear that Khaemwese and his exploits as a very clever man in the time of Ramesses II were the stuff of legend. Once more, the great king and his court provide the background for magical happenings and fantastic adventures. Throughout, Ramesses is depicted as the common-sense ruler who is full of understanding and knows how to solve problems.

In one episode Khaemwese, by trickery, makes off with a book of magic belonging to a dead prince named Naneferkaptah. Delighted with his prize, he shows it to Ramesses and boasts of the way in which he came by it. His father advises him most strongly to return the book to Naneferkaptah. Khaemwese ignores the advice, and we know that trouble will follow. And so it does.

The story goes on to tell how Khaemwese becomes infatuated with Tabubu, a lady who turns out to be a priestess of the goddess Bastet. He follows her to Bubastis in the hope of having his way with her, but she teases him along with half-promises until he undertakes to make over to her, by legal contract, all his property. Tabubu's demands, however, are increasingly exacting. Next, she obliges him to get his children to sign the contract in agreement. Then, she forces him to kill his children; for, as she says, "I don't want them left

41

to fight with my children over your property." Poor Khaemwese, his resolve and independence reduced to jelly, agrees, and he and Tabubu sit down to a feast while they hear the dogs and cats squabbling over his children's bodies in the yard outside.

At this point it seemed to Khaemwese as if he would achieve his desire, but just then Tabubu screamed, and he woke up to find himself lying in the open with no clothes on. At that very moment, who should drive past in his chariot but Ramesses. Khaemwese felt he should jump up in respect but could not bring himself to do so because he was nude. "Why are you in this state?" said Ramesses. "It is Naneferkaptah who has done it all to me," was Khaemwese's reply. So he was sent off to Memphis where he found his children safe and well.

Ramesses, having heard the whole story, reminded Khaemwese of his previous advice and urged him to return the book to Naneferkaptah. And that is what Khaemwese did.

Classical authors who wrote about Egypt inevitably picked up stories and whispers of stories about Ramesses, and they included tantalising passages which celebrate the fame of the long-dead Pharaoh without necessarily saying anything true about him. Herodotus, the great fifth-century Greek historian, who travelled in Egypt to collect material at first-hand, was always ready to accept and pass on a good story. None was better than that about a king called Rhampsinitus, who may historically represent a confusion or conflation of both Ramesses II and Ramesses III, who lived not quite a century later.

The essence of the story is the outwitting of Ramesses, or Rhampsinitus, by the son of a man who had constructed an impregnable treasure-house for the king. The son learnt the secret of entering the strong room, and he, at first with his brother, set about steady, though restrained, robbery. By cleverness he outwitted every move made by Ramesses to apprehend him, even when the king sent his daughter to trap him by pretending to be a lady of easy virtue. In the end Ramesses gave up, admitting defeat, and promised the thief a pardon and a fine reward if he were to reveal himself. This he did, and Ramesses told him that he thought him the cleverest of men. "The Egyptians," he maintained, "beat the rest of the world in wisdom, and this man beats all the Egyptians."

This story seems to have little recognizable fact in it. Some commentators find references which point to the great mortuary temple of Ramesses III at Medinet Habu in Western Thebes, but the treasure-house could equally have been located within the precinct of Ramesses II's own mortuary temple, known as the Ramesseum.

Herodotus was on better ground in mentioning that Rhampsinitus was best memorialized by the western court of the Temple of Hephaestus, before which he had placed two statues of 25 cubits in height, that is, about 36 feet. Now, the Greeks equated their god Hephaestus with the Egyptian god Ptah, whom we have already met through Khaemwese, the High Priest in Memphis. Here, therefore, Herodotus is talking of the great Ptah temple in Memphis, which, as we well know from surviving remains, was added to substantially by Ramesses II. There are also several colossal statues of the king in and around the site of ancient Memphis. The best known is the great alabaster colossus, now lying prone and housed in a special building. It was originally about 42 feet tall. A second, very impressive, granite colossus was moved some years ago into Cairo and now stands dominating the square outside Cairo's main railway terminus. It is about 34 feet tall. Biggest of all the Memphite statues of Ramesses was sadly broken to pieces, probably in antiquity. One of its great fists is now in the British Museum, and from it, the height of the original has been estimated at about 70 feet. We should also not forget the somewhat smaller colossus which has been rehabilitated for the exhibition in Memphis, Tennessee.

Great statues were certainly favoured by Ramesses II, and, as we shall shortly see, the surviving examples still memorialize the great king, impressing visitors to Egypt, whether at Tanis in the Delta, at Thebes in various temples, or at Abu Simbel. They also impressed ancient visitors to Egypt. Diodorus of Sicily, a Greek historian of the first century B.C., writes at length about a building which he calls the tomb of Osymandyas. There can be little doubt that the structure in question is none other than Ramesses II's mortuary temple, the Ramesseum. Although he visited Egypt, Diodorus does not seem to have got as far south as Thebes, and his account of this tomb of Osymandyas is based on hearsay. "Why Osymandyas?" you may ask. This name, undoubtedly, is based on that part of Ramesses' full titulary which Egyptologists call the prenomen. It is, in a sense, the name by which the king can best be recognized. We talk all the time about Ramesses II, but the name Ramesses, from the royal point of view, was almost as common as Smith. There were eleven Ramesses kings during the Nineteenth and Twentieth Dynasties. But the prenomen of Ramesses II was the name by which he was truly identified. It was User-ma'at-Re, "One great of Truth is Re," and it may have been pronounced, in the manner of speaking of the mid-Nineteenth Dynasty, as Usimare. From Usimare to Osymandyas is but a short step.

Those of you who know something of English poetry of the early nineteenth century may call to mind a sonnet of Percy Bysshe Shelley which is called *Ozymandias*. This is where we find the ancient form of Ramesses II seeping into the consciousness of civilized Europe three thousand years after the death of the great king. And in what a strange and round-about way!

Let us go back to Diodorus the Sicilian for a moment. In the course of his second-hand description of the Ramesseum, he talks of a seated statue of the king carved from a single piece of black stone of Syene, that is, the black granite-like stone found in the neighbourhood of Aswan. He says that it is the largest statue in Egypt, and after purveying the other details, he gives the sense of the inscription as follows: "King of Kings, Osymandyas am I. If anyone wants to know how great I am and where I lie, let him exceed my works."

Now, back to the poet Shelley. The sonnet starts:

> I met a traveller from an antique land Who said: 'Two vast and trunkless legs of stone Stand in the dust.... Near them, on the sand, Half sunk, a shattered visage lies....'

A few lines later, he continues:

> And on the pedestal these words appear: 'My name is Ozymandias, King of Kings: Look on my works, ye Mighty, and despair.'

Nobody now doubts that in writing this sonnet Shelley made use of Diodorus' account, taking it either directly from the Greek text or from some secondary source. "King of Kings, Osymandyas am I. If anyone wants to know how great I am and where I lie, let him exceed my works." But what prompted Shelley to write about Ozymandias, for at his time of writing, probably 1817, Egypt had only recently been made easily accessible to Europeans, and it was to be several years before the hieroglyphic script was deciphered?

It used to be said that the inspiration for Shelley's sonnet was a colossal bust of Ramesses II, from the Ramesseum, which was presented to the British Museum in 1817, but there is no evidence that Shelley ever saw it. In any case, the opening words of the sonnet make it clear that Shelley heard about it from "a traveller from an antique land," who presumably had seen the wreck of a colossal statue in Egypt. This traveller may well have been William Hamilton, who had travelled in Egypt in the years following the disastrous Napoleonic invasion of that country and had published his account in a volume called *Aegyptiaca* in 1809.

Speaking of colossal Egyptian statues, he describes the head of one which he identifies as being in the temple called the Memnonium - a name erroneously given to the Ramesseum at that time. Of it he says:

> It is certainly the most beautiful and perfect piece of Egyptian sculpture that can be seen throughout the whole country. We were struck by its extraordinary delicacy; the very uncommon expression visible in its features.... It is of granite.... Its proportions are not so colossal as those of the two which are together in the plain [that is, those called the Colossi of Memnon]; and the place in which it is to be found exactly answers to the [the sacred precinct of Memnon]...a space within a ruined temple...strewn with fragments of columns, traces of walls, pedestals, doorways and statues....

The head here described by William Hamilton is certainly the one which arrived in the British Museum in 1817; and it is not unreasonable to think that Shelley may have known about the piece and the temple directly from Hamilton or from reading Hamilton's account in *Aegyptiaca*. But there is here, as in almost every episode involving Ramesses II in his mythical existence in the traditions and stories of late antiquity, a notable mix-up of fact, fiction, and pure invention. To begin with, the fine head, so much admired by Hamilton, was never identified as Ozymandias when it came to the British Museum. On the contrary, it was dubbed "The Younger Memnon," and this name persisted for a great part of the nineteenth century, although it was known that the subject of the sculpture was Ramesses II. Even now, we sometimes call it the Younger Memnon for sentimental reasons, and partly out of sheer perversity.

Furthermore, if you are to look for the original statue described by Diodorus and said to have a foot measuring over seven cubits, you must focus on the remains of a truly vast seated colossus which once dominated the first court of the Ramesseum. Here is what the "traveller from an antique land" had seen and what Shelley, with poetic genius and not a little poetic licence, immortalized in verse.

In a sense, Shelley's sonnet and the arrival of the colossal bust in the British Museum signalled the rebirth of the Ramesses legend in modern times. It was not long before the brilliant French scholar, Jean-François Champollion, announced his decipherment of the hieroglyphic script, followed shortly by his reading of the name of Ramesses on Egyptian monuments. By the 1840's Egyptologists had succeeded in translating a great many ancient Egyptian inscriptions, including some dealing with Ramesses II and his reign.

It is not surprising that Ramesses made his mark in the scholarly world so decisively and so quickly. Among the standing monuments easily visible to visiting scholars and available for study without excavation, were many buildings and statues of Usimare, Ramesses II, Ozymandias. His name was easily recognizable, the scale of his monuments compelled recognition. He was indubitably "Ramesses the Great." The splendour of his works led romantically inclined writers to describe him, for example, as the Louis XIV of antiquity, *le Roi Soleil*, the Sun King. In fact, Ramesses was being judged according to his own estimation. His own propaganda was working after three thousand years. He would have been pleased.

Let us look at some of the buildings and monuments that contributed to the first appraisal of the Pharaoh who, above all, typified the grandeur that was said to be Egypt.

As the Ramesseum has already attracted our attention, we may begin here, approaching it from the modern town of Luxor by crossing the Nile and driving a mile or so over the flood-plain of the river, past the great Colossi of Memnon, and turning a little way to the north. On our left are the hills of the Theban Necropolis, which hold the tombs of the nobles who served Ramesses and his fellow monarchs of the New Kingdom.

Here, within a huge mud-brick enclosure wall, are the remains, principally, of the temple built to serve as the cult-chapel of the king after his death. It was common practice to provide a mortuary or funerary temple to accompany the tomb of every dead king. In earlier times such temples were built close to the tomb, which was often a pyramid. In the New Kingdom, however, the kings of the Eighteenth, Nineteenth, and Twentieth Dynasties were buried in the Valley of the Kings, where there was no space for individual mortuary temples. Consequently, the temples were built some distance away, on the edge of the desert, where there was much more room for grandiose construction.

In the mortuary temple, elaborate daily rituals took place aimed at honouring the cult of the dead king, worshipping the great god of Thebes, Amun, and providing huge offerings of food and drink for the posthumous benefit of the dead, but divine, monarch. Ramesses made sure that his temple was worthy of his long reign, of his fame, and of the mighty exploits which had distinguished his life. It was monumental in every respect, suitably embellished with scenes and texts illustrating what he persisted in regarding as his great triumph over the Hittites at the Battle of Qadesh, and liberally provided with colossal sculptures, which included the one later dignified as Ozymandias, which, according to modern estimates, weighed at least 1000 tons.

The great reputation which Ramesses has acquired in modern times is based on three considerations, all of which are patently demonstrated in the Ramesseum and elsewhere. Firstly, he was a great builder. Secondly, he was lavish in presenting his greatness to the world through colossal sculpture. Thirdly, he vaunted his success at Qadesh so vigorously that it might well seem to have been the greatest victory of all times. The main record ends this way:

> Attaining Egypt in peace at Piramesse, resting in his palace of life and power like Re who is in his horizon, the deities of this land coming to him, adoring and saying: 'Welcome our much-loved son, King of Upper and Lower Egypt, Usimare-Setepenre, son of Re, Ramesses-meryamun'; and they gave to him millions of jubilees for ever on the throne of Re, all lands and all foreign countries subdued beneath his sandals, for ever and ever.

The three factors mentioned above should be held in mind as we proceed with our tour of some of his major constructions.

Before we leave Western Thebes and recross the Nile to Luxor, we should consider briefly one further monument. It is his own tomb in the Valley of the Kings. It is not one of the tombs visited today by the modern traveller to Egypt. It is a long, corridor-like tomb, extending deep into the rock, but in a very ruinous condition. So it has been probably since antiquity, and we know that it had been comprehensively plundered, perhaps within a century of the burial. After at least one protective move, the great king's body, stripped of all its funerary finery, was included in an impressive collection of royal bodies reburied in a hidden place during the Twenty-first Dynasty. And here, among his peers, was Ramesses II himself, a poor, sad shell of a man, helpless and naked, but still displaying a face that could be recognized from his many monuments. He had survived, he was remembered, his name still rang clear in the halls of history.

Back in Luxor we find Ramesses mightily represented in the two great temples of Karnak and of Luxor, cult shrines of Amun-Re and of his divine wife, Mut, and their son Khons. At Karnak, Ramesses has left his work in many parts of this vast conglomerate of divine buildings. We approach the complex along an avenue of ram-headed sphinxes; between the paws of each is a small figure of the king - an avenue which was planned by Ramesses to run up to the great pylon forming the entrance to the over-powering Hypostyle Hall. As seen today, the avenue is interrupted by another pylon or gateway built at a much later date.

Just before we enter the Hypostyle Hall, we cannot fail to be struck by a standing colossus of Ramesses II with his daughter Bintanat. This fine statue was later usurped by the High Priest Pinudjem in the Twenty-first Dynasty. The usurpation of a statue means the hijacking of its identity by the addition of someone else's name and, possibly, the destruction by erasure of the names of the original subject.

It is ironic that Ramesses was usurped in the form of this great statue, because he was himself not averse to taking over other kings' monuments by usurpation. In a sense, he took over the Hypostyle Hall to be his own monument by completing the decoration of the columns and walls, a work that had been started by his father, Sethos (or Seti) I. Some of Ramesses' wall reliefs are lively and well carved, but, in general, they compare badly with those of Sethos.

To see temple architecture of Ramesses II in its greatest glory, we should pass from Karnak to Luxor to look at the pylon and court which he added to the temple of Amenophis III. Visitors in the early nineteenth century found a very romantic ruin, heavily encumbered with mounds of debris and ramshackle dwellings of the modern inhabitants of Luxor.

The huge formal entrance, or pylon, was originally embellished in the most imposing manner, a model of what a temple entrance should be. In fact, a record of the façade can be found on one of the walls of the great court. First, there were the two great wings of the pylon decorated with vast reliefs illustrating the ubiquitous Battle of Qadesh. Placed in great recesses in the pylon and towering high above it, were immense flag-poles with pennants streaming from their tops. Then, in front of the pylon pointing high to heaven, were two, monolithic, granite obelisks and on each side of the doorway, huge seated colossi and a pair of equally imposing standing figures of Ramesses. The effect, when the temple additions were completed, must have been stupendous. Even now, with one of the obelisks in exile dominating the Place de la Concorde in Paris and with only one of the standing figures still in place, the impression is memorable, especially if you visit it in the early morning or in the evening when the temple is flood-lit.

Studies in recent years have shown that Ramesses II, through his temple building and particularly through his colossal sculpture, built up a series of cults in which he, through assimilation with certain Egyptian deities, became himself the object of worship, even during his lifetime. The temple-building activity carried out during his reign was unsurpassed by any other ancient Egyptian king, and it secured for Ramesses a firm and substantial basis for glory while he was alive and fame when he was dead.

It is always hazardous to assign motives to people in the past when the evidence is sketchy or ambivalent. Should we think, for example, that Ramesses consciously set out to glorify himself and establish a myth of divinity for subsequent ages? I very much doubt it. Nevertheless, that was the effect of much that was achieved on Ramesses' behalf during his reign. He evidently had an excellent public-relations staff which, no doubt, based its endeavours on the known opinions of the king. It seems highly likely that the correct estimates of what was needed were made early in his long reign of 67 years, for the events and ideas which had marked his early years were exploited again and again. Building went on throughout his reign, but nothing occurred to surpass the so-called victory of Qadesh which happened in Year 5.

Even in the earliest architectural works of the reign, the grandiloquent tendencies are evident. At Abydos, the most sacred place in ancient Egypt, where Ramesses' first enterprise was the completion of the noble temple started by his father, Sethos I, he outdid his parent in the scale of his construction, although in style and delicacy of architecture and decoration, the later work falls far short of the earlier. At Abydos, in Sethos' temple, the ancestor kings of Egypt were celebrated in a famous scene in which their names were listed chronologically beginning with Menes, first king of the First Dynasty. This scene may well have stimulated in Ramesses' mind ideas of fame in posterity, for a similar list was put up in the temple he built for himself a few hundred yards from that of his father. The second Abydos temple is notable in being built of limestone (whereas most of Ramesses' other temples were of sandstone) and in having exceptionally fine low-relief scenes. Their appearance is still most striking, especially as much colour is preserved.

The vaunting of Ramesses II in his own lifetime by building and by religious means reached a special level outside Egypt proper, in Nubia, the district that lay beyond Egypt's southern boundary at Aswan. Its consideration in this alien region will form the culmination of our study of Ramesses in myth and fact. But before we travel south to Nubia, let us briefly lament the fact that so little can be said of the secular sides of Ramesses' work and life. Egypt is dominated today by the religious monuments of its past. Temples and tombs survive today because they were built of stone for eternity. Palaces and houses and other secular buildings were mostly constructed of mud-brick. We know from many ancient records, including the Bible, that the Residence and administrative capital of the great king was named Piramesse and that it was in the Delta. By all reports it was a magnificent city. A contemporary account written on papyrus has this to say about it:

> His Majesty (may he live, be prosperous, and healthy) has constructed a palace named 'Great-of-Victories.' It lies between Djahy [Syria] and Ta-Mery [Egypt] and is stocked with food and provisions. It is planned like Thebes in Upper Egypt, and its continuation is like Memphis. The sun rises and sets within its horizon. All have deserted their own towns and come to live in its neighbourhood. Its west is the Temple of Amun, its south is the Temple of Seth.

In contemplating the greatness and fame of Piramesse, it is remarkable to consider that until very recently the very location of the place was lost. Egyptologists of earlier generations thought it was at Tanis, the Biblical Zoan, where many monuments of Ramesses II may be seen. Recent archaeological researches, however, have shown beyond reasonable doubt that Piramesse and its predecessor, the Hyksos city of Avaris, were sited in the neighbourhood of modern Qantir. There is now ample evidence to show that here there were magnificent palaces, temples, and all the constructions of a great city of the time of the Nineteenth and Twentieth Dynasties. It has also been demonstrated that the region was subsequently abandoned because the branch of the Nile, on which Piramesse stood, had silted up. Its *raison d'être* as a major city and port, therefore, disappeared, and the focus shifted to a new site with a potentially good harbour. This was Tanis, and to Tanis was transported, lock, stock, and barrel, a great part of the monumental statuary which had been brought to his Residence by Ramesses from Memphis and elsewhere.

With the physical remains of Piramesse, numerous small, but specific, cults of Ramesses II were also moved to Tanis. There they continued for generations, perpetuating in a somewhat anomalous manner, the fame and divinity of a king long beyond the time of reasonable expectation.

As I mentioned earlier, Ramesses II developed a very particular style of grandeur and divinity in Nubia. It was a process of divinization which developed as Ramesses' long reign continued. There is good reason to believe that in constructing temples in this extra-territorial region of Egypt, the intention was primarily to establish, for the edification of the non-Egyptian inhabitants of Nubia, the might of the Egyptian king supported by the great gods, Amun, Re-Herakhty, and Ptah - gods which were transformed at this time into imperial deities. In these temples the commonplace scenes showing Ramesses honouring the gods were later in his reign supplemented by scenes in which the king himself became the recipient of the same. This development is particularly clear in the temple built by the Nubian viceroy, Setau, between Years 35 and 50 at a place called Wadi es-Sebua, "Valley of the Lions," so-called because of the avenue of sphinxes - royal-headed lions which formed the processional way to the temple from the river. Here the king, without equivocation, substitutes for certain expected deities in scenes of offering.

What is clear at Wadi es-Sebua may be seen developing in Abu Simbel, the most dramatic of Ramesses' monuments in Egypt. This vast rock-cut temple, known specially for its monumental façade and for the fact that it was moved complete to a much higher location after the flooding of Nubia in the 1960's, was started in the early years of the reign but was not completed until about the thirty-fifth year.

The great façade, with its four colossal figures of the king cut from the living rock, is, in a sense, conventional in that the pylon façade of a temple built in the open would have colossal figures placed in front of it. Here, because of the situation, a local variant was effected. Each statue is over 65 feet in height, finely proportioned, and excellently carved with the midget visitor in mind. The eyes of the king are so angled that they look down at the visitor and not straight ahead to the distant horizon. So far, then, nothing is specially divine, and the statues are not by their inscriptions invested with the kind of divine cult found, for example, at Piramesse.

The temple proper extends about 180 feet into the cliff with a series of halls, side-chambers, vestibules, and, ultimately, the sanctuary. It may be sensibly assumed that the sanctuary was the last part of the temple to be carved out of the rock, and here are figures of four gods, the joint objects of worship - Re-Herakhty, Amun, Ptah, and Ramesses himself. Here, then, there is no beating about the divine bush: Ramesses is placed in equality with the three other great gods, and his position is made clear in scenes in and adjacent to the sanctuary. It is the apogee of his divinity, expressed openly and unambiguously.

What then are we to make of the myth and reality of Ramesses II? One thing is clear: it is impossible to get at all close to this great man, to determine his character, to penetrate the physiognomy of his abundant portraiture, to establish his likes and dislikes. What we have is what we have been allowed to have according to the conventions and traditions governing the public presentation of an Egyptian Pharaoh.

Nevertheless, he succeeded, as no other Pharaoh did, in establishing a memory of himself - I deliberately do not use the word reputation - which long outlived his reign and which survived in ripples or echoes as late as the Graeco-Roman Period, one thousand years after his death. And again, in modern times, even before hieroglyphs were deciphered and scholars could read his name, he made his mark on visitors to Egypt - the traveller in an antique land. Why should this have happened?

If the historian looks at the 67 years of Ramesses' reign, he will find few high points to plot in compiling a graph of achievement. The great events which seem to be required to establish the importance of a reign can be counted on the fingers of both hands. Internally Egypt was evidently in a very settled state; administration was apparently good, the land was prosperous, there were no serious crises to scar the record. A good, prosperous, peaceful reign does not make headlines, but it does provide an opportunity for a long-living king to make his mark in other ways.

Self-promotion was not a matter for disapprobation in ancient Egypt, and Ramesses was ceaselessly promoted throughout his long reign, to such an extent that he became a legend in his lifetime - in fact, a suitable subject for divinity and a divinity far beyond the usual identification of the ruling Pharaoh with the god Horus. By historical accident rather than by clever planning, the cults of the divine Ramesses persisted in places like Tanis and Abu Simbel long after his death. His posthumous fame was far greater than that of any of his predecessors, nurtured, no doubt, by the ever-present and unavoidable temples and statues clearly marked with his name.

And so he is remembered today. His monuments draw the curious to gaze and wonder. This is the reality of his legend. And whether he planned his fame or not, he would be mightily pleased to know that his name still lives triumphantly more than three thousand years after his death.

ROYAL PAINTERS : DEIR EL-MEDINA IN DYNASTY XIX

C.A. Keller

Introduction

The tomb paintings of the Egyptian New Kingdom are among the most widely-known (and readily appreciated) artistic remains of ancient Egypt. With a relatively simple kit composed of pigments, ink, water, a rush pen, and palette, the ancient Egyptian draughtsman was able to render textures as varied as fish scales, animal hair and fur, and the diaphanous garments of female guests at the funerary banquets. The juxtaposition of this type of naturalistic detail with the formalized organization of the scenes is one of the most striking attributes of ancient Egyptian tomb painting and has its roots in the fundamentally magical purposes of the painted representations: to ensure a continuous supply of offerings to the deceased, as well as to provide him with the information (and paraphernalia) necessary to effect successful transformations into the forms appropriate for the desired type of afterlife.

For these reasons the paintings had to conform to traditional canons of iconography, form, and proportion. If the information contained in the painting or relief was not "correct," then it would be ineffective in accomplishing its purposes. In order to learn both the proper method of rendering the sacred images and their appropriate wall arrangement, the draughtmen-to-be received instruction (along with the scribes-in-training) at training institutions, which were often located in temple or palace precincts. One such school was located in the workmen's village at the site now called Deir el-Medina, and was founded in order to train the scribes, draughtsmen, and sculptors responsible for the decoration of the royal tombs of the New Kingdom.

Although the village of Deir el-Medina was occupied for most of the New Kingdom (c. 1500-1085 BC), the focus of the present study will be on Dynasty XIX, and the reign of Ramesses II in particular, for his reign appears to have contained the high point of the village in terms of its economic prosperity - if one can judge by the sheer number and quality of the private monuments that were produced by the workmen at that time. These private monuments were fabricated and decorated by the same artists and craftsmen responsible for the royal tombs themselves. And it is by reviewing contemporary monuments from both royal and private contexts that a better understanding and appreciation of the artistic methods and achievements of the XIXth Dynasty draughtsmen of Deir el-Medina may be obtained.[1]

---

1 The present paper is an outgrowth of research conducted in the US, Europe, and Egypt during portions of 1975, 1980-81, and 1987 and was partially funded by PL-480 funds administered by the Smithsonian Institution. I would like here to express my appreciation to the American Research Center in Egypt, Inc., the American Council of Learned Societies, and the University of California, Berkeley, who in large part funded the projects; to the Egyptian Antiquities Organization for permission to conduct research in Egypt; and to the institutions whose archival materials and objects were made available to me during these study tours. Permission to reproduce the objects and photographs included in the plates accompanying this paper has been acknowledged where appropriate. A greatly expanded version of this paper will appear in an enlarged study of the Deir el-Medina draughtsman, which is now in progress.

Training, Methods, and Materials

The *sš-kd* "outline draughtsman" (or "painter" as the title has also been translated) was only one of several craft occupations practiced at Deir el-Medina.[2] This group of workmen, which also included relief sculptors, carpenters, and stonecutters, was organized into a bipartite "crew" under the administrative supervision of the "chiefs" (i.e., the two chief workmen, the "scribe(s) of the tomb", and occasionally the master draughtsman), whose task it was to keep track of the progress of the work on the tomb(s) under construction at any given time.[3] This all important work was funded by the state, with the workmen receiving payments in kind (chiefly grain, but also including many different types of commodities), which were issued at more or less regular intervals. shelter, various types of domestic assistance, and other types of support were also received by the workmen in exchange for their labor. The payments in kind could be used by the family of the workman to whom it was issued or passed on to others in exchange for other commodities.[4]

Membership in the crew was chiefly governed by heredity, which was in keeping with the ancient Egyptian ideal of the son being a "staff of old age" for the father who had raised (and often trained) him to take over upon the older workman's retirement. Thus not only the son benefited from this arrangement, which enabled him to step right into a more potentially lucrative profession that he otherwise might, but the father could be supported in a state befitting his own higher status.

Once admitted to the status of draughtsman-in-training, the young man spent years in imitating the models set before him by his teachers. These patterns (or, models) were drawn on *ostraca* (the "waste paper" of ancient Thebes). And the student attempted to copy them exactly, or as well as his as yet unpracticed hand would allow, at any rate. Many examples of both the models and the students' attempts at imitation have survived from the village, such as an example now in the Medelhavsmuseet in Stockholm, originally published by Peterson (plates 1 and 2),[5] that bears the teacher's rendering of the cartouches of the deified Amenhotep I on the *recto* and the student's clumsy imitation on the *verso*. And on another (unfortunately fragmentary) example of a "teaching" ostracon preserved in the collection of the IFAO in Cairo, which depicts the chin and neck area of a leftward-facing male profile, the master's correction has been added in white over the laboriously drawn and colored work of the student.[6]

---

2 OC 25581, *verso* 1 ff., where two draughtsmen are enumerated among some *rmṯ.w-jst hmww*, "specialized (or, skilled) crew members," who are to be recruited for work on the tomb.

3 For a discussion of the composition of the *ḥwntyw*, "chiefs/captains," of the tomb, see J. Cerny, *A Community of Workmen at Thebes in the Ramesside Period*, Cairo, 1973, p. 231 ff.; for a recent reconsideration of the topic, see R. Ventura, *Living in a City of the Dead*, Freiburg/Göttingen, 1986, pp. 73-76.

4 For the most complete treatment of the economic side of village life at Deir el-Medina to date, see J.J. Janssen, *Commodity Prices from the Ramesside Period*, Leiden, 1975, and the review by P.J. Frandsen, *Acta Orientalia* 40 (1979), p. 279 ff.

5 B.J. Peterson, *Zeichnungen aus einer Totenstadt*, Stockholm, 1973, cat. no. 138 = MM 14 116; p. 104 and *tafel* 73. I am grateful to Dr. Peterson for permission to include ostraca from the Medelhavsmuseet collection in the present study.

6 OIFAO 2509 = J. Vandier d'Abbadie, *Catalogue des ostraca figurés de Deir el-Médineh*,

In contrast, other figured ostraca appear to have served as true sketchpads, being covered with a plethora of unrelated images, such as an example in the Metropolitan Museum of Art, New York, (plate 3), bearing a tangle of various images, including a very elegant profile (facing right), two crocodiles, and a portion of the titulary of Ramesses II.[7] One might contrast this piece (which was probably discarded after the various jottings on both sides were of no further interest) with an example of the figured ostracon as a finished object in and of itself, as illustrated by the charmingly executed drawing of the ram of Amun that bears the name and title of the late Dynasty XIX Chief Workman Hay, now in Cairo. (plate 4).[8] The "finished" appearance of the images on the latter piece, coupled with the dedicatory text, may indicate its use as a small *ex voto*.

Particularly interesting in the context of this presentation are representations of three-dimensional objects, which were decorated by the draughtsmen themselves. Now in Stockholm are two figured ostraca that preserve drawings of a *shabti* and the upper portion of a heart scarab[9] an the lower portion of a heart scarab,[10] respectively. On the *recto* of the former piece, in the position where the name of the client might have been expected to appear, the name and title of the "Draughtsman of Amun Rahotep" has been inserted in at least one place on the *shabti* (plate 5). And on the upper portion of the heart scarab, which has been sketched on the *verso*, the name and title of his brother, the "Draughtsman of Amun Nebre" has been inscribed. In addition, the name and title of what may be a third draughtsman, whose name begins with *P3* ... has been written on the lower portion of the *shabti* inscription. Even though this partially preserved name may actually be simply a variant of Rahotep, in which the definite article *P3* has been prefixed to the basic form of the personal name (resulting in the form Perahotep), a reference to either (Pe)rahotep and Nebre's father, Pay, or to their remaining brother, Peraemheb, both of whose names begin with the same element, is also a possibility. This draughtsman family is known to have been active during the first half of Dynasty XIX, with the majority of attestations falling into the long reign of Ramesses II.[11] In light of the prominence of (Pe)rahotep's name (and that of at least one other member of his family) in the texts on these objects, it is quite

---

DFIFAO 2:2, CAIRO, 1937, P. 105 and pl. LXIII.

7 OMMA 14.6.204 (unpublished). The *verso* of the ostracon preserves a text dated to a "year 60," presumably of Ramesses II. My thanks to Dr. Christine Lilyquist, Senior Research Curator, and Dr. Dorothea Arnold, Associate Curator in-charge, for permission to examine and publish this - and other pieces - from the Egyptian collection of the Metropolitan Museum of Art, New York, in the present article.

8 Cairo Museum Temporary Register 23/2/22/1, see most recently: R. Freed, *Ramesses the Great: His Life and World*, Memphis, 1987, cat. no. 12: p. 143. I thank Mr. Mohammed Mohsan, Dr. Mohammed Saleh, and Mr. Mohammed Gomaa for facilitating my study of this - and other objects - in the Egyptian Museum, Cairo, during 1980-81 and 1987.

9 MM 14 120 = Peterson, *Zeichnungen*, cat. no. 139: pp. 105-6; *tafel* 76.

10 MM 14 121 = Peterson, *Zeichnungen*, cat. no. 140: p. 106; *tafel* 76.

11 For this draughtsman family, see most recently: L. Habachi, *Tavole d'offerta are e bacili da libagione* Torino, 1977, cat. no. 22029: p. 37. The study by M. Tosi, *Una Stripe de pittore a Tebe*, Torino, 1972 has incorrect genealogical information on pp. 32-4 (a fact already noted by Bogoslovsky in *ZÄS* 107 [1980], p. 94) but provides a short, nicely illustrated popular account of the Deir el-Medina draughtsmen.

possible that either Perahotep or Nebre was the artist responsible for these drawings, which were probably preliminary studies for the inscriptions to be placed on the actual three-dimensional objects.[12]

Further examples of two-dimensional representations of three-dimensional objects that were decorated by the draughtsmen are two sketches now in the Metropolitan Museum of Art, New York, which document the form and decorative schemes of private coffins of the period. On the smaller of the two ostraca[13] (plate 6) the layout for the texts on an anthropoid coffin is preserved. Omitting the larger figural representations of divinities that were placed in the interstices, the artist has compressed the organizational scheme of the texts into a small black ink study that could be conveniently held in the hand; blanks were left in the appropriate positions for the insertion of the name (and possibly titles) of the person for whom the coffin was intended.[14]

A larger red ink drawing depicts a male innermost lid (or, "*couvercle planche*") lying within the box of an anthropoid coffin (plate 7).[15] An innermost lid is a lifesize wooden-backed plastered and painted image of the deceased that was placed directly over the mummy as it lay in the inner coffin. This particular sketch portrays such an object, which in this case represents the deceased in the ceremonial dress he wore during life, rather than in the mummiform guise in which he was usually represented on his anthropoid coffins. These innermost lids were a regular part of the funerary outfit of a well equipped burial of the Ramesside and Third Intermediate Periods (1314-730 BC). However, those examples that depict the deceased in the dress of the living are peculiar to early Dynasty XIX,[16] as is the example belonging to Iyneferti, the wife of Sennedjem, illustrated in Plate 8.[17]

The use of ostraca (or papyrus) drawings as small-scale patterns for the transference of images to large-scale contexts, such as tomb or temple walls, is well illustrated by the squared-up depiction of the frequently encountered motto "all life, stability and dominion" from an XVIIIth Dynasty context at Deir el-Bahri, and now in the Metropolitan Museum, New York.[18] An example from Deir el-Medina itself is provided by a very fragmentary

---

12 It is also possible that OT 57431 also preserves the work of Nebre but in this case his hieroglyphic hand. See J. López, *Ostraca ieratici n. 57320-57449* (fasc. 3), Torino, 1982, p. 41, *tav.* 138. The text is a short fragment of "The Instruction of Amenemhat I," and the words "by the Draughtsman in the Place of Truth Nebre" appear near the end of the text. For further discussion of this ostracon, see below, pp. 61-62.

13 OMMA 29.2.24 (unpublished); reference in Wm. C. Hayes, *The Scepter of Egypt* Part II New York, 1959, p. 392.

14 For such objects, see conveniently, Hayes, *Scepter* II, figs. 264 and 265, for the anthropoid coffins of Iyneferti and her son, Khonsu, respectively.

15 OMMA 23.7.1 (unpublished); reference in Hayes, *Scepter* II p. 392, who identified the subject as a "seminude corpse of a man lying extended in an open anthropoid coffin." However, the subject depicted is clearly an innermost lid of the type possessed by the Workman Sennedjem; for this object, see most recently: R. Freed, *Ramesses the Great*, cat. no. 61: pp. 194-195.

16 A. Niwinski in *Lexikon der Ägyptologie* (W. Helck and E. Otto, eds.), 440 ff.

17 MMA acc. no. 86.1.5A-C; see above, note 15.

18 OMMA 23.3.4 = Hayes, *Scepter* II, p. 174 and p. 175, fig. 96.

ostracon that preserves only the left arm of a rightward-facing male figure, grasping a sceptre; the sketch includes a grid,[19] though whether it over- or underlies the figure is not clear from the published drawing. Also of interest as a pattern for use in scaling figures up or down is a papyrus fragment, now in Turin, which preserves a portion of (at least) two registers of black ink hieroglyphic signs with a juxtaposed red grid.[20]

The last sketch to be discussed in this context is preserved on a small limestone flake in the Louvre.[21] The drawing depicts the Abydene reliquary of the God Osiris borne in procession. Two versions of the image appear, superimposed on one another. The earlier (red) version was used to "block out" the scene; major elements were positioned, but no details were indicated. The "final" version was rendered in black ink, using the red version as a guide, and stands out from the latter because of its greater color intensity.

The final two types of figured ostraca discussed immediately above (i.e., the gridded sketches and those that preserve both preliminary and final versions of the image) are intimately connected with the work performed by the draughtsmen in the royal tombs, in that they most directly reflect the process followed by these artists to create the painted images that adorned the walls and ceilings of these monuments. Having reached this point of contact with the draughtsmen's artistic methodology, the time has come to consider the professional activity of the XIXth Dynasty draughtsman in their major work sites: the Valleys of the Kings and Queens.

The Draughtsmen in the Royal Wadis

In order to place the draughtsmen in their appropriate artistic context, it is necessary to consider *their* work in the royal tombs with reference to the contributions made by the other Deir el-Medina craftsmen. The production of a XIXth Dynasty royal tomb was a complex, multi-stage process that involved the skills and labor of several types of specialists.[22] The following brief summary of the steps involved in this procedure will serve to illustrate the intricate nature of the undertaking. After the tomb site had been selected by a committee composed of local officials (including the vizier and the main administrative officials of the crew of workmen), the stonecutters then hollowed out the

---

19 Vandier d'Abbadie, *Ostraca figurés* (1937), cat. no. 2601: pp. 123-4; pl. XXX.

20 P. Turin A5708 (unpublished). I thank Drs. Donadoni-Roveri and Roccati for the opportunity to study and photograph this piece.

21 Louvre ostracon 1345 = Vandier d'Abbadie, *Ostraca figurés* (1937), cat. no. 2603: p. 124; pl. LXXXII.

22 For a discussion of the earlier stages of royal tomb construction, see J. Cerny, *The Valley of the Kings* (Cairo, 1973). Many of these intermediate stages are still to be observed in the unfinished tomb of Horemheb (KV 57), see: E. Hornung, *Das Grab des Haremhab im Tal der Könige* (Bern, 1971). Popular accounts of the tomb-building/ decorating process are to be found in M. Bierbrier, *The Tomb-builders of the Pharaohs* (London, 1982), p. 43 ff. and E. Hornung, *Tal der Könige* (Zürich/München, 1982), p. 70 ff. An additional short description of the process, which stresses the textual sources, is: E.S. Bogoslovsky, *ZÄS* 107 (1980) p. 91 ff. The short description that follows in the body of this paper is necessarily brief and omits many details.

passages and chambers according to plans prepared by the scribe and/or the chief draughtsman.[23]

The walls and ceilings were given a "quarry" finish, and the actual drawing surface was prepared for the draughtsmen by the plasterers, who laid down a series of plaster layers of progressively finer quality. The wall area was then subdivided into design units, most often by snapping a string that had been dipped in red ink against the wall. The resulting lines (both horizontal and vertical) are easily recognizable by the small spatter marks that surround them. However, occasionally a straight-edge was also used, particularly when shorter intervals were to be connected. Within these larger demarcated areas, additional compositional guides could be added, as may be observed in the details from the tomb of Horemheb (KV57) reproduced in Plates 9 and 10. Although full grids are known from royal tombs of Dynasty XVIII, such as the example in Plate 11 from the tomb of Amenhotep III (KV 22), there is little physical evidence to prove that the draughtsmen of the Ramesside Period used them to facilitate the execution of large-scale figures in the royal tombs of the latter period.[24]

After having executed any proportional/placement guides that were desired, the draughtsmen approached the wall to begin the preliminary sketches. Although most of the surviving evidence would seem to suggest that red and (subsequently) black were the only colors used for this purpose, recent investigations in the tomb of Ramesses XI by J. Romer and M. Ciccarello have demonstrated that yellow ochre was used for the initial sketches, with red being utilized for a secondary stage of the work.[25] However, in the vast majority of cases only the red placement sketches and the black detailed drawings can be seen today. Plate 12 reproduces a series of columns of hieroglyphic text from the tomb of Sety I (KV 17); the initial "spattered" lines, darker ruled lines, red ink placement sketches that

---

23 For the association of the Scribe of the Tomb Amennakhte with the Turin plan of the tomb of Ramesses IV, see C. Keller, *JARCE* XXI (1984), p. 125, note 73. For the Master Draughtsman Amenhotep (his son) engaged in the preparing of a plan of a royal tomb, see O. Gardiner 70 = Cerny and Gardiner, *Hieratic Ostraca* (Oxford, 1957), 48.1, *recto* 3 ff.

24 For recent research into the proportional systems of the late Dynasty XVIII – early Dynasty XIX royal tombs, see G. Robins, *GM* 65 (1983), pp. 91-96; *GM* 68 (1983), pp. 85-90; and *GM* 72 (1984), pp. 27-32. In her recent *Egyptian Painting and Relief* (Alyesbury, 1986), p. 21, she remarks on the paucity of evidence for grids as compositional/proportional devices during Dynasty XIX in the private tombs. However, at least for a later period, evidence from the tomb of Ramesses XI (KV 4), indicates that the grids may have been deliberately erased before the relief sculptors began their work in order to reduce the number of extraneous lines that might confuse the sculptors - and thus impede the work. Certainly a grid was used in conjunction with the kneeling figure of Amen-Re-Harakhti that accompanies the Pinodjem graffito in KV 4, as indicated by M. Ciccarello, Theban Royal Tomb Project: *The Graffito of Pinutem I in the Tomb of Ramesses XI* (Brooklyn, no date), p. 5.

25 M. Ciccarello, op. cit., p. 4 ff. The low contrast of the yellow hue with the whitewashed plaster walls would have made it an ideal color to use in the initial stages of placing the figures on the wall. The tendency for the whiter plaster background to take on a yellowish tinge over time has decreased the contrast even further and, as a result, has made the yellow sketches rather difficult to discern today (and even more difficult to photograph). Closer examination of other unfinished tomb walls in the royal necropoleis might reveal additional instance of its use.

render only very cursive hieroglyphic forms, and the "final", more detailed black drawings, which the relief sculptor was supposed to follow, are all present.

In the normal course of events the relief sculptor would take over at this point to produce the sculpted forms, which were based generally (though not always exactly) on the work of the draughtsmen. (plate 13) Finally, the draughtsmen would return to the wall to clothe the pallid reliefs in vivid colors (plate 14). The less skilled artists probably filled in solid blocks of color, while the master draughtsman (and other more experienced hands) executed the detailed work. Only at this time was the work considered complete.

Although from the above description one might assume that the draughtsmen pursued an easy occupation, their work in the royal tombs was not without problems. Frequent eye problems, sometimes culminating in blindness, a scourge of ancient Egypt, were all too common among the workmen and would have been especially catastrophic for a draughtsman. Hence the urgency of the note written by the Draughtsman Pay to one of his sons:

> Do not neglect me. Do not tire from weeping for me. ...My Lord Amun [has turned] away from me. Bring me some honey for my eyes, some salve(?), while it is freshly made, and also some genuine eye paint. Am I not your father? I am ill. I am longing for my sight, but it is gone.[26]

Even from this necessarily brief description of the royal tomb decoration process it is clear that the work of an individual draughtsman would be difficult to distinguish from that of his contemporaries. The interaction between the draughtsman and sculptor teams, on the one hand, and the hierarchical assignment to various tasks within the group of draughtsmen themselves, on the other, combined to ensure a sense of stylistic uniformity, which was, by its very nature, disassociated from the individuals who created it.[27] However, the contributions of individual draughtsmen, and those of the more skilled members of the group in particular, have not been entirely obscured by the result of the interactive process of royal tomb decoration in use at this period. And while it may not be possible to attach specific names to the draughtsmen responsible for individual paintings in the royal tombs of Dynasty XIX, as has been done for their Dynasty XX successors,[28] some strides may be taken towards a closer evaluation of the individual contributions made by the draughtsmen of Dynasty XIX. But before this topic may be addressed, it is necessary to investigate the work of the draughtsmen in their other main center of activity: Deir el-Medina.

---

26 O. Berlin 11247 = G. Roeder (ed.) *Hieratische Papyri aus den Königlichen Museen zu Berlin*, Leipzig, 1911, pl. XXV/XXVa. The work of the draughtsmen would have become progressively more difficult as they moved farther and farther away from natural sunlight. For the means used to illuminate the work, see Cerny, *Valley of the Kings*, p. 43 ff.

27 It therefore existed in a realm other than that of the immediate present. And such a theoretical basis may have been as decisive as any more purely aesthetic consideration (such as the desire to achieve overall stylistic unity) or even more "practical" considerations (such as timesaving factors) in the development of an interactive process of royal tomb decoration.

28 C. Keller, *NARCE* 115 (1981), p. 7 ff.

The Draughtsmen at Deir el-Medina

During the Ramesside Period, the workmen's village at Deir el-Medina housed a crew numbering some 60 individuals and their families.[29] The village itself was set at the bottom of a small *wadi* flanked on the east and west by the local cemeteries. The village chapels and administrative area were situated at the north. The main Ramesside cemetery was on the west, and the tombs of the workmen cascaded down the hill towards the village on a series of artificial terraces. (plate 15) The tomb complexes themselves were composed of the same elements constructed elsewhere in the Theban necropolis. An open courtyard, entered by means of a pylon-like gateway, provided access to the partly freestanding and partly rock cut tomb chapel, which was located at the side opposite the entrance. The chapel was usually topped with a small masonry or mudbrick pyramid containing a niche cut into its eastern face, into which a stela dedicated to the rising sun might be set. (plate 16), and which was crowned with a small limestone pyramidion inscribed on all sides with solar texts and representations.[30] The burial apartments were reached by shafts sunk into floor of either the outer court or the chapel itself.

The interiors of both the chapel and the burial chamber(s) were decorated with paintings, or more rarely, with painted reliefs. Few of the painted tomb chapels have survived, since their above ground location rendered them far more susceptible to destruction than the subterranean burial chambers. However, if the tomb chapel of the Sculptor Ipuy (Tt. 217)[31] may be regarded as not too atypical, then the iconography of the Deir el-Medina tomb chapel did not differ substantially from those of their contemporaries elsewhere in the necropolis, which featured scenes of the tomb owner and his family and friends in the company of the gods; engaged in supervising typical day-to-day activities, such as fishing, trading, or (especially relevant in the case of Ipuy) workshop production; and the ceremonies connected with the funeral.

The paintings in the small vaulted burial chambers, on the other hand, were mostly large scale representations of texts and vignettes from the *Book of the Dead*, with a few scenes drawn from other religious sources.[32] The practice of decorating the burial chamber, as well as the chapel, was, with few exceptions, not followed elsewhere in the necropolis; the

---

29 For a description of the site and a full-size plan, see M. Tosi and A. Roccati, *Stele e altre epigrafi di Deir el Medina*, Torino, 1972, p. 11 ff. A recent description of life in the village may be found in D. Valbelle, *"Les Ouvriers de la Tombe"*, Cairo, 1985, p. 229 ff. And a well illustrated popular account of the site and its inhabitants is: M. Bierbrier, *The Tomb-builders of the Pharaohs*, London, 1982.

30 Such as the "lucarne" stela of the Draughtsman Pay, now in Turin (cat. 50048 = Tosi and Roccati, *Stele*, pp. 82-3, 281) and the pyramidion of the Scribe Ramose, who was also active during the reign of Ramesses II (Turin cat. 1603 = M. Tosi, *La Capella di Maia* (Torino, 1972), pp. 12-13.

31 N. de G. Davies, *Two Ramesside Tombs at Thebes* New York, 1927, pp. 33-76.

32 As, for example in the tombs of Pashed (Tt 3) = A.-P. Zivie, *La Tombe de Pached à Deir el-Médineh*, Cairo, 1979; and Sennedjem (Tt 1) = B. Bruyère, *La Tombe de Sennedjem à Deir el-Médineh*, Cairo, 1959 and Fahmy 'Abd el Wahab, *La Tombe de Sennedjem ...croquis de position*, Cairo, 1959. Both tombs date to the early XIXth Dynasty. See p. 54 and note 54 for an example of private utilization of a vignette of probable royal origin.

possibility that this procedure was adopted by the workmen under the influence of their work in the royal tombs will be discussed below.[33]

In addition to decorating the private tombs at Deir el-Medina, the draughtsmen were probably also commissioned to decorate other structures at the site;[34] the chapels situated at the northern end of the wadi,[35] as well as the houses of the workmen themselves,[36] most likely fell into this category. Economic texts that have survived provide at least a partial list of private objects that were embellished by the draughtsmen. these include: various types of architectural elements and furniture, statuary, stelae, and examples of funerary objects, such as: coffins, mummy masks, funerary shrines, *shabtis*, and *Books of the Dead*.[37] In fact, beginning already in late Dynasty XVIII there had been a gradual shift towards producing a larger proportion of objects of strictly mortuary purposes for incorporation into the burial equipment. Of course, such objects as coffins, canopic chests, and *shabtis* had long been so included. However, up to that time it had also been the tradition to place in the tomb many objects that had actually been used by the deceased during his lifetime, such as: domestic furniture, used clothing, personal jewelry, and tools.[38] By the reign of Ramesses II, however, nearly all of the objects included in the burial of the Workman Sennedjem had been fabricated (or at least redecorated) with his burial in mind.[39] So that we now encounter a proliferation of inner and outer coffins, funerary shrines, *shabtis*, pottery decorated especially for the tomb, and funerary furniture - all embellished with funerary motifs and texts, of which extracts from the *Book of the Dead* and prayers using the *ḥtp-di-*

---

33 See below, pp. 58 f.

34 The lexicographical terminology of many of these structures is discussed in: J.J. Janssen and P.J. Pestman, *JESHO* XI:2 (1962), p. 158 ff.

35 For references to the chapels at Deir el-Medina and their decoration, see *PM* I:2, (2nd ed.) pp. 689-91. Some fragments of painted plaster giving an idea of the various types of subjects are to be found in: Bruyère, *Rapports (1929)* (Cairo, 1930), p. 25: fig. 4.

36 For some of the painted decoration of houses at Deir el-Medina, see: Bruyère, *FIFAO* XVI (Cairo, 1939), p. 57 ff. and pls. IX-X; much the same painted fragments are to be seen in Wm. S. Smith with W.K. Simpson (ed.), *The Art and Architecture of Ancient Egypt*[2] (Baltimore and Harmondsworth, 1981), p. 291 and fig. 288.

37 For the cost involved in the decoration of many of these items, see J.J. Janssen, *Commodity Prices*, p. 182 (woman's bed); p. 190 (a stool/chair); p. 241 ff (a funerary bed); pp. 245-6 (a *Prt-m-hrw*/*Book of the Dead*); p. 248 (a female statue); p. 390 (a door); and p. 392 (a set of doorjambs). For references to the cost of the decoration of other funerary objects, see below, note 45.

38 See, for example, the contents of the tomb of the "Chief in the Great Place" Kha (Tt 8) in E. Schiaparelli, *Realazione sui lavori della missione archeologica italiana in egitto (1903-1930)*, vol. II: *La Tomba intatta dell'architetto Cha nella necropoli di Tebe*, Torino, 1927.

39 List of the objects found in the tomb published by Ed. Toda in G. Daressy, *ASAE* XX (1920), p. 147-60. See also, a recent account of the objects from the tomb by D. Valbelle, *Ouvriers*, p. 294 ff. (with, unfortunately, a few errors contained in the museum numbers). A partial list of the *shabtis* from the tomb of Sennedjem (and from other XIXth Dynasty origins) was compiled by D. Spanel in *SAK* 13 (1986), pp. 252-3.

nsw formula were by far the most common.[40] One depiction of the production and decoration of some of the articles mentioned above has survived from the tomb of the Sculptor Ipuy (Tt 217) at Deir el-Medina, a detail of which appears in Plate 17.

The decoration of such objects as those from the tomb of Sennedjem was apparently undertaken as private commissions by the Deir el-Medina draughtsmen, who performed these tasks in exchange for payment *in kind*. Evidence of the private negotiations (and the eventual prices) of the cost of decorating these objects has survived in the form of hieratic texts on *ostraca* and provides a look at one aspect of village economics during Dynasty XIX. For instance, in year 2 of Merneptah (Ramesses II's son and successor), we learn

> what the Draughtsman Neferhotep gave to Horemwia (namely): one painted stela of (Nofretari), May she live! (And) he gave me a wooden coffer in exchange for it. In addition, (I) decorated two coffins for the Riverbank (*mryt*) for him, and he made a bed for me..."[41]

In the above text, the amounts of the commodities involved in the series of exchanges were specified. However, sometimes the exact price was left open, at least at the beginning of such negotiations:

> "A message from the Draughtsman Pay to his son the Draughtsman Peraemheb: Take steps to look for the two faience heart-amulets, concerning which I said to you that I would pay their price to their owner, consisting of whatever he asks for..."[42]

Since we know from numerous texts that the Deir el-Medina workmen were issued wages at more or less regular intervals,[43] from storehouses under the control of the vizier, the goods obtained from decorating the monuments and other objects for their fellow workmen represented additional income to the draughtsmen. Indeed, the decoration of a complete coffin "set" (including: a large wooden funerary shrine, an inner and outer coffin, an innermost lid, and a funerary mask)[44] of Dynasty XIX date could net the draughtsman fortunate enough to receive such commissions goods worth several times his monthly grain

---

40 For examples of the decorated funerary objects from the tomb of Sennedjem, see Hayes, *Scepter* II, pp. 414-418, 425, 428-430 with accompanying illustrations, and Freed, *Ramesses the Great*, pp. 188-95, 197. For an example of the sharing of motifs between the tomb paintings and the decorated funerary objects placed within, see below, p. 17 and Plates 18 and 19.

41 O. Michaelides 13 = H. Goedicke and E.F. Wente, *Ostraca Michaelides*, Wiesbaden, 1962, pls. 46-47: J.J. Janssen, op. cit., pp. 85-86; S. Allam, *Hieratische Ostraka u. Papyri aus der Ramessidenzeit*, Tübingen, 1973, pp. 209-210.

42 Cerny and Gardiner, *Hieratic Ostraca*, pls. 54 and 54a.

43 See above, p. 49.

44 See above, note 39, for references to illustrations of some of these objects from the tomb of Sennedjem. See also Janssen, *Commodity Prices*, p. 210 ff. and Valbelle, *Ouvriers*, p. 294 ff. for discussions of objects from the same tomb; the former stresses the lexicography, while the latter aims at a complete inventory of the types of objects present for each of the several burials discovered in the tomb.

ration.[45] From this point of view alone, one can see why admission to the more skilled occupations, such as scribe, relief sculptor, and draughtsman, might be jealously guarded[46] and reserved for one's own sons or those of relatives and close friends, who could be counted upon to help support an aged former practitioner of one of these professions.

Having now passed in review some of the tasks that occupies the draughtsmen in their village context, it is now time to investigate points of contact that might exist between the works produced during their "off" hours by the draughtsmen at Deir el-Medina (as exemplified by the painted tombs and chapels and decorated funerary and votive objects) and that body of work that was the *raison d'être* for their existence as an occupational unit: the paintings in the Valleys of the Kings and the Queens.

The Draughtsmen: Their Styles and Subjects

Since the Deir el-Medina draughtsmen's major task was the decoration of the royal burial apartments, it is understandable that it is in the burial chambers of the Deir el-Medina tombs that one observes those elements that most clearly link them with the royal tombs. In general, these similarities are not shared with contemporary private tombs in the rest of the Theban necropolis. And this fact is not surprising when one remembers that the same group of artists were responsible with the first two groups of tombs, but not for the latter. Yet it is interesting to note that the influence appears to move in both directions. Generally speaking, it was royal artistic style (as exemplified by the style(s) of painting in the royal tombs of Dynasty XIX) and iconography that has left the greater mark on the tombs at Deir el-Medina. However, specific iconographic items originating (or at least having a longer documented history) in the private sphere can occasionally be seen in the royal sepulchres.

The fact that the burial chambers of the Deir el-Medina tombs were extensively decorated at all (as opposed to the custom in the rest of the Theban necropolis, which limited decoration to the tomb chapel and usually excluded the burial chamber from the decorative scheme) certainly bespeaks the influence of royal decorative practice.[47] In the king's tomb,

---

45 See Janssen, op. cit., pp. 223-8 (for the amount received for the decoration of an *wt*, "anthropoid coffin"); pp. 233-5 (for the amount of an *wt ʿ3* (or, *mnʿnḫ*) "outer coffin"); pp. 235-8 (for the decoration of a *swḥt*, "innermost lid"); pp. 238-9 (for the decoration of a *ḏbȝt*, "outer wooden shrine/sarcophagus"); and p. 462 ff. (for the value of the monthly grain ration).

46 See above, p. 49.

47 Only a very few burial chambers in private tombs of the New Kingdom were decorated, and the best known of these are of XVIIIth Dynasty date. The three examples most often cited belonged to Hatshepsut's steward, Senenmut (Tts 71 and 353), the Vizier Amenuser, who served Tuthmosis III (Tts 61 and 131), and Sennefer, mayor of Thebes under Amenhotep II (Tt 96). But even during this period, which predates our study, there existed very close connections between these particular private tombs and the contemporary royal sepulchres. In the case of the two officials possessing two tombs each, Senenmut and Amenuser, the decoration in the burial chamber of each man's "second" tomb was clearly derived from royal sources. In the burial chamber of Senemut's tomb 353, the ceiling bears astronomical texts (see R.A. Parker, *The Calendars of Ancient Egypt*, Chicago, 1950, pl. I), similar to those that will later appear in the royal tombs (e.g., that of Sety I [KV 17]; see *PM* I:2 (2nd ed.), pp. 542-3) and temples (i.e., the Ramesseum; see Parker, *Calendars*, pls. II-III) of the Ramesside Period. And in Tt 131 of Amenuser, the walls of the burial chamber were embellished with a papyrus-inspired version of the *Amduat* (see E. Hornung, *NAWG* [1961],

60

the burial chamber was known as *Pr-n-nwb* "the House of Gold",[48] an appellation that probably possessed a compound imagery: 1) the burial chamber as the place of rebirth of the king as the Sun-god; 2) the burial chamber as the location of the golden shrines that - as in the tomb of Tutankhamun[49] and in the Turin plan of Ramesses IV[50], - surrounded the stone sarcophagus and the golden coffins that held the body of the king; and 3) the golden color of the burial chamber walls, long a traditional practice, that served to stress the papyrus origin of the religious texts and representations that covered the mural surfaces.

Similarly, the private burial chambers at Deir el-Medina were embellished with funerary texts, in the latter case with vignettes and texts culled from the *Book of the Dead*, and the walls were also colored yellow to reflect the papyrus originals. While the texts selected for enlargement in the private tombs were usually *not* derived from royal prototypes, the analogy holds, and is even reinforced by the adoption of the gold background color for the tomb walls. The same decorative scheme was also utilized for the funerary objects, such as *shabtis*, coffins, and shrines, which were placed in these tombs. For example, Plate 18 depicts a painting from the soffit of the entrance into the burial chamber of the tomb of Sennedjem,[51] and Plate 19 a detail from the foot of the inner coffin of his son Khonsu, which was found in this tomb and is now in the Metropolitan Museum of Art, New York.[52] Both vignettes depict the same scene: the Disk of the Horizon in the arms of the Goddess Nut.

However, there are, in fact, a few instances where the Deir el-Medina draughtsmen of Dynasty XIX *did* use excerpts from royal tomb iconography for the decoration of their own

---

nr. 5, pp. 99-120), which is stylistically similar to those in the tombs of Tuthmosis III (KV 34) (*PM* I:2 (2nd ed.), p. 553) and Amenhotep II (KV 35) *PM* I:2 (2nd ed.), p. 554). In the case of Sennefer, the artist(s) who executed the paintings in his burial chambers (see *Sennefer: Der Grabkammer des Burgermeister von Theben*, Mainz, 1986, were clearly among those responsible for the lifesize figures on the pillars in the burial chamber of Amenhotep II, his sovereign [see *PM* I:2 (2nd ed.), p. 554]). Since all three of these officials were of the highest rank and had access to royal resources (including the labor force) and workshops, it would have been a natural outcome of their close association with royal construction projects for their own tomb decoration to partake of royal style and iconography.

48 As on the Turin plan of the tomb of Ramesses IV (KV 2), see H. Carter and A.H. Gardiner, *JEA* 4 (1917), p. 139. Gardiner opined that the reason for this appellation was the opulent burial equipment of the deceased ruler, while Carter suggested that the ground color of the walls was the deciding factor.

49 See, conveniently, C. Desroches-Noblecourt, *Tutankhamen* New York, 1963 p. 74 and fig. 37.

50 P. Turin cat. 1885 *recto*; see Carter and Gardiner, op. cit., p. 130 ff and pl. XXIX. For a color version of the plan, see E. Scamuzzi, *Museo Egizio do Torino* (New York), pl. LXXXVII.

51 For permission to conduct photography in the royal and private tombs at Thebes, I would like to express my appreciation to the Permanent Committee of the Egyptian Antiquities Organization, Dr. Ahmed Kadry and Dr. Gamal Mokhtar, presidents, and all the members of the EAO who facilitated my work at Luxor in 1975, 1980-81 and 1986.

52 MMA accession no. 86.1.2AB. The slide from which this photograph was taken is my own; I thank Dr. Lilyquist for permission to reproduce it here.

tombs. For example, in the tomb of the Sculptor Nakhtamun (Tt 335)[53] a mummiform ram-headed god is flanked by the Goddesses Isis and Nephthys; the accompanying text identifies him as both Re and Osiris. The same scene is found in the tomb of Queen Nofretari (QV 66).[54]

Stylistic affinities between the tomb groups can also be traced. Particularly striking is the similarity between the large scale figures in the tombs of Sety I (KV 17) and the workman Sennedjem (Tt 1), and several tombs of wives of Ramesses II. Since the "style of Sety I", with its aristocratic profile, small eyes, and small, slightly curving mouth, is also well established from other sites throughout Egypt (notable, of course, at Abydos), this particular stylistic influence can probably be viewed as having moved from the realm of a promulgated royal style towards this specific private application. the depiction of the deity *3wtj-ḥntj-Dw3t* "the offerer who is before the Duat"[55] from KV 17 (plate 20) is stylistically quite similar to a carefully executed depiction of the God Osiris from the tomb of Sennedjem (plate 21). And a head of the Goddess Isis (plate 22) from the tomb of an anonymous queen of Ramesses II (QV 40) was painted in a style similar to that of a rendition of Sennedjem's mummy (plate 23). Even the rendering of anatomical details, such as the knees of the God Anubis and Sennedjem (which appear in a detail from the latter's tomb in Plate 24) have their royal counterpart (prototype ?) in the knees of the king and gods in the tomb of Sety I (plate 25). It would seem, therefore, that the figural style of the Deir el-Medina tombs was, largely determined by that adopted for the contemporary royal tombs.

The influence of private tomb decorative practice on its royal counterpart can sometimes be observed in the area of specific iconographic details. The distribution of scenes such as that of Anubis attending the mummy (a common component of burial chamber decoration at Deir el-Medina), which also appears in the XIXth Dynasty tombs of Siptah (KV 47)[56] and Tausert (KV 14),[57] as well as some of the wives of Ramesses II in the Valley of the Queens,[58] suggests that the inclusion of this particular vignette in the royal tombs was a secondary phenomenon.

In at least one instance, the transfer of color utilization from the private to the royal sphere can be documented. The so-called "monochrome" tomb style,[59] in which the palette is

53 M. Tosi, op. cit., p. 27, fig. 21, and Bruyère, *Rapport (1924-25)*, p. 136, fig. 92.

54 G. Thausing and H. Goedicke, *Nofretari: eine Dokumentation der Wandgemälde ihres Grabes* (Graz, 1971), pl. 41.

55 From the ninth hour; see: E. Hornung, *Das Amduat* (Wiesbaden, 1963), Teil I, p. 162; Teil II, p. 158.

56 PM I:2 (2nd ed.), p. 565 (4) and (5).

57 PM I:2 (2nd ed.), p. 530 (19).

58 As in the tomb of Queen Nofertari (QV 66); see *PM* I:2 (2nd ed.), p. 762 (2) to (4) for references. Most recent published photos in Thausing and Goedicke, *Nofretari*, pl. 22. The closest parallels for this depiction occur both in the tomb of Sennedjem and on objects from the tomb, notably the funerary shrines of Sennedjem and his son Khonsu, some details of which are shown in A. Lhote and Hassia, *Les Chefs d'oeuvre de la peinture égyptienne*, Paris, 1954, pls 63 and 162 and pl. 12, respectively.

59 As defined by B. Bruyère in: *Tombes thébaines de Deir el-Médineh à décoration monochrome,*

limited to yellow, black, and red on a white background, can be seen in some 22 of the Deir el-Medina tombs, where it appears to have had a fairly wide period of use,[60] though the vast majority of the private tombs decorated in this manner date to Dynasty XIX, and to the reign of Ramesses II in particular.[61] One might not expect to find this rather flat color scheme in a royal context; however, a small niche at the rear of the tomb of Queen Nofretari was indeed decorated in this manner.[62] The rather careless style of its execution links it to paintings in the tombs of Khabekhnet (Tt 2)[63] and Nefer'abu (Tt 5).[64] However, the relatively constricted area in which the design had to be executed and the small scale of the figures may also have had some bearing on the lack of artistic quality present in the niche (particularly when compared with the majority of the paintings in the tomb).

The monochrome tombs are of particular interest to this study because, as was pointed out by Bruyere,[65] they contain the names of many of the draughtsmen of this period. This fact is all the more remarkable since the draughtsmen are not (save in the case of Tt 323) the tomb owners themselves, but are depicted as taking part in the funeral procession and the funerary banquet, along with members of the deceased's family and associates. Indeed, the percentage of *sš-ḳd.w* depicted in the monochrome tombs far outranks their frequency of appearance in the polychrome chapels. Bruyère did not think that this situation could be fortuitous. In fact, he was moved to posit that the paintings in the monochrome tombs might be linked to the specific painters (or families of painters) represented.[66] It might be worthwhile pausing at this point to review the individuals involved in order to determine whether any connections might, in fact, be established between the particular draughtsmen represented in these tombs and the paintings executed therein.

The draughtsmen who appear with greatest frequency in the monochrome tombs at Deir el-Medina were members of two well known draughtsman families of Dynasty XIX: the

---

Cairo, 1952, p. 7 ff.

60 See the list of monochrome tombs in Bruyère, *Tombes thébaines*, pp. 11-12.

61 Bruyère, loc. cit. Of the 22 monochrome tombs listed by Bruyère, the only tombs that do *not* date to the period Sety I-Ramesses II are those of Penamun (Tt 213) and Amenpahapi (Tt 355); Tt 211 (of Paneb) is problematic; the original owner may have dated to early Dynasty XIX, but Paneb himself was active as chief workman rather later in the XIXth Dynasty.

62 Thausing and Goedicke, *Nofretari*, pls. 88-90.

63 Bruyère, *Tombes thébaines*, pls. IV-XII.

64 J. Vandier, *La Tombe de Nefer-abou*, Cairo, 1935, pls. IV, VI, VIII, XVIII (left).

65 Bruyère, *Tombes thébaines*, pp. 18-19.

66 Bruyère, *Tombes thébaines*, p. 18. On the following page Bruyère states that the same hands who executed the monochrome tomb paintings were also responsible for the work in the polychrome chapels as well. Therefore, an in-depth assessment of the style(s) of the Deir el-Medina draughtsmen of Dynasty XIX would also have to involve the detailed examination of the polychrome chapels and burial chambers as well. Since that task is beyond the scope of the present project, the discussion of the XIXth Dynasty painting styles that follows in the body of this paper will be almost entirely concerned with the relationships that can be established between the paintings in the monochrome tombs and those in the contemporary royal tombs.

family founded by the Draughtsman Ipu, and including his son Pay, the latter's sons Nebre, (Pe)rahotep and Peraemheb, Nebre's sons Nakhtamun and Khay, and several younger Ipu's;[67] and the family descended from the Draughtsman Amenemhat, which includes the Draughtsman Pashed the Elder, his son Maaninakhtef, and the latter's son, Pashed the Younger; and the family of a second Pashed, son of Mehnakhte, himself only occasionally titled *sš-ḳd*, that comprised himself, and his sons Amenmose and (User) satet.[68] (Members of both families appear in the detail from the tomb of Nefer'abu [Tt 5] shown in Plate 26; the names and titles of the draughtsmen Rahotep, Maaninakhtef, Ipu, and Pashed are written above the heads of the first four figures from the left.) There are a few other draughtsmen who make single appearances in the monochrome tombs, but cannot be linked to either of the families just enumerated, such as the Draughtsman Paherypedjet, who is described in the detail from the tomb of Nebenmaat shown in Plate 27 as a "son" of Nebre, and the Draughtsman Satet, mentioned in the tomb of Pashed, son of Hehnakhte, (Tt 292).[69]

A breakdown of their appearances is as follows: the Draughtsman Pay appears in the tomb of Amennakhte (Tt 218) only. However, his sons Nebre and Perahotep are depicted with greater frequency, namely: in the tombs of Ken (Tt 4), Amennakhte, Nebenma'at (Tt 219), and some female relatives of the Scribe Ramose (Tt 250); and the tombs of Ken, Nefer'abu (Tt 5), Amennakhte, and the Sculptor Nakhtamun (Tt 335), respectively. The Draughtsman Nakhtamun and his brother Khay, both sons of Nebre, appear only in the tomb of Nebenma'at, and Ipu, a grandson of Pay (possibly the son of Perahotep) in the tomb of Nefer'abu. It is interesting to note that, in at least one case, the chronology of these tombs comes into play: members of the two elder generations (Pay and Nebre) appear in the tomb of Amennakhte, who was the father of Nebenma'at, in whose tomb the brothers Nebre and Perahotep and the former's son Nakhtamun and Khay appear. In most cases the draughtsman nearest in age to the tomb owner is given the most prominent role. Thus, in the tomb of Amennakhte, it is the latter's contemporary, the draughtsman Pay who, acting as the *ḥry-ḥb* priest, reads the *Opening of the Mouth* text before the mummy of Amennakhte; Pay's sons Nebre and Perahotep are merely two out of a whole group of

---

67 For this family, see most recently, L. Habachi, op. cit., pp. 30 and 37; and J. Malek, *RdÉ* 31 (1979), pp. 153-6.

68 For the family of Pashed (Tt 323), see the genealogy of Janssen in *Commodity Prices*, pp. 38-9; for that of Pashed (Tt 292), see: E.S. Bogoslovsky, *VDI* 1972:1, pp. 96-9 and Bierbrier, *The Late New Kingdom in Egypt*, Warminster, 1975, pp. 24-6. However, it should be noted that the latter Pashed is hardly ever referred to as *sš-ḳd*, and, for this reason, this family is not included in the following discussion.

69 Since Paherypedjet appears nowhere else on the numerous monuments of the family of Nebre, he is probably, in reality, the son of Huy, who is mentioned on stela Turin 50069 (Tosi and Roccati, *Stele*, pp. 105-6) and on the stela of his brother, Kaha, in the British Museum (BM 144 = T.G.H. James, *Hieroglyphic Texts*, Part IX, London, 1970, pp. 46-7 and pl. XXXIX). Paherypedjet also appears in the textual record on O. Brooklyn 37.188OE and OBM 5644 = Cerny and Gardiner, *Hieratic Ostraca*, pl. 86.3 (see Janssen, *Commodity Prices*, pp. 30 and 80; and M. Gutgesell, *Die Datierung der Ostraka und Papyri aus Deir el-Medina und ihre ökonomische Interpretation*, Hildesheim, 1983, p. 484). The kinship terminology in use at Deir el-Medina during this period was fairly limited and was also utilized to express simply generational (rather than strictly familial) relationships, see: M.L. Bierbrier, *JEA* 66 (1980), p. 100 ff. For Satet, see: B. Bruyère, *Tombes thébaines*, pp. 18-19; and for a possible additional appearance of (User)satet, see Bruyère, *Rapport (1923-1924)* Cairo, 1925, p. 72, 7[0].

participants in the funeral procession.[70] In contrast, in the tomb of Nebenma'at, Amennakhte's son, Pay does not appear at all, but Nebre and his wife Pashed are depicted seated at an offering table while their sons Nakhtamun and Khay stand before them.[71]

Apart from their family tomb (Tt 323), the Draughtsman Maaninakhtef and his father (or his son) Pashed appear in the monochrome corpus only in the tomb of Nefer'abu, where the former is described as the "brother" of the tomb owner, and the latter bears only the title *sš-ḳd*, with no genealogical/generational affiliation. (See plate 26) Several members of this draughtsman family appear on other monuments of the Nefer'abu family, probably indicating a relatively close temporal and professional relationship.[72] Since, other than these two instances, members of this second draughtsman family make no other appearance in the monochrome tombs, one might suggest, on the basis of the somewhat unequal distribution, that the family founded by Pay was by far the more prominent of the two draughtsman families; it was certainly the more capable of producing draughtsmen, at any rate.

It might be possible to press the association of these particular draughtsmen with the monochrome tombs further by attempting to tie them with the tombs in which they appear, not only as participants in the action, but also as the authors of the paintings.[73] One begins this process by noting that, based purely on tomb appearances, the family of Pay is associated with the tombs of Amennakhte, Nebenma'at, Ken, Nakhtamun, the female members of the family of Ramose, and Nefer'abu; the Pashed family, on the other hand, is apparently tied to their own family tomb and to that of Nefer'abu as well.

Since the tomb of Nefer'abu possesses two chambers decorated in the monochrome style, it is tempting to attempt to "share" the artistic responsibility for the paintings in this tomb by assigning one chamber to each of the two draughtsman families. In fact, the paintings in the upper chamber do closely resemble those in the tombs of Nakhtamun and Nebenma'at[74] (the identity of whose styles may be judged by comparing Plate 28, which derives from the tomb of Nakhtamun, with Plate 29, from the tomb of Nebenma'at). These tombs have been associated with the family of Pay according to the criterion of the appearance by members of this family in the tomb paintings. By the process of elimination one might posit that the other (i.e., lower) chamber had been decorated by the other family (i.e., that of Pashed). In fact, the style of the paintings in the lower chamber does appear to differ slightly from those in the upper. In the lower chamber, a style reminiscent of that of the draughtsmen who executed the paintings in the tomb of Paneb (Tt 211) appears to be

---

70 Bruyère, *Rapport (1927)*, Cairo, 1928, pp. 64-5 and fig. 46 (Nebre and Perahotep); pp. 67-8 and fig. 47 (Pay).

71 B. Bruyère, *Rapport (1927)*, Cairo, 1928, pp. 69-70 and fig. 48.

72 For stela BM 150+1754, see T.G.H. James, *Hieroglyphic Texts*, Part IX, London, 1970, pp. 34-5 and pl. XXX; for stela BM 305, see op. cit., pp. 36-7 and pl. XXXII.1. Of course, it is possible that the "Pashed" depicted in Tt 5 is, in fact, Pashed, son of Hehnakhte (of Tt 292), rather than his homograph from Tt 323. However, the presence of Maaninakhtef (the latter's father/son) speaks against this option.

73 As was tentatively suggested by Bruyère in *Tombes thébaines*, p. 18.

74 For the upper chamber paintings in the tomb of Nefer'abu (Tt 5), see Vandier, *Nefer-abou*, pls. IV.2 and VI; for Nebenma'at (Tt 219), see Ch. Maystre, *La Tombe de Nebenmât*, Cairo, 1936, pls. IV and V; for Nakhtamun (Tt 335), see M. Tosi, *Stirpe*, figs. 16 and 22.

present[75] (though it should be emphasized that this association is based only upon a preliminary survey). This latter style is rather closer, in general, to that exemplified by the paintings in the tombs of Sennedjem and Arinefer (Tt 291) at Deir el-Medina, the tomb of Sety I in the Valley of the Kings, and several of the tombs of wives of Ramesses II in the Valley of Queens.

Of course, it must be stressed that, while the number of draughtsmen who worked on any given private tomb would probably have been limited, the number of hands responsible for the paintings in the contemporary royal tomb(s) would have been rather larger. So that one would expect to find a larger stylistic range present in a royal than in a private tomb one the size of Sety I in particular. Therefore, one is hardly justified in attributing the paintings in any royal tomb, in their entirety, to the hand of a single artist, even if he should be the master draughtsman.

It would be very satisfying if, at this point in the discussion, the association of any of the aforementioned draughtsman could be definitively linked with any of the royal tombs listed in the preceding paragraph. Given the large scale, interactive process followed in the decoration of the royal tombs, however, the most one can hope for is that some small details held in common might emerge. The assessment of the personal artistic styles of the Deir el-Medina draughtsmen of Dynasty XX has been facilitated by the relatively large number of signed figured ostraca that have survived. These signed pieces could be compared with unsigned sketches executed in the same style and, finally, to painting details in the contemporary royal and private tombs decorated by the draughtsmen of this later period, with the result that it is now possible to speak of figures in the royal tombs (at least partly) executed by known individual draughtsman.[76]

In contrast, few signed ostraca of this type have come down to us from Dynasty XIX. One example now in Brussels[77] bears a sketch of the cobra Goddess Mertseger on the *recto* and the inscription: *ir.n sš-ḳd m St-M3ʿt Mn* "made by the Draughtsman in the Place of Truth Men" on the *verso*, which may indicate his authorship of the drawing. However, as in many instances, *jr.n* may here signify "dedicated by", rather than "made by", which is the literal meaning of the expression. The Draughtsman Men is known also from a stela in Turin,[78] where he is designated as the "father" of a certain Servant in the Place of Truth Perahotep, whose brother was Burekhonef,[79] also a draughtsman. Men is thought to have been active near the end of Dynasty XIX, which would provide a date for this piece. However, there exists a complication: it is also possible that *Mn* is to be understood here as a shortened form of *Mnn3*. If the latter is in fact true, then the drawing of Mertseger might then be attributed to one of the like-named members of the Menna/Merysakhmet family of

75 For the lower chamber of Nefer'abu (Tt 5), see Vandier, *Nefer-abou*, pls. XI, XVI, XXII; for the tomb of Paneb (Tt 211), see Bruyère, *Tombes thébaines*, pls. XV-XXV.

76 K. Keller, *NARCE* 115 (1981), p. 7 ff.

77 E.6573 = M. Werbrouck, *BMRAH* no. 25 (1953), pp. 102-3 and figs. 25-6.

78 Cat. 50033 = Tosi and Roccati, *Stele*, pp. 66-7 and p. 274. Men is also mentioned in Spiegelberg, *Graffiti*, no. 711, in conjunction with the *sš-ḳd* Noferhotep, who was active in late Dynasty XIX-early Dynasty XX.

79 Burekhonef is also known from ODM 215, 228, and 260 and 0. Brussels E.301 and Spiegelberg, *Graffiti*, no. 313. His career appears to span the late XIXth - early XXth Dynasty. See also Janssen, *Commodity Prices*, p. 43.

draughtsmen, and thus may be somewhat more difficult to establish with precision.[80] In any case, there is little that can be done to establish a drawing style on the basis of one sketch that bears what may be either a true artist's signature or a short dedication text.

It might be of use, however, at this juncture to recall the Medelhavsmuseet ostracon that bears the sketches of the *shabti* and the heart scarab,[81] upon which the names of the draughtsmen Perahotep and Nebre were written (plate 5). In this case one might be somewhat more justified in assuming that either Perahotep or Nebre was the artist responsible for these sketches, for several reasons at least: 1) the title *sš-ḳd* is consistently used, thus calling attention to drawing skills; 2) these sketches are just the type that a draughtsmen *might* compose as preliminary layouts for his decoration of a completed three-dimensional object; 3) the script on both the *verso* and *recto* is the same.

If one compares the features of the *shabti* as depicted on the *recto* of the piece with those of the seated deity from the tomb of queen Nebettawey, a wife of Ramesses II, shown in Plate 30,[82] the resemblance is clear. therefore, it is suggested that this particular painting in the Valley of the Queens be assigned to the hand of either the Draughtsman Perahotep or that of his brother, Nebre. (Yet this one association, no matter how firm, does not seem so very important when compared with the vast majority of the (as yet) unattributed body of material represented by the paintings in the royal tombs of the XIXth Dynasty.)

In light of the above discussion it becomes clear that the association of individual draughtsman with specific works of art in the XIXth Dynasty Deir el-Medina/Kings Valley/Queens Valley corpus remains somewhat speculative. Ongoing and more detailed analyses of the paintings in tombs and on discrete objects from these sites should yield more specific conclusions regarding the attribution of the paintings to specific hands. And even if it is not possible to assign a name to these individual hands, it should be possible to delineate the range of activity and career span of these stylistically individual (if as yet unidentifiable) draughtsmen.

---

80 For the Menna/Merysekhmet family, see Janssen, op. cit., pp. 62-3 and in *Gleanings from Deir el-Medina* (Leiden, 1982), p. 116 ff. For an alternative view, see E.S. Bogoslovsky, *ZÄS* 107 (1980), p. 101.

81 See above, p. 52, for a fuller discussion of the piece.

82 QV 60 = *PM* I:2 (2nd ed.), p. 761 (6).

Plate 1

The cartouches of Amenhotep I as drawn by the "instructor".
OMM 14 116 <u>recto</u>
Photograph courtesy of the Medelhavsmuseet,
Stockholm; reproduced by permission.

Plate 2

The cartouches of Amenhotep I as drawn by the "student".
OMM 14 116 <u>verso</u>
Photograph courtesy of the Medelhavsmuseet,
Stockholm; reproduced by permission.

Plate 3

"Sketchpad" ostracon. OMMA 14.6.204 <u>recto</u>
Gift of Theodore M. Davis, 1913. Photograph from a slide by the author; reproduced by permission of the Egyptian Department, Metropolitan Museum of Art, New York.

Plate 4

Drawing of the Ram of Amun-Re, dedicated by the Chief Workman Hay.
O. Cairo Temporary Register 23/2/22/1
Author's photograph.

70

Plate 5

Sketch of a <u>shabti</u> bearing the name of (Pe)rahotep.
OMM 14 120 <u>recto</u>
Photograph courtesy of the Medelhavsmuseet,
Stockholm; reproduced by permission.

71

Plate 6

Sketch of the layout for the textual decoration of an anthropoid coffin.
OMMA 29.2.24 <u>recto</u>
Rogers Fund, 1929
Photograph courtesy of the Egyptian Department,
Metropolitan Musuem of Art, New York.

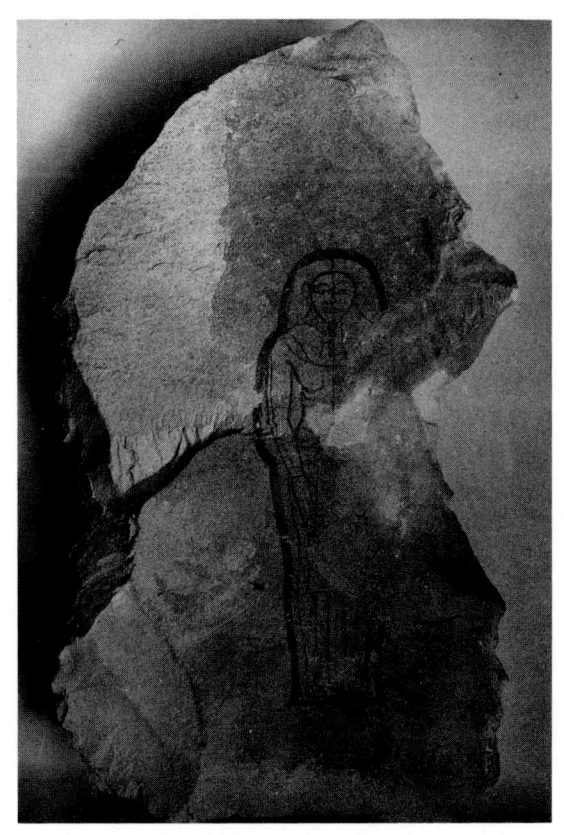

Plate 7

Sketch of an innermost lid (or, <u>couvercle planche</u>) lying within the box of an anthropoid coffin.
OMMA 23.7.1
Gift of the Earl of Carnarvon, 1923
Photograph courtesy of the Egyptian Department,
Metropolitan Museum of Art, New York.

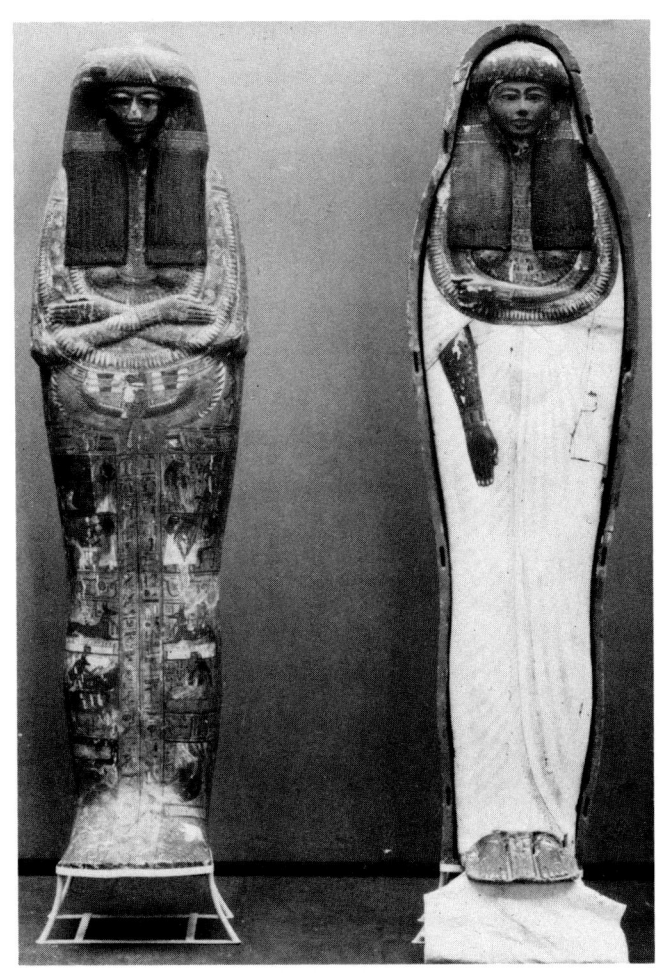

Plate 8

The anthropoid coffin and innermost lid of Iyneferti, the wife of Sennedjem.
MMA 86.1.5A-C
Museum Purchase, 1886
Photograph courtesy of the Egyptian Department,
Metropolitan Museum of Art, New York.

74

Plate 9

Section of the <u>Book of Gates</u> in the tomb of Horemheb (KV 57), showing guidelines for the placement of figures and texts.
Author's photograph.

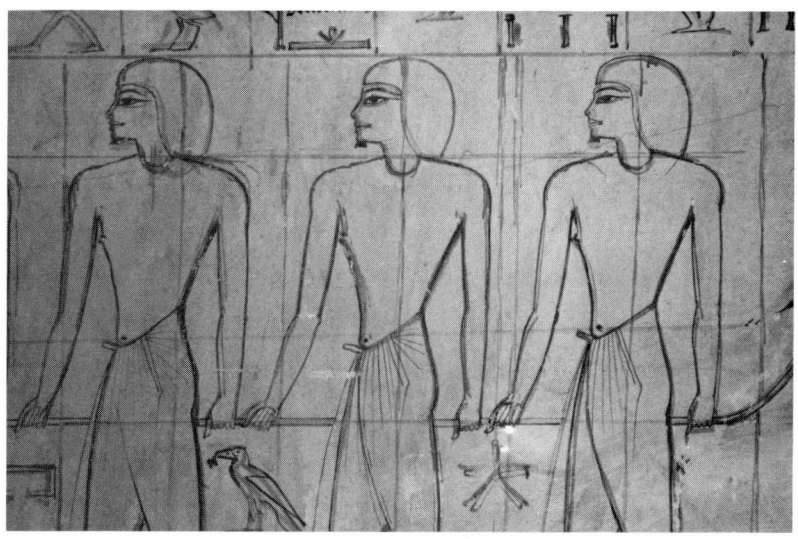

Plate 10

Detail from the <u>Book of Gates</u> in the tomb of Horemheb (KV 57), showing placement lines, which have been partly ruled and partly handdrawn.
Author's photograph.

Plate 11

Detail from a pillar in the burial chamber in the tomb of Amenhotep III (KV 22). The underlying grid has been exposed as the result of the loss of the outer layers of the painted surface.
Author's photograph.

Plate 12

Vertical columns of hieroglyphic text from the tomb of Sety I (KV 17). The initial "spattered" red demarcation lines, subsequent black ruled lines, and the red and black preliminary sketches are all visible.
Author's photograph.

Plate 13

Detail of the Solar Barque in the tomb of Horemheb
(KV 57). The carving of the relief, based on the
preliminary sketches, remains uncompleted.
Author's photograph.

Plate 14

Portion of an unfinished wall painting in the tomb of Horemheb (KV 57). The paint was applied in a series of solid
color blocks and the details and figural outlines would have been added later.
Photograph from a slide by the author.

Plate 15

View of the village at Deir el-Medina, looking towards the East. Portions of the western cemetery terraces are visible at right.
Photograph from a slide by the author.

Plate 16

The reconstructed tomb chapel of Nakhtmin (Tt 291) at Deir el-Medina.
Photograph from a slide by the author.

78

Plate 17

Detail of a wall painting from the tomb of the Sculptor Ipuy (Tt 217) at Deir el-Medina. The fabrication of religious and funerary objects is depicted.
Photograph from a slide by the author.

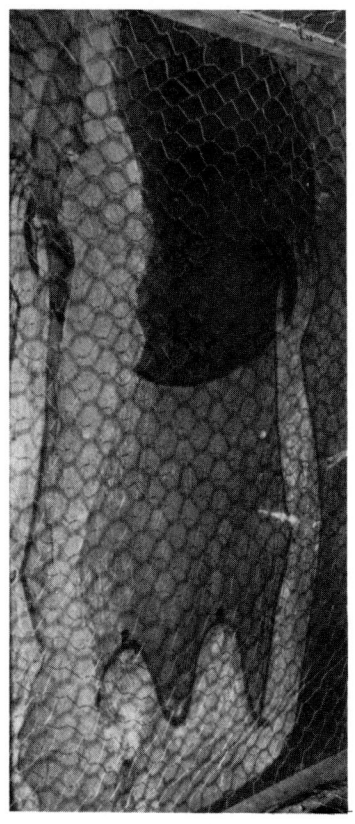

Plate 18

Painting from the soffit of the door into the burial chamber of the tomb of Sennedjem (Tt 1).
The Disk of the Horizon in the arms of Nut.
Photograph from a slide by the author.

Plate 19

Detail of the painted decoration on the foot of the inner coffin of Khonsu, the son of Sennedjem, depicting the Disk in the arms of Nut.
Photograph from a slide by the author; reproduced by permission of the Egyptian Department, Metropolitan Museum of Art, New York.

Plate 20

Drawing depicting "The Offerer before the Duat" in the tomb of Sety I (KV 17).
Author's photograph.

Plate 21

Detail of a painted representation of the God Osiris in the tomb of Sennedjem (Tt1) at Deir el-Medina.
Author's photograph.

Plate 22

Detail of a painted relief of the Goddess Isis in the tomb
of an Anonymous Queen of Ramesses II (QV 40).
Author's photograph.

Plate 23

Detail of the mummy of Sennedjem, from his tomb
(Tt 1) at Deir el-Medina.
Author's photograph.

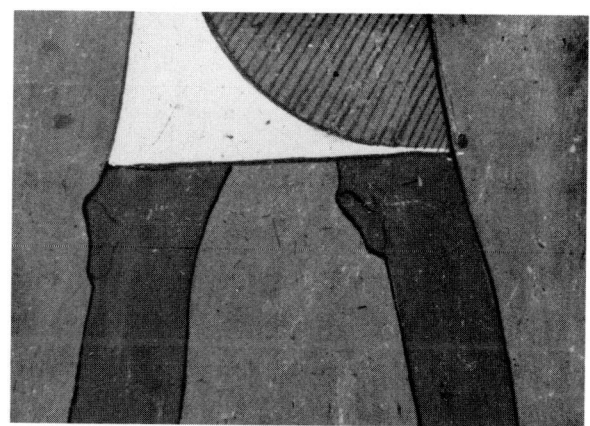

Plate 24

The knees of the God Anubis, a painted detail from the tomb of Sennedjem (Tt 1) at Deir el-Medina.
Author's photograph.

Plate 25

The knees of Sety I, from a pillar in the "unfinished chamber" of his tomb (KV 17).
Author's photograph.

Plate 26

Detail of a wall painting in the tomb of Nefer'abu (Tt 5) at Deir el-Medina, depicting a file of mourners that includes four draughtsmen at left.
Photograph from a slide by the author.

Plate 27

Detail of the wall decoration in the tomb of Nebenma'at (Tt 219), depicting the Draughtsman Nebre, his wife Pashed, and "son" Paherypedjet.
From MMA neg no. T. 3792.
Photography by the Egyptian Expedition, Metropolitan Museum of Art, New York.

Plate 28

Painted wall scene in the tomb of Nakhtamun (Tt 335) at Deir el-Medina: Piay before a ram-headed form of the God Anubis. From MMA neg. no. T. 3809.
Photography by the Egyptian Expedition, Metropolitan Museum of Art, New York.

Plate 29

Portion of a wall painting in the tomb of Nebenma'at (Tt 219), depicting the son and daughter-in-law before the tomb owner and his wife. From MMA neg. no. T. 3798. Photography by the Egyptian Expedition, Metropolitan Museum of Art, New York.

Plate 30

Two seated divinities, from a wall painting in the tomb of Queen Nebettawey (QV 60), a wife of Ramesses II. Author's photograph.

TOWARDS A RECONSTRUCTION OF RAMESSIDE MEMPHIS

Kenneth A. Kitchen

The present study is not based upon close personal inspection of the modern terrain of ancient Memphis - a privilege always denied to this writer - but upon scrutiny of the combined evidence culled alike from published documents from antiquity and the still limited data furnished by the available reports of excavations and surveys, not least the Egypt Exploration Society centenary survey-project, in which the Institute of Egyptian Art and Archaeology of Memphis State University, Tennessee, has appropriately participated. But despite its limitations, it is hoped that this study will at least provide a tangible model to be improved upon in future years, as new fieldwork yields fresh data.

The Precinct of Ptah

Today, very little is visible of the splendid monumental buildings that once adorned ancient Memphis. The most obvious monumental ruins are the still visible parts of the precinct and Temple of Ptah. So, we begin here and work our way outwards (Fig. 3).

The main axis of the great Temple of Ptah, as built by Amenophis III, the Ramesside kings, and Late-Period rulers, runs along a basically east-west line. The account given by Herodotus makes this clear through his sequence of structures (A, B, C), to which other elements can readily be added:

A. The eastern entrance-gate of the Temple of Hephaestus (Ptah), described as the finest and biggest of the four entrances, more elaborately decorated than the others; its builder was Asychis (Herodotus ii 136).[1] This grandiose scale suggests that we have here the principal entrance to the temple.

B. Sesostris (Ramesses II) is said to have brought enormous masses of stone for building the temple (Herodotus ii 108)[2] and to have set up colossi of himself and his queen, with their sons, in front of the temple (Herodotus ii 110).[3]

C. Rhampsinitus (also Ramesses II) is reported to have erected the entrance-gate and two colossi at the west end of Ptah's precinct (Herodotus ii 121).[4] This feature is generally admitted to be the pylon of the existing West Hall of the Temple of Ptah preceded by colossi, of whose bases Petrie saw one.[5] In contrast to A and B, clearly C is not the main or front entry to the great Temple of Ptah in Ramesside and later Egypt.

1 A. de Selincourt (transl.). *Herodotus, the Histories*, Penguin Classics, Harmondsworth, 1954, p. 155.

2 *Ibid.*, p. 141.

3 *Ibid.*, p. 142.

4 *Ibid.*, p. 147.

5 W.M.F. Petrie, *Memphis I, 1908*, London, 1909, p. 2.

D. Later than Herodotus is the eastern propylon of Ptolemy IV, of which Petrie found traces well to the east of the still existing main precinct of Ptah.[6] This eastern extension again points to the east entry being the front or principal entry, oriented directly toward the then course of the Nile (cf. also, Fig. 2).

E. Conversely, the oldest finds from the main temple came towards its west end, but at some distance east of the West Hall site of Ramesses II (whose foundations included earlier remains, such as popular votive stelae of Tuthmosis IV's reign[7]). The oldest remains of the main temple proper were two handsome blocks of Amenophis III offering to Sekhmet, Ptah's co-templar consort.[8]

F. There is the possibility of a processional way having traversed the west end of the Ptah precinct from north to south, running from a presumed northwest gate (north wall) down southward behind the West Hall to a southwest gate in the south enclosure wall, immediately adjacent to the small temple of Ramesses II dug by Habachi and Anthes.[9] Such a processional line may have intersected with the West Hall of Ramesses II (and any ancillary buildings) and would have, perhaps, separated it from the rear of the real sanctuary of the main New-Kingdom Temple of Ptah, somewhat further east. Thus, the West Hall is not integral to the Temple of Ptah proper - rather, it had its own separate function and identity, as did the *Akh-menu* temple of Tuthmosis III at Karnak behind the main sanctuary of Amun and, even more so, the completely separate eastern Temple of Ra-Horakhti at Karnak.

The resultant history of the Temple of Ptah may now be set out as follows. Before Amenophis III, the old traditional Temple of Ptah had been sited from early times up in the old city (cf. Fig. 2), further west than the precinct partly visible today - somewhere along the line of Mitrahina south through Kom Fakhry. This is clear from the recent surveys, which indicate that - before the New Kingdom - the Nile may have run through what is now the New-Kingdom temple-site. By the early New Kingdom, the gradual eastward shift of the bed of the Nile had left an increasing area of new land along the eastern side of the old city. Not later than the reign of Tuthmosis IV, a popular shrine had, perhaps, been established (for whatever reason) down on the new plain, from which come the modest votive stelae found by Petrie in the foundations of the later Ramesside West Hall. One stela[10] features Tuthmosis I, which might be the initial date of this shadowy early shrine.

Under Amenophis III came a major new initiative. A brand new main Temple of Ptah was now founded in the plain, comfortably to the east of the popular shrine (?) existing in his father's reign. At some juncture, Amenophis III also made his eldest son, Tuthmosis, High Priest of Ptah - a signal honour for the main cult of Egypt's ancient administrative capital and a means of keeping close royal check on the reforms and new buildings.[11] With these

6 *Ibid.*, pp. 2, 14, pl. 45.

7 *Ibid.*, p. 7, pls. 7, 8.

8 Petrie, *Meydum and Memphis III, 1910*, London, 1910, p. 39, pl. 29: 2, 3.

9 D.G. Jeffreys, *The Survey of Memphis, Part I; the Archaeological Report*, London, 1985, fig. 63, down left side of map.

10 Petrie, *Memphis I*, pl. 7:46.

11 H. Kees, *Das Priestertum im Ägyptischen Staat*, Leiden/Cologne, 1953, pp. 66-67, with

developments there probably went an upgrading in the status of the Apis Bulls. It is from this reign that individual tombs for the Apis Bulls are first attested archaeologically. Ptah's new precinct was conveniently nearer to the royal palaces on the plain by the river (Tuthmosis I onward) than his old temple would have been. During the Amarna Period, there may have been an Aten-temple at Memphis, unless the blocks found as early as the 1850's,[12] reused in a pavement, had been shipped in from elsewhere as building material by later kings. But the Memphite copy of Haremhab's coronation-inscription was surely set up in the new temple, reopened after the Amarna interlude.[13] It mentions the erecting of a quartzite stela of the ruler "opposite the great *idr* of [....]."[14]

Sethos I inaugurated a fresh phase in the building and history of the New-Kingdom temple. In both Thebes and Memphis, he set up parallel foundations having closely matching names (we lack evidence for Heliopolis as yet). In Thebes at Karnak, he erected, in front of Amenophis III's great pylon, the building "Glorious (*Akh*) is Sethos I in the Domain of Amun" (*Pr-Imn*), familiar to us today as the Great Hypostyle Hall. At Memphis Sethos I erected a building with the precisely parallel name "Glorious (*Akh*) is Sethos I in the Domain of Ptah" (*Pr-Ptḥ*) but known to us only by a scarab (from Mitrahina) and a plaque.[15] These tiny pieces may have come from looted foundation deposits of this building. As a clearly parallel foundation to the great hall at Karnak, it may be suggested that the Memphite building was also a great columned hall, erected in front of the temple of Amenophis III and Haremhab, just as the Karnak great hall fronts and incorporates works of those two kings. The Memphite great hall will have been built of limestone (not sandstone, like its Theban counterpart), and so it has long since disappeared into the limekilns.

Ramesses II, in turn, treated both the Theban and Memphite foundations of his father in exactly the same way. They now had their names changed to "Glorious is Ramesses II in the Domain of" Amun and Ptah, respectively. This probably means that to Ramesses II fell the task of completing what his father had left unfinished (as at Karnak), hence he appropriated the whole. The evidence for the name-change at Memphis is provided by Papyrus Bulaq 19 (Cairo CGC 58096), which records the issue of red jasper pieces for inlay (pomegranates and another fruit, *bw*) in the temple "Glorious is Ramesses II in the Domain of Ptah," not later than his Year 43, ç. 1237 BC.[16] In general terms, in his great text, "The Blessing of Ptah," Ramesses II claims:

references.

12 Sir Charles Nicholson, *Aegyptiaca...University of Sydney*, London, 1891, pp. 113 ff., with relevant plates.

13 Petrie, *Memphis I*, pl. 6; W. Helck, *Urkunden der 18. Dynastie* (*Urk. IV*), Hefte 21-22, Berlin, 1958, pp. 2121-2124.

14 Helck, op. cit., p. 2123:12-13.

15 K.A. Kitchen, *Ramesside Inscriptions* (hereinafter, *KRI*), I, Oxford, 1969/75, p. 124:5, 10, § 63. For the little "oratory" of Sethos I for Ptah and the two goddesses personifying "Memphis" and a "Rampart," on south side of the south wall of the precinct, see latterly, J. Berlandini, *BSFÉ* No. 99 (1984), pp. 28-52.

16 *KRI*, VII 1987, pp. 102-103; cf. Helck, *Materialien zur Wirtschaftsgeschichte des Neuen Reiches*, I (*Abhandlungen, Akad., Mainz, 1960*), Wiesbaden, 1961, p. 135, 2, but omit the mention of Louvre C. 94.

<u>A</u>. "I enlarged your Temple in Hatkuptah [Memphis], constructed in eternal work, of excellent workmanship, of stone, finished-off with gold and real gemstones.

I laid out (??) your esplanade on the North, with two noble twin halls?/walls? (ḏrity) opposite you, their doors like the horizon of heaven, causing the common people to adore you.

<u>B</u>. I make for you a noble temple within Inbu [Memphis], divine is your image in the mysterious shrine, reposing on its great seat.

I equipped it with priests and prophets, serfs, fields, cattle, I made it festive with sacred offerings, myriads of things."[17]

Section A of this citation may well be a generalised account of the work on "Glorious is [Sethos I] Ramesses II in the Domain of Ptah," as it was certainly an enlargement of the New-Kingdom Temple of Ptah. It also suggests that Ramesses II organised the precinct on the north side of the temple, building a pair of ḏrity there - whatever they may have been (an obscure term).

Section B is clearly some other structure, a separate foundation. It is not described as being in Hatkuptah (precinct of Ptah and, by extension, Memphis) but in Inbu, a wider term for Memphis city ["(White) Walls"]. Two candidates for this entity seem, at first sight, possible. One is the West Hall of Ramesses II, the other is his funerary or (better) memorial temple in Western Memphis. As the West Hall is part of Ptah's precinct, it can be ruled out as not being the structure of Section B. While separate from the Temple of Ptah, the West Hall was still in that precinct, hence would come under the rubric of <u>A</u>, enlargements to the main centre of Ptah's worship. One may suggest that the West Hall was a jubilee-hall, analogous to one erected at Pi-Ramesse, and that parallel ceremonies were conducted in the two centres when Ramesses II celebrated one or other of his numerous jubilees. It was expensively built - the walls with black basalt footings, friezes and waterspouts,[18] and granite column-bases having the king's cartouches upon ḥb-signs. [19] The rest, doubtless of limestone, has long since disappeared.

Thus, the edifice mentioned in Section B above may more probably be identified as Ramesses II's Memphite funerary temple (on which, see below). This was sited well to the west of the main precinct of Ptah.

Returning to the main precinct, Ramesses II appears to have fairly littered the area and its environs with colossi and minor chapels. The red-granite dyad of the king with Ptah (now Ny Carlsberg AEIN 1483) was found by Petrie near the supposed North Gate of the precinct,[20] along with another dyad, a sphinx, and part of a colossus. The colossi, seen at a distance along the east (front) façade of the main Ptah-temple by Herodotus (ii 110), probably fronted the great hall "Glorious is Ramesses II in the Domain of Ptah." Whether

17 Text, *KRI*, II, pp. 278-279.

18 Petrie, *Memphis I*, pls. 21, 23, 24; texts, *KRI*, II, pp. 488-492.

19 Petrie, op. cit., pl. 25; *KRI*, II, p. 492.

20 W.M.F. Petrie, *Tarkhan I and Memphis V*, London, 1913, p. 32, pls. 77-78.

they also correspond in any way to the spots signifying four colossi before an east-facing facade on a recent plan,[21] I cannot tell; these seem rather far east in relation to the axis of the main north-south avenue.

On the south side of the precinct and beyond it, there is a rash of works by this king; the barest summary must suffice. Outside the southwest corner of the existing (and later) precinct wall, is a Ptah-chapel from not before the 40's of the reign, as the king here includes the distinctive epithets "God, Ruler of Heliopolis" in his nomen.[22] Opposite, and a little north (within the walls), is the oratory of Sethos I.[23] Roughly halfway along the south stretch of the precinct wall, was once a gateway giving onto the main southward processional way. That gateway was once adorned by the famous colossi of Ramesses II - the limestone one lying prostrate in the "shed" museum on site and the granite one now standing in Cairo's Railway Station Square (Meidan el-Mehatta).[24] One small temple of Ramesses II is close to the east of this roadway, while a Hathor-temple of his is further off to the west.[25] Near the "shed" museum of the limestone colossus, can be seen various items of mainly granite statuary of this king, mainly broken up. One splendid granite figure, recently restored, may have stood outside one of the lesser southern shrines just mentioned.[26]

Merenptah's best known contributions to Memphis are his separate temple and palace, situated to the southeast of Ptah's precinct (Fig. 2 at M).[27] However, he may also have been the Pheron of Herodotus (ii 111), who set up two obelisks before the Temple of Ptah.

To complete the picture, we must briefly continue the story beyond the 19th Dynasty. In the great Papyrus Harris I, 45:3 ff., Ramesses III mentions clearly that he built, "a mansion anew, on your esplanade (wb3), a place of repose" (st htp) - or way-station - "at your [Ptah's] wish, for whenever you appear,"[28] One may suggest that this building was the direct Memphite counterpart to the temple of Ramesses III in the Karnak forecourt of Amun, situated on what was then an esplanade (not a walled court), serving as way-station for Amun's processions. Here at Memphis, one may suggest provisionally that Ramesses III's corresponding building was on the south side of the main west-east axis of the Temple of Ptah and close to the route south across the precinct to the South Gate and the south-continuing processional way. Other works by Ramesses III at Memphis are noted in Papyrus Harris I but have not yet been traced, while other traces actually found are of

21 Jeffreys, *Survey of Memphis*, I, 1985, fig. 63.

22 Ibid., pp. 72-73, figs. 30-36, with references.

23 Ibid., pp. 73-74, fig. 37.

24 For the roadway, cf. ibid., pp. 74-75, figs. 15, 40-44, with references.

25 See ibid., figs. 15, 42, and p. 74, figs. 38-39, respectively.

26 See R.E. Freed, *Ramesses the Great, His Life and World*, Memphis, Tennessee, 1987, pp. 1-10.

27 B. Porter and R. Moss, ed. J. Malek, *Topographical Bibliography...* , III, Oxford, 1981, pp. 854-857.

28 W. Erichsen, *Papyrus Harris I*, Brussels, 1933, p. 50; J. H. Breasted, *Ancient Records of Egypt*, IV, Chicago, 1907, §311.

small import so far. But we may note, in passing, fragments of a granite gateway of Ramesses VI from somewhere north of the west-east axis of the main temple.[29]

Leaving aside the known structures of the 21st-dynasty king Siamun, south of Ptah's main precinct, we reach the enigmatic Asychis of Herodotus. The Asychis who built a brick pyramid may well have been Shepseskaf of the 4th Dynasty. Equally clearly, the Asychis who erected a vast sculptured gateway out in front of the Ramesside structures of the Temple of Ptah was not Shepseskaf. So, we have two kings, Asychis, run together in his tourist notes by Herodotus.[30] Asychis II was clearly post-Ramesside and also earlier than Anysis and the invasion of Egypt by S(h)abako of the 25th Dynasty. Therefore, he was a strong king of the Third Intermediate Period. All indications point to Shoshenq I. First, the archaeological parallel: at Thebes, Shoshenq I enclosed the Ramesside esplanade as a vast forecourt and planned an entrance, later replaced by the present Pylon I (Nectanebo or Ptolemaic). At Memphis, he could equally have enclosed the esplanade before the Ramesside hall, and the entrance gateway covered with scenes (as is the "Bubastite Gate" at Karnak) at the east entrance would be the one that so impressed Herodotus. Second, textual evidence: Shoshenq's great Theban forecourt was named the "Mansion of Hedjkheperre Setepenre in Thebes," where mention is made of a "Mansion of [millions of years, of] Hedjkheperre Setepenre which is in Memphis."[31] Just as did the 19th Dynasty, so in turn Shoshenq I founded parallel edifices in Memphis and Thebes fronting the older structures. To finish with this precinct, Amasis II remodelled or added to the original temple of Amenophis III; and much later, Ptolemy IV added an outer gateway to the east of everything else so far built, as already noted above. During the Late Period (precisely as at Karnak in Thebes), various kings added minor structures around and within the main precinct (e.g., Shabako); these lesser works need no further attention here.

Temples and Cults Elsewhere in Memphis

1. Hathor of the Southern Sycamore

In Papyrus Harris I, we learn that Ptah would sail in his river-barge to visit Hathor of the Southern Sycamore[32] (cf. Fig. 2) and specifically, "on the South of Inbu" (Memphis). This could have been no mere five-minute journey; comparison with Amun's river-journeys at Thebes would suggest that Hathor's famous temple may lie some two miles or more south of the precinct of Ptah, even if not so far as Dahshur, as Sethe once suggested.[33]

2. Neith North of the Wall

This rather elusive phrase suggests a shrine of the goddess Neith, somewhere north of Mitrahina and north of the original "White Wall(s)" of Menes - the opposite of Ptah "South of his Wall."[34]

---

29 Petrie, *Meydum and Memphis III*, pp. 39-40, pl. 31; *KRI*, VI, p. 281.

30 K.A. Kitchen, "A Note on Asychis," in J. Baines, T.G.H. James, A. Leahy, A.F. Shore (eds.), *Pyramid Studies and Other Essays presented to I.E.S. Edwards*, London, 1988, pp. 148-151.

31 K.A. Kitchen, *Third Intermediate Period in Egypt*, Warminster, 1972, 1986, p. 301 and n. 313.

32 Page 49:2-3; Erichsen, *Papyrus Harris I*, p. 55; cf. Breasted, *Ancient Records*, IV, § 331.

33 As quoted by Sir A.H. Gardiner, *Ancient Egyptian Onomastica*, II, Oxford, 1947, pp. 123* ff.

34 Reference, Helck, *Materialien zur Wirtschaftsgeschichte des Neuen Reiches*, I, p. 141, 6.

3. Ankhtawy and Funerary Temples of the Kings

On this point, Amenhotep, an officer of Amenophis III, is absolutely explicit:[35] the local memorial temple of Amenophis III "United with Ptah" was erected "in the inundation-area ($b^c\dot{h}$) on the west of Hatkuptah [central Memphis], on territory of Ankhtawy." The $b^c\dot{h}$ proper would be the lower cultivable (and floodable) ground west of the main city-ridge (now represented by the mounds, or *koms*, of Mitrahina and Fakhry), while Ankhtawy seemingly included this plus the immediately neighbouring desert edge on which such funerary temples might well stand, running up westward into the Saqqara necropolis plateau. On the Berlin "*Trauerrelief*" from the New-Kingdom tombs of the nobles at nearby Saqqara, comes the prayer:[36] "receive(?) me in the Isle of the Just, the Necropolis of Ankhtawy." So, the general location of Ankhtawy (when it is not merely used as a further synonym for Memphis) seems clear.

Furthermore, a Cairo fragment, as interpreted by Helck,[37] would appear to vouch for a similar temple of Haremhab in this $b^c\dot{h}$ area. Therefore, it is logical to place the Memphite funerary temple of Ramesses II in this same area.[38]

4. Ro-Setjau and Sokar's Shetayet-Shrine

The general area of Ro-Setjau appears to have covered the area south from the Giza pyramid-plateau proper as far as Zawiyet el-Aryan.[39] At more than one point in this area, deposits of shabti-figures were left in the desert sands by high officials and even in the names of Queen Nefertari and Prince Khaemwaset from Ramesses II's own family. Also in this area, rather more than a mile south from the Great Pyramid, Petrie found limestone foundation-blocks.[40] Further north, Petrie also found granite fragments of some other totally destroyed building.[41] And more such traces have been found, also, south of the first site.[42] Recent study may suggest that one or other of these structures was the famous Shetayet shrine of the god Sokar, where his great gilded Henu-barque was kept and whence it was taken ceremonially to Memphis at the Festival of Sokar.[43] If so, then the area was

---

35 Cf. text, in Helck, *Urkunden der 18. Dynastie*, pp. 1793, 1795.

36 Text cited by A. Badawi, *Memphis als zweite Landeshauptstadt im Neuen Reich*, Cairo, 1948, p. 64.

37 Helck, *Materialien zur Wirtschaftsgeschichte des Neuen Reiches*, I, p. 138, 3.

38 References, Helck, op. cit., p. 138 f., 5, but omit Louvre C.94 (a Heliopolitan shrine); *KRI*, III, p. 169.

39 Cf. C.M. Zivie, "Ro-Setau," in W. Helck, W. Westendorf (eds.), *Lexikon der Ägyptologie*, V, Wiesbaden, 1983, cols. 304-306.

40 Cf. W.M.F. Petrie, *Gizeh and Rifeh 1907*, London, 1907, pp. 1, 24.

41 Ibid., p. 9.

42 I.E.S. Edwards, "The Setayet of Rosetau," in L.H. Lesko (ed.), *Egyptological Studies in Honor of Richard A. Parker*, Hanover/London, 1986, p. 35, n. 50.

43 For the possible interrelations of Ro-Setjau, the Shetayet shrine of Sokar, and desert

one of high sanctity (like Abydos), where it would be deemed advantageous to bury shabtis near a sanctuary and tomb of the god, as at Abydos and in the Serapeum.[44]

Many other minor Memphite cults can be traced in texts, etc., but our knowledge of these and their locations is too limited to justify review here.

Civil Districts of the City

1. Peru-nefer and the Docks

It has long been known that this term ("bon voyage") is the name of a royal dockyard at Memphis, together with its adjoining suburb,[45] generally placed on the south side of the city, perhaps southeast from Ptah's precinct, if certain assumptions are granted. These are as follows. First, the "wharf of the charioteer, Herynefer, which is on the South of Memphis,"[46] is in, or part of, the Peru-nefer dockland area. Second, the "foreign Aphrodite" and "Tyrian camp" and its Tyrian Phoenician inhabitants[47] are to be linked with the earlier cult of Astarte, attested as belonging to Peru-nefer as early as Amenophis II[48] and in the late 18th Dynasty.[49] Baal is another foreign deity with a New-Kingdom cult there.[50] Third, Petrie[51] offered rather circumstantial evidence for locating the Tyrian camp of Herodotus near the temple and palace of Merenptah, southeast of the main Ptah precinct, namely the occurrence nearby of 7th-century Greek pottery and his identification of Aphrodite as being the Egyptian Hathor, attested (when he wrote) only at that point in Memphis (his pl. 28). Now, of course, she is amply attested elsewhere on this vast site.

---

burials of shabti-figures by high officials, etc., see the paper by I.E.S. Edwards, "The Shetayet of Rosetau," in L.H. Lesko (ed.), *Egyptological studies in Honor of Richard A. Parker*, pp. 27-36.

44 Cf. B.J. Kemp, "Abydos", in W. Helck, W. Westendorf (eds.), *Lexikon der Ägyptologie*, I, 1972, cols. 36-37; *KRI*, II, pp. 367-376 passim.

45 Cf. S.R.K. Glanville, *ZÄS* 68 (1932), pp. 27-30, § 86; Helck, "Perunefer," in Helck, Westendorf (eds.), *Lexikon der Ägyptologie*, IV, 1982, col. 990; cf. Jeffreys, *Survey of Memphis*, I, pp. 48, 107, nn. 385-388.

46 The "*Rechnungen*" under Sethos I, *KRI*, I, p. 271:9.

47 Herodotus ii 112; Petrie, *Memphis I*, p. 3.

48 Cf. G. Daressy, *ASAE* 11 (1912), p. 258, deity No. 4.

49 C.R. Lepsius, *Denkmäler aus Aegypten und Aethiopen, Texte*, I, p. 16.

50 Helck, *Materialien zur Wirtschaftsgeschichte des Neuen Reiches*, I, p. 143:1-n. Cf. also, R.A. Caminos, *Late-Egyptian Miscellanies*, Oxford, 1954, p. 337.

51 Petrie, *Memphis I*, pp. 3-4.

2. The City Districts

(a) The South District. (See Figs. 4, 5.) For this area, the most informative source is a group of papyri that preserve part of some official accounts from the first three years of the reign of Sethos I, first edited by Spiegelberg[52] and subsequently revised slightly and included in the writer's *Ramesside Inscriptions*, I. Almost the whole of the timber-accounts relate to the South District, and none unquestionably to any other district. We have knowledge of twelve District Officers - ten explicitly belong to the South District, one probably does (Ru), and one possibly (Meryre). The area under the control of a District Officer (*wˁrtw*) can be clearly called "The South District" (*t3 iwyt rsi*) of the "District Officer PN" (so, e.g., Ramose, *KRI*, I, p. 273:4). Less precisely, one may simply read of "The District of the District Officer PN" (e.g., *KRI*, I, p. 277:12, Mahu).

Used as a broad general term, "The South District" (e.g., ibid., p. 263:2) can serve as the overall heading to the several specific wards overseen by a series of District Officers (loc. cit.). As a result, we find that we have here a whole "South District" of the city, divided up into sub-districts or wards, each ward under its own officer - at least seven or eight, and most probaby eleven or twelve such officers. Apart from houses, streets (*ḫ3r*, Coptic *hir*) are named as well as chapels (*ḫnw*), (cf. ibid., p. 273:9). Doubtless, the wharf of the charioteer Herynefer (ibid., p. 271:9) should also be included in the overall area.

At present, it is not possible to map out these sub-districts with certainty, partly because the fixed sequences are few, partly because lacunae destroy the possibility of other sequences. But twice we find the sequence, Anhurmose + Amenmose + Hori (ibid., p. 264:5, 7 & 9, 11; p. 267:1, 3, 5). A third series goes Anhurmose + X [=Amenmose?] + Hori + Mahu (ibid., p. 263:4, 6/&, 9, 11). This itinerary then doubled back to Hori's district, then that of Ramose (p. 263:15; p. 264:1, 3), and may be presumed to have returned to that of Anhurmose. The last suggestion is inspired by a sequence from Ramose into Anhurmose (273:5/6, 9, 11, 13, 15). From the ward of Hori (264:11, 15), a longer foraging-expedition appears to have circled round a series of wards in order (265:1 to 266:13). The link from the wharf of Herynefer up via Meryre to Mahu remains tenuous but possible (271:7 to 272:1, 10). Other short sequences can be seen on Fig. 4 in the wards of Ru, Pawah, and Ahmose. The "map" offered in Fig. 4 is frankly theoretical, and other formulations could be offered. The other point is that the overall orientation of the whole scheme as given is not certain - the wharf could as easily be located on the north or east (see Fig. 5) as on the south; we simply have no indications about this. However, it is hoped that this bold projection will be an amusing stimulus to students of ancient Memphis!

Looking at the men in charge of these wards, we have possible evidence of nepotism: officers include Ru and Ptah-roi, son of Ru; also, Hori and Amenmose, (son of) Hori, even adjoining Hori (e.g., p. 264:7-10, 11). So, perhaps a father on occasion managed to have his son appointed to a ward immediately adjacent to one run by himself.

The size and scope of these sub-districts is uncertain. In the largest traceable grouping, under Anhurmose (but not all placed on the "map"), we find at least eleven properties - nine houses and two chapels. The minimum is one large property, a granary, placed under a former porter, Meryre (p. 272:1). For the overall South District in the timber-accounts, we learn of over 70 houses (but not all located on the "map"), five or six chapels, and royal estates of Haremhab, Ramesses I, and Sethos I, etc. And these must represent only a proportion of the buildings and institutions to be found in the area - not everyone need have had timber available for requisition.

---

52 W. Spiegelberg, *Rechnungen aus der Zeit Setis I*, Strassburg, 1896.

One may sketch the social spectrum visible in this area. Among the Egyptian notables, we find properties of a vizier (Nebamun), a chief lector and administrator (Iuny), a steward of property (Ruru), a chief of the *Medjayu*-militia (Amenwahsu), a troop-commander of Kush (Khay), a deputy of Pharaoh's granary (Hori), and others. There are lesser bureaucrats, particularly those attached to royal foundations. Other military personnel appear, mainly of middle rank: many standard-bearers, some charioteers and stable masters, the occasional other soldier. Among those in practical callings are a chief builder, three "merchants," a fowler, and the agent for a wharf. Remarkably, only a few religious personnel appear: one priest (w^cb), besides the chapels ($ḥnw$) of Ptah, Amun, and Qasarti. No further analysis can be pursued here. But the peremptory requisitioning of timber from all these properties perhaps makes it possible to suggest that these houses (with their back yards and spare timbers) were, in fact, state-owned and went with the job held by their tenants. One is reminded of a passage in the Late-Egyptian Miscellanies[53] where the pupil promises his teacher, "I will build you a new villa (upon) the ground of your Lord..." - i.e., on royal land - perhaps giving Pharaoh certain rights over the leases? While town houses (and their offices) may have been government property (like those in our accounts) put at the disposal of appointees to various posts, it is also clear that well-placed officials gained enough wealth to build and equip their own luxurious suburban villas, from the idealised accounts given in the Miscellanies.[54]

(b) The District of Pharaoh, Which is Called the Fine District (cf. Fig. 2).[55]

It is a very short step to make the suggestion that this "Fine District of Pharaoh" is essentially the area of the royal palaces and estates in Memphis. Given the known location of the palace-complex of Merenptah eastward of Ptah's precinct (as well as south of it), one may also suggest that the New-Kingdom palaces occupied a privileged position close to the new course of the river, east of what became the New-Kingdom precinct of Ptah. Going on the analogy of how early royal tombs and later royal temples tended to be built in runs from north to south in Western Thebes, one may further suggest that the original (and long-used) palace of Tuthmosis I was the northernmost of the series, which, thereafter, extended ever further south until that of Merenptah is reached. The estates of Haremhab, Ramesses I, Sethos I, and Ramesses II should then have lain somewhere north of Merenptah's precinct.

(c) The District of Ptah may well have been the precinct of the New-Kingdom Temple of Ptah, at the centre of the New-Kingdom metropolis.

(d) Northern District. Its existence rests principally on the slender evidence of the phrase, (the goddess) "Neith North of the Wall," which (so far) I can trace only on Cairo CGC 1484 of the Old Kingdom.[56] Paser's titles regarding Neith on one monument[57] do not provide

53 Papyrus Lansing 11:3 ff.; A. Gardiner, *Late-Egyptian Miscellanies*, Brussels, 1937, p. 110; Caminos, *Late-Egyptian Miscellanies*, p. 410.

54 Papyrus Anastasi IV, 3:7, 8:9, and P. Lansing, 12:1 ff.; Gardiner, *op. cit.*, pp. 37, 43, 110, and Caminos, *op. cit.*, pp. 138, 164, 412.

55 Spiegelberg, *Rechnungen aus der Zeit des Setis I*, p. 57.

56 Which is A. Mariette, *Les Mastabas de l'Ancien Empire*, 1882-9, pp. 307-309, in *Wb.*, *Belegstellen*, II, 125:11 (p. 180).

57 In *KRI*, III, pp. 13:11, 14:6.

evidence for a location.[58] And Petrie[59] does not document his northern location for the Temple of Neith.[60]

3. The Suburbs.

The Miscellanies, several of Memphite origin, several times sketch the ideal life of the wealthy official with his private villa in its own grounds.[61] It may be suggested that these delectable properties formed garden-suburbs, spreading to north and south of the main central districts of the city proper.

4. The Memphite Necropolis in the New Kingdom.

The long line of Old-Kingdom pyramids from Giza to south Saqqara formed the backdrop to the burial-places of the inhabitants of Memphis during the New Kingdom. The prime site was that part of the desert plateau directly opposite Memphis itself, at least distance from the city, coming under the same name as its Ankhtawy quarter: the part of central Saqqara immediately east of the Pyramid-precinct of Sekhemkhet, adjoining the south side of the causeway of Unis. Here lay streets of the tomb-chapels[62] of the very great (Haremhab as general; Tia and Tia, the sister and brother-in-law of Ramesses II; Neferronpet, vizier of Ramesses II; Harmin, harim-chief of Sethos I; and many more), with the humbler tombs of hangers-on and of lesser officials and artisans tucked around and in between the more pretentious tombs of the great.[63] Rather further north, between the Archaic Cemetery of the first two dynasties and the pyramids of Teti and Queen Iput, was located a further cemetery of higher middle-rank administrators explored by Loret and including the tombs of petty officials, such as Mose, whose great legal texts are so celebrated.[64] Along the cliff-face that formed the southeast boundary of this part of the plateau, high officials of the 18th Dynasty cut rock-tombs, like their Theban contemporaries; these date from about the reigns of Amenophis III and IV.[65] An

58 Despite Helck, *Materialien...*, I, p. 141,   6.

59 Petrie, *Memphis I*, p. 3.

60 Seemingly accepted without much question by Jeffreys, *Survey of Memphis*, I, p. 44 end, and by C.M. Zivie, "Memphis," in Helck, Westendorf (eds.), *Lexikon der Ägyptologie*, IV, 1980, col. 32 end.

61 E.g., in Caminos, *Late-Egyptian Miscellanies*, pp. 138, 164, 400, 410, 412 f.

62 For the type of tomb-chapel, cf. Kitchen, in M. Görg and E. Pusch (eds.), *Festschrift Elmar Edel*, 1979, pp. 272-284.

63 Cf. the reports by G.T. Martin, in *JEA* 62 (1976), pp. 5-13, and *JEA* since; G.T. Martin et alii, *The Tomb-Chapels of Paser and Ra'ia at Saqqara*, 1985. Cf. Porter & Moss, (ed.) Malek, *Topographical Bibliography...*, III, 1979, pp. 653 ff.

64 This tomb, see G.A. Gaballa, *The Memphite Tomb-Chapel of Mose*, 1977; other tombs, V. Loret, *BIE*, 3rd series, 10 (1899), pp. 95-100; Porter and Moss, (ed.) Malek, op. cit., pp. 552 ff.

65 Cf. (e.g.) A.-P. Zivie, *ASAE* 68 (1982), pp. 63-69.

intriguing gap in our knowledge (which later explorers might care to investigate) is presented by the segment of plateau right opposite the precinct of old Djoser himself, north of the Unis causeway and southeast of Userkaf's pyramid (marked "?" on Fig. 1). Who knows what and who may have been buried here? Other tombs and monuments were scattered all the way south as far as the complex of Pepy II.

Then, some original archaeology. Ramesses II's scholar-son, Prince Khaemwaset, surveyed many of the pyramids and set inscriptions prominently upon them under his father's patronage, naming the ancient owner and renewing the endowment of the cult - this latter detail may underlie the comments about food supplies in a text on the Great Pyramid made to Herodotus by his tourist-guide.

5. In Conclusion, we return to the city itself. The chapels already mentioned may have been small popular places of worship, metropolitan equivalents of the little chapels familiar to us from Deir el-Medina in Western Thebes. On the bazaars, streets, and squares, we have practically no information; we know of the arsenal but not its location.[66]

Finally, as pure scholarly whimsy, I present here a pair of "maps" (Fig. 6) of a shrine of Ptah and of the Shetayet precinct of Sokar (with *Pr-Ḥnw*) which is based on the data on Memphite gods and shrines given in a text in the great Temple of Sethos I at Abydos and long ago studied by Kees.[67] Whether these two plans bear any relation to reality can safely be left to the verdict of colleagues and to the impact of future discoveries in the area of ancient Memphis itself.

---

66 Arsenal, cf. S. Sauneron, *BIFAO* 54 (1954), pp. 7-12.

67 H. Kees, in *Rec. Trav.* 37 (1915), pp. 57-76.

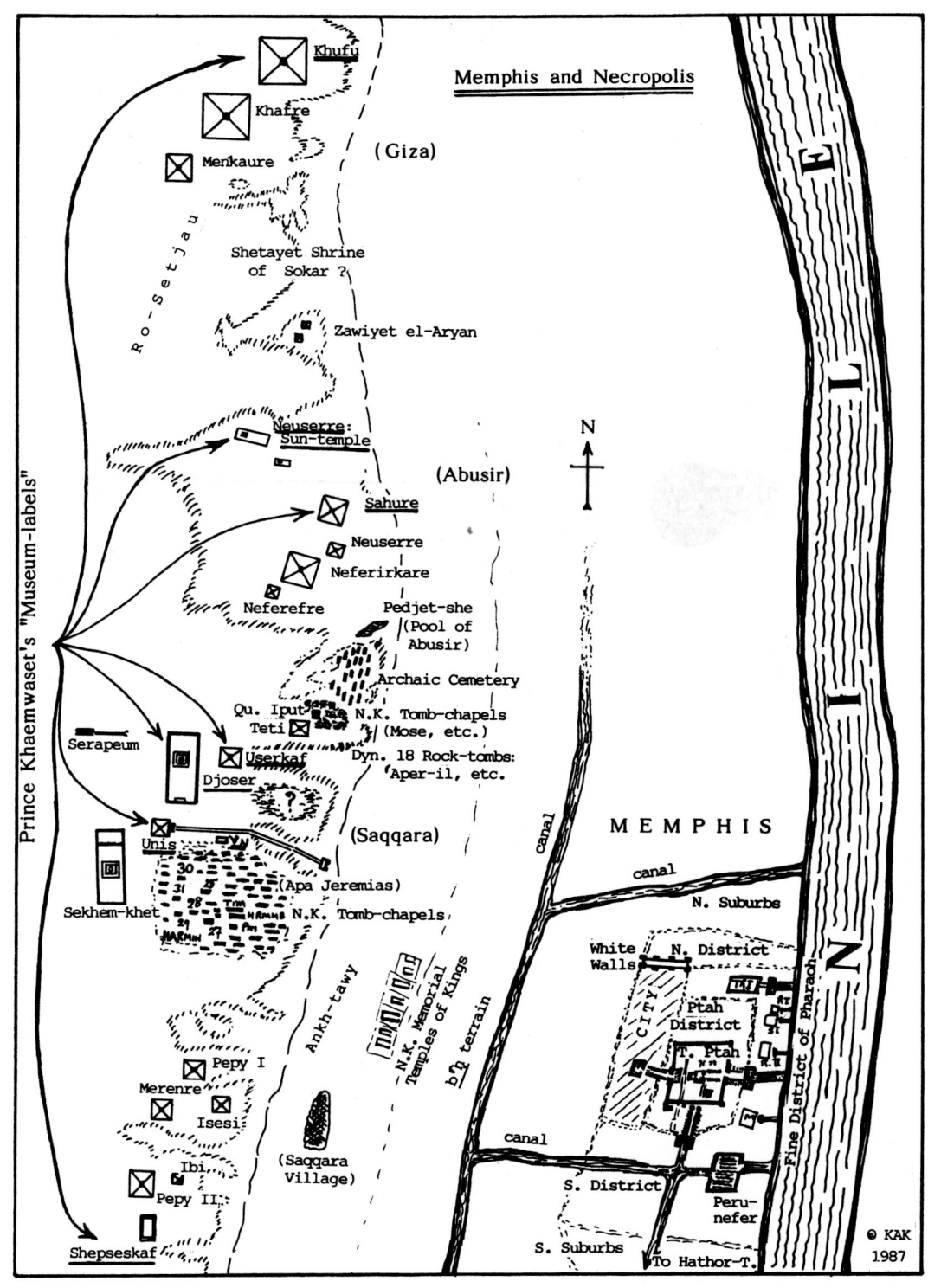

Fig. 1 Memphis and its Necropolis, Old to New Kingdoms

The following labels appear on the map:

Memphis and Necropolis

Khufu
Khafre
Menkaure
(Giza)
Ro-Setjau
Shetayet Shrine of Sokar ?
Zawiyet el-Aryan
Neuserre: Sun-temple
(Abusir)
Sahure
Neuserre
Neferirkare
Neferefre
Pedjet-she (Pool of Abusir)
Archaic Cemetery
Qu. Iput
Teti
N.K. Tomb-chapels (Mose, etc.)
Dyn. 18 Rock-tombs: Aper-il, etc.
Serapeum
Userkaf
Djoser
(Saqqara)
Unis
30
(Apa Jeremias)
Sekhem-khet
N.K. Tomb-chapels
Prince Khaemwaset's "Museum-labels"
Ankh-tawy
N.K. Memorial Temples of Kings
ḥ terrain
Pepy I
Merenre
Isesi
Ibi
Pepy II
(Saqqara Village)
Shepseskaf

N

N I L E

canal
MEMPHIS
canal
N. Suburbs
White Walls
N. District
CITY
Ptah District
T. Ptah
Fine District of Pharaoh
canal
S. District
Peru-nefer
S. Suburbs
To Hathor-T.
© KAK 1987

99

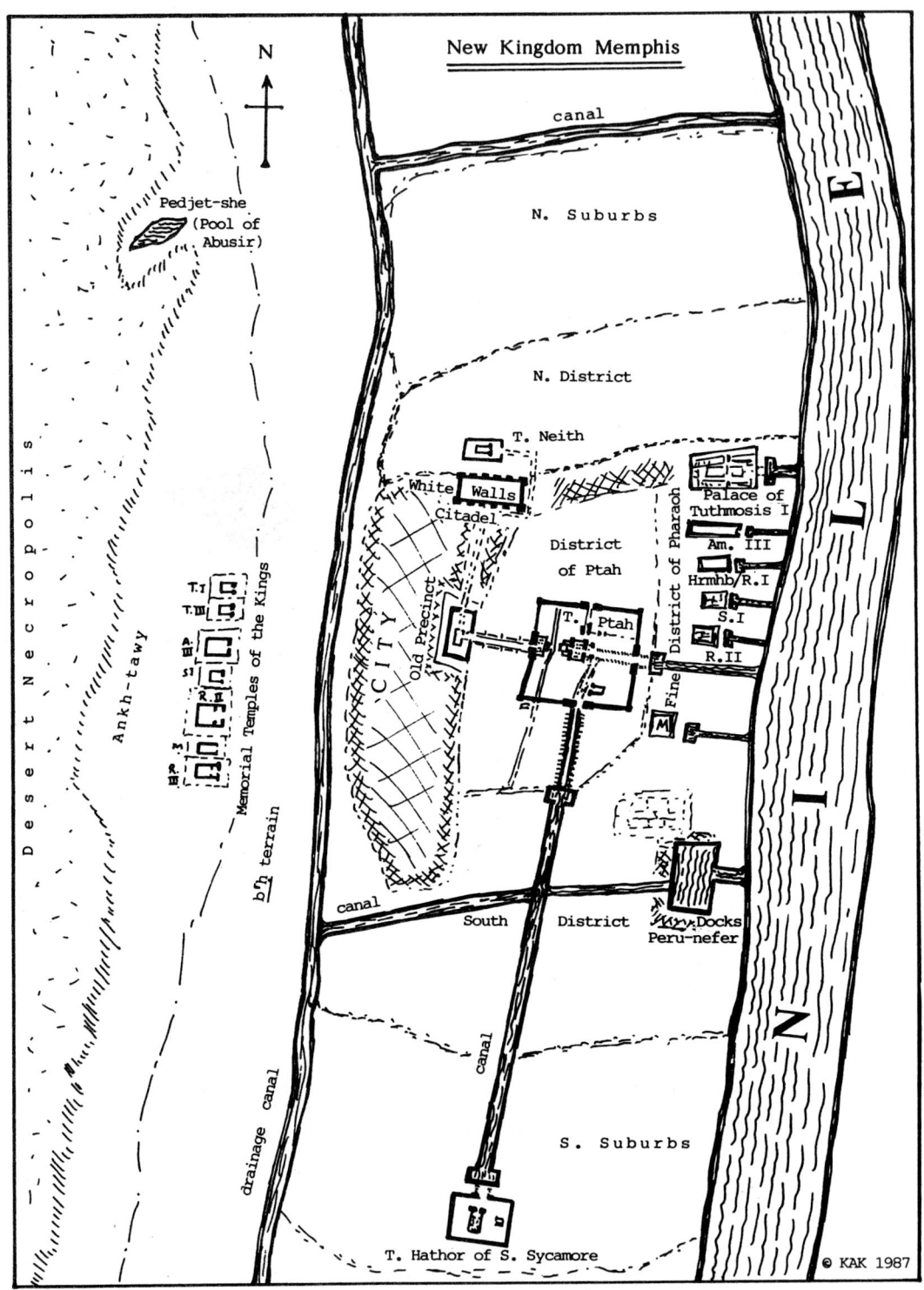

Fig. 2 The City of Memphis in the New Kingdom, Theoretical Reconstruction

100

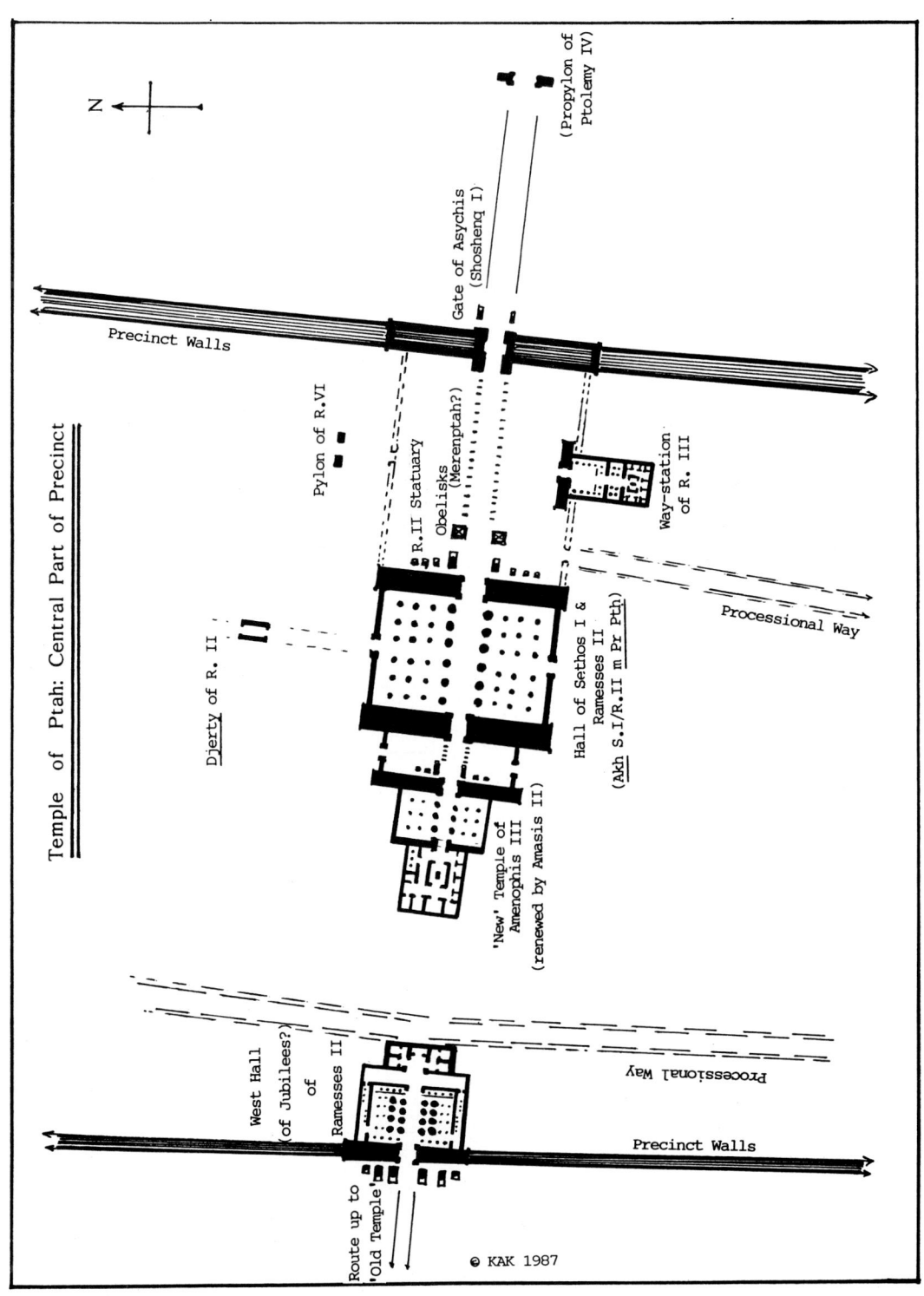

Fig. 3 Memphis, Theoretical Reconstruction of the Great Temple of Ptah, New Kingdom

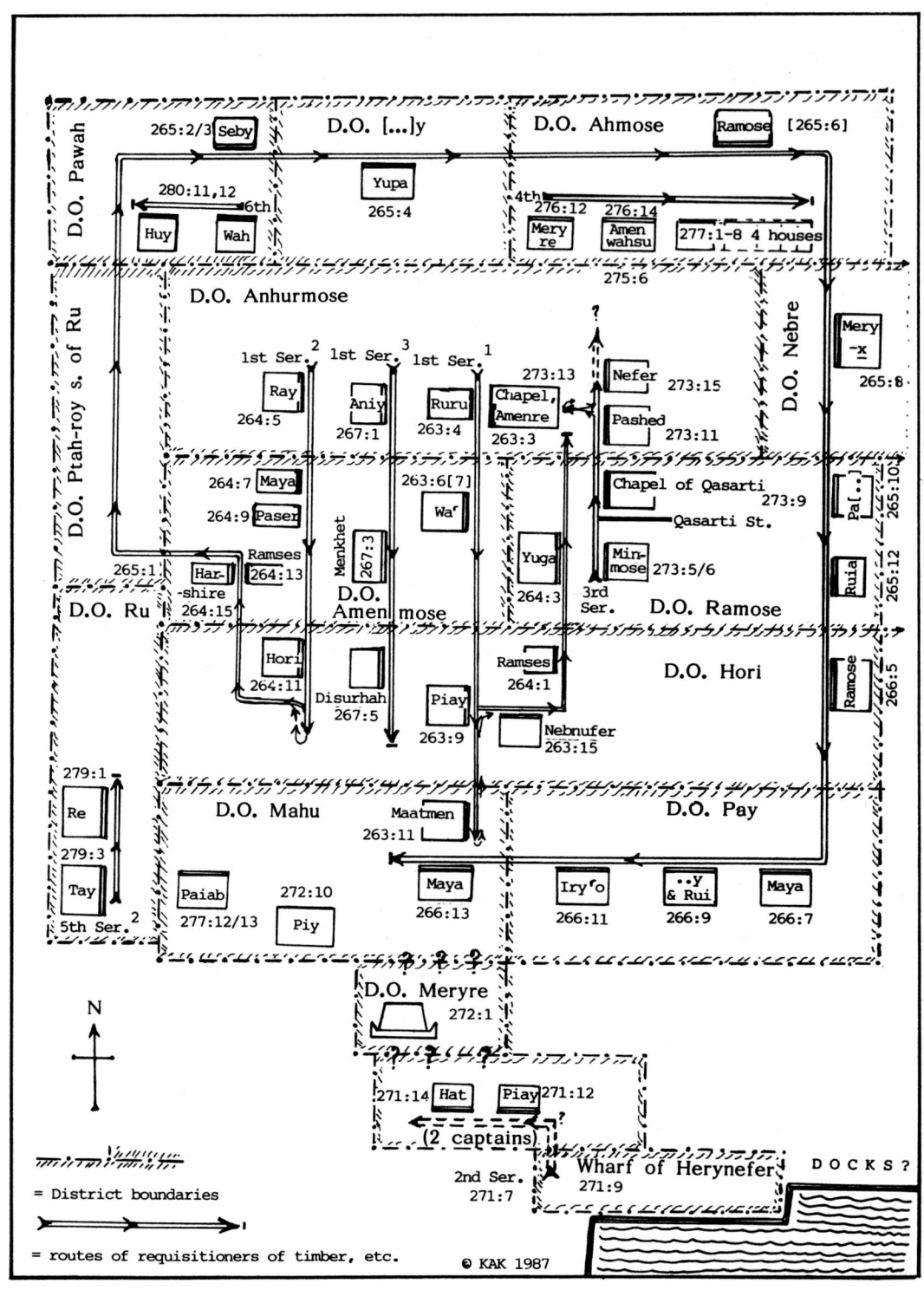

Fig. 4 Theoretical Reconstruction of Part of the South District of Memphis : based on Requisitioning-Accounts of Sethos I (=KRI,I, pp. 263-281)

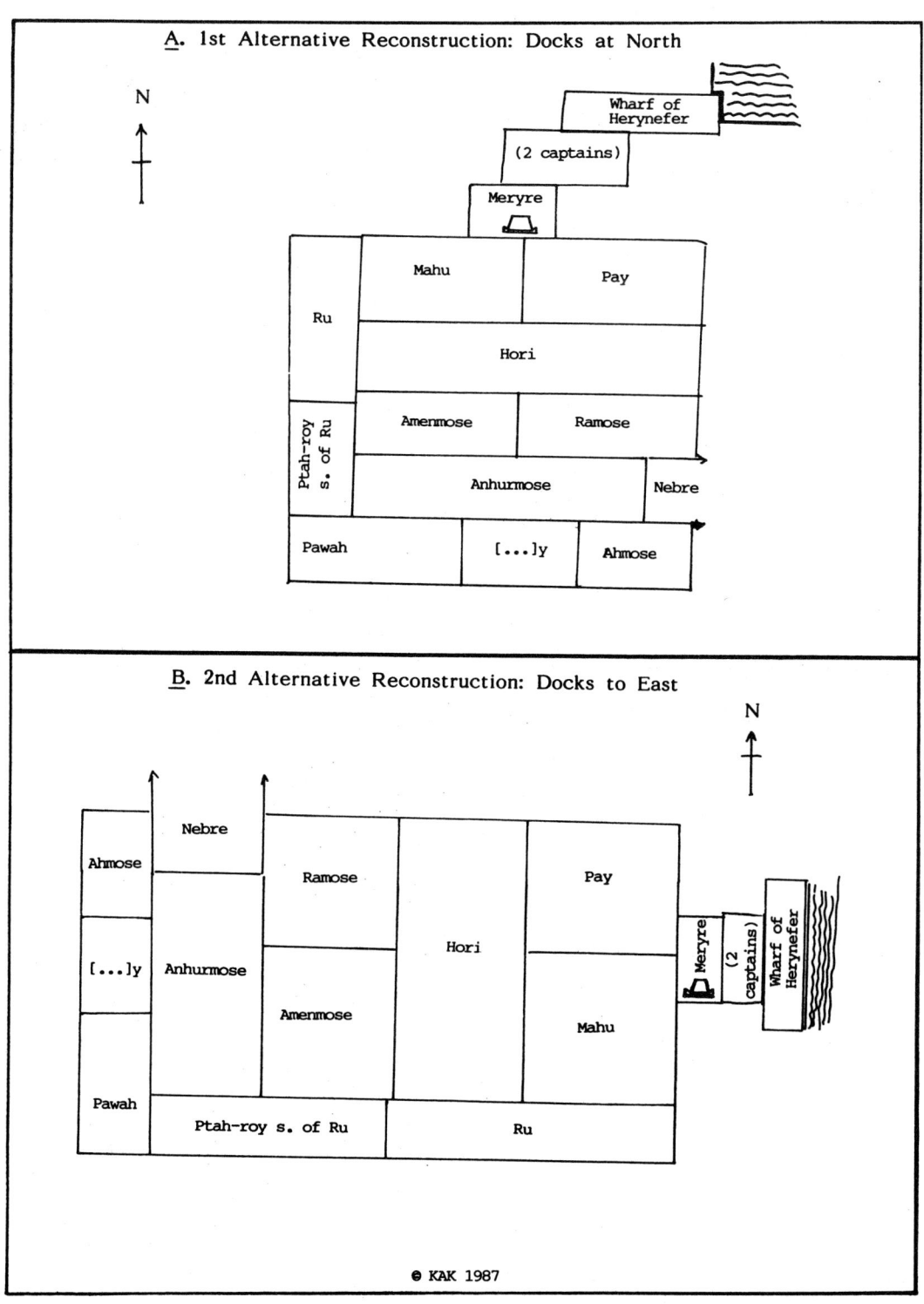

Fig. 5 Alternative Orientations of the Data in Fig. 4 (S. District)

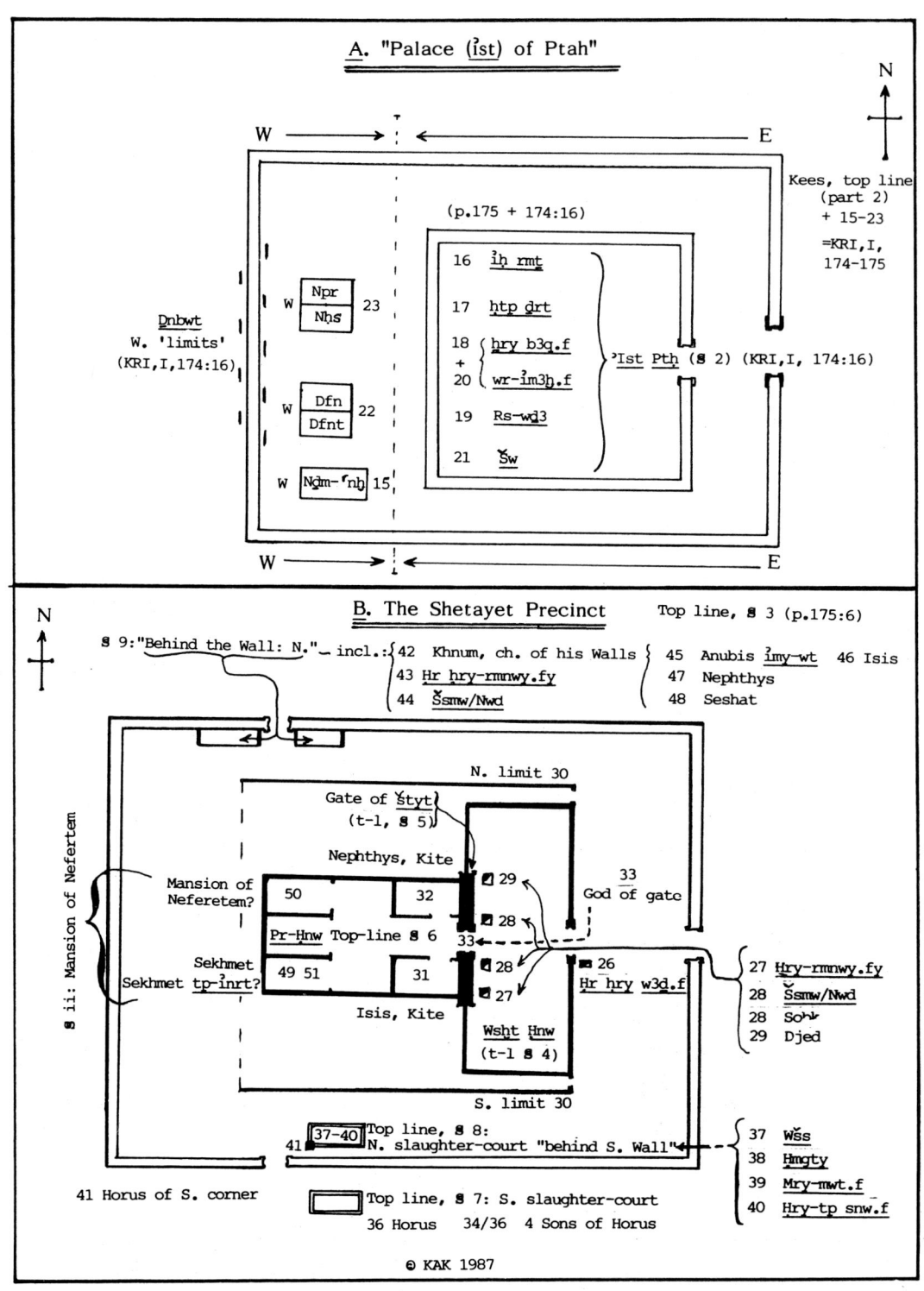

Fig. 6   Theoretical Reconstructions of Sanctuaries of Ptah & Sokar at Memphis, based on the Abydos List (Kees, <u>RT</u> 37(1915),74ff. = KRI,I, 173-176)

RELATIONS BETWEEN IHNASYA AND MEMPHIS DURING THE RAMESSIDE PERIOD

Dr. Gamal Mokhtar

In the long course of Egypt's ancient history, a number of cities along the river Nile and its branches flourished, played an outstanding role in its history, and exercised a strong influence over the life and civilization of the whole country. One of those was the ancient Egyptian city *Nn-nswt*, the classical Herakleopolis Magna and the Ihnasya el-Medina of today. Although this city had never been a national capital like Memphis or Thebes, or a center of religious development as Heliopolis or Abydos, its role, especially in some periods of Egyptian history, was great and striking. The present Ihnasya is located to the west of the Nile, not far from the entrance to the Fayum region and about 70 miles south of Cairo. So, Ihnasya, like Memphis, lies nearly on the boundary between Upper and Lower Egypt, a fact which helped to make both of them central capitals.[1]

The Herakleopolitan kings paid great attention to Memphis. It may be that those kings, for political reasons, tried to appease the people of Memphis and even considered themselves as the direct and legal successors of the Memphite kings. They assumed Memphite names, and we know that at least one of those kings, Merikare, was buried at Saqqara in the neighbourhood of the pyramid of Teti, where a cemetery of the First Intermediate Period existed.[2] However, it is unlikely that the Memphite people accepted this attitude since the rise of Ihnasya was a signal of the decline of the Memphite supremacy.

Although we can see on the Palermo Stone, that there was a temple of Herishaf, god of Ihnasya, since the First Dynasty,[3] yet from a glance at the present day remains of the temple of Herishef, it is clear that the original structure belongs to the XII Dynasty, reconstructed and developed during the XIX dynasty.[4]

Ramesses II's traces are everywhere in the temple. It was he who rebuilt the whole facade, added the colossi along both sides of the court and the two immense triads representing him, drew the large scenes of the Heb Sed festival, and raised the granite columns of the portico, as well as other alterations.[5]

---

1 The rise, prosperity, and importance of cities are not accidental, but mostly due to the geographical situation and surrounding physical conditions and features. The ancient Egyptians recognized the importance of such central positions between the North and South as is clear from the designations and names given, for example, to Memphis, ^{c}nh-$t3wy$ and $mh3t$-$t3wy$ ("the life of the two lands" and "the balance of the two lands") and to present day el-Lisht, It-$t3wy$ ("the seizer of the two lands"). See A. Badawy, *Memphis als zweite Landeshauptstadt im neuen Reich*, Cairo, 1948, p. 5.

2 See J. Quibell, *Excavations at Saqqara, 1905/06*, Cairo, 1907, p. 1-3, 17-26, pl. XIII, XV; *Excavations at Saqqara 1906/07*, p. 72, pl. VI; Firth and Gunn, *Teti Pyramid Cemeteries* I, Cairo, 1926, pp. 187, 202, 257; II, pl. XXVII.

3 See H. Schäfer, *Ein Bruchstück Altägyptischer Annalen, Abh. d. Kgl. preuss. Akad. der Wiss.*, 1962, 120.

4 W. F. Petrie suggested that the first stage was during the XVIII Dynasty, while the second stage was that of Ramesses II.

5 Rebuilding might have occurred in the Libyan period, which gave special attention to

Most interesting are the two triads of red granite found in front of the court which show Ramesses II between Ptah and Sekhmet. The one, which once lay to the west of the temple and which Barsanti transported in 1905, is now in the garden of the Cairo Museum. It is larger than the one which was lying to the east of the temple and is in much better condition. It is a big statue, 10 feet in height, 8 feet in breadth, and about 13 tons in weight. The front, back, and base of the triad were engraved with inscriptions bearing the different cartouches of the king who was beloved of nine different gods, for the most part Memphite gods and Herishef, god of Ihnasya. The eastern triad, on the other hand, was found in a very bad condition, and only its upper half was intact. It also represents Ramesses II between Ptah and Sekhmet, but in a seated posture.[6]

Two seated colossal quartzite statues bearing the names of Ramesses II were found in the portico of the temple. One was found by Naville in the northeastern corner and is now in the Philadelphia Museum.[7] The other was found by Petrie in the same area but was badly damaged and is now in the Cairo Museum.[8] That of Philadelphia is one of the best monuments found in Ihnasya. Nothing is missing save the head and parts of the elbows. It is an impressive work of art with some colours preserved. In the inscription below the throne, the king is said to be beloved by Herishef.

Columns from the Herishef temple are scattered now, for example, in the Museum of Fine Arts in Boston and the Philadelphia Museum.[9]

In February, 1915, during the digging for *sebakh*, two colossal statues of Ramesses II were found on a mound covered with sherds. This mound, called Kom El-Akareb ("Mound of the Scorpions"), located south of the Temple of Herishef, dates from the Roman Period. These statues represent the king sitting. They were transported by Barsanti in 1917 to the Cairo Museum, where they are now exhibited in its garden.[10]

During the XIX Dynasty, Ihnasya enjoyed an extraordinary military and strategic importance,[11] as may be seen from the burial of a great number of military men and officials of high rank in its cemetery, Sedment, and the existence of a fortified camp of Shardana mercenaries (named by the Egyptians $nhtw$-$^{c}3$ = the great fortress) near Ihnasya. It was during the XIX Dynasty, also, that an important personality from Ihnasya, named *Iwny*, was appointed to the post of "King's Son of Kush."[12]

Ihnasya, and perhaps during the XXX Dynasty, whose kings showed unusual activity in building.

6 See W.F. Petrie, *Ehnasya*, pp. 9-10; G. Daressy, "L'Obélisque de Qaha," *ASAE* XIX, 1919, pp. 133 ff.; G. Maspero, *Guide*, 1915, p. 3, no. A.

7 E. Naville, *Ahnas*, p. 11; P. Miller, "A Statue of Ramses II in the University Museum," *JEA* XXV, pp. 1-7, 3 plates; also, *University Museum of Philadelphia, Bulletin* XV, no. 2, 3.

8 W.F. Petrie, *Ehnasya*, pl. XIX, pp. 10, 15, 21, 22.

9 G. Mokhtar, *Ihnasya el-Medina (Herakleopolis Magna)*, Cairo, 1983, pl. VI.

10 Statues J.E. 45975 and J.E. 45976; see Daressy-Barsanti, *ASAE* XVII, 1917,

11 That means at the beginning of the Libyan invasion.

12 See G. Mohktar, *Ihnasya*, pp. 121-122.

Many important military men belonging to the XIX Dynasty were buried in Sedment. From that period is tomb no. 2010, in which were found many objects, among them a plaque with the name of General Hori. From the XIX Dynasty date also the tombs of General Sety (no. 198), Pahemneter (no. 33), and of Parahotep and Rahotep (no. 201). They are two viziers of Ramesses II at Memphis and Pi Ramesu (most probably Kantir). The large tomb of the two viziers from the time of Ramesses II consisted of eight rooms.[13] In the tomb of the Royal Scribe Ramesses, from the time of Sety I, were found more than two hundred ushabtis.[14]

Since the Archaic Period and the Old Kingdom, Herishef, the god of Ihnasya, was highly esteemed in the Memphite region. He might even have had a chapel at Memphis. In the mastaba of Prince Neb-kaw-Hor in Saqqara, one of the offering bearers is seen bringing "the pure bread of Herishef" in addition to "the pure bread of the House of Ptah." Names such as Herishef-hotep, Herishef-nakht, and Herishef-shema also appear in the various cemeteries of the Memphite nome. On the other hand, Ptah, Sekhmet, and Nefertum were represented on several monuments from Ihnasya. On the back of the triad of Ramesses II, found in Ihnasya and now in the Cairo Museum Garden, he is said to be beloved by Ptah, Lord of Truth, King of the Two Lands, great of love, and also of Ptah-Tatenen.[15]

---

13 Their relations with the high priests of Memphis and Abydos were treated in H. Kees, *Priestertum*, Leiden, 1953, pp. 101 ff.; see also, A. Weil, *Die Veziere*, Strasbourg, 1908, pp. 96-100; P. Lacau, "Recherches généalogiques," *Rec. de Trav.* XXXI, 1909, pp. 202 ff., and XXXII, 1910, pp. 35 ff.; A Scharff, "Ein Denkstein der Viziers Rahotep," *ZÄS* LXX, 1934, pp. 47 ff.

14 For those tombs, see W.F. Petrie, *Sedment*, London, 1924. Pillars from the tomb of Sety are now in the The Oriental Institute (Chicago) and the Philadelphia Museum.

15 The relation between the gods of Ihnasya and Memphis can be traced easily in their titles, epithets, and mythological trends.

RAMESSIDE TRADITIONS IN THE ARTS OF THE
THIRD INTERMEDIATE PERIOD

Karol Myśliwiec

The end of the XXth Dynasty does not signify a turning point in the history of Egyptian culture. On the contrary, the Third Intermediate Period is known to have been a time of nostalgia and search for the best traditions of the past. Among the artistic manifestations of this trend, there are representations of some XVIIIth Dynasty kings, as well as their names, occurring in the painted decoration of many wooden coffins belonging to Dynasties XXI-XXII. The king depicted or mentioned most frequently is Amenhotep I, less frequently Tuthmosis III, and quite sporadically Horemheb.[1] Their large-scale representations decorate the bottom of numerous coffin cases, and their small-size figures frequently occur on the coffin's outer faces. The king is always depicted in the attitude of Osiris, wrapped either in the falcon dress[2] or the white tightly fitting mummy cloth.[3] He holds various insignia in his hands and wears various types of royal headdresses, some of which are very sophisticated. Particularly popular are all the variations of ostrich-feather crowns, e.g. the *ḥmḥm* and the *3tf*.[4] These are usually set on either the *nms* headcloth or a short wig. Another royal crown occurring frequently in these representations is the *ḫprš*.[5]

On some coffins there are analogous figures depicted without any royal names, most often described as Osiris.[6] They imply a close affinity, if not identity, of this god with the much venerated kings of the XVIIIth Dynasty, a concept which must have been present in the theological conscious-ness of the two dynasties following the Ramesside Period. The tradition of depicting those deified kings in a funerary context remains, however, purely Ramesside. Scenes showing Amenhotep I and his mother Ahmes Nefertari, less frequently other kings of the XVIIIth Dynasty, belong to the standard items in the decoration of the Theban tombs of the XIXth and XXth Dynasties.[7] Nevertheless, the king, who was merely one of the numerous gods represented in Ramesside tombs as equally important, appears promoted to a central position on the coffins of the two following dynasties. Does it only signify a new iconographic feature of the cult developed in the times of the Ramessides, or should it be interpreted as an expression of an increasing devotion to the earlier kings - symbols of a "golden age?" The question of which elements, Ramesside or earlier, predominate in the artistic, and more generally - the cultural heritage of the Third

---

1 K. Myśliwiec, *Royal Portraiture of the Dynasties XXI-XXX*, Mainz 1988, the frontispiece and pls. I-III, VI.

2 Id. Ib., the frontispiece and pls. II, III.

3 Id. Ib., pls. I, VI.

4 Id. Ib., the frontispiece and pls. II, III.

5 Id. Ib., pls. I, VI b.

6 Id. Ib., pls. IV b, V b.

7 Id., *Le Portrait royal dans le bas-relief du Nouvel Empire*. Varsovie 1976, 28-30.

Intermediate Period, returns again and again in art historical studies concerning this period. Several aspects of this problem constitute the subject of this essay. A diachronical presentation of some specific iconographic patterns may help one to better understand the complexity of this problem.

One of the details subject to variations in the Ramesside Period and later is the "blue crown" (ḫprš) of the king. The deified kings of the XVIIIth Dynasty are sometimes depicted as wearing this crown, both in Ramesside tombs and on coffins of a later date. A Ramesside example is recorded, i.e. in the tomb of Amenemonet (TT 277), where Amenhotep III is the deified king receiving offerings from the tomb owner.[8] Two additional elements appear sometimes in the iconography of this crown from the beginning of the XIXth Dynasty on. These are a solar disc at the top and an ostrich feather on either side of the crown[9] (fig. 1). Being symbols of the gods Re and Osiris, rulers of the realms of the living and the dead, these emblems endow the Egyptian crown of coronation and victory[10] with a more universal character.

Another interesting change in the iconography of this crown occurs almost immediately after the Ramesside Period and is first observed in Memphis. It concerns the arrangement of the uraeus on the crown. As early as the time of Siamun, the snake's circular coils, occurring on the ḫprš throughout the New Kingdom[11] (fig. 2), appear to be replaced by two parallel horizontal coils (in a representation of Siamun on a lintel from Memphis[12] [fig. 3, pl. I, b]). The latest known example of the New Kingdom pattern dates from the time of Shoshenq I (on a relief from Hiba[13] [pl. I, a]). Since then, the horizontal arrangement of the snake's body becomes a rule in royal iconography whenever the king appears in a "blue crown." The latest known examples of this pattern are found on the reliefs of Darius I (particularly in the Hibis temple), where a similarly coiled uraeus decorates not only the ḫprš, but also all the other headdresses.[14] After the XXVIIth Dynasty this pattern becomes simplified to a single coil (fig. 4), the earliest examples of which are known from the rule of Psammuthis or Achoris, XXIXth Dynasty (in their chapel at Karnak).[15] This scheme

8 J. Vandier d'Abbadie, *Deux Tombes ramessides à Gournet-Murraï*, *M.I.F.A.O.* 87, Le Caire 1954, 24-25, pls. XIX-XX.

9 Recorded, for example, in the reliefs of:
-Seti I (Calverley-Gardiner, *Abydos*, IV, pl. 44);
-Merenptah (J.E. Quibell, "Lintel of Merenptah at Mitrahineh," *ASAE* 8, 1907, 120-121 and plate after p. 192);
-Seti II (G. Roeder, *Hermopolis 1929-1939*. Hildesheim 1959, Taf. 63, 65);
-Ramesses III (*Medinet Habu* IV, pl. 237 [B]; V, part 1, pls. 254, 335; VII, pl. 609).

10 Cf. J. Leclant, "Sur un Contrepoids de *menat* au nom de Taharqa

(Allaitement et 'apparition' royale)," *Mélanges Mariette*, Le Caire 1961, *Bd'E* 32, 266, n. 11.

11 K. Mysliwiec, *Royal Portraiture* o.c., n. 243.

12 Id. Ib., pl. XII b.

13 Id. Ib., pl. XV b.

14 Id. Ib., n. 244.

15 Id. Ib., pl. LXXII a-b.

appears to be universally applied in royal iconography through the fourth century B.C., right up to the beginning of the Ptolemaic Period (pl. I, c).[16] Taking into consideration this criterion, one may propose a new dating of the bronze statuette in the Atkins Museum of Fine Arts (Kansas City, Missouri), attributed so far to Achoris.[17] Given the horizontal composition of the snake's double coil in the king's ḫprš-crown, we may ascribe it most probably to the XXVIth Dynasty, less probably to the XXVIIth and certainly not to the XXVth Dynasty, during which the "blue crown" disappeared completely from the royal iconography.

The absence of the ḫprš in Egyptian art of the Kushite Period is a problem in itself, and it leads to a number of reflections. It is the tightly fitted skullcap, the favorite headdress of the Napatan kings (pl. II), that is believed to have replaced the crown of coronation and victory during the XXVth Dynasty.[18] This observation does not prove to be absolutely accurate, for in a particular context in which earlier Egyptian records most frequently show the king wearing the ḫprš, a Kushite king (Taharka) is represented with the nmś-headcloth and not the skullcap. This fact is to be seen on the reliefs decorating the granite stand for a bark at Gebel Barkal (pl. III, a-b).[19] Applying, in the case of Taharka, a pattern which differs from the well known Ramesside archetypes and their later copies, the Napatan artist could have had in mind an XVIIIth Dynasty model which has recently been found in three examples on the still unpublished reliefs with a well preserved polychromy from the temple of Tuthmosis III at Deir el-Bahari.[20] The decoration of the stand depicted at Deir el-Bahari shows, as usual, four figures of the king supporting the sky but wearing, quite exceptionally, the nmś-headcloth, just as the figures of Taharka at Gebel Barkal.

The artist sculpting in Napata preferred this version to the popular Ramesside pattern, in which the first of the four royal figures wears the "Kushite"-like skullcap and the others, the ḫprš. This pattern is recorded in the reliefs of Seti I (Abydos)[21] and Ramesses III (Medinet Habu).[22] The difference between the leading figure and the three followers extends in this case to the king's dress as well. The leader wears a panther skin, typical of priests of high rank, whereas the remaining kings have the usual short apron. The artist of Taharka even ignored a Ramesside prototype which iconographically appears to be much closer to the solution chosen at Napata. This prototype is found in the decoration of a bark stand

16 Id. Ib., chapter VIII, type "c."

17 Id. Ib., chapter VI, sources, Achoris, statuary: attributed to Achoris, no. 5, b (William Rockhill Nelson Gallery of Art, Atkins Museum of Fine Art, Kansas City, Missouri, no. 53-13).

18 Cf. J. Leclant, *Mon. Thébains*, 323, n. 7-8, and 324, n. 3; E. R. Russman, *The Representation of the King in the XXVth Dynasty*, Bruxelles-Brooklyn 1974, 27-28. For the history and the meaning of the hrps, compare W.V. Davies, "The Origin of the Blue Crown," *JEA* 68, 1982, 69-76.

19 K. Myśliwiec, "Das Königsporträt des Taharka in Napata," *MDAIK* 39, 1983, 157, pls. 45-46.

20 To be published by Joanna Wiercińska in her dissertation on the decoration of the hypostyle hall in New Kingdom temples. I wish to thank Professor Jadwiga Lipińska for this information.

21 Calverley-Gardiner, *Abydos* II, pls. 5, 10, 11, 23.

22 *Medinet Habu*. IV, pl. 229.

represented in the temple of Seti I at Abydos, where the king wearing the skullcap is followed by three kings having the *nmś* on their heads.[23] Although these headdresses would fit the general conventions of Kushite iconography perfectly, a version without the cap was chosen by the Napatan artist, who seems to have been anxious to appear more orthodox than his predecessors in Thebes.

These observations would suggest that on one hand the art traditions of the XVIIIth Dynasty could have been an important source of inspiration for the artists of the XXVth Dynasty, and on the other hand the skullcap was not really used in places where the Egyptians would have liked to see the "blue crown."

The popularity of this particular headdress in Kushite royal iconography may be explained in the context of religious traditions of the XXVth Dynasty. As has been observed by several scholars, the religious centre which played a special role during that period was Memphis.[24] Fragments of the temples built by subsequent Kushite kings have been found there,[25] Shabako boasted of having personally found the ancient record of Memphite theology,[26] and Taharka's coronation took place in the ancient capital of Egypt.[27]

The great god of Memphis enjoyed the particular respect of the Kushite pharaohs. The "*ḥb-sd*" porch of Shabako in Karnak was built as part of the temple of Ptah,[28] and the official titles of Taharka assimilated the king to Nefertem, the divine son of Ptah and Sekhmet.[29] In this respect Taharka resembles Ramesses II, whose monumental statue from Ehnas el-Medina shows him in the place of the youngest member of the Memphite triad (Nefertem) between Ptah and Sekhmet.[30] The inscription of Ramesses II in the great temple at Abu Simbel describes him as "son of Re, who came out from Tatenen, and (was) born by Sekhmet."[31]

Beside Atum, Re, and Horus, Ptah belongs to the gods with a clearly royal character. He is the only Egyptian god to wear the straight royal beard, and one of his most popular epithets

---

23 Calverley-Gardiner, *Abydos* II, pls. 15, 18.

24 *LÄ* III, 894, n. 25.

25 J. Leclant and J. Yoyotte, "Notes d'histoire et de civilisation égyptiennes. A propos d'un ouvrage récent," *BIFAO* 51, Le Caire 1952, 28, n. 3 and 4; cf. J. Leclant in *Mélanges Mariette* o.c., 281-282.

26 J. Leclant and J. Yoyotte, "Notes d'histoire" o.c., 28, n. 4.

27 Id. Ib., 28, n. 2; J. Leclant in *Mélanges Mariette* o.c., 279.

28 *PM*, II (2nd ed.), 197.

29 J. Leclant and J. Yoyotte, "Notes d'histoire" o.c., 28, n. 2;

J. Leclant in *Mélanges Mariette* o.c., 279-280.

30 Now in the gardens of the Egyptian Museum, Cairo, TN 8/2/21/20 (garden register no. 149); cf. *PM* IV, 118, and W.M.F. Petrie, *Ehnasya 1904*, London 1905, 9-10 (described as a granite triad of Ramesses II between Ptah and Harsaphes).

31 *LD* III, 194, second line.

calls him "the king of the Two Lands" (*nsw.t t3wj*). Ever since the Ramesside Period, he had been one of the gods frequently associated with the royal jubilee feast.[32] The text of a hymn to Ptah (pap. Berlin 3048), copied from a Late Ramesside original in the Third Intermediate Period, represents the god as the king who united Egypt into a single kingdom and as the ruler of the united country.[33] These associations are emphasized in the famous Shabako text qualifying Ptah as an earthly king, e.g. in line 4: "He is (the binder) of the Upper and Lower Land of Egypt, the uniter who has risen as the king of Upper Egypt and as the king of Lower Egypt".[34]

The resemblance of the Egyptian king to various gods was underlined by the iconography of various royal crowns. The pharaoh is often depicted as wearing the double crown of Atum, the feather crowns of Osiris or Amun, etc.; but none of his headdresses has so far been identified with the skullcap of Ptah. A possible connection between the headdress of this god and the skullcap of the king may be deduced from the Ramesside reliefs which represent them together as partners wearing the same type of cap.[35] If a slight difference in details (i.e. the colour of the cap, usually yellow in royal inconography, and blue in the representations of Ptah, or the shape of the tabs in front of the ears, being rounded on the cap of the king, and square on that of the god) may leave some doubts concerning the affinity between both headdresses, a representation in the tomb of Amen-her-khepshef, son of Ramesses III (Valley of the Queens, TT 55), provides a convincing argument in its favour (fig. 6).[36] Not only are Ptah and the king depicted with skullcaps of analogous shape, but also the headdress of the god is also decorated with the royal uraeus. The only difference is the composition of the snake's coils on each of them and the presence of a hawk figure on the occiput of the king. We may, therefore, presume that the royal tightly fitted cap, a headdress known in Egypt long before the appearance of the "blue crown,[37] identifies the king with the Memphite god.

Why would the headdress of Ptah be so popular in royal iconography of the XXVth Dynasty? As has already been observed by some scholars, the Napatan rulers of Egypt tried to imitate the Memphite pharaohs of the Old Kingdom in many respects, i.e. in the construction of their names.[38] Ptah was a god with evident royal features (e.g. the straight beard), and his role in the "political theology" grew remarkably during the Ramesside Period. Royal jubilees were frequently associated with those of Ptah-Tatenen, and in some Ramesside temples (Seti I at Abydos and Ramesses II at Derr) Ptah appears to be the

---

32 M. Sandman Holmberg, *The God Ptah*, Lund 1946, 80-93; comp. W. Helck, "Ramessidische Inschriften aus Karnak," *ZÄS* 82, 1958, 139.

33 W. Wolf, "Der Berliner Ptah-Hymnus," *ZÄS* 64, 1929, 17-44;
cf. M. Sandman
Holmberg, o.c., 83-84.

34 M. Sandman Holmberg, o.c., 80.

35 E.g. Seti I (Calverley-Gardiner, *Abydos* IV, pls. 44, 46) and Ramesses III (*Medinet Habu* V, part 1, pl. 343; VI, pl. 412).

36 F. Hassanein and M. Nelson, *La Tombe du prince Amon-/her/-khepchef*, Le Caire 1976, 49, pl. XV, cf. pl. II.

37 E.R. Russmann, *The Representation* o.c., 29-32.

38 J. Leclant in *Mélanges Mariette* o.c., 282-283.

main god in the scene with the *iśd* tree,[39] which places him on a par with Atum, Re-Harakhte, Amun, and Thoth in this respect.[40] Ramesses II had introduced the cult of Ptah to Nubia. In his temples at Gerf Hussein, Derr, Abu Simbel, and Wadi es-Seboua, the Memphite god was worshipped as either a principal deity or a subsidiary god.[41] Napata could, therefore, have known well the political importance and the general regality of the "Lord of Maat" (Truth) and "the one with a beautiful face." The desire for a physical resemblance to Ptah may have been the reason for the unprecedented popularity of this god's headdress in the iconography of Napatan rulers. Besides the association with Ptah, the headdress could also have had a more universal meaning, for it occurs in the iconography of Min[42] and of Amun - "King of the Gods" as well.[43] The latter god's skullcap had a kind of horizontal band[44] that eventually became a typical element of the "Kushite headdress."

After the XXVth Dynasty, the skullcap retains its popularity in royal iconography, particularly in Lower Egypt (e.g. the reliefs of Psammetichus I, Psammetichus II, and Nectanebo I).[45] This fact would confirm our conclusion that this headdress was associated more with the Memphite god than with the Kushite kings.

Another iconographic feature of Kushite propaganda was the double uraeus at the king's head. As an element of royal iconography, the double uraeus was not, however, an invention of the XXVth Dynasty. It had several New Kingdom antecedents.[46] Two cobras sometimes accompany the *ḫprš* crown of Seti I (fig. 5),[47] Ramesses II,[48] and Ramesses III,[49] and they appear on the wooden ushebti figures of Ramesses VI.[50] The heads of the two

---

39 Calverley-Gardiner, *Abydos* IV, pl. 25 (comp. A. Champdor, *Die altägyptische Malerei*, Leipzig 1957, 139); W. Helck, "Ramessidische Inschriften" o.c., 121, no. 10.

40 W.Helck, "Ramessidische Inschriften" o.c., 132.

41 M. Sandman Holmberg, o.c., 241-243.

42 E.g. in *Medinet Habu* VII, pl. 530.

43 *Medinet Habu* V, part 1, pl. 326; VI, the frontispiece; VII, pl. 496 (A) and 512 (A).

44 See n. 43.

45 K. Myśliwiec, *Royal Portraiture* o.c., pls. 53-55 a-c, 86 a-c.

46 J. Leclant, "Une Statuette d'Amon-Rê-Montou au nom de la divine adoratrice Chepenoupet," *Mélanges Maspero* I,4, Le Caire 1961, 79, n. 2; Id., *Mon. Thébains*, 325, n. 4.

47 Calverley-Gardiner, *Abydos* III, pl. 38.

48 H.H. Nelson (ed. W.J. Murnane), *The Great Hypostyle Hall at Karnak* I, part 1: *The Wall Reliefs*, Chicago 1981, pl. 53.

49 One cobra at one side of the crown - a parallel piece was probably set at its other side: *Medinet Habu* II, pl. 98; III, pls. 197, 199, 223; V, part 1, pl. 313; VI, pl. 455; comp. J. Leclant, the publications quoted in n. 46 above.

50 J.-F. Aubert, L. Aubert, *Statuettes égyptiennes chaouabtis, ouchebtis*, Paris 1974, 119.

cobras decorating the *ḫprš* crown, occasionally wear the white or the red crown, sometimes exceptionally the *3tf* crown.[51] Another possible source of inspiration for this feature of Kushite iconography could have been the double uraeus usually occurring at the forehead of some divinities (Monthu, Neith) and Egyptian queens.[52] The Kushites only adopted the Egyptian archetypes and probably gave them a new geographical and political meaning.

In spite of the popularity of the double uraeus in the representations of the Kushite kings, some reliefs show them with only one cobra at the forehead, especially when the kings are wearing a crown other than the skullcap. Such is also the case with the numerous ushebti figures of Taharka found in his pyramid at Nuri (pl. III, c-f).[53] These statuettes are visible signs of an archaizing tendency and orthodoxy with respect to ancient models. Their material (various kinds of stone), considerable dimensions, and iconography imitate the New Kingdom archetypes, among which the ushebtis of the XXth Dynasty may have served as direct models.[54] One can hardly believe that they were made in Napata and not in an Egyptian artistic centre. Their inscription, which is a version of the VIth chapter of the Book of the Dead, has an additional formula at the end that occurs earlier only on the ushebtis of Ramesses IV.[55] In their search for the most "classical" prototypes, the creators of these figurines did not imitate the example of Ramesses VI, whose ushebtis sometimes have two uraei,[56] just as the statues of the Kushite kings. The inspiration evidently came from the earlier Ramesside example. After the reign of Taharka, two cobras appear, however, once again on royal ushebtis, those of Taharka's grandson Senkamenisken, who never became king of Egypt.[57]

A continuation of Ramesside traditions during the Third Intermediate Period may be traced not only in royal iconography, but also in the representations of royal children. Shoshenq, a son of Osorkon II and a high priest at Memphis, is depicted in the reliefs decorating his Memphite funeral chapel[58] wearing the same kind of headdress as the sons of Ramesses III, who are represented in their Theban tombs.[59]

The choice and the composition of some scenes sculpted on the walls of the few preserved monumental buildings belonging to the Third Intermediate Period also suggest some

---

51 Cf. n. 47-49.

52 J. Leclant, *Mon Thébains*, 325, n. 4; Id. in *Mélanges Maspero* o.c., 79, n. 1.

53 K. Myśliwiec, "Das Königsporträt" o.c., 152-157, pl. 36-44.

54 J.-F. Aubert, L. Aubert, o.c., 78-82, 114-120, 129-131, 188-192.

55 Id. Ib., 118, 191.

56 Cf. n. 50.

57 J.-F. Aubert, L. Aubert, o.c., 192.

58 A. Badawi, Das Grab des Kronprinzen Scheschonk, Sohnes Osorkon's II. und Hohenpriesters von Memphis, *ASAE* 54, 1956, 153-177.

59 E.g. in the tomb of Amon-her-khepshef (cf. the publication quoted in n. 36, pl. IV and p. 32; comp. A. Champdor, o.c., 79) and Montu-her-khepshef (J. Romer, *Valley of the Kings*, London 1981, photo opposite p. 96; Id., *Ancient Lives. The Story of the Pharaohs' Tombmakers*, London 1984, fig. 30).

general conclusions concerning the character of the Ramesside inspirations in the art of this period. Two examples seem to be particularly instructive in this respect.

The first one is the representation of a goddess nursing the king, a kind of scene which becomes surprisingly popular in post-Ramesside reliefs at Karnak (pl. IV).[60] This item, much in vogue during the XVIIIth Dynasty and still present in the decoration of some early Ramesside temples until Ramesses II,[61] seems to disappear from the repertory of later Ramesside reliefs. Its "renaissance" in the Third Intermediate Period suggests that the traditions of the XVIIIth and early XIXth Dynasties were particularly vivid after the XXth Dynasty.

The other example is the scene with the *išd* tree, known from many New Kingdom temples. The latest known record of this representation is a particularly fine relief of Osorkon III and Takeloth III sculpted in the chapel of Osiris-Hekadjet at Karnak (pl. V, a-b).[62] This double scene confirms our previous observations. Its symmetrical and antithetical composition follows a Ramesside pattern sometimes applied in temple reliefs depicting this ceremony. This sort of parallelism is found in some Theban temples, e.g. in the reliefs of Ramesses II at Karnak (possibly also in the Ramesseum)[63] and in those of Ramesses IV at Medinet Habu.[64] In the passage of the second pylon at Karnak, such scenes decorate two walls facing each other, and in Medinet Habu they are located symmetrically on the fronts of the north and south towers of the pylon. With respect to its composition, the double scene of Osorkon III and Takeloth III represents a simple synthesis of the two parallel scenes occurring in the Ramesside examples. However, the contents of the double scene reveal a clear affinity with the early Ramesside models. One of the two gods represented there antithetically is Amun, the other - Atum. The latter frequently appears as the main god in the scenes with the *išd* tree on the reliefs of Ramesses II (the Ramesseum, Karnak)[65] but does not occur in a similar function on those of Ramesses IV.[66]

All these examples seem to prove that the artists of the Third Intermediate Period were perfectly conscious of the various iconographic traditions of the past. They did not copy the most popular or typical schemes, but chose arche-types which they considered the best and the most appropriate for the sake of their religious and political propaganda. Trying to restore the best models of the past, they clearly preferred those of the XVIIIth and early XIXth Dynasties to those of the later Ramesside Period. This tendency finds confirmation in the style of both reliefs and statuary of the Third Intermediate Period, particularly those of the Dynasties XXI-XXIII (e.g. pl. VI).[67] During this period the facial features of the

---

60 *PM*, II2, 36 (129), II, 2, and (130), III; (131), III, as well as 205 (11) and 206 (15).

61 J. Leclant in *Mélanges Mariette* o.c., 263-265.

62 W. Helck, o.c., 124, no. 18; K. Mysliwiec, Die Rolle des Atum in der "išd"-Baum-Szene, *MDAIK* 36, 1980, Taf. 88-89.

63 K. Mysliwiec, Die Rolle o.c., 350-353 (no. 2), 352-353 (no. 3).

64 *Medinet Habu*, II, pls. 84, 104, 119.

65 Cf. W. Helck, o.c., 120 (no. 8) and the two examples quoted in our n. 63.

66 Cf. for example the scenes with the "išd" at Medinet Habu quoted in n. 64, and *Medinet Habu*, VI, pl. 448.

67 Comp. K. Myśliwiec, *Royal portraiture* o.c., pls. VII-XXVI.

kings and gods follow the stylistic patterns of the late XVIIIth Dynasty, which are characterized by a soft rendering of the shapes and an organic concept of particular details. These characteris-tics are well known from the art of Akhenaten[68] and from a "renaissance" of similar trends in the time of Ramesses II.[69] Their revival is a remarkable feature of post-Ramesside artistic production, although a continuation of the Ramesside tradition as a whole is also visible.

---

68 Id., *Le portrait royal* o.c., pls. LXX-LXXXVIII.

69 Id. Ib., 111-112, 116, 143 and pls. CIII-CXXI.

DESCRIPTIONS OF THE PLATES

Pl. I. Various arrangements of the uraeus on the "blue crown" as represented on post-Ramesside reliefs:

    a) Shoshenq I (XXIInd Dynasty). Relief from El-Hiba.
       Ägyptologisches Institut der Universität Heidel-
       berg, Inv. nos. 922 and 562. Photo

    b) Siamun (XXIst Dynasty). Detail of a relief on a
       lintel from Memphis. Egyptian Museum, Cairo, JE
       40033. Photo: A. Bodytko, Polish Centre of
       Mediterranean Archaeology, Cairo.

    c) Alexander the Great. Detail of a relief in his
       chapel at Luxor. Photo: Z. Doliński, Polish
       Centre of Mediterranean Archaeology, Cairo.

Pl.II. The "Kushite" skullcap. Relief of Shebitku (XXVth Dynasty) in the chapel of Osiris-Hekadjet at Karnak. Photo: D. Johannes, German Archaeological Institute, Cairo.

Pl.III. Representation of Taharqa (XXVth Dynasty) with one or two uraei: a-b) Relief on the bark stand at Gebel Barkal. c-f) Ushebtis found in the king's pyramid at Nuri. Museum of Fine Arts, Boston: c) 20.227, d) 21.2912, e) 20.230, f) 20.226. Photos: K. Myśliwiec.

Pl.IV Goddess Mut suckling Shoshenq I (XXIInd Dynasty). Relief in the "Bubastide Portal" at Karnak. Photo: D. Johannes, German Archaeological Institute, Cairo.

Pl.V. a-b) Double-scene with the "išd"-tree in the chapel of Osiris-Hekadjet at Karnak, representing the kings Osorkon III and Takeloth 10th III (XXIIIrd Dynasty). Photo: D. Johannes, German Archaeological Institute, Cairo.

Pl.VI. Osorkon III and his son Takeloth, the future king Takeloth II block found in Karnak. Centre Franco-Egyptien d'Etude des Temples de Karnak, no. 14546. Photo: Courtesy Centre Franco-Egyptien, Karnak.

Plate I

a.

b.

c.

Plate II

120

Plate III

a.

b.

c.

d.

e.

f.

Plate IV

Plate V

b.

a.

123

Figures 1-5

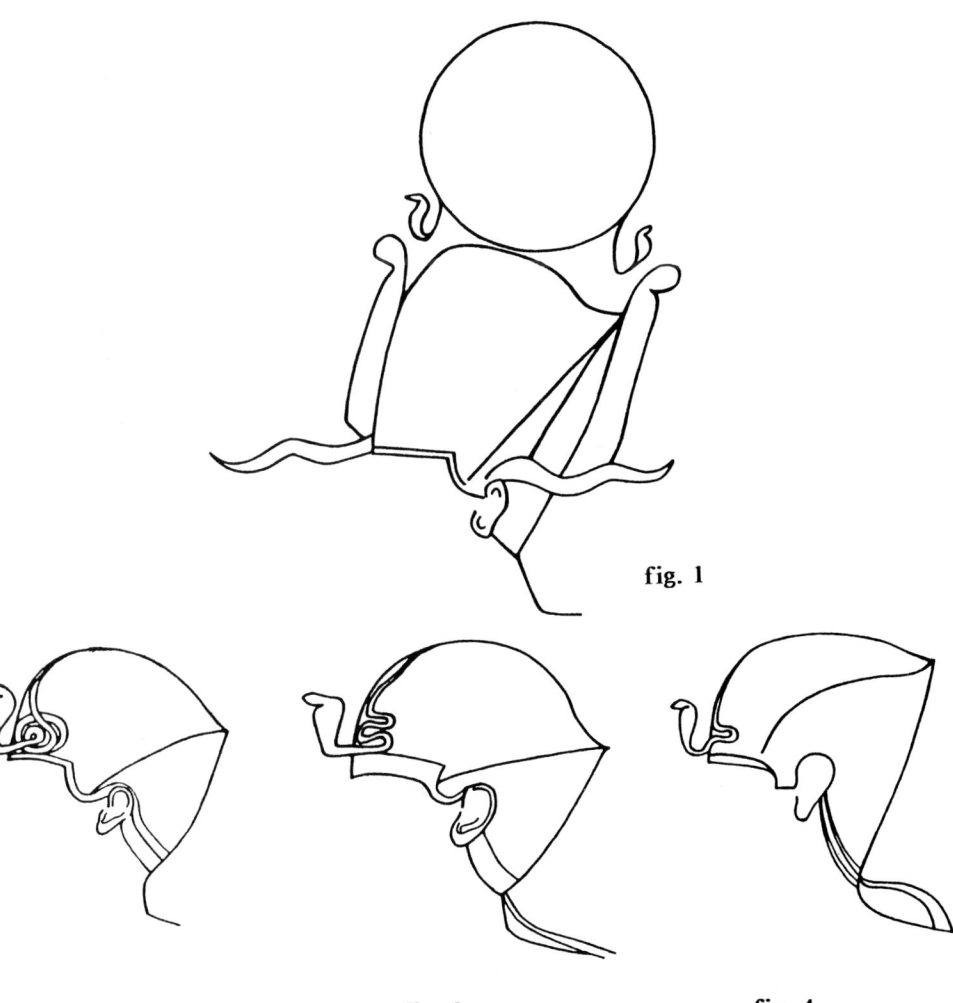

fig. 1

fig. 2

fig. 3

fig. 4

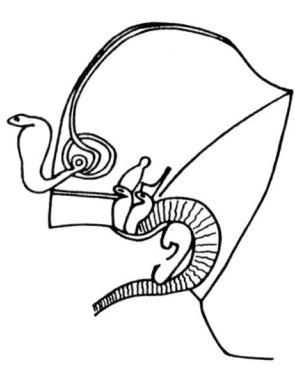

fig. 5

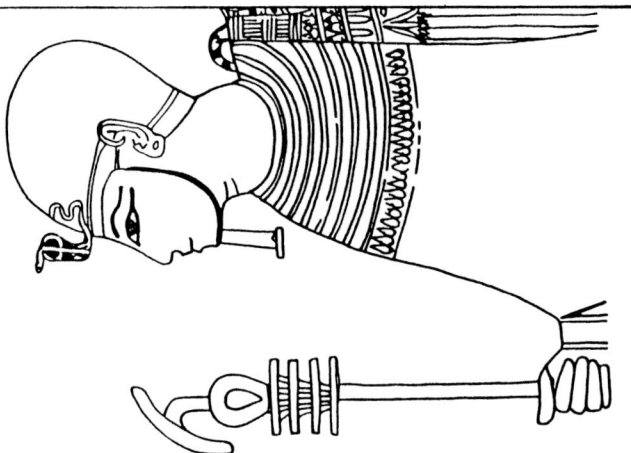

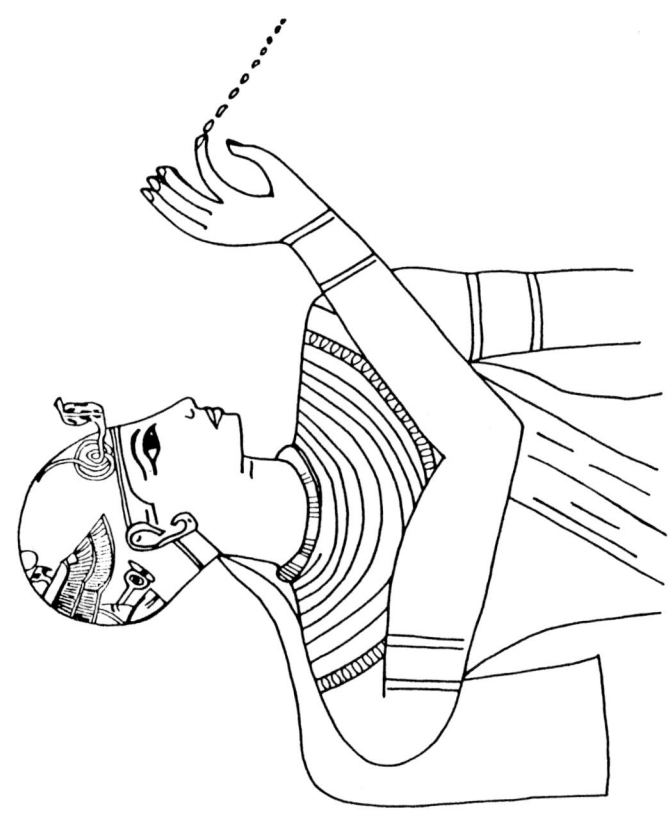

Figure 6

126

ABOU SIMBEL, RAMSES, ET LES DAMES DE LA COURONNE

Ch. Desroches Noblecourt

Suivant la formule consacrée "*on ne prête qu'aux riches*", on a voulu reconnaître à Ramsès, fils de Séthi, un nombre considérable d'enfants où les filles paraissent même en quantité plus importante que les garçons.[1] Au fil des études consacrées à ce sujet, la cohorte des héritiers - et des héritières connues - du Grand Roi semble en tous cas atteindre des proportions un peu moins considérables qu'on ne pouvait le prévoir. Il doit en être de même pour ses épouses secondaires et ses "favorites" d'un moment, au sujet desquelles, au reste, nous savons encore bien peu de choses.

Mon propos est, ici très précisément, consacré aux Dames les plus proches du Pharaon, c'est-à-dire à la mère (mais non à la, ou aux soeurs), aux deux premières Grandes Epouses Royales (princesses dont on ignore semble-t-il l'origine) et à celles des filles aînées qui paraissent avoir joué, - auprès de lui, - un rôle officiel, sinon d'importance.

Après avoir procédé à une enquête dans les principaux sites où Pharaon a fait ériger des sanctuaires, on s'aperçoit assurément que l'ensemble incomparable constitué par les deux fondations religieuses d'Abou Simbel réunit et abrite des *témoignages essentiels de son règne*.

Nulle part ailleurs, la bataille de Qadesh présentée avec toute la rigueur du "Bulletin"[2] fraîchement dicté, n'est aussi bien figurée pour ses étapes principales, dans un style narratif aussi nouveau, hérité de l'imagerie amarnienne. Les allusions nécessaires à rappeler l'activité guerrière dans les régions d'Asie ou contre les Libyens et les expéditions punitives en Nubie sont évoquées essentiellement grâce à des détails typiques rendus dans le respect de la plus haute qualité esthétique.

La répartition des membres de la famille en Abou Simbel

Cependant Ramsès n'a pas seulement sacrifié à "l'Histoire" événementielle!

Les préoccupations religieuses, les nombreux messages qu'il a voulu concrétiser dans la pierre pour aboutir à l'expression affirmée de sa complète divinisation sur terre,[3] sont exprimés avec force dans les deux sanctuaires creusés au sein des deux mamelons rocheux de *Meha*, au sud, et d'*Ibchek*, au nord (Fig. 1).

Avant toute autre chose, l'impression que l'on ressent à l'approche des deux temples, lorsque l'on arrive par le Nil, est celle d'un gigantesque et puissant maître, le géniteur d'une famille prolifique et attentive. Cet ensemble préfigure, à la façon égyptienne, la vision qui plus tard sera traduite dans l'imagination des derniers conquérants gréco-romains par l'image du génie du Nil entouré de ses rejetons évoquant la richesse de l'Inondation annuelle.[4]

Ramsès, comme cela n'avait encore jamais été réalisé, fit entourer la simple ouverture qui, auparavant pour les sanctuaires rupestres, donnait accès à un *spéos*, par un décor en ronde-bosse[5] formé des statues des membres de sa famille, très soigneusement sélectionnés. C'est, avant tout, ce décor (Fig. 2) qu'il faut interroger pour comprendre son message.

Tout d'abord, - et pour suivre en cela l'exemple amarnien, - point de rappel du père, bien que l'on soit assuré depuis longtemps par les témoignages subsistants, du souci de Ramsès d'en entretenir le culte et le souvenir.[6]

En revanche, l'effigie de sa mère est présente à deux reprises sur la façade du Grand Temple (Fig. 2): elle est debout, à gauche du premier colosse sud (Fig. 4), près de l'entrée, puis à droite du dernier colosse nord.

On sait qu'au début de son règne, Ramsès possédait déjà deux Grandes Epouses Royales: Isis-Nofret, - sans doute la première épousée, - et Nofretari. Fait étrange: *nulle part en Abou Simbel, ne figure Isis-Nofret*. C'est, en quelque sorte, la reine absente, mais non la reine morte. En revanche, Nofretari, - qui bénéficie aussi d'un temple au nord du site, - apparaît à deux reprises sur la façade à la place d'honneur (Fig. 2), à droite du premier colosse sud et à gauche du premier colosse nord (Fig. 3), encadrant ainsi l'entrée du *spéos*. De surcroît, à l'intérieur du temple, on peut admirer sa silhouette sur le premier pilier sud de la salle-cour. On la retrouve, de même, à deux reprises, accueillant avec le roi, la barque divine dans la "salle hypostyle".

Une place est seulement faite au premier fils de chacune des deux premières Grandes Epouses (Fig. 2). L'aîné de tous *Amonherkhopshef*,[7] mis au monde par Nofretari, est représenté en flabellifère, entre les jambes du premier colosse sud. Le puîné, enfanté par Isis-Nofret, figure dans la même position, entre les jambes du premier colosse nord: il s'agit du prince *Ramsès*.[8]

Les autres personnages de la façade sont strictement des filles (Fig. 2).

- à gauche du second colosse sud, on trouve *Nebet-Taouy*, fille de Nofretari.

- à droite, la fille aînée d'Isis-Nofret, *Bentanta*. La même sera, par la suite sculptée sur le dernier pilier sud de l'hypostyle: on constate, alors, qu'elle est devenue à son tour "Epouse Royale" et est désignée comme telle sur le relief.

- entre les jambes du dernier colosse sud apparaît une autre princesse, anonyme. En se fondant sur la sculpture analogue d'une autre princesse entre les jambes du dernier colosse nord,

- et qui s'appelle *Nofretari* (II), fille de la reine du même nom,

- L. Christophe a suggéré que la princesse anonyme pourrait être une fille d'Isis-Nofret, celle qui porte le nom de sa mère (et qui figure à la sixième place dans les listes des filles du roi). Il s'agit très probablement de la future soeur-épouse de Mineptah: *Isis-Nofret II*.

- à droite du premier colosse nord à partir de la porte d'entrée, faisant pendant à la reine Nofretari, on peut voir la statue de *Baket-Mout*,[9] fille de celle-ci.

- à gauche du second colosse nord, enfin, apparaît la princesse *Meryt-Amon*, autre fille de Nofretari.

Ainsi donc, sur la façade du Grand Temple, *entre* les jambes des colosses, figurent les deux fils aînés des deux premières Grandes Epouses Royales, et les deux filles qui portent le nom de leurs mères respectives. Ces quatre statuettes sculptées sont de taille réduite. Quant aux autres effigies de dimensions plus importantes et *encadrant* les jambes des colosses, ce sont celles de la reine mère *Touy*, de la Grande Epouse Royale *Nofretari* et celles des princesses *Bentanta*, sans doute *Isis-Nofret II*, *Baket-Mout*, *Nebet-Taouy*, *Meryt-Amon*, et *Nofretari II*. Les quatre dernières filles citées sont nées de la Grande Epouse Nofretari.

On peut ainsi constater que, sur la façade du Grand Temple qui constitue comme une sorte de "pancarte", une préférence va aux filles de Nofretari. A l'intérieur, on ne trouve pas davantage mention de la reine Isis-Nofret, bien que dans le défilé conventionnel des filles du roi, - en pendant au défilé de ses fils, - on discerne les enfants des deux lits. De même, *Bentanta* figure sur un pilier du Grand Temple.

Quant à la façade du Petit Temple (Fig. 5),[10] elle est consacrée au couple royal et aux seuls enfants de Nofretari. Des princes flanquent les quatre colosses du roi: *Amonherkhopshef*, l'aîné et le douzième, *Rêherounemef*, puis *Mery-Rê* et *Mery-Atoum* (le dix-septième, signalé comme défunt). En ce qui concerne la reine, ses deux statues sont encadrées de *Meryt-Amon* et de *Henout-Taouy* (signalée comme défunte).

Nofretari apparaît ainsi à quatre reprises sur les deux façades, *Meryt-Amon*, trois fois. Hommage certain du roi, au grand jour pourrait-on dire, à ses deux préférées. Dans le même contexte, c'est également sur la façade du Grand Temple que le roi tint à consigner son mariage contracté avec la fille du roi hittite, union à l'importance si exceptionnelle. La façade flanquée des deux autels niches consacrées au dieu Amon (sud) et à Horakhty (nord) et de surcroît encadrée, au sud, par la chapelle de Thot, et au nord par la chapelle solaire, ne présentait plus de surface libre à utiliser au moment de l'union avec la fille de Tadoukhepa. Aussi Ramsès fit-il graver la célèbre Stèle du Mariage sur le refend sud, perpendiculaire à la niche consacrée au dieu Amon. L'étrangère devint exceptionnellement Grande Epouse Royale.

Ce rapide survol nous permet de partir du principe que le site d'Abou Simbel a conservé les images de Dames de la Couronne qui jouèrent, auprès du grand roi, un rôle de premier plan (ou, du moins, dont on attendait qu'elles jouassent ce rôle), ainsi que nous allons le constater.

La mère royale Touy

La mère de Pharaon, Epouse du Dieu et Grande Epouse Royale de Séthi le Premier, occupe aussi bien dans ce Grand Temple que partout ailleurs où ses traces subsistent encore, une place éminente. Les mêmes égards ne furent pas témoignés à la grand-mère maternelle de Ramsès, *Sat-Rê*, mère de Séthi Ier,[11] dont le monument principal est constitué, à ce jour, par la petite tombe, dont le décor est presque exclusivement exécuté au trait. Dans la Vallée des Reines:[12] on était encore à l'aube de la nouvelle dynastie.

En Abou Simbel, les allusions d'importance aux Dames de la famille commencent donc par la figuration de Touy, dont on sait qu'elle fut aussi communément appelée *Mout-Touy* et même *Mouty*.[13] Je pense avoir identifié une magnifique statue de la douairière portraiturée - fait exceptionnel, - en porte-enseigne. Haute d'un mètre, en granite rose, cette statue,[14] maintenant entrée dans une collection particulière des U.S.A., représente incontestablement une souveraine traitée dans le style de la meilleure époque ramesside. Elle est coiffée de la dépouille de vautour posée sur sa volumineuse perruque:[15] sur la hampe, le roi est non seulement cité comme le rejeton d'Amon,[16] mais aussi étant bien *mis au monde par la déesse Mout*. Ramsès a voulu gravir un échelon supplémentaire: la théogamie en sa faveur n'a pas seulement été due a l'intervention du puissant dieu de Thèbes. La reine-mère devait bien passer pour la réelle incarnation de la divine mère Mout, - d'où le nom qui lui était fréquemment attribué, de son vivant.

Au reste, ne voit-on pas, dans la première salle-cour du Grand Temple d'Abou Simbel (Fig. 6), les traces visibles de cette sublime étape dans l'affirmation de la nature complètement divine du roi. En effet, Ramsès n'hésite pas à transformer une diade (ou Amon et Mout, côte à côte, recevaient l'hommage du souverain), en une triade composée du dieu et de la déesse, entre lesquels il fit postérieurement introduire sa propre image en guise du dieu-fils Khonsou. Les traces de la transformation sont très visibles sur les murs du *spéos*.[17]

Aussi n'était-il pas surprenant qu'il lui consacrât un temple que j'ai pu définitivement identifier en 1972, grâce à la découverte (dans le pseudo temple de Séthi jouxtant, au nord, le Ramesseum) d'un fragment de grès portant la dédicace du roi mentionnant la *"fondation qu'il avait faite pour sa mère"*.[18] Le nom de Nofretari mentionné sur un chapiteau hathorique trouvé sur le même terrain me permettait d'interprêter ce monument comportant deux petits sanctuaires jumelés comme étant, de surcroît, une double fondation dédiée à la mère du roi, mais aussi à la Grande Epouse favorite.

Au reste, leurs deux images (Fig. 7) côte à côte, apparaissent près de la porte, à l'intérieur de l'hypostyle du Ramesseum, affairées à jouer du sistre en direction de leur temple, vers le nord.[19] Dans ce temple du Ramesseum (*Per Imen*) près de colosses qui flanquaient les portes du deuxième pylône, le roi avait aussi dû faire figurer sa mère.[20] Les vestiges retrouvés à Tanis, provenant de *Per Ramsès* témoignent du souci qu'avait Ramsès de faire portraiturer sa mère en transformant même les effigies de grandes Dames des temps antérieurs.[21] La douairière fut inhumée en une place de choix dans la Vallée des Reines.[22] Le plan de sa tombe (Fig. 8) présente les proportions les plus majestueuses et les plus harmonieuses de toute la nécropole, préfigurant, avec plus de régularité, les lignes empruntées pour celle de Nofretari.[23]

La sépulture entièrement pillée, saccagée même, livra des vestiges d'importance: quelques inscriptions à son nom sur les murs très meurtris, des fragments de magnifiques canopes d'albâtre dont un bouchon à l'effigie de la reine, des débris de vases d'onguents en calcite, en verre complètement transparent, permettant d'évoquer la splendeur de l'équipement funéraire des shaouabtis, des jarres à vin brisées....[24] Partout les allusions à l'essence "divine" de la reine-mère ont disparu: elle est seulement citée comme Touy et non en tant que *Mout-Touy*. Bien que Grande Mère et Epouse Royale, profondément vénérée, elle est redevenue une mortelle, fille de (*Thou)ia* et du lieutenant général de la charrerie, *Raïa*[25] et l'identité de ses parents ne fait pas mystère. Elle doit s'appliquer, durant les épreuves du grand voyage, à gagner, comme telle, son Eternité. Le nom de Touy lui fut, en certaines occasions appliqué de son vivant: par exemple lorsqu'elle écrivit au souverain hittite,[26] à l'époque des échanges en vue de l'établissement du traité de paix et c'est bien par le simple vocable du *Touy* (Tuja) qu'elle fut mentionnée sur les lettres officielles.

Soeur(s) de Ramsès

Aucune femme investie de l'identité de réelle soeur du roi ne figure en Abou Simbel. Pas plus que les grands-mères, la (ou les) soeur(s) de Ramsès ne fut semble-t-il appellée à jouer un rôle dans la "geste" religieuse du Pharaon. On sait que H. Sourouzian[27] a démontré l'identité du *Henout-mi-Rê* comme *fille*-épouse du roi et non comme soeur-épouse ainsi qu'on le croyait auparavant.

Reste uniquement (et jusqu'à présent) sa soeur très certainement aînée, *Thya*,[28] - dont les récentes fouilles de G. Martin[29] ont fait réapparaître les reliques de la splendide tombe de famille à Saqqarah, - étant mariée à celui qui semble avoir été un des précepteurs de son souverain "dès l'oeuf"[30] et investi de très hautes responsabilités (notamment au Ramesseum). Thya ne semble avoir joué aucun rôle religieux auprès de son royal frère.

La Grande Epouse Royale Nofretari

Il n'est pas question de revenir ici sur ce que l'on sait[31] de la belle reine, mais seulement de clarifier, si possible, certains points de son histoire. La magnificence de ses portraits, dans sa tombe,[32] l'attachante plastique de ses statues et le fait que l'autre Grande Epouse Royale contemporaine, Isis-Nofret était tenue dans l'ombre et ne figurait jamais sur les monuments de l'époque, ont souvent incité les égyptologues à supposer l'existence d'un véritable roman d'amour entre Ramsès et Nofretari, de même qu'une rivalité entre cette dernière et Isis-Nofret.[33]

Si l'on peut aisément imaginer une très logique attirance dont le roi aurait fait montre à l'égard d'un femme aussi exceptionnellement séduisante qu'avait dû lêtre Nofretari, on imagine mal une rivalité entre les deux Dames aussi visiblement attestée et éternisée par des monuments religieux chargés d'un message bien supérieur et étranger à de simples contingences humaines.

A tenir compte, avant tout, du strict protocole qui devait régner à la cour du pharaon, *il faut surtout prendre en considération le fait que Nofretari était la mère du prince aîné*, le premier des enfants mâles mis au monde, *Amonherkhopshef*.[34] Elle était devenue la nouvelle mère royale par excellence et c'était naturellement d'elle que devaient dépendre certains rites de la Couronne. Elle conservera ces prérogatives, sans aucun doute, jusqu'à sa mort, alors que, - bien avant, comme nous le verrons, - d'autres Grandes Epouses avaient également pris place auprès du pharaon. Ses statues, comme on en voit de très suggestifs exemples au temple de Louxor, devaient avoir été consacrées dans la majorité des temples d'Egypte, subsistant à côté de celles des nouvelles Grandes Epouses Royales. Lorsque le roi ordonna d'aménager la sépulture de Nofretari, les peintres décorateurs se conformèrent aux exigences de l'iconographie rituelle. Ainsi qu'elle en avait été coiffée au moment de son intronisation en déesse Sothis,[35] la reine figure dans son caveau portant, la plupart du temps, les deux hautes plumes coiffant la silhouette humaine qui évoquait la radieuse étoile (Fig. 9). Cependant, *Nofretari ne possède plus les hautes cornes effilées qui enserraient le disque solaire visibles sur la presque totalité de ses effigies durant sa vie terrestre* (Fig. 10).

Tout se passe comme si ces cornes pointues, le nom même de la *Spdt*[36] l'indique, - lui avaient été retirées parce qu'elle n'était plus appelée à jouer le rôle qu'elle avait si souvent tenu, elle et ses semblables, auprès du royal époux. Aussi, à la lumière de cet indice, convient-il de bien observer la stèle rupestre d'Hekanakht,[37] gravée sur la muraille rocheuse de Meha[38] en Abou Simbel (Fig. 11).

Certes, au registre supérieur, Ramsès est accompagné de la fille de Nofretari, toute jeune Epouse Royale: *Meryt-Amon*; les deux hautes plumes sont sur sa tête, mais on ne distingue pas encore les cornes. En revanche, au registre inférieur (Fig. 12), Nofretari, assise, recevant les hommages du vice-roi, porte bien encore la coiffure complète de la déesse Sothis; son rôle d'épouse protectrice semble être encore actif.

Il demeure encore nombre de chapitres inconnus relatifs à l'existence de celle qui fut certainement une bien-aimée de Ramsès. Qui était-elle? Comment disparut-elle? Comme pour presque tous ces personnages royaux, même les plus célèbres, nous ne savons quasiment rien.[39] Y eut-il vraiment agression contre certaines de ses images, après sa mort, et si c'était le cas, par qui aurait-elle été perpétrée? On a même cru voir dans le martelage[40] du nom de la reine sur la célèbre statue de Ramsès à Turin, une vengeance du fils d'Isis-Nofret, - après le décès de Nofretari, sans doute, mais surtout après la mort du prince héritier *Amonherkhopshef*, survenue en l'an XXXIX. Mais les preuves ne sont pas suffisantes pour pouvoir conclure dans ce sens.

La Grande Epouse Isis-Nofret I

Peut-être fut-elle l'aînée des Grandes Epouses Royales: première les preuves ne sont pas suffisantes, mais elle donna à Ramsès la première fille royale *Bentanta*. Ses fils (postérieurs à la naissance du fils aîné de Nofretari): *Ramsès, Khaemouaset* étaient déjà représentés dans le temple de el Beit Ouali remontant à l'an I du règne. On ne connaît pas son origine (pas davantage que celle de Nofretari). Une indication peut-être: le fait que le nom de *Bentanta* donné à son premier enfant, et qui signifie "fille de la déesse Anat",[41] pourrait laisser supposer qu'elle tirerait ses origines du Proche-Orient,[42] dont les principales formes divines étaient vénérées par le roi. Rien n'est certain.

Elle ne figure en Abou Simbel (Fig. 2) *que* par personne interposée, en l'occurrence sa fille aînée dont il vient d'être question, et sans doute, sa fille cadette, *Isis-Nofret II*. Néanmoins la place du deuxième fils de Ramsès, qu'elle mit au monde (s'appelant également *Ramsès*) a été réservée, en Abou Simbel (Fig. 2), en parallèle avec celle qui fut donnée à son demi-frère aîné, *Amonherkhopshef*, prince héritier de l'époque, fils de Nofretari.

J'ai proposé plus haut d'interpréter l'absence d'Isis-Nofret sur les monuments des premières grandes époques du règne,[43] non pas comme une disgrâce, ni comme une rivalité entre les premières Grandes Epouses, mais surtout parce qu'au début du règne, elle n'était pas la mère du prince héritier.[44] Cette hypothèse est confirmée par les deux stèles d'Assouan (Fig. 13) et du Gebel Silsileh (Fig. 14) où Isis-Nofret apparaît, enfin, aux côtés de Pharaon, escortée de sa fille aînée *Bentanta*, de ses fils *Ramsès* et *Khaemouaset* et du petit *Mineptah* après la mort d'*Amonherkhopshef*, l'aîné de Nofretari (c'est-à-dire en l'an XXXVI pour la stèle d'Assouan et pour celle du Gebel Silsileh en l'an XXXIX).[45]

Il convient aussi de remarquer la situation géographique des sanctuaires où apparaissent successivement les mères des héritiers:

> - au début du règne, Nofretari est la première Grande Epouse Royale représentée au nord de la deuxième cataracte, à l'endroit où le grand évènement annuel de l'Inondation est sanctionné par les rites qui devaient se dérouler entre les deux temples d'Abou Simbel.[46]

> - au moment où l'héritier en titre, fils de Nofretari disparaît, les fils d'Isis-Nofret deviennent prépondérants! Isis-Nofret apparaît alors aux côtés de Ramsès, escortée de sa fille aînée *Bentanta* déjà naturellement Grande Epouse Royale, mais aussi de ses fils, nouveaux et successifs prétendants au trône. L'évènement n'est plus consigné aux portes de la Nubie égyptienne, mais près de celles qui introduisent dans l'Egypte métropolitaine, au Gebel Silsileh surtout, où les importantes cérémonies que l'on sait, sanctionnaient l'étiage du fleuve et l'appel au retour de la bienfaisante Inondation.[47]

Remarquons en dernier, que les deux grandes Dames royales portent chacune les hautes plumes et les *cornes* de Sothis: argument supplémentaire pour rappeler que la reine Isis-Nofret avait retrouvé une place officielle éminente auprès du souverain et qu'elle ne devait pas encore être morte à cette époque.[48]

Isis-Nofret ainsi "réhabilitée" fut certainement honorée avec insistance, si ce n'est avec ostentation par ses fils. Si l'on n'a pas encore repéré sa sépulture dans la Vallée des Reines, on est assuré qu'elle y fut enterrée et que sa tombe fut aménagée à la même époque que celle du fils de Ramsès, *Ramsès Mery-Toum*, Grand Prêtre d'Héliopolis.[49]

La Grande Epouse Royale Isis-Nofret II

Des deux statues d'Aménophis III, usurpées par Mineptah,[50] celle qui est actuellement privée de tête est supposée représenter le treizième fils de Ramsès. Elle est gravée, - sur son côté gauche, - d'une élégante silhouette de princesse devant laquelle une inscription nous apprend qu'il s'agit de la Grande Epouse Royale, maîtresse des Deux Terres, Isis-Nofret. Il ne semble pas très convaincant d'y voir la reine mère de Mineptah et d'imaginer qu'il avait voulu, à cette place, commémorer le souvenir de sa mère défunte. Il est plus normal de penser qu'il a désiré, comme son père en avait coutume, y faire figurer sa propre épouse qui s'appelait elle aussi Isis-Nofret. L'inscription, au reste, *ne fait pas mention de mère royale*. Nous sommes donc en présence de la fille d'Isis-Nofret et soeur de Mineptah[51] figurant en Abou Simbel (Fig. 2) et qui devint l'épouse de ce dernier. L'union survint certainement du vivant de Ramsès. Elle était peut-être un peu plus âgée que son frère. On apprend aussi par le papyrus de Leiden I, lettre n°362[52] qu'en l'an LII de Ramsès, elle n'était pas encore Grande Epouse Royale de son frère, puisque ce dernier n'était pas encore monté sur le trône. La statue usurpée aurait naturellement été remaniée aprés l'intronisation.

Avant la découverte des statues de Louxor, on connaissait seulement l'existence d'Isis-Nofret II, en tant que reine et Grande Epouse Royale de Mineptah par les inscriptions du grand *spéos* du Gebel Silsileh.[53]

La Grande Epouse Royale Bentanta

Il apparaît bien que Bentanta, fille aînée d'Isis-Nofret fut aussi l'aînée des filles de Ramsès II. Il semble également qu'elle fut promue Grande Epouse Royale un peu avant *Meryt-Amon*: toutes deux figurent assurément sur la façade du Grand Temple d'Abou Simbel (Fig. 2), mais Bentanta apparaît, à nouveau, en tant que Grande Epouse sur le dernier pilier sud-ouest de la salle-cour (*Meryt-Amon* n'est représentée à l'intérieur de ce temple, que dans le défilé des filles, avec Bentanta qui est en tête). Bentanta venait vraisemblablement d'être intronisée Grande Epouse Royale, comme le sera plus tard *Meryt-Amon* (stèle de Hekanakht).

Elle bénéficia certainement d'une place d'honneur pendant tout le règne. Indépendamment du rang qui lui fut logiquement affecté dans les défilés des princesses ornant les temples du roi, en Nubie (Abou Simbel, Derr, Ouadi es-Seboua) et en Egypte métropolitaine (Louxor, Abydos) son effigie de Grande Epouse Royale flanque certaines statues monumentales du roi à Ouadi es-Seboua (Fig. 15), devant le pylône remontant, au plus tôt, aux entours de l'an XL du règne, et avant cette date à Louxor, à deux reprises dans les colonnades est et ouest de la grande cour (on la devine, encore simple princesse, derrière le couple royal, au cours des festivités de Min, face sud de la tour est du premier pylône),[54] puis à Per Ramsès du Delta.

Elle est à l'honneur aux côtés de sa mère à Assouan et au Gebel Silsileh à partir des années trente-six, mais son intronisation comme nouvelle Grande Epouse Royale dut se produire bien avant ce qui a pu être établi jusqu'à présent. En effet, on sait maintenant par une inscription de jarre de vin retrouvée dans la tombe de la reine *Touy*, que la douairière fut ensevelie peu après l'an XXII du règne de son fils. Or, le 27 mars 1987, le "nettoyage" autour de l'entrée de cette tombe dans la Vallée des Reines a permis de découvrir, parmi les débris de l'équipement funéraire rejetés à l'exterieur par les pillards antiques, un fragment de vase en fritte émaillée bleu turquoise foncé, portant les traces de l'inscription au nom de la Fille Royale, Grande Epouse Royale Ben(tanta).

Elle était donc investie de cette fonction au moins dès l'an XXII[55] et même peut-être un peu avant et, en tout cas, bien avant la mort de sa mère. Sans doute, comme la plupart des Grandes Epouses Royales vécut-elle à Per Ramsès et passa-t-elle des séjours au grand harem de Mi-Our. Mais elle fut enterrée dans la Vallée des Reines (*Ta Set Neferou*) comme, semble-t-il la majorité des Grandes Epouses Royales. L'ampleur et la qualité[56] de son caveau témoignent du rang qu'elle occupait parmi les Dames royales: cette sépulture (n°71) est comparable en importance a celle de *Meryt-Amon*. On peut l'inscrire au troisième rang après celle du *Touy* et de *Nofretari*. Faut-il aussi y reconnaître les égards particuliers qui lui furent témoignés parce qu'elle mit au monde une fille pour Ramsès? En effet, en dégageant la sépulture entièrement brûlée, à l'époque arabe semble-t-il, nous avons mis au jour à nouveau ses magnifiques effigies, lesquelles éclairées à jour frisant, - bien que totalement noircies, - révèlent une plastique rendue avec un talent remarquable et où les différents âges de la reine paraissent être consignés dans le traité des visages. A deux reprises une jeune princesse est représentée dans la salle du sarcophage, une fois précédant Bentanta en adoration devant Nephthys, une autre fois derrière la reine qui se dirige vers l'insigne d'Abydos, gardé par Anubis. Au-dessus de la charmante princesse (Fig. 16), l'inscription *s3t.f n ḥt.f* ne laisse aucun doute sur les liens de parenté qui unissaient la jeune fille et le grand roi. Cet exemple confirme le phénomène déjà constaté, en tous cas à l'époque d'Akhénaton,[57] lequel semble avoir été l'époux rituel, - mais aussi fécondateur, - d'au moins deux de ses filles aînées: Meryt-Aton et Ankhsenpaaten. Jusqu'à présent le nom de cette fille et petite-fille de Ramsès demeure inconnu.

La Grande Epouse Royale Bentanta II

Si l'on se réfère à la plus belle des statues au nom de Mineptah (représentant à l'origine Aménophis III) trouvée devant le pylône de Louxor[58] (maintenant au musée de Louxor), on peut contempler l'image d'une "*fille royale, soeur royale, Grande Epouse Royale, Bentanta*". Le titre de Grande Epouse indique clairement le rôle qu'elle joua auprès de Mineptah. S'il était question de sa soeur aînée, fille d'Isis-Nofret, cette dernière aurait dû avoir approximativement soixante-douze ans à l'accession au trone de Mineptah.[59] Elle n'aurait vraiment pu jouer aucun rôle effectif auprès de lui. Aussi H. Sourouzian envisage-t-elle plutôt d'y voir seulement l'image *commémorative* de la grande soeur ayant épousé Ramsès II, peut-être encore vivante à l'époque où la statue fut remployée et rappelant le souvenir de leur commune mère.[60]

Pour ma part, en considérant les suggestions qui viennent d'être exposées et en me référant à la coutume adoptée par les reines de la famille de Ramsès qui semblent avoir donné à telles de leurs filles le nom qu'elles portaient elles-mêmes (cf. *Isis-Nofret II* et *Nofretari II*), j'inclinerais à penser que nous sommes peut-être en présence d'une seconde épouse de Mineptah, fille de Bentanta et de Ramsès et qui peut-être, ne serait autre que la princesse anonyme figurant dans la tombe de sa mère, n°71 de la Vallée des Reines (Fig. 16).[61]

Sur les deux statues de Louxor, usurpées par Mineptah on pourrait donc constater la continuation du phénomène qui, à propos des Grandes Epouses Royales, semble être attesté au moins dès le règne de Ramsès II, ainsi Isis-Nofret I et Nofretari I, *Bentanta I* et *Meryt-Amon* (cf. les statues de Hiéraconpolis et de Tanis). Mineptah aurait, sur l'une des statues d'Aménophis III, usurpée par ses soins, fait figurer *Isis-Nofret II* et sur l'autre Bentanta II.

La Grande Epouse Royale Meryt-Amon

Tout comme *Bentanta*, Meryt-Amon fut représentée sur la façade du Grand Temple d'Abou Simbel (Fig. 2) pour occuper une place exactement parallèle à celle de la statue de sa soeur aînée.

On a vu (Fig. 11) que Meryt-Amon figure aussi en Abou Simbel sur une stèle rupestre près de l'entrée du Grand Temple. Escortant son père faisant l'offrande à la triade divine, en tant que Grande Epouse Royale, elle domine ainsi, coiffée des hautes plumes, *mais sans les cornes effilées*, le registre inférieur (Fig. 12) où Nofretari reçoit les hommages du vice-roi Hekanakht qui cessa ses fonctions en l'an XXV. Cette scène devait avoir été gravée peu de temps après l'apparition de *Bentanta* comme Epouse Royale sur le pilier sud-ouest avant l'an XXII. La stèle rupestre pourrait donc à son tour rappeler la "promotion" de Meryt-Amon comme Epouse Royale, commémorant ainsi un évènement parallèle à celui qui avait été consigné pour *Bentanta* sur le pilier sud-ouest de la salle-cour.

Pour l'une et l'autre des deux princesses l'évènement fut donc relativement contemporain. Nous savons qu'Isis-Nofret était encore bien présente en l'an XXII et nous avons la preuve que Nofretari n'avait pas davantage disparu. C'est un fait certain: les deux nouvelles Grandes Epouses Royales, *Bentanta* et Meryt-Amon, bénéficièrent de leur nouvel état du vivant de leurs mères respectives. On les voit, par exemple, représentées l'une et l'autre encadrant deux colosses de Ramsès provenant d'Héracléopolis, actuellement exposés dans le jardin du musée du Caire.[62] Toutes deux, investies des mêmes titres, dans la même attitude, debout, les bras le long du corps et la perruque ornée de l'importante mèche latérale: elles apparaissent ainsi dans l'éclat de leur jeune beauté. Sur une statue de Tanis (Petrie I, V) elles figuraient également en parallèle.

Le hasard a réalisé au cours d'une construction moderne à Akhmîn, ce qu'une longue recherche n'avait pu antérieurement provoquer: le creusement de fondations a fait découvrir à quelque six mètres de profondeur, les vestiges majestueux d'une statue monumentale (d'environ 7 m) de Meryt-Amon (Fig. 17), Grande Epouse Royale[63] porteuse de titres analogues à ceux, - incomplets, - qui figurent sur le pilier dorsal de la statue de reine trouvée au Ramesseum.[64] Ainsi vient d'être identifiée la princesse anonyme si connue du musée du Caire, surnommée parfois la "*Reine Blanche*" ou la "*Reine à la menat*". *Meryt-Amon* apparaît alors, dans toute sa fleur. Sur les deux effigies d'Akhmîn et du Ramesseum, la couleur en partie conservée fait encore frémir les lèvres de la princesse épouse, aux rondes boucles d'oreille.

L'importance de ces monuments semble indéniable et souligne la position exceptionnelle que devait occuper auprès du roi, la fille aînée de Nofretari. En Abou Simbel, a Akhmîn, au Ramesseum et à Louxor (une fois flanquant un colosse sud de la cour et contre le colosse debout de la tour occidentale du pylône, (Fig. 18),[65] elle figure également à Tanis, sur un colosse en grès rouge de Ramsès. Contre la jambe gauche du roi subsiste encore l'image de son épouse hittite *Maâthorneferourê*;[66] sur une autre statue on voit, semble-t-il, les traces de la reine hittite et entre les jambes du souverain, fut aussi réservée l'image de Meryt-Amon. Le nom aurait subi des martelages, ce qui devrait prouver, d'après L. Christophe, que la princesse aurait été supplantée par la fille de Tadoukhepa dès l'an XXXIV. Il s'agit peut-être seulement d'une statue réutilisée au moment de l'union de Ramsès avec la fille du grand prince du Kheta.[67]

En tenant compte des éléments que nous venons de passer en revue, on demeure surpris devant les proportions modestes de la tombe n°68 de la Vallée des Reines par rapport au caveau de *Bentanta* et encore plus de celui de *Nebet-Taouy*.

La Grande Epouse Royale Nebet-Taouy

Cette princesse qui figure naturellement en bonne place dans les défilés des princesses conservés dans les temples du roi, est signalée comme défunte (*Wsir et m3ᶜ-ḥrw*) dans le *spéos* nubien de Derr. Sa tombe n°60[68] de la Vallée des Reines conservant encore une partie de son décor a été bien tardivement aménagée en église primitive, mais les peintures chrétiennes n'ont pas entièrement fait disparaître le decor antique: les locaux présentent un plan qui s'éloigne de celui de ses mère et grand-mère. Par sa tombe, nous apprenons seulement que la princesse devint à une époque encore indéterminée, Grande Epouse Royale.[69]

Ainsi donc de toutes les filles royales évoquées en ronde bosse sur la façade des deux temples d'Abou Simbel, deux seules semblent n'avoir jamais occupé de haut rang: *Henout-Taouy*, probablement morte très jeune et *Baket-Mout*[70] dont nous ne pouvons *rien* dire, et sa tombe n'ayant pas encore été retrouvée.

Maathorneferourê, Grande Epouse Royale

La princese hittite, dont la légende déformée semble avoir traversé les siècles[71] paraît être, à notre connaissance, la seule Grande Epouse Royale étrangère de Ramsès[72] (mariée à Pharaon en l'an XXXIV). Non pas détrônée, mais suivie par une de ses soeurs cadettes qui vint aussi partager la couche de Pharaon, il semble qu'elle vécut à Per Ramsès un certain temps et qu'elle rejoignit le Grand Harem de Mi-Our où elle aurait pu achever ses jours.[73]

Les cérémonies du mariage de la princesse escortée par son père, -sur la stèle figurée en Abou Simbel (Fig. 19), - soulignent encore l'importance de l'évènement dont les échos se répandirent sur toute l'Egypte[74] et dans les pays voisins. Le rôle qu'elle dût alors tenir auprès du roi est rappelé par une statue colossale du souverain (Fig. 20), - transportée ultérieurement à Tanis, - où l'on distingue contre la jambe gauche du colosse, l'image en haut relief de Maathorneferourê, (son nom égyptien) et ses titres.[75]

Une information que m'a très aimablement communiquée le professeur E. Edel[76] fait état d'un échange de lettres entre Ramsès II et Hattoushilish concernant la grossesse de la princesse. On apprend que cette dernière mit au monde une fille qui semble avoir reçu le nom abrégé de sa mère: *Neferourê*. Il existe en effet une princesse de ce nom très visible par exemple dans le défilé des filles de Ramsès en Abydos.[77]

Ayant mis au monde une héritière royale, la Grande Epouse hittite devait certainement avoir eu droit à une sépulture officielle dans la Vallée des Reines, mais le caveau, s'il existe bien, n'a pas encore été retrouvé.

Ce dont on est assuré, est qu'elle devait avoir possédé un palais dans la cité de son roi à Per Ramsès.

La Grande Epouse Royale Henout-mì-Rê

Cette dernière Grande Epouse de Ramsès recensée à ce jour, ne figure pas en Abou Simbel et n'apparaît pas dans les défilés de princesses d'une façon certaine. Il ne semble pas que son action à la cour ait laissé de traces marquantes. Son personnage a pourtant posé des problèmes. Tout d'abord sur son identité, car elle n'était vraiment connue que par son image sculptée contre la statue de la reine *Touy*, que l'on croyait être sa mère, statue conservée au musée du Vatican.[78] Ile était pourtant mentionnée sur un colosse de granite rose du musée d'Alexandrie. Récemment H. Sourouzian, en publiant ce colosse, a prouvé qu'il s'agissait bien, en fait, d'une des dernières filles nées de Ramsès II, apparue certainement à la fin du règne.[79]

Sa tombe avait été aménagée dans la Vallée des Reines[80]: on en était d'avance assuré, comme on le sait, par le témoignage du Papyrus Salt 124 où le chef des ouvriers, Pa-neb était accusé d'avoir pénétré dans la tombe d'Henout-mì-Rê, dans la *Set Neferou*, et d' avoir volé une oie-*ser*.[81] Mais une première preuve tangible en fut donnée par la découverte, au sud-ouest de l'entrée de la tombe n°75 en 1985, d'un fragment de canope, au nom de la fille, Grande Epouse Royale, Henout-mì-Rê. Une année après sa tombe était indentifiée (caveau n°75). Après son premier pillage, la sépulture fut remise en état, mais les temps étaient moins opulents. Sans doute est-ce la raison pour laquelle le mobilier dut être complété à moindres frais: le fragment de canope portant des traces d'usurpation montre qu'il avait, à l'origine, appartenu à un précédent propriétaire.

A quel mobile Ramsès avait-il répondu en faisant figurer l'image d'une de ses dernières filles, aux côtés de sa propre mère, très vénérée? C'était certainement lui reconnaître l'importance à laquelle elle avait droit. En la plaçant près de *Touy* dont on sait qu'elle semble avoir toujours été proche de Nofretari, c'était peut-être aussi indiquer par là son ascendance. Etait-ce un des derniers enfants de Nofretari ou tout au moins une héritière d'une de ses filles-épouses? H. Sourouzian a supposé que sa mère aurait pu être une fille de *Touy*, encore inconnue.

D'autre part, il conviendrait d'établir la date à laquelle a été inaugurée la statue de *Touy*. Si l'évènement s'était passé du vivant de la reine, les figurations seraient antérieures à l'an XXII et cela paraît très peu probable, d'autant que, dans les inscriptions, Ramsès II y est appelé "*Maître des Jubilés*", indiquant assurément que la sculpture doit être postérieure à l'an XXX.

Quoi qu'il en soit, on pourrait envisager que Pharaon voulait la rattacher au groupe des Dames ayant fait partie de son cercle "d'honneur". N'ayant semble-t-il, plus la place de faire figurer en Abou Simbel celle à laquelle il avait témoigné cette nouvelle faveur, il l'avait fait sculpter près de la statue dédiée à sa mère, trônant dans un de ses monuments principaux (le Ramesseum?)

Le rôle religieux de la Grande Epouse Royale: Auprès du roi vivant

Nous revenons maintenant vers les deux temples d'Abou Simbel qui ont été notre point de départ. Après avoir étudié et publié le Petit Temple, Ch. Kuentz et moi-même avions bien été persuadés que le Grand et le Petit Temples étaient complémentaires, au même titre certainement que les sanctuaires respectifs d'Aménophis III à Soleb et de Tiyi à Sedeinga, en Nubie soudanaise.[82]

Il nous est vite apparu qu'un des mobiles essentiels de leur implantation et de leur aménagement en ces lieux était d'aider, de provoquer aussi, le cas échéant le renouvellement annuel du souverain et enfin de favoriser les grandes festivités au moment de l'arrivée des hautes eaux du début de l'année. Nofretari, dans son sanctuaire, s'incorporait à la Grande Déesse remettant au monde un souverain à la jouvence affirmée, réapparaissant sur le trône d'Horus doté d'une nouvelle vigueur, au jour de l'an neuf.[83]

Cependant, il convenait de mener plus avant l'enquête et de mieux préciser encore le rôle confié à la souveraine de prédilection, choisie entre toutes par Ramsès.

Sur la façade du Petit Temple, l'image vibrante de la reine, comme surgissant de la montagne à l'aube d'un matin radieux, avait été automatiquement interprétée comme l'apparition incarnée d'Hathor d'*Ibchek*.[84]

A considérer avec attention la coiffure de Nofretari, aussi bien à cet endroit, qu'à l'intérieur du vestibule où elle est couronnée par Hathor et Isis (Fig. 21), la reine est, en réalité, dans cette grotte sacrée, *traitée en Sothis*, dont elle porte la coiffure. On observe d'abord les deux hautes plumes *droites* qu'il serait fautif de continuer à confondre avec les plumes d'autruche à l'extrémité recourbée portées par Hathor.[85] De surcroît, les hautes cornes effilées ne peuvent être assimilées à celles, plus courtes et lyriformes, de la Grande Vache, nourrice divine.

L'image de Sothis est donc bien affirmée dans le Petit Temple du nord. La reine incarne la belle Étoile près de laquelle - et par laquelle - le Soleil apparaît, au Jour de l'An.

Auprès du roi défunt

Tout porte à croire que la Grande Epouse Royale en activité, lors du trépas de Ramsès, dût certainement mimer les rites de renaissance pour le pharaon défunt. Ces rites, dans le monde des Transformations, constituaient la réplique symbolique de l'oeuvre d'Isis, la plus auguste des veuves, auprès d'Osiris défunt. Les reliefs du temple de Séthi Ier en Abydos ont conservé les allusions essentielles à ces actes relatifs au grand mystère. Des images plus nombreuses et plus détaillées apparaissent naturellement, entre autres, dans les chapelles osiriennes de l'île de Philae. Le roi défunt, - comme le dieu mort, - devait, pour passer à l'éternité solaire, connaître les mêmes avatars, suivre le périple chthonien inauguré par Osiris. A défaut du mobilier funéraire disparu de Ramsès, tournons-nous vers celui de Toutankhamon dont les éléments[86] devaient constituer l'essentiel du bagage nécessaire au défunt en voie de transformation pour s'intégrer à l'impérissable soleil.

Bornons-nous à considérer les principaux tableaux du petit naos doré du jeune roi (Fig. 22), où toutes les scènes retracent, au moyen de symboles tirés de l'iconographie civile amarnienne, les différentes étapes du voyage "infernal".[87] Il faut d'abord s'arrêter à la présentation, par le souveraine, de la *menat* et du sistre, instrument appelé, dans cette scène, la "*Grande de Magie*", et réunissant à eux seuls l'éveil de l'*éros* et la fécondation de la future mère solaire. Puis sont figurées les différentes passes rituelles auxquelles la veuve Ankhsenamon procède afin de revigorer le corps blessé par le Malin. Alors vient l'acte de procréation au cours duquel Pharaon, assis et encore dolent, mais réveillé par la magicienne (portant la coiffure de Sothis) verse, dans la main de l'amoureuse tournée vers lui, le liquide fécondateur. Ce seront ensuite les scènes (Fig. 23) où, pendant la gestation du soleil à venir, la veuve attentive indique au désincarné en transformation[88] les mauvais génies à détruire dans les marécages primordiaux. Enfin pour réapparaître, Pharaon à nouveau debout, encore vacillant, est guidé par la reine qui l'entraîne vers l'aube de la vie éternelle.[89]

Conclusions

Ainsi les deux temples d'Abou Simbel (Fig. 24) nous permettent de saisir, entre autres, l'action de la Grande Epouse Royale dans le rituel de l'essentielle festivité pour le renouvellement sur terre de Pharaon. Ce dernier a tenu à consigner dans cet endroit de prédilection les personnages et les évènements qui semblent avoir marqué le plus profondément sa longue existence. Si longue que bien au-delà des limites du temps marquées par les deux sanctuaires nubiens, il faut interroger la Vallée des Reines pour connaître celles que Ramsès avait désignées pour être ensevelies dans la "Place des *Neferou*", sous la protection particulière de la déesse dont elles avaient été appelées à jouer le rôle. Un des buts de la rénovation de la Vallée[90] est, entre autres, de faire sortir de l'ombre ces grandes Dames. On sait, par exemple, que *Henout-Taouy* qui décéda très jeune, y fut ensevelie et ne devint jamais Grande Epouse Royale. D'autres princesses sont restées anonymes, comme la supposée propriétaire du caveau n°40[91], préparé avec le plus grand soin et où elle ne fut, semble-t-il, jamais enterrée. Non loin de là l'épouse royale *Tanedjmy*, inconnue, fut inhumée dans un caveau[92] dont, du décor, seule subsiste la silhouette de la princesse surmontée par son cartouche. D'autres tombes très détériorées, aux propriétaires encore non identifiées paraissent appartenir au même règne.[93] Certaines encore, comme *Isis-Nofret et Baket-Mout*, qui furent très probablement enterrées dans la Vallée (nous en possédons en tout cas l'indication pour *Isis-Nofret*), manquent à l'appel.

Les recherches sur les Dames de la Couronne auprès du grand Ramsès sont donc loin d'être closes, mais nous avons pu apporter certaines précisions dans l'identification de quelques unes d'entre elles. Ces précisions - ou rectifications - peuvent se résumer par les points suivants:

- à l'encontre de ce qui a pu être supposé antérieurement, la Grande Epouse Royale *Isis-Nofret* ne semble pas, apparemment avoir été l'objet d'une féroce rivalité qui en aurait fait la victime désignée de *Nofretari*. La raison de son absence marquée dans les monuments connus du début du règne (jusqu'à la première fête *Sed* du roi et le décès d'*Aamonherkhopshef*) serait, avant tout, qu'elle n'était pas la mère du prince aîné, héritier de *Nofretari* et prétendant au trône.

- *Isis-Nofret* ne serait pas davantage morte au moment où *Bentanta* fut consacrée Grande Epouse Royale, puisqu'elle apparaît, bien vivante, aux côtés de cette dernière sur les stèles d'Assouan et du Gebel Silsileh.

- *Isis-Nofret* aurait-elle été d'origine étrangère pour avoir donné à sa fille aînée (son premier enfant semble-t-il) un prénom cananéen, "*Fille de la déesse Anta (Anat)*"? Cette origine étrangère aurait-elle aidé à son éclipse provisoire, aux côtés d'une Grande Epouse égyptienne, mère du "Dauphin"?

- *Nofretari* disparut très probablement avant le mariage avec la princesse hittite, mais ne semble pas, ainsi qu'on a pu le supposer, être quasiment mourante au moment où la stèle rupestre d'Hekanakht fut dédiée contre la roche d'Abou Simbel. On pourrait plutôt voir dans cette scène le rappel (avant l'an XXV) de l'*intronisation* comme Epouse Royale, de *Meryt-Amon*, fille aînée de *Nofretari* (intronisation postérieure à celle de *Bentanta* dont la place put encore être consignée dans le Grand Temple). Détail important: *Meryt-Amon* porte les deux hautes plumes sur sa perruque, mais cette dernière est privée des élégantes cornes de Sothis que *Nofretari* arbore encore au registre inférieur de la stèle.

- *Bentanta* fut intronisée Grande Epouse Royale avant l'an XXII du règne de son père, - dernière date consignée sur les jarres à vin du mobilier funéraire de sa grand-mère paternelle, *Mout-Touy*. En effet, elle déposa, selon toute probabilité, dans cette tombe un petit vase portant son nom et ses titres.

- Ces deux derniers exemples nous permettent d'affirmer que ni *Nofretari*, ni *Isis-Nofret* n'étaient mortes, lorsque deux autres nouvelles Grande Epouses Royales furent intronisées. L'établissement d'une fille royale comme Grande Epouse ne se fait donc pas assurément à la mort de sa mère[94], ce qui était déjà prouvé avec le cas de Sat-Amon, de sa soeur Isis (57), et des trois princesses amarniennes. *Bentanta* semble bien avoir été choisie pour devenir Grande Epouse Royale un peu avant que *Meryt-Amon* ne le devienne à son tour, car seule l'image de *Bentanta* appelée à cette auguste fonction apparaît sur le dernier pilier sud de la salle-cour en Abou Simbel (Grand Temple), en réplique du premier pilier sud, portant l'image de *Nofretari* (mais seul le titre "d'Epouse Royale" lui est encore affecté sur ce pilier; c'est le début de la "promotion"!).

- Les deux princesses, filles des deux premières Grandes Epouses apparaissent en parallèle assez régulièrement: sur la façade du Grand Temple nubien, *Bentanta* près du colosse de l'extrême sud et *Meryt-Amon* près du colosse de l'extrême nord.

- Le parallélisme est très visible, encore, sur les deux colosses usurpés par Ramsès et retrouvés à Héracléopolis: sur ces statues, elles sont alors toutes deux appelées "Grande Epouse Royale". Si elles apparaissent toutes deux, sans discrimination, c'est sans doute qu'il n'est pas question pour elles d'être les mères des princes héritiers, donc sur ce point "monarchique", il n'est pas question de préséance.

- Il est aussi instructif de remarquer un parallélisme très évident entre les deux petites statuettes de princesses figurant entre les jambes des deux colosses du sud et du nord d'Aboul Simbel, dont il vient d'être question. La présence (au nord) de *Nofretari II*, fille de la première *Nofretari*, permet de supposer que la princesse anonyme du sud serait bien *Isis-Nofret II*, fille de la première du nom et qui devint une des deux futures Grandes Epouse de Mineptah. Une question non résolue: pourquoi figurerait-elle anonyme sur la façade? Je pense qu'il s'agirait d'un oubli, (rectifié sur la surface anciennement peinte), car elle défile bien dans les listes des filles de Ramsès en Abou Simbel, dans la salle-cour et à Derr ici et là, au sixième rang, par deux fois.

- Il ne semble pas que l'on puisse rejeter les hypothèses qui avaient été considérées comme mal fondées à propos des mariages *consommés* entre les pharaons et leurs filles devenues Grandes Epouses Royales. Des preuves étaient apparues pour le règne d'Aménophis IV. On ne peut plus en douter, maintenant, lorsqu'on se reporte à l'apparition d'une nouvelle princesse qui figure à deux reprises dans la tombe de *Bentanta* et qui est indiquée comme *s3t nswt n ḥt.f*, "Fille royale de son ventre".

- L'existence de cette nouvelle princesse dont le nom n'est pas mentionné dans la tombe de sa mère, nous permettrait d'avancer une suggestion grâce aux deux statues d'Aménophis III (usurpée par Mineptah) trouvées sur le parvis du temple de Louxor, flanquées, chacune, de l'image d'une Grande Epouse Royale. L'une, nommée *Isis-Nofret*, doit être la nièce et soeur-épouse de Mineptah, *Isis-Nofret II* figurant, entre autres en Abou Simbel et à Derr. L'autre est appelée *Bentanta*. On a pu supposer qu'à défaut de faire représenter sa mère morte, Mineptah aurait pu rendre aussi hommage aux femmes de sa famille en faisant figurer sa soeur aînée. Cette dernière, cependant, n'aurait pu être en même temps son épouse car son âge aurait été, à cette époque, mémorable. N'est-il pas plus logique de penser qu'il s'agit là d'une autre nièce et très jeune demi-soeur de Mineptah, fille de la grande *Bentanta* et de Ramsès, et qui, pour suivre l'exemple de son père, aurait porté le nom de celle qui l'avait mise au monde: ce serait *Bentanta II*.

- L'importance extrême de l'union avec la fille du souverain hittite est soulignée par le titre suprême donné à la puissante *Maathorneferourê* qu'il nomme d'emblée Grande Epouse Royale. Cet évènement sanctionne évidemment, avant tout, le traité de paix entre les deux pays. Cependant, Ramsès n'hésite pas à mentionner, après le nom et les titres égyptiens affectés à la princesse, son état de "*Fille du Grand du pays du Kheta*".[95] L'étrangère est glorifiée, sans doute aussi parce que, pour suivre E. Edel, elle aurait donné à Pharaon une héritière, laquelle, suivant la coutume égyptienne appliquée à trois reprises pour les filles de Ramsès, semble avoir porté le nom abrégé (ou même pas du tout abrégé) de sa mère: *Neferourê*.

- Enfin, une des dernières filles de Ramsès devenue Grande Epouse Royale pourrait avoir été *Henout-mì-Rê* laquelle, suivant la récente étude d'H. Sourouzian, ne fut pas la soeur, mais une fille de Ramsès. Elle mourut tard dans le règne, ou même peut-être après le décès de son père, ce qui expliquerait la pauvreté du fragment d'un des ses canopes qui paraît provenir d'un mobilier usurpé et réutilisé pour panser les blessures du pillage.

- Les Dames de la Cour mises officiellement en rapport avec la mère royale *Touy* sont, avant tout: *Nofretari* en Abou Simbel et au Ramesseum, *Meryt-Amon* qui encadre le colosse nord de Ramsès avec *Touy*, toujours en Abou Simbel et enfin, la petite *Henout-mì-Rê* sur la statue du Vatican: aurait-elle été la fille de *Meryt-Amon*?

- Enfin, si l'on a pu remarquer l'importance occupée par la mère royale et le culte qui lui fut réservé, en revanche, il semble assuré, maintenant que le roi, tout en témoignant à sa - ou à ses - soeur(s) l'attention qu'il convenait, ne leur réserva pas un rôle à jouer en tant que telles dans l'imposant rituel confié, auprès de lui, aux grandes Dames royales du palais.

1 K.A. KITCHEN, *Pharaoh Triumphant*, Warminster, 1982, p. 252, cite le nombre approximatif de quatre-vingt-dix. Kitchen (*JEA* 1975, p. 27) réfutait déjà le nombre de 111 fils et de 59 filles avancé par certains auteurs. Il se réfère aux trente fils attestés à Ouadi es-Seboua et estime que le roi dut probablement revendiquer 45 à 46 fils à côté de 40 filles: au total 85 à 86 enfants. Il rappelle néanmoins que l'*ostracon* n°666 du Louvre faisait allusion à 15 princesses supplémentaires. Ce document pourrait élever le nombre des enfants du roi à 101.

2 Voir la grande planche, aux multiples plis, donnant toute l'illustration du "*Bulletin*", dans le temple du roi en Abou Simbel. Ch. DESROCHES NOBLECOURT, J. CERNY, S. DONADONI, *La bataille de Kadesh*, C.E.D.A.E., Le Caire, 1971, pl. IV.

3 Le culte jumelé de Ramsès, de Rê et aussi d'Amon est extrêmement perceptible en Abou Simbel. Le temple est évidemment un sanctuaire "mémorial" et ne paraît pas avoir jamais été affecté aux cérémonies de la fête *Sed*, comme on a pu le supposer. Voir ce que je propose dans la préface de: *Le Grand Temple d'Abou Simbel*, I, 1, Architecture, C.E.D.A.E., Le Caire, 1984, p. VI-VII.

4 Ch.DESROCHES NOBLECOURT et Ch.KUENTZ, *Le Petit Temple d'Abou Simbel*, mémoires du C.E.D.A.E. I, Le Caire, 1968, p. 229, n. 566.

5 Pour l'architecture du Grand Temple, consulter H. EL-ACHIRIE et J. JACQUET, *Le Grand Temple d'Abou Simbel*, I, 1, Architecture, C.E.D.A.E., Collection Scientifique, Le Caire, 1984.

6 Ce que L.CHRISTOPHE avait déjà naturellement bien noté, in *B.I.E.* XXVIII, p. 115.

7 Ce prince, dont le nom est transformé en *Sethherkhopshef* dans la correspondance avec les Hittites, demeurera l'héritier jusqu'aux environs de l'an XXXIX.

8 Au moment du troisième jubilé de son père, à Assouan, le prince ne portait pas encore le titre de *semsou* (héritier du trône). Il en fut investi à la mort d'*Amonherkhopshef*. On sait par le papyrus de Leiden I, 350 qu'il vivait encore en l'an II du règne de son père. Ceci contredit l'étude de J. Janssen, lequel avait proposé l'an XXVI comme dernière année de la vie du prince (J. JANSSEN, *La reine Nofretari et la succession de Ramsès II par Merenptah, CdE* XXXVIII, 1963, p. 35). De même L. Christophe supposait que le prince Ramsès serait mort avant le trépas du troisième Apis de la XIXe dynastie et enseveli en l'an XXVI (*BIE* XXVIII, p. 126).

9 *Baket-Mout* apparaît, sur la liste d'Abou Simbel, comme la deuxième fille de *Nofretari* et sur la liste du temple de Derr, comme la troisième fille du roi après (*Bentanta* et *Meryt-Amon*) (le début de la liste est détérioré).

10 Ch.DESROCHES NOBLECOURT et Ch.KUENTZ, *op. cit.*, p. 1-25.

11 Les titres de *Sat-Rê* influencés par ceux des Dames de la cour des rois Aménophis III et IV, furent étudiés par G.MASPERO, *Etudes de mythologie et d'archéologie*, IV, p. 327-332.

12 Tombe n°38 de la Vallée des Reines, dont la publication par I. Franco et M. El-Fekhry est en préparation.

13 L.CHRISTOPHE, *BIE* XXXVIII, fasc. 2, 1956/57 (1965) p. 109 et L. HABACHI, *La reine Touy, femme de Séthi Ier et ses proches parents inconnus*, RdE 21, 1969, p. 27-47.

Ch. DESROCHES NOBLECOURT, Revue du Louvre, 1974, n°1, p. 43-46.

14 Ch. DESROCHES NOBLECOURT, *Touy, mère de Ramsès II, la reine Tanedjmy et les reliques de l'expérience amarnienne*, L'égyptologie en 1979, axes prioritaires de recherches, tome 2, C.N.R.S., Paris, 1982, p. 239 et fig. 65.

15 Les proportions des ailes, assez courtes, sont très comparables à celles des ailes qui recouvrent la tête de canope découverte dans sa tombe. Cf. catalogue de l'exposition *Ramsès le Grand* à Paris, Grand Palais, 1976, objet n°V, p. 29-31.

16 Suivant la théogamie classique que Ramsès avait fait naturellement représenter à son profit sur les reliefs usurpés et réutilisés à Medinet Habou (L. HABACHI, *MDAIK* 8, 1975, p. 206).

17 L. HABACHI, *Features of the Deification of Ramesses II, ADAIK*, Band 5, Gluckstadt, 1969, pl. III (photo C.E.D.A.E.) et fig. 7 p. 9. De même, sur le mur nord-ouest de la même salle-cour, il s'est introduit entre Ptah et Sekhmet, sous l'aspect de Nefertoum.

18 Ch. DESROCHES NOBLECOURT, *Les temples de la Nubie submergée et la rive gauche de Thèbes*, Courrier du C.N.R.S. no. 9, juillet 1973, p. 32 et catalogue de l'exposition *Ramsès le Grand* à Paris, Grand Palais, 1976.

19 Ch. DESROCHES NOBLECOURT, *Touy, mère de Ramsès II*...,C.N.R.S., 1982, p. 243 et fig. 64.

20 H. CARTER, *ASAE* 2, 1901, p. 194 et Ch. LEBLANC, *Le tombeau d'Osymandias et la statuaire du Ramesseum*, Mélanges G.E. Mokhtar, *BdE* XCVII, I.F.A.O., Le Caire, 1985, p. 78-79.

21 Ainsi la grande statue de Touy, assise, du musée du Caire qui a figuré parmi les chefs-d'oeuvre de l'exposition *Ramsès le Grand* à Paris (cf. catalogue, 1976, p. 24-27).

22 Au coeur de la Vallée, face à l'Est religieux du thalweg.

23 Ch. DESROCHES NOBLECOURT, *Touy, mère de Ramsès II*..., C.N.R.S., 1982, tome 2, fig. 58.

24 Ch. DESROCHES NOBLECOURT, Courrier du C.N.R.S. n°9, juillet 1973.

25 GABALLA et KITCHEN, *Ramesside Varia, CdE* XLIII, n°86, juillet 1968, pp. 251-270 et catalogue de l'exposition *Ramsès le Grand*, 1976, pp. 20-23, (R. SCHUMANN-ANTELME et Ch. LEBLANC).

26 Ceci se passait autour et un peu avant l'an XXII comme le prouve une date portée sur une jarre de vin trouvée dans la tombe de la reine. Cf. Ch. DESROCHES NOBLECOURT, Courrier du C.N.R.S. n°9, juillet 1973, p. 32 et E. EDEL, *Zwei Originalbriefe der Königsmutter Tuja Keilschrift, SAK* 1, 1974, p. 105-146 et spécialement p. 130. Voir la publication de la jarre dans le catalogue de l'exposition *Ramsès le Grand* à Paris, 1976, n°LII, p. 264 et surtout 265, reprise par K.A. KITCHEN, *Pharaoh Triumphant*, 1982, p. 80.

27 H. SOUROUZIAN, *Henout-mì-Rê, fille de Ramsès II et Grande Epouse du roi, ASAE* LXIX, Le Caire, 1983, pp. 365-371 et pl. I.

28 K.A. KITCHEN, *Pharaoh Triumphant*, p. 98: "chanteuse d'Amon... attachée au culte d'Amon dans la résidence du Delta", elle avait également des liens avec Héliopolis et Memphis.

29 G.T. MARTIN, *The Tomb of Tia and Tia*, Preliminary Report, 1983, *JEA* 70, 1984, p. 5-12.

30 Sur une petite stèle en schiste conservée au Louvre (n°7717).

31 Ch. DESROCHES NOBLECOURT, catalogue de l'exposition *Ramsès le Grand*, à Paris, 1976, p. XXI-XXX et D. HARLE, p. 208-221, K.A. KITCHEN, *Pharaoh Triumphant*, p. 98-sqq.

32 G. THAUSING et H. GOEDICKE, *Nofretari, eine Dokumentation der Wandgemalde ihres Grabes*, Graz, 1971 (les couleurs ne sont pas toutes fidèles et les fonds blancs éclatants ne sont pas respectés); comparer avec K. LANGE, M. HIRMER, Ch. DESROCHES NOBLECOURT, *L'Egypte*, Flammarion, Paris, 1968 (pl. LV. LVI, LVII, LVIII).

33 Les derniers auteurs en date qui ont émis cette supposition sont L. CHRISTOPHE, *BIE* 38, 1965, p. 118-sqq puis K.A. KITCHEN, *Pharaoh Triumphant*, p. 98.

34 Pour le prince héritier, désigné *s3 smsw*, en comparaison avec l'aîné des fils *s3 tpy*, cf. K. SETHE, *Untersuchungen* I, 59, note 1. On sait qu'au moment où se préparait le traité de paix avec les Hittites, ce prince *Amonherkhopshef* était appelé dans la correspondance échangée: *Seth-her-khopshef*.

35 Voir plus bas: le rôle de la reine du vivant du roi. Déjà la reine Tiyi apparaît sous la forme humaine de Sothis debout aux côtés d'Aménophis III et de la déesse Hathor, tous deux assis durant les cérémonies de la fête *Sed* figurée aux murs du tombeau de Kherouef, Ch. NIMS... WENTE et *alii, Theban Tomb 192, OIP* 102, Chicago, pl. 24, 25, 26.

36 Voir, à ce propos, le jeu de mots que j'indique dans mon étude sur les quatre objets en calcite du Louvre, parmi lesquels figure la petite chienne Sothis: Ch. DESROCHES NOBLECOURT, *Quatre objets proto-dynastiques provenant d'un trésor funéraire*, Revue du Louvre et des Musées de France, n°2, 1979, p. 114-115.

37 Cette stèle fut gravée avant l'an XXV, date à laquelle Hekanakht fut remplacé par le vizir Pasar. Elle porte le n°46 des fac-similés du C.E.D.A.E. (J. CERNY) et figure sur l'important relevé photogrammétrique montrant les positions respectives des deux temples, des stèles et des graffiti rupestres que j'ai fait établir par l'Institut Géographique National de Paris: Ch. DESROCHES NOBLECOURT et Ch. KUENTZ, *Le Petit Temple d'Abou Simbel*, Mémoire du C.E.D.A.E. II, pl. CXXVII (c'est la sixième stèle à gauche du Grand Temple). Les premières reproductions sont de J. F. CHAMPOLLION, *Monuments de l'Egypte et de la Nubie*, pl. 4, n°1 et de R. LEPSIUS, *Denkmäler* III, 195 d.

38 Le volumineux mamelon dans lequel le Grand Temple a été creusé portait, rappelons-le, le nom de *Meha* (l'Horus de Meha était un des quatre Horus de Nubie, ceux de Bouhen, Meha, Miam et Baki). Le plus petit, celui du nord, ayant reçu dans ses flancs le Petit Temple de la reine, était le rocher d'*Ibchek*.

39 On sait que la reine occupa une certaine place dans la vie politique du royaume et qu'au moment des échanges de correspondance avec la famille royale hittite, *Nofretari (Naptera)* écrivit au moins deux lettres à Pudukhipa, l'épouse du roi, cf. E. EDEL, *SAK* 1 (KBOI.29 et 74 e). Une correspondance parallèle a été retrouvée: celle du fils aîné de *Nofretari* et celle du vizir Pasar: E. EDEL, *Der Brief des aegyptischen*

Wesirs Pasijara an den Hethiter Konig Hattusili und verwandte Keilschriftbrief, Gottingen, 1978.

40 J. JANSSEN, *Nofretari et la succession de Ramesès II par Merneptah*, CdE XXXVIII, 1963, p. 30-sqq. La raison d'une rivalité entre les fils de *Nofretari* et ceux d'Isis-Nofret ne peut pas davantage s'expliquer par les soi-disant martelages du nom de la reine.

41 Cette traduction fut proposée par E. du ROUGE, *Mémoires sur l'origine égyptienne de l'alphabet phénicien*, Paris, 1874, p. 33, puis reprise par W. GROFF, *La fille de Pharaon*, BIE 3è série, n°7, 1896, Le Caire, 1877, p. 65.

42 A propos de ce nom théophore cananéen, il faut rappeler que le vingt-troisième fils de Ramsès, *Sa-Monthou* épousa Iryeth, la fille de *Ben-Anath* ("Fils d'Anat"), un capitaine de marine syrien (K.A. KITCHEN, *Pharaoh Triumphant*, p. 111).

43 Ainsi dans le temple de Louxor où *Nofretari*, près des statues qui subsistent, est figurée au moins deux fois, de même que *Bentanta*. On ne trouve aucune allusion à *Isis-Nofret*.

44 Dans la correspondance avec les Hittites dès l'an XXI, *Isis-Nofret* semble complètement écartée. Ceci ne prouverait *en aucune manière* que la rein était morte, ainsi que le supposait E. EDEL, *SAK* 1, p. 130.

45 Pour la stèle d'Assouan: *LD* III, 175 h et celle du Gebel Silsileh, *LD* III, 174 e, voir aussi, I. ROSELLINI, *Monumenti dell'Egitto e della Nubia*, III, pl. XXI. *L'étude des dates de ces stèles est faite par F. GOMMA, Chaemwaset, Sohn Ramses II. und Hohenpriester von Memphis*, Äg. Abh. 1973, Wiesbaden (Gebel Silsileh, p. 120, fig. 29 et Assouan p. 131, fig. 31 a).

46 Ch. DESROCHES NOBLECOURT et Ch. KUENTZ, *Le Petit Temple d'Abou Simbel*, p. 109 à 124. Les deux temples d'Abou Simbel étaient en étroite corrélation, leurs axes se croisant dans le Nil.

47 P. BARGUET, *Les stèles du Nil au Gebel Silsileh*, BIFAO L, 1952, p. 49-69. A propos des festivités des fêtes *Sed* et des promesses de Hauts Nils, H. BRUNNER, *ZÄS* 93, 1966, p. 7-79, repris par K.A. KITCHEN, *JEA* 61, 1975, p. 71. Voir aussi Ch. DESROCHES NOBLECOURT et Ch. KUENTZ, *Le Petit Temple d'Abou Simbel*, p. 112-113.

48 L. Christophe en effet pensait que la reine avait dû mourir beaucoup plus tôt, estimant que seuls devaient avoir figuré sur la façade d'Abou Simbel, les membres *vivants* de la famille de Ramsès II. Il situait le décès d'*Isis-Nofret* avant l'an XXII (*BIE* 1965, p. 118). Pour sa part K.A. Kitchen (*Pharaoh Triumphant*, p. 100) estimait qu'elle dût mourir autour de l'an XXXVII pour laisser la place à sa fille aînée *Bentanta*. On verra qu'il n'en était rien, cette dernière étant investie de cette fonction dès au moins l'an XXII.

49 J. CERNY, *A community of workmen at Thebes in the Ramesside Period*, BdE L, I.F.A.O., Le Caire, 1973, p. 82 a 3 et 4.

50 Abdel Kader MUHAMMAD, *Preliminary Report on the Excavations carried out in the Temple of Luxor*, ASAE 1968, p. 227-279, pl. LXXI-LXXII-LXXIV.

51 *Isis-Nofret II* figure en Abou Simbel et dans les listes des princesses de Derr, de Louxor et d'Abydos.

52 J. JANSSEN, *Nine Letters from the time of Ramses II*, OMRO 41, p. 32.

53 J.F. CHAMPOLLION, *Monuments* II, CXIV et *LD* III, 186.

54 Ch. KUENTZ, *La face sud du massif est du pylône de Ramsès II à Louxor*, C.E.D.A.E., Collection Scientifique, Le Caire, 1971, pl. XXIV.

55 Son image en Epouse Royale, à l'intérieur de la salle du Grand Temple d'Abou Simbel, aurait pu être sculptée avant l'an XX, ce qui fixerait son intronisation avant celle de *Meryt-Amon* qui aurait aussi été choisie pour cette fonction avant l'an XXV.

56 En dépit de la détérioration par le feu qu'elle subit dans chacune de ses salles. La publication de cette tombe est préparée par Ch. DESROCHES NOBLECOURT et R. SCHUMANN-ANTELME.

57 Peut-être même depuis l'Ancien Empire: K. SETHE, *ZÄS*, 1912, p. 160. Ch. DESROCHES NOBLECOURT, *La femme au temps des Pharaons*, Stock, Paris, 1986 (l'inceste royal entre père et fille), p. 45-47, puis p. 83 pour les filles de Ramsès III. Pour la parure de ces filles favorites: Ch. DESROCHES NOBLECOURT, *Interprétation et datation d'une scène gravée...provenant du palais d'Ugarit*, Ugaritica III, 1956, Paris, p. 197-205. Voir aussi B. VAN DE WALLE, *La princesse Isis, fille et épouse d'Aménophis III*, CdE XLIII, 86, 1968, p. 36-54 et J.R. HARRIS, *CdE* XLIX, 97, 1974, p. 30, n. 6.

58 C'est la statue dont la tête est conservée. Cf. Abdeld Kader MUHAMMAD, *ASAE* 60, 1968, p. 261, 276-7 et pl. LXXII, LXXIV et *The Luxor Museum of Ancient Art*, catalogue, Le Caire 1979, n°129.

59 Ainsi que l'a démontré R. SCHUMANN ANTELME dans sa communication au Congrès des Egyptologues à Munich en 1985: *Bentanta, fille et épouse de Ramsès*.

60 H. SOUROUZIAN, *ASAE* LXIX, Le Caire, 1983, p. 371 et n. 4.

61 Cl. LALOUETTE (*L'Empire des Ramsès*, Fayard, Paris, 1986) reconnaît à Mineptah deux épouses, *Isis-Nofret* et *Bentanta*, mais sans aucun commentaire.

62 Exposées sur le côté gauche du jardin, devant le tombeau de Mariette Pacha (J.E. 45.975) et remontant primitivement au Moyen Empire.

63 Voir Y. AL-MASRI, *Preliminary Report on the Excavations in Akhmim by the Egyptian Antiquities Organization*, ASAE LXIX, 1983, p. 7-11.

64 Voir entre autres le catalogue de l'exposition *Ramsès le Grand* à Paris, 1976, pp. 72-75 (photo inversée). La meilleure photographie est publiée par K. LANGE, M. HIRMER et alii, *L'Egypte*, Flammarion, Paris, 1968, pl. LIV.

65 San parler naturellement de sa présence dans le défilés-listes des princesses.

66 *RT* IX, 1887, p. 13 et L. CHRISTOPH, *BIE* XXXVIII, 1956, p. 120, n°2.

67 Voir plus loin au chapitre *Maathorneferourê* et P. MONTET, Kêmi V, 1935, pl. VII et p. 10. Le fouilleur de Tanis parle de "légende de la princesse qui fut effacée pour graver une inscription nouvelle parvenue en bon état".

68 M. DEWACHTER, Archeologia n°53, Décembre 1972, p. 18-24, Ch. LEBLANC, *ASAE* 1983, p. 40-82, pl. IV à VI et Ch. LEBLANC et F. HASSANEIN, *La Vallée des Reines*, Archeologia n°205, Septembre 1985, p. 29-sqq.

69 Une peinture de sa tombe, relevée du temps de Champollion, nous a conservé son image coiffée de la couronne de fleurs dressées, insigne de grandes favorites royales, voir Ch. DESROCHES NOBLECOURT, Ugaritica III (1956), p. 203, fig. 171. Pour cette couronne de fleurs des déesses, ornement qui apparaît souvent dans la parure des filles-épouses royales, voir ensuite, GRIST, *The identity of Queen Tiyi, JEA* 71, 1985, p. 179.

70 Pourtant cette dernière, figurant dans les défilés-listes des princesses à Derr et en Abydos, n'est pas signalée comme déja défunte (tombe n° 73, cf. Ch. LEBLANCE et F. HASSANEIN, Archaeologia n° 205, p. 29-30).

71 G. LEFEBVRE, *Romans et contes égyptiens de l'époque pharaonique,* Maisonneuve, Paris, 1949, p. 222 et K.A. KITCHEN, *Pharaoh Triumphant*, p. 229.

72 Si notre hypothèse concernant *Isis-Nofret I* ne peut être retenue.

73 K.A. KITCHEN, *Pharaoh Triumphant*, p. 83-89, 92-95.

74 Des copies de la fameuse Stèle du Mariage d'Abou Simbel figurent aussi, comme on le sait, à Elephantine, à Karnak et à Aksha; à ce propos cf. L. CHRISTOPHE, *BIE* XXVIII, p. 119. Référence est faite à la princesse hittite deux fois en Abou Simbel: sur la Stèle du Mariage et une autre fois (une allusion, sans que son nom soit mentionné) sur la stèle dite "Bénédiction de Ptah", dans la salle-cour du Grand Temple.

75 Il existe aussi une autre statue à laquelle nous avons fait allusion en étudiant *Meryt-Amon* et qui porte aussi, entre les jambes du roi, l'effigie de cette fille-épouse. Les vestiges de l'image de *Maathorneferourê* de la premiere statue sont reproduits en couleurs dans le récent livre de G. GOYON, *La découverte des trésors de Tanis*, Persea, Paris, 1987, p. 48 P. MONTET, Kêmi V, pl. VIII (Photo en noir et blanc).

76 Par sa lettre du 26 IX 1986 ce dont je le remercie vivement.

77 Cf. H. GAUTHIER, *Livre des Rois* III, 1, p. III. Ce nom de *Neferourê*, considéré comme abrégé, correspond, peut-être, à la réelle appelation de sa mère que l'on aurait fait précéder, dans son cartouche, de la formule abrégée "Celle qui voit Hours (et Seth)" bien connue pour les reines dès l'Ancien Empire. Cf. Ch. DESROCHES NOBLECOURT, *Hommage d'un poète à la princesse lointaine*, Kêmi II, 1952, principalement p. 43-44.

78 BOTTI-ROMANELLI, Scul. Mus. Greg. Eg. n°28.

79 Elle figure peut-être dans le défilé des princesse d'Abydos comme le suggère H. SOUROUZIAN (*ASAE* LXIX, Le Caire, 1983, p. 371). K.A. KITCHEN (*op.cit.* p. 257) la considérait encore comme soeur du roi.

80 Cette tombe (caveau n°75 de la Vallée des Reines, qui doit être publié par Ch. LEBLANC) fut sans doute pillée au moins à deux reprises dans l'antiquité. Le sarcophage fut retrouvé à Médinet Habou dans la tombe du prêtre Horsies de la XXIIè dynastie. Il porte au musée du Caire le numéro JE 60.137. Elle y est citée comme "*fille du roi et Epouse du roi*".

81 J. CERNY, *JEA* 15, 1929, p. 246.

82 Ch. DESROCHES NOBLECOURT et Ch. KUENTZ, *Le Petit Temple d'Abou Simbel*, p. 82.

83 Ch. DESROCHES NOBLECOURT et Ch. KUENTZ, op.cit. p. 114-119 et Ch. DESROCHES NOBLECOURT, *La femme au temps des Pharaons*, Stock, Paris 1986, p. 69-73.

84 Ch. DESROCHES NOBLECOURT et Ch. KUENTZ, op.cit. p. 1-2. Champollion l'appelait le "*Spéos d'Hathor*". Aucune inscription n'indique que ce temple soit dédié à la déesse Hathor, cependant, l'ambiance du décor évoque bien la déesse (op. 110-111).

85 On peut clairement constater une impossible confusion en contemplant les deux déesses Hathor et Sothis figurées près d'Aménophis dans la tombe de Kherouef, cf. note 36; Ch. NIMS, WENTE et *alii, Theban Tomb 192, OIP* 102, Chicago, pl. 24 à 26.

86 On est assuré que les objets rituels contenus dans ce trésor devaient faire partie du bagage traditionnel que les pharaons possédaient dans leurs caveaux: les vestiges retrouvés dans les autres tombes royales pillées en sont la preuve.

87 J'avais présenté le schéma général des rites évoqués sur les flancs de la chapelle dorée de Toutankhamon, dans mon *Toutankhamon, vie et mort d'un pharaon*, Hachette, paris, 1963, chapitre 8 et principalement p. 269-270. Cette interprétation a été suivie par W. WESTENDORFF, *Bemerkungen zur "Kammer der Wiedergeburt"*, in *Tutanchamunsgrab, ZÄS* 84, Berlin, 1967. J'ai repris le sujet dans *La femme au temps des Pharaons* Stock, paris, 1986, p. 73-75. Pour les seigneurs, des scènes d'inspiration civile servaient à atteindre le même but, cf. Ch. DESROCHES NOBLECOURT, M. NELSON, F. HASSANEIN, et *alii, Reconstitution du caveau de Sennefer dit "Tombe aux Vignes"*, Fondation Kodak-Pathé, Paris, 1985, p. 7-9 et p. 51 à 77: les rites de régénérescence. J'ai repris le commentaire des vignettes du naos plaqué d'or dans le catalogue de la tombe de Sennefer exposée à partir du 2 août 1987.

88 Ce désincarné est redevenu le "foetus" du soleil dans le sein de la Déesse qui lui donnera la vie perpétuelle.

89 L'image de renaissance de Pharaon est traduite avec des éléments analogues sur le dossier du "pseudo trône" de Toutankhamon. On peut y admirer la reine, en Sothis, appliquant les derniers onguents sur une épaule du jeune roi encore assis, mais déjà coiffé de la couronne de gloire *hmhm*, évoquant la phosphorescence du soleil levant. Cf. Ch. DESROCHES NOBLECOURT, *Isis-Sothis, le chien, la vigne et la tradition millénaire, in MIFAO* CLV, 1980 (Livre du Centenaire), p. 19-20 et fig. 14.

90 Ch. DESROCHES NOBLECOURT, *La Vallée des Reines retrouvera-t-elle sa splendeur passée?*, Archeologia n°209, Janvier 1986, principalement p. 34-36.

91 Publication en préparation par Ch. DESROCHES NOBLECOURT et R. SCHUMANN-ANTELME.

92 Caveau n°33, cf. Ch. DESROCHES NOBLECOURT, *Touy, mère de Ramsès II, la reine Taned jmy et les reliques de l'expérience amarnienne*, L'égyptologie en 1979..., tome 2, C.N.R.S. Paris, 1982, p. 226-231 et fig. 56-57. Voir aussi Ch. LEBLANC, Archeologia n°205, p. 27-28.

93 Telle la tombe n°58; Ch. LEBLANC, *op. cit.* p. 28-29.

94 Une opinion contraire avait été émise par W. HELCK *Amarna Probleme, CdE* XLIV, 89, 1969, p. 200-sqq, suivi par F. GOMAA et H. SOUROUZIAN, *ASAE* 1983, p. 370, notes 1 et

95 Ainsi en savons-nous plus sur son origine que pour *Isis-Nofret I* et *Nofretari I*!

Figure 1

Les deux temples d'Abou-Simbel en 1956. (Avant leur exhaussement)

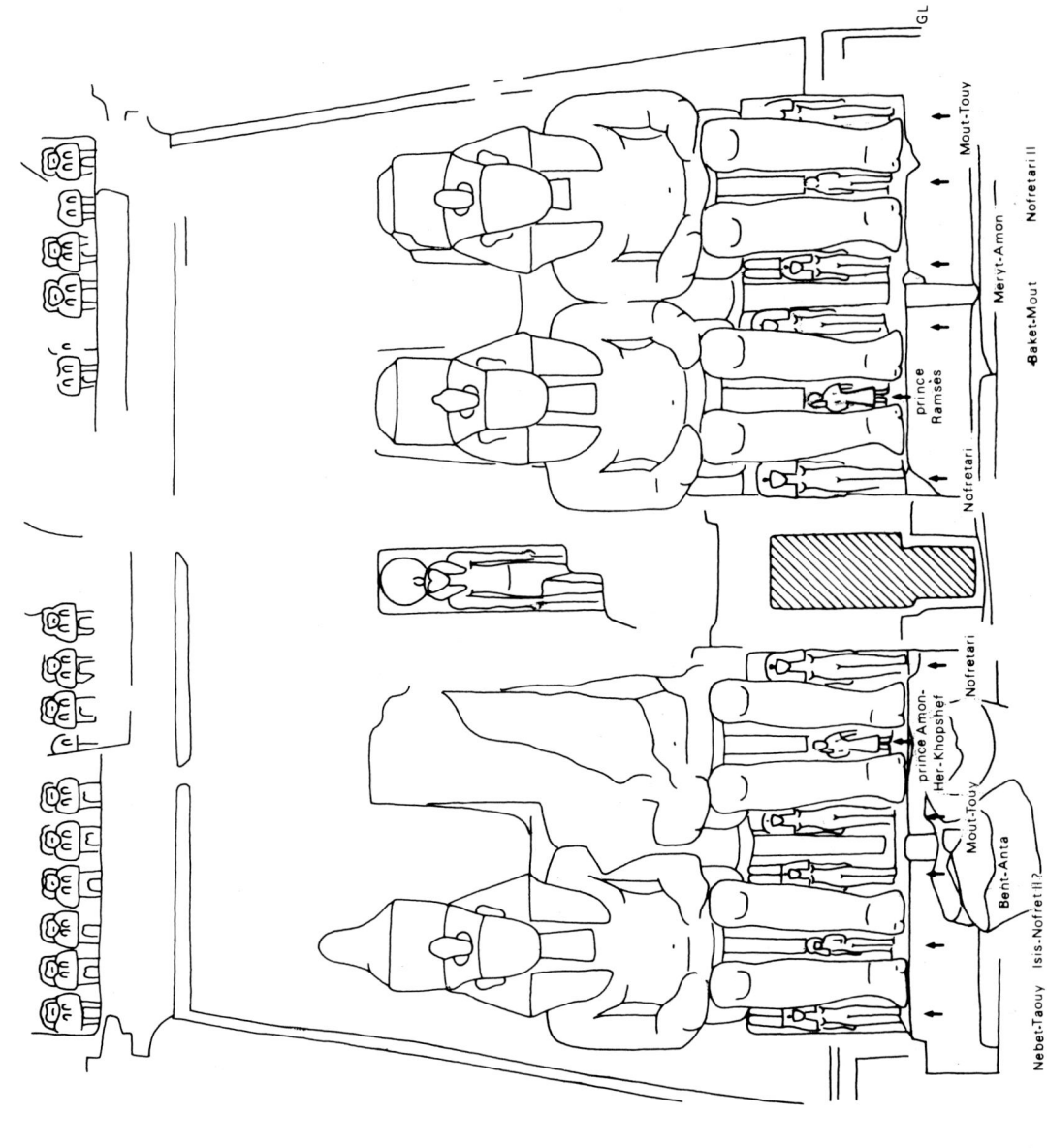

Figure 2

Grand Temple d'Abou Simbel.
Implantation des personnages
royaux sur la façade (dessin de Guy
Lecuyot)

Figure 3

Grand Temple d'Abou Simbel, La reine Nofretari contre le premier colosse nord, à droite de la porte d'entrée.

Figure 4

Abou Simbel, Grand Temple, Mout-Touy, Mère Royale, Epouse (à gauche du second colosse sud)

151

Figure 5

Abou Simbel
Façade du petit Temple.

Figure 6

Abou Simbel, Grand Temple, Salle-cour.
Image du roi divinisé sous la forme de
Khonsou introduit entre Amon et Mout.

152

Figure 7

Ramesseum, salle hypostyle. Nofretari accompagnée la reine mère Touy, jouant des sistres

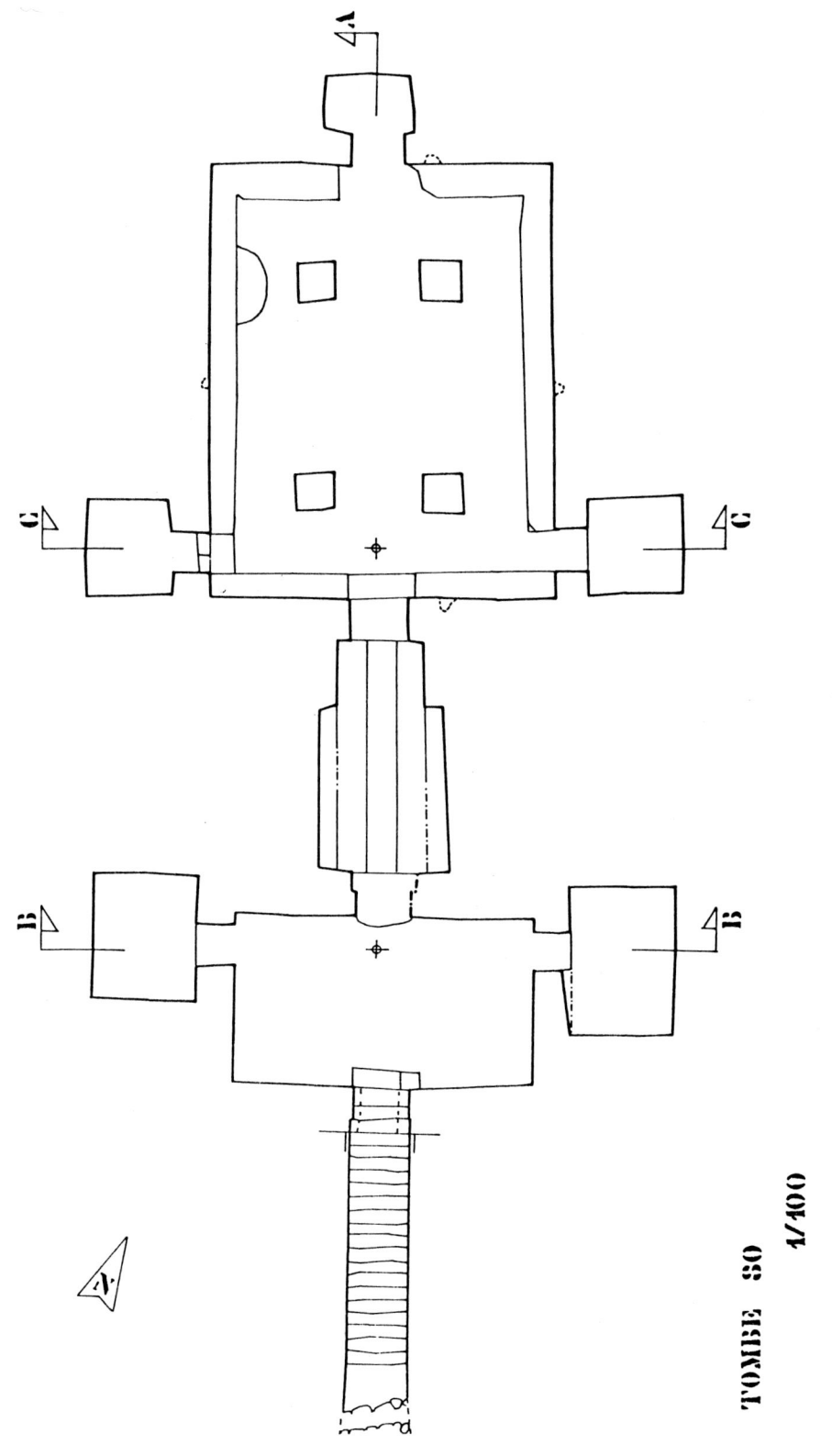

TOMBE 80

1/400

Figure 8

Vallée des Reines, plan de la Tombe de la reine-Mère Touy (n°80)

Figure 9

Abou Simbel. Petit Temple de la
reine Nofretari, figurée vivante, (sa
coiffure est ornée des deux hautes
cornes de Sothis).

Figure 10

Vallée de Reines, Tombe de Nofretari
(m° 66).
Figuration de la reine morte guidée par
Horus. (Sa coiffure est démunie des
hautes cornes de Sothis).

Figure 11

Abou Simbel, extérieur du Grand Temple.
détail de la stèle rupestre de Hekanakht.
Au registre supérieur: Ramsès suivi de l'Epouse Royale Meryt-Amon (coiffée des plumes, sans les cornes).

Figure 12

Abou Simbel...Détail de la stèle de Hekanakht.
Au registre inférieur, la reine Nofretari, coiffée des hautes plumes et cornes.

157

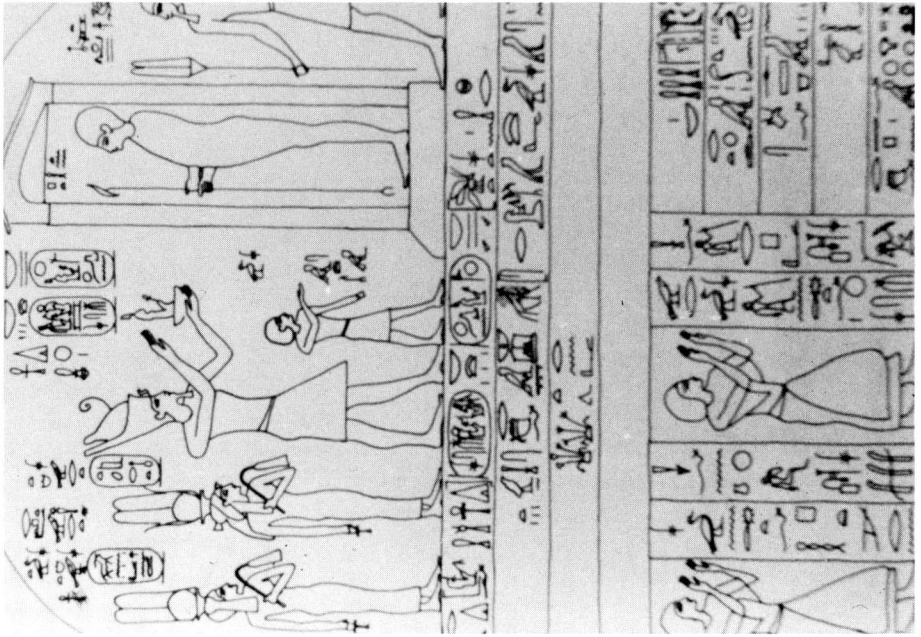

Figure 14

Gebel Silsileh, stèle rupestre. Ramsès devant Ptah. en compagnie de Khaemonaset, (officiant), d'Isis Nofret, de Bentanta, du prince Ramsès et de Merenptah.

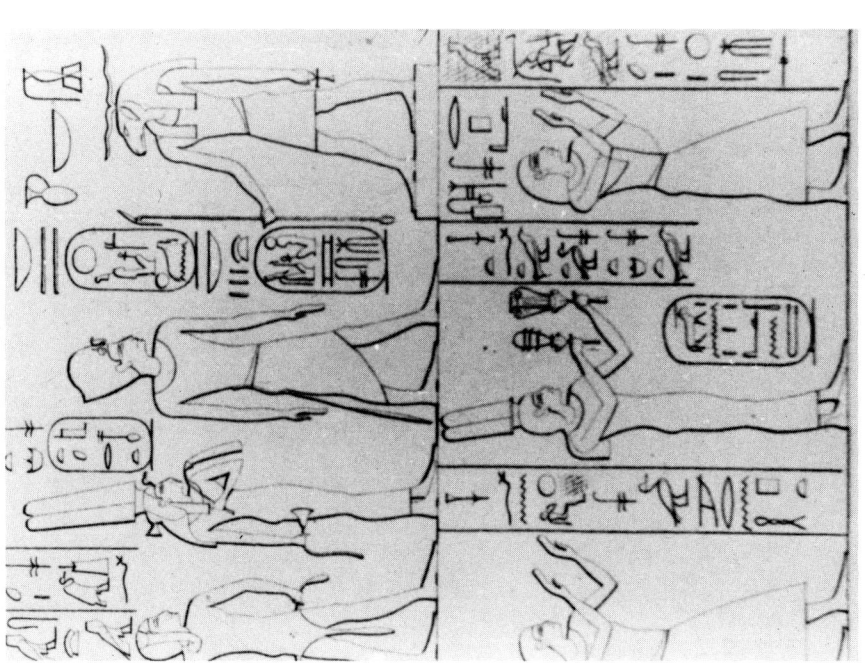

Figure 13

Assouan, Stèle rupestre. Ramsés devant Khnoum, en compagnie d'Isis Nofret, de Khaemonaset, de Bentanta, du prince Ramsès et du jeune Mineptah.

Figure 15

Temple de Ouadi es Seboua la façade.
Le colosse de Ramsès flanqué de le statue de la Grande
Epouse Royale, Bentanta.

Figure 16

Valleé de reine, Tombe de Bentanta (n° 71)
La Grand Epouse Royale, Bentanta, accompagnee de sa
fille, issue de Ramsès.

Figure 17

Akhmim. Découverte de la statue colossale Meryt-Amon, tombée au sol.

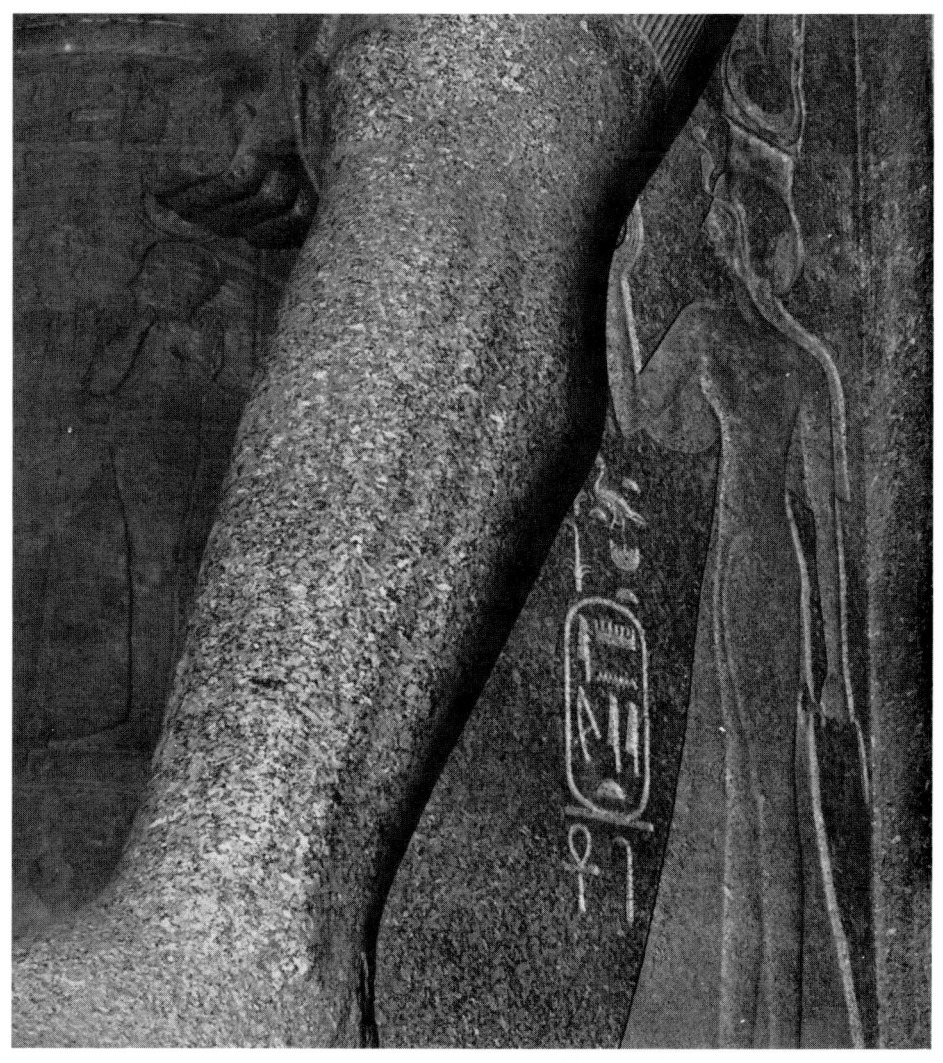

Figure 18

Temple de Louxor. La Fille-Grande Epouse Royale, Meryt-Amon, (contre le colosse de Ramsès, devant la tour occidentale du pylône).

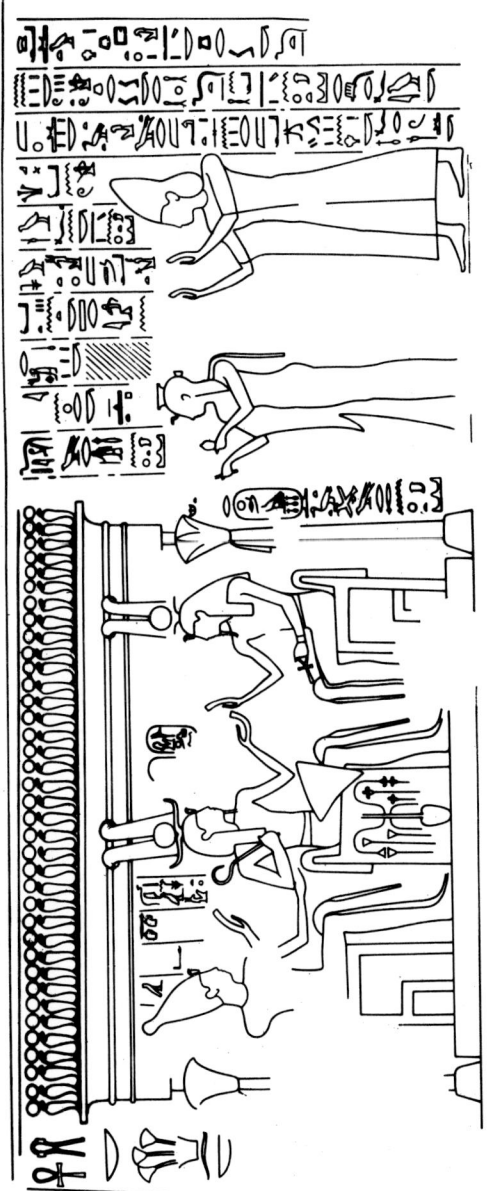

Figure 19

Abou Simbel, Grand Temple. (Sommet de la Stèle du mariage)
Maat Hor Neferou Rê, escortée de son père, se présente devant Ramsès, qui apparaît comme une émanation du divin.

162

Figure 20

Tanis. Contre la jambe d'un colosse de Ramsès, vestiges
de l'image de "la Grande Epouse Royale, Maat Hor
Neferou Rê fille du Grande Kheta."

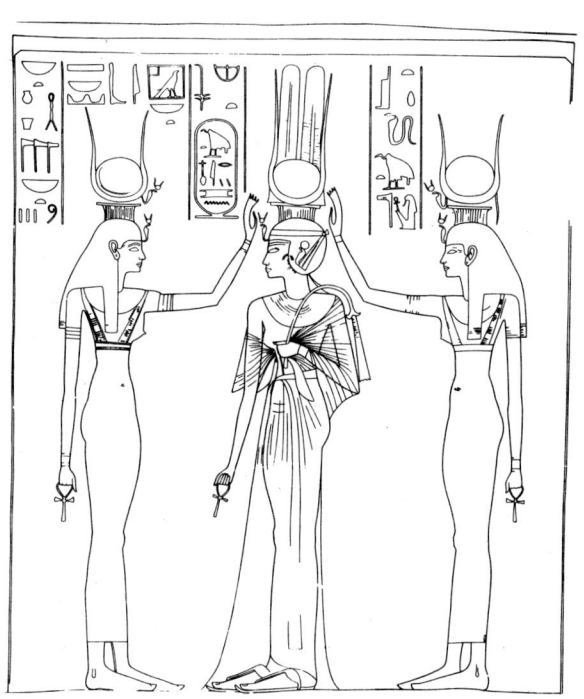

Figure 21

Abou Simbel, Petit Temple. Isis et Hathor
transforment Nofretari en une vivante déesse Sothis.

163

Figure 22

Naos doré de Toutankhamon
(Musée du Caire)

a	b
d	c

a) présentation de la "Grande de Magie" à
Toutankhamon
b–c) Ankhesenamon "revitalise" le défunt par des
fleurs et des amulettes
d) le roi transmet la semence à la divine épouse

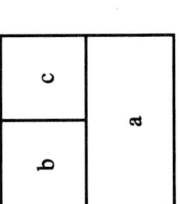

Figure 23

Naos doré de Toutankhamon
(Musée du Caire)

b	c
a	

a) dans le marécage primordial la divine veuve assiste
   son epoux dans sa lutte contre les démons
b) le roi est victorieux des épreuves
c) le défunt va sortir alors des ténèbres assisté par
   Ankhesenamon.

Figure 24

Les deux Temples d'Abou Simbel. Vus du nord, après
leur exhaussement.

166

MIRROR OF THE COSMOS: THE PALACE OF MERENPTAH

David O'Connor

University Museum, University of Pennsylvania

I

Introduction

The Royal Cities

Neither the palace of Pharaoh Merenptah nor other palaces of the New Kingdom can be discussed in isolation from their contexts, the royal cities of the period. By the New Kingdom, any major city was considered to be the domain of its particular god or goddess. The city's main temple, with its high pylons or gate towers, high roofline, and massive, often towered, enclosure wall, visually dominated the town-scape and, beyond this, the flat alluvial land surrounding the city. On a national scale, the result was that - in Assman's striking image - the Egyptian landscape was characterized by a series of castle-like temples expressing a kind of theocratic feudalism (1984a, 36). In these circumstances, every city naturally derived cosmological significance from the temple or temples which dominated it (ibid., 25-36); but this was true in a heightened sense of the royal cities, for they had the unique attributes of being the national centers of pharaonic government and of housing the chief royal residences. The royal cities in question included Thebes in southern Egypt, burial place of virtually all New Kingdom pharaohs and cult center of the imperial god Amun-Ra, under whose tutelage an empire extending into both western Asia and northeast Africa had been won and held. In the north, at the apex of the Delta, was Memphis, home of the god Ptah, of whom, according to a particularly sophisticated theory, other primary gods could be considered merely the members or agents (Assman 1984b, 680; with reference). Closely linked to Memphis was nearby Heliopolis, not strictly a royal city in the sense used here but cult-center of Ra the sun-god, with whom the pharaohs for millennia had a unique relationship (Kakosy 1977). Finally, in the eastern Delta, Ramesses II founded Pi-Ramesses, wherein were celebrated the cults of Seth, the ancient god of the region, Amun-Ra, Ra, Ptah, and a divine Ramesses, a hypostasis of the king himself (Uphill 1984). Another new royal city, but much more short-lived, was at Tell el Amarna in Middle Egypt, where Akhenaten founded the city of Akhetaton as the center of his government and his monotheistic cult; it did not long survive his death.

Eulogies, often included in hymns to a god, were written about cities, and especially the royal cities which each emerge in these eulogies as an *axis mundi*, a microcosm of the macrocosmos and a model of the universe. In cross-cultural terms, such cities in Egypt and elsewhere

> dramatized the cosmogony by reproducing on earth a reduced version of the cosmos ... (as) ... a focus of creative force.... Here communication was likely to be effected most expeditiously between cosmic planes, between earth and heaven and between earth and the netherworld (Wheatly 1971, 417; generally an excellent introduction to such cities; cf. also O'Connor 1982).

This is certainly the image of the royal city conveyed by the eulogies, in which each is not only an ideal city in itself but also a center of cosmic power, conceptually expanding out to fill the entire universe. Thus, Thebes is not only the pattern or norm for every city, it is also the place of primaeval water and earth from which emerged the mound upon which the creation of the universe took place; mankind itself had its birth in this holy city (Barucq and Daumas 1980, 213-214). Pi-Ramesses is also the perfect city, modelled on Thebes and as enduring as Memphis, while its limits are those of the universe itself, for the sun - the course of which defines that universe - rises and sets within it (Wilson 1969, 470-471). The citations could continue to cover the other royal cities, but the basic themes are the same whichever city is involved.

Was this image of the royal city as a model of the universe and a mirror of the cosmos and its workings only an intellectual abstraction or a powerful but poetic metaphor; or did, in fact, the material form and disposition of the chief structures of each royal city and the lives of its inhabitants literally replicate the cosmos and mimic its workings as they were conceived by the Egyptians? This question brings us to the royal palace, or rather palaces, characteristic of each royal city. Apart from the main temples, such palaces were the principal monumental buildings within the city, and if the cosmological aspects of the city were to find any material expression outside of the temples, it would most likely be through the palaces. But before turning to the nature and role of the palace, we must first consider the one certain manifestation of a "cosmos on earth," the Egyptian temple.

Temple and Cosmos: An Integrative Role

There are several reasons for such a consideration. First, reviewing the cosmic aspects of temples reminds us of the specifically Egyptian world-view which was given material form in the temple and, conceptually at least, had such a powerful impact upon the Egyptian idea of a royal city. Second, the fact that the Egyptians were so capable of making, in the form of the temple, a dramatically three-dimensional statement about their complex view of the cosmos and its workings raises the possibility that they could do the same with the royal palace. Third, as I hope to show below, with special reference to the uniquely well preserved data from Merenptah's palace, the New Kingdom temple in reality did provide a model for the royal palaces of the period, and our understanding of the palace is, therefore, enhanced by understanding what the temple itself represented. Finally, this relationship between temple and palace arose from an important function that they shared, the function of integrating the earthly reality of ritual and governing processes with the supra-reality of the cosmic processes. This integration ensured that the latter would endow the former with meaning, authority, and, above all, effective power. The mechanisms of integration were two-fold, combining both speech and image, spoken evocations of supernatural knowledge and power and material evocations of the same. It may be doubted that speech and image could be separated in the Egyptian mind, so far as the arousal of supernatural power was concerned; utterance was vitally important (Assman 1984a, 61-63), but equally so were the images that were a manifestation of a deity and that, in two or three-dimensional form, evoked both the cosmos of which the deity was an essential element and the cosmic processes in which all deities were involved. More specifically, the liturgy (speech and action) performed in a temple, combined with the plan, architectural form, and "decoration" of the temple (i.e., the image that the temple itself was) rendered the liturgy cosmically effective and, by extension, integrated the farflung network of administrative and economic institutions characteristic of temples into the workings of the cosmos. Similarly, I would suggest, the ceremonies conducted within a palace, combined with the plan, architectural form, and "decoration" of the palace, rendered these rituals of government cosmically meaningful and effective and, by extension, integrated the administrative and economic structure of Egypt and its empire into the cosmos.

The cosmological aspects of New Kingdom temples (Figure 9) are well-known and are similar in gods' temples and in those dedicated to royal funerary cults in association with a god's cult, as on the west bank at Thebes (Stadelmann 1979). In sketching this

168

cosmological significance, I will, therefore, draw on useful early studies (e.g., Rochemonteix 1887; Nelson 1944) and on more recent reviews, such as Baines' (1976) and Assman's (1984a, 35-63), the latter particularly useful in bringing out significant differences as well as similarities between New Kingdom and Late Period (Ptolemaic-Roman) temples. However, some of the nuances or interpretations mentioned below are my own.

The integrative role of the temple is clear if we consider it as functioning simultaneously on three levels. At the utilitarian level, the temple proper is a structural setting laid out so as to conform to and make possible the performance of specific rituals and so as to house the sacred images, cult objects, and offerings needed for those rituals. At the level of ritual itself, the temple is the essential setting for cult activities that meet the basic needs of the gods and stimulate their reciprocal benevolence toward Egypt and toward the cosmos of which it is a part. Finally, in order to combine with utterance and act so as to render ritual and cult supernaturally effective, the temple reproduces in material form the universe itself, including the processes which brought it into being and which maintain it in place, mainly by periodic frequent renewals.

The temple proper represents the cosmos in terms of both space and time. The typical plan consists of one or two courts, each with a pylon or double-towered entryway, followed by the roofed section of the temple. The latter culminates in a sanctuary, containing the naos for the chief cult-image and preceded usually by a chamber for a sacred boat, a portable shrine. The sanctuary is fully enclosed within the temple and buried in darkness so that it can be protected as fully as possible against contamination from the impure world outside and from supernatural evil. Such dangers might travel even in air and along beams of light; so, in general, the flow of light and air into the temple was strictly controlled (through roof slots and relatively small windows set high in the walls). *Sacred* light and air, that energized the universe, was permitted, either purified ritually through such openings as were allowed or generated by the rituals themselves in the form of flame and incense. The floor of the temple sloped up gently to the sanctuary, representing the primaeval mound upon which the creation of the cosmos took place, while the sanctuary was identified as the cosmic horizon, where the sun rose, renewing the universe, and set, temporarily placing it in suspension. The doors of both shrine and sanctuary were identified as the gates of heaven, opening to permit the sun to blaze forth, closing behind it as it sank into the west.

Before the sanctuary extended two or more columned halls, functionally for the laying out of offerings and the performance of ritual but cosmologically representing the sacred world that came into being at the time of creation. The walls of these halls were covered with repetitive ritual scenes which, if projected outwards in three dimensions, reveal this sacred world as filled with innumerable deities, each the recipient (often many times over) of offerings or other ritual attention from the kings, each in turn bestowing upon him (and via him Egypt and the universe) a concrete benefit. These are also the gods responsible for maintaining the orderly universe and it literally rises around them. The temple floors are plain -- perhaps the pure surface of the primaeval mound -- but thrusting up from them are columns, often gigantic, shaped to represent aquatic plants (lotus, papyrus) growing out of water; the primaeval swamp where creation occurred is evoked, but surely also the inundated Nile river plain, the annual miracle upon which the Egyptian cosmos at least depended. These columns and the doorways are also cosmic supports, for they underpin lintels and ultimately a flat ceiling, all richly embellished with celestial iconography - star-studded skies, the sky goddess Nut, winged sun-disks, the soaring vulture goddess Nekhbet; this model of the universe is brought to completion by the sky that floats over it. This is the sacred realm that is illuminated and regenerated into life every time the sanctuary doors are opened and the divine image, as creator and renewer, is envisioned as shining forth upon it.

The roofed area opens onto a large open court, drenched in sunshine, the walls being covered with scenes depicting the public festivals of the temple's god (and other gods); such festivals might be confined to this court, before a select audience, or on other occasions involve a procession through the town surrounding the temple, before an awed and excited populace. This court might be considered the transitional zone between the sacred world and that of men, and the festivals themselves linked earth and heaven, for the image travelled in a portable shrine in the shape of a boat, a clear reference to the sun-god traversing, defining, and expressing his domination over the universe in *his* boat.

Sometimes another court preceded the "festival court," and typically it, as well as the the temple pylons and the temples' exterior walls, were covered with scenes evoking the terrestrial realm. These dealt especially with pharaoh's victories and domination over foreign lands, but culminated in scenes of offerings, and implicitly referred also to the governance of Egypt itself. So the temple as a whole embodies the place of creation, the sacred world of the gods, the orderly world of Egypt, and the subjugated world of the foreigners, thus arriving at the fringes of the orderly universe, far beyond these stretches limitless chaos and non-being (Hornung 1971, 171-196), forever pressing in upon this perfectly balanced, functioning cosmos.

The above description and interpretation has been given in spatial terms, but this schematized universe can be described equally (and perhaps for the Egyptian more appropriately) in terms of time. Egyptian concepts of time are complex and rich, productive of much scholarly debate (e.g., compare Assman 1984, 90-97; 1975; with Wente 1982, 222 and Westendorf 1983), but the following may reasonably be inferred about the temple. The external "historical" scenes, although idealized into icons of order defeating chaos, usually remain specific enough to link the temple to historical time, the time of Egypt and its neighbors, while the festivals of the first or second court equally link sacred time and the everyday world of Egypt. Otherwise, however, the temple embodies the two cosmically powerful, complementary concepts of *neheh* time and *djet* time. The former is cyclical and is manifest dramatically in the course of the sun, appearing and disappearing, energizing the cosmos into renewed life, and letting it slip, temporarily, into threatening death-like darkness. *Djet* time is typical of those aspects of the cosmos that do not periodically change, that are in a special sense complete; creation is complete, although it is periodically renewed, Osiris is complete, for his miraculous revival from death endures forever. Both concepts of time are fused together in the daily ritual, which continually evokes -- side by side -- the myths of the sun-god in his various forms and of Osiris (Moret 1902) and fuse further in the form of the temple. The pylon literally is the cosmic horizon, and so is the sanctuary within the temple; they embody cyclical time. The sanctuary as primaeval mound and the sacred world frozen in stone that stretches before it eternally endure unchanged; they embody *djet* time.

The preceding analysis has been lengthy, but it is necessary, for it not only dramatizes the Egyptian ability to produce a three-dimensional image of their cosmos, but many of the concepts involved, I believe, are relevant to understanding the nature and functions of the royal palace also.

The Royal Palace in the New Kingdom

Merenptah's palace, because of its (in some ways) unique state of preservation, is a key datum for any analysis of the New Kingdom palace in general. Egyptian royal palaces have received comparatively slight scholarly attention. The authoritative *Lexikon der Ägyptologie*, for example, dedicates some sixteen and two-thirds columns to the concept, architecture, *et al.* of "*Tempel*" (*Lexikon VI*, 355-365, 377-379, 407-414) but only some two and a half columns to those of "*Palast*" (*Lexikon IV*, 644-646); Vandier's useful and detailed survey of the religious and secular architecture of Egypt devotes 307 pages to the New Kingdom temples, including brief descriptions of ritual palaces in royal funerary temples (1955, 661-971), but only some 18 pages to the palaces of New Kingdom pharaohs (ibid., 1004-1022). This comparative lack of attention is in large part because of archaeological reasons. Temples were often built of stone, and as a result some have survived substantially intact while extensive fragments of others remain available for study. Royal palaces were of mudbrick, inherently survive much less well, and were, in any case, typically located in the urban agglomerations surrounding temples, agglomerations which have rarely been explored archaeologically. Moreover, of the small number of excavated palaces, some -- such as Merenptah's -- remain largely unpublished.

Even the small amount of data available, however, may be a productive field of research, for the palace in general was evidently not only a major building complex of some significance; it is also likely that it combined utilitarian and cosmological attributes, because of the complex nature of the pharaoh for whom palaces were built. The pharaoh had a critical and unique position within the Egyptian world view (usefully summarized in Barta 1980, 485-494). He was not only absolute political and military leader of the state, but he was also believed to be the son, heir, and appointed delegate of the gods on earth, a unique status expressed forcefully by the fact that the king was also the sole ritualist, all priests being but embodiments of him when they performed the temple cult.

These historical realities were expressed in a theory of kingship which formally emphasized the divine aspect of kingship but implicitly recognized the dual nature of a pharaoh. Each individual pharaoh was recognizably human and mortal; he was born and nurtured, needed food, shelter, and the satisfaction of his human needs, was an active participant in political process and eventually aged and died. But, as "the" pharaoh, each ruler was simultaneously divine as well as human, for reasons well outlined recently by Bell (1985). The coronation made manifest in each pharaoh what had only been immanent earlier in his life, namely that he was flooded with the *ka* -- roughly, soul or being -- of ideal kingship, which had been made by a creator god as a vital part of the orderly universe. Thereafter, each king was "*ex officio* a god" (ibid., 258) and, in particular, was recognized as Horus, son of Osiris, and as a being who could be ritually transformed into Amun-Ra, the solar god, creator of the universe, and lord of the Egyptian state and its empire. The divine aspect of the pharaoh was present in all his activities but was given greater prominence in certain specific contexts, e.g., in religious ritual, in ceremonies at court, and in major governmental ceremonies such as the formal announcement of some major initiative, the reception of Egyptian and imperial tribute, the ceremonies following a victorious campaign, and the appointment, promotion, and rewarding of high officials. In some instances, and perhaps in more than we realize, the identification of pharaoh with sun-god could be pushed very far indeed. For example, Akhenaten can appear to be "on earth the incarnation of Aten the sun-god" (Kitchen 1982, 175; cf. also Bell 1985, 291-293), while Ramesses II "seemingly made of [himself] a manifestation of the sun-god on earth" (Kitchen 1982, 178).

While Merenptah's palace offers much direct evidence of great value, much of its meaning must be elucidated by comparison with other known palaces of the New Kingdom. Of the latter, it should first be noted that nearly all our archaeological evidence is confined to the later Eighteenth, Nineteenth, and Twentieth Dynasties; and second, that palaces varied considerably in size, function, and plan (Arnold 1982; Vandier 1955, 1004-1022; Badawy 1968, 35-55). Some were residential, i.e., true living areas; others were recreational and might not be actually lived in for extended periods; some were administrative, and focused upon practical relationships between king and bureaucracy; some were ceremonial, intended mainly for the performance of rituals of kingship; and some were more specifically ritual, in that they were used by the king when he took part in the cult activity of a great temple. The divisions between these various functions were not completely rigid, but each of the individual known palaces seems predominantly to belong to one or the other of the types just listed. Despite this variety, however, there are certain key features of plan, architectural form, and decoration that occur in *all* the palaces and create a recurrent unity overlying the functional variability and its effects. Our understanding of these recurrent features and their significance is perhaps best enhanced by Merenptah's palace. The data on this palace are not well-known, and I shall dedicate the rest of this essay to a more detailed description of them than has been available hitherto and to a preliminary interpretation of the functions of the palace. Eventually, we plan to fully publish this site on behalf of the University Museum, the sponsor of the original excavation and repository of the relevant archives.

II

The Palace of Merenptah

Ramesses II (1279-1213 B.C.), as husband of several queens and other ladies as well, fathered an extraordinarily large number of children over his long reign, and naturally a number of his sons predeceased him. When, through a process combining both attrition and his father's favor, Merenptah became Ramesses' Heir-Apparent in ca. 1223 B.C., he had been preceded by at least four earlier Heirs-Apparent. Merenptah stayed the distance, becoming in effect the de-facto ruler of Egypt during Ramesses' last years and formally ascending the throne when he was in his sixties, a relatively advanced age for ancient Egypt. Not surprisingly, Merenptah had a short reign (1213-1204 B.C.), but it was a distinguished one. A substantial Libyan invasion was defeated, the Palestinian empire held, and Nubian rebels crushed; Egypt was prosperous, and Merenptah undertook an active building program including a grandiose tomb, an impressive funerary temple (both at Thebes), and the Memphis palace discussed here (Kitchen 1982, 111-112, 215-216; Krauss 1980).

The existence of this palace was discovered in 1914 by C.E. Edgar, an official of the Egyptian Antiquities Organization, who excavated a small segment (room 5 on Fisher's plan) which had been accidentally exposed. Clarence S. Fisher had been engaged that year as Egyptian curator of the University Museum, was scouting for a likely site, and, attracted by this discovery, applied for and received a permit to excavate this sector of Memphis. The palace proper, as we know it, and the "South Portal" of its enclosure wall were excavated 1915-1918, while in 1919-1920 Fisher carried out additional excavations intended to trace an assumed continuation of the palace towards the west. In this he was unsuccessful in that, while excavating extensions of the five building levels of urban character he had already found over the palace, he did not penetrate as far as the floor level of the palace remains. The palace was of mudbrick, but many stone elements (columns, doorways, etc.) were found *in situ* or approximately so, and all (?) of these were removed and divided between the Cairo and the University Museums. The palace site itself, at Kom Qala'a, remained visible until recent times; Anthes located it "without difficulty" in 1956 (Anthes 1965, 38) and in 1985 it was still recognizable as "two separate hollows in the ground" (Jeffreys 1985, 20).

Despite its considerable size (a little over 30% of a hectare) and the rich architectural detail it preserved, the palace of Merenptah has not received much scholarly discussion because Fisher never published a final and full report on his excavation. He did publish a relatively extensive description of the palace, succinctly summarizing some of its chief points of interest (Fisher 1917) and later two interesting, if brief, discussions of the palace throne room (Fisher 1921, 1924). These have been made of brief use in various publications (e.g., Ricke 1932, 65; Vandier 1955, 1005-1006), and the general area of the palace has been discussed by Anthes (1965, 25-40) and Jeffreys (1985, 19-20, 63-64). However, there is a wealth of archival information on the palace (plans, photographs, field diaries, and notes) as well as some important architectural elevations that Fisher brought close to completion. To fully digest this material and publish it adequately is a formidable task which the Egyptian Section of the University Museum will address in the near future. This interim description, however, will expand the information hitherto available and provide a better basis for a comparative discussion.

The Palace and the City

The palace was part of a larger complex that was enclosed by substantial brick walls laid out in trapezoidal shape, the whole apparently attributable to Merenptah. The relationship of this enclosure to the rest of New Kingdom Memphis -- a still poorly known entity -- is best discussed with reference to Jeffrey's recently published *Survey of Memphis I* (cf. also Kitchen, this volume). A fundamental starting point is Jeffrey's plausible argument that, at the opening of the New Kingdom, Memphis, the city, lay west of the western wall of the present Ptah temple enclosure and faced out upon a flat marshy plain left by a river channel that was slowly moving eastwards over the decades (Jeffreys 1985, 48-51; Smith and Jeffreys 1986, 91-94). It was upon this plain that New Kingdom Memphis developed; by the time the Merenptah palace enclosure was built, it lay east of a series of at least four major temple enclosures running in a north to south direction (Kom Aziz, the north Birka, the middle Birka -- the Ptah temple enclosure itself -- and the south Birka; cf. Jeffreys 1985, 44-45, 33-38), all presumably founded in the later Eighteenth Dynasty and much expanded in Ramesside times. There was apparently little space between these enclosures save between Kom Aziz and the north Birka, separated by Kom Tuman, the site of a very large palace in the later first millennium B.C.: it is hinted that it might have been functioning as a palace site as early as the Eighteenth Dynasty (Jeffreys 1985, 41). Might this, in fact, have been the site of the famous Memphite palace of Tuthmosis I, still in use as late as the reigns of Tutankhamun and perhaps Seti I (Helck 1958, 7-8)? Certainly, for both pharaohs and crown princes, Memphis was of increasing importance as a residential and administrative center in the Eighteenth Dynasty, while in the Nineteenth and Twentieth it shared its status as a royal city with Pi-Ramesses (ibid., 5-9).

The western sector of New Kingdom Memphis would then have been occupied largely by temples, ancillary chapels and shrines, and perhaps a royal palace complex; the location of Merenptah's palace shows the river bank must have lain considerably further to the east, but presumably it was felt appropriate that the new temples should remain close to the ancient urban nucleus and its venerable holy places and could be served by access canals running from the river. The eastern sector, between the temples and the river, is occupied by Koms Dafbaby, Nawa, and Arba'in which have yielded no definite evidence for New Kingdom monumental structures such as temples (Jeffreys 1985, 43-44, 38-40, 31-33); so it is likely that this sector -- including Kom Qala'a -- was the principal urban zone, occupied by residences, offices, and perhaps magazines. This would be natural, for since the river was the principal means of communication, cities tended to develop ribbon-like along its shores, rather than spread back into the hinterland (cf. the urban pattern at Tell el Amarna, Kemp 1985, figure on 311-312 f.). There may have been even further suburbs north and south (Kitchen 1982, 114). Merenptah's palace complex would, therefore, have stood in the southern part of an urban, otherwise non-monumental zone; whether other Nineteenth Dynasty palaces lay further north in this zone (as in Kitchen's imaginative reconstruction 1982, 114) is uncertain, and new temples on the still eastward moving flood plain in the Twentieth Dynasty are unlikely, given the very restrained building programs of this dynasty (Kitchen 1973, 245-254).

The Palace Complex of Merenptah

The palace of Merenptah, large in itself, appears to be part of a much larger complex. The area of this complex (over 6 ha. or 15 acres) is defined by brick walls forming a trapezoidal enclosure (Figure 7). The reality of its southern and eastern walls have been established by excavation, and both are dated to Merenptah's reign, the former by *in situ* inscriptions, the latter by its orientation with the palace (Jeffreys 1985, 66-67 and Figure 63; Anthes 1965, 35-40). The northern and western walls appear to be reconstructions on Jeffrey's part. The eccentric trapezoidal shape, if true, also reflects the relatively late date of the enclosure, for it was caused by the effort to parallel the orientation of already existing features, i.e., the east enclosure wall of the Ptah temple, a roadway running along the east-west axis (projected) of that temple, and a roadway in the south leading to a small temple of Ramesses II (Jeffreys 1985, 33 ff.; 65-67; 69 and 77, with Figure 63; 22; 72-73).

Significantly, the excavated palace of Merenptah was not the central feature of this enclosure; rather, it was built close to the enclosure's eastern wall, 6.3 meters east of a substantial wall shielding the east side of the palace (Figure 1). What else lay within the vast enclosed area is debatable, but a centrally located building also dated to Merenptah; its sole excavated feature is a courtyard about 35 meters wide, with a stone gateway on its south and a stone doorway on its north, both inscribed with Merenptah's names (Petrie 1909a, 11-12; Jeffreys 1985, Figures 13, 63). It has often been suggested that this court was part of a temple, e.g., by Petrie (op. cit.) and more recently by Anthes (1965, 35-38), Jeffreys (1985, 19-20), and Uphill (1970, 155; 1984, 16, "T.34"; cf. also Porter, Moss, and Malek 1981, 854-855). This opinion, however, has not been universally accepted; Ricke thought Merenptah's palace stood within "a larger palace district" (1932, 64; cf. also Badawy 1968, 54), and Fisher believed that the "temple" really belonged "to the Merenptah palace complex" (1919-1920 Field Diary, 12/4/19; cf. also Fisher 1917, 226-227). In fact, Fisher devoted much of the 1919-1920 season to excaating the area between "temple" and palace, expecting to find palace remains below the later urban levels, and he planned to continue westward into the "temple" area itself (1919-1920 Field Diary, 9/30-10/2, 1919; 11/10-21, 1919; 12/11, 1919). Unfortunately, the season closed before either aim was achieved, and Fisher did not resume his excavations.

Neither Fisher nor anyone else appears to have argued, in detail, the case for the "temple" being really a palace, but this is, I believe, the most likely possibility. Petrie identified the structure as a temple because of a possible reference to it in Herodotus (1909a, 3-4) and of two, New Kingdom dedicatory stelae to Hathor, found approximately *in situ* (1909a, 4 and 12, and Plate XXVIII, 21 and 22). The first proof is of no value, but the second should not be ignored; the stelae invoke "Hathor, Lady of the Sycamore" in one case and "Hathor, Mistress of *Htpt*" (in Heliopolis; Gardiner 1947, II, 137*) in the other. However, since there were many later structures in the courtyard (Petrie 1909a, 11-12), the stelae may have been brought from elsewhere to be re-used; and, in fact, the principal temple of Hathor, "Lady of the Sycamore," possibly lay southwest of the Merenptah enclosure and the palace it contained (Jeffreys 1985, 6). The lintel from the gateway depicted Merenptah enthroned (a sed-festival scene?; Petrie 1909b, Plate XXI) which might well occur in a temple but could equally well occur in a palace; related if not identical scenes occurred on lintels in Merenptah's palace (archival records). Similarly, the jambs of the doorway into the "temple," referring iconographically to the unity of Egypt and textually to the length of Merenptah's reign and to his rulership ("appearing in glory upon the Horus [throne] like Ra"; Petrie 1909a, Plate XXIX), would be as appropriate for a palace as a temple. Finally, Petrie also made "to the west of the court of the temple of Merenptah a wide cutting...to water level, to try to recover the side wall of the court." He found it "ruined and built over; but among the ruins were two colossal Negro heads in limestone..." (Petrie 1909a, 14, Plate XX). These clearly came from a set of emblematic heads of foreigners projecting from a wall surface. They might have come from the setting of a "Window of Appearance," which were found in ritual or cult-palaces attached to temples and in at least certain types of other palaces, such as administrative ones (Arnold 1977; Stadelmann 1973; Kemp 1976); or even perhaps come from consoles (sometimes supporting statuary) set into a wall (Hölscher 1941, 40 and Plate 33F, the latter the closest parallel in structural form to the Memphis examples). Uphill suggests the Memphis heads come from a "Window of Appearance" but is not clear as to whether he thinks they came from the "temple" or the palace (Uphill 1984, 134-135); the find spot of the heads indicates the original location was the "temple." Moreover, such elements would not only be appropriate in a palace, but have always -- to my knowledge -- been associated with palaces or palace-like features within temples, never directly with a temple proper. We might, therefore, suspect that the "temple" had some kind of a palace to its west or that the "temple" itself was, in fact, a palace. The fact that the walls of the "temple," in so far as they were revealed, were of brick and not stone also fits better with a palace than with a significant temple.

On balance, then, it is reasonable to argue that the excavated palace of Merenptah flanked yet another palace which, to judge from its central location, was the more important of the two and perhaps considerably larger and more complex than the excavated example.

The Palace of Merenptah

With the palace proper, we move from informed speculation to archaeological reality, and we can improve upon Fisher's published descriptions in several areas (Figure 1).

Fisher nowhere published any over-all impression of the external appearance of the palace but in fact did quite a lot of work on reconstructing this. He was very much aided by the fact the palace had been destroyed by fire "not many years" after Merenptah's death, and many architectural elements such as columns and monumental doorways had survived, sometimes fallen but substantially intact (Fisher 1917, 227). Only the lower parts of the mudbrick walls had survived, but Fisher was able to calculate accurately the heights of the columns and door frames in the different parts of the palace and so arrive at a probable (and varied) roof height. The only variable that he appears not to have taken into account was the possibility that the roof was formed by barrel vaults, as later proved to be indisputably the case in the two successive palaces of Ramesses III at Medinet Habu (Hölscher 1941, 38-39 and 44 ff.). Fisher argued that Merenptah's palace had a flat wooden roof (Fisher 1917, 227; 1921, 31), similar to those of at least parts of the palaces of Amenhotep III at Malkata (Smith 1981, 294-295) and, in fact, although he did not state them, there are good reasons to support his belief.

First, although the subsidiary chambers of Merenptah's palace (rooms 1-4, 6, 8-12, 14, 16-17, 21-22) never exceeded 3.65 meters in width and, therefore, could have supported vaults similar to those typically spanning 3.65 meters at Medinet Habu, the larger halls (5, 7, 18, and 20) had columns which, in general, were significantly further apart than was the case at Medinet Habu and, in any case, none of the stone beams needed to support the vaults of the columned halls at Medinet Habu appear to have been recovered at Memphis. Second, in room 20 Fisher actually found "ceiling stucco" adhering to the wall west of the southern doorway, stucco which still bore the marks of a wooden roof on its underside (Fisher's notes on decorated stucco throughout the palace). Third, and most importantly, Fisher found, apparently throughout the entire palace, that the collapsed or still partially standing stone architectural elements were buried in a "bed of charcoal, ashes and mud-bricks" which evidently had come from a burning and collapsing wooden roof topped by brick (Fisher 1921, 30).

I will assume here, therefore, that Fisher's renderings of the actual roof heights are correct, when shown, as they are through most if not all of an important series of elevations he drew: north-south through room 20 and into court 19, east-west across the north end of court 19, north-south through the entire palace, and finally east-west across the throne room (7) and its flanking chambers (University Museum archives). In addition, a careful scale model of the throne room (7) was prepared (Fisher 1921, 1924) and is still on exhibit in the Museum.

Based on these data, the external appearance of the palace may be described as follows (Figure 8). A low ramp led from an open area (a court[?] cf. Fisher 1917, 225) into a columned vestibule room (20), itself with a ceiling height of 6.42 meters, but which had apparently supported a second storey equipped with a window, facing inwards over court 19 and supplied with a massive stone balustrade supporting two tall (4.50 meters) but relatively thin columns. Fisher did not depict the roof line of the second storey, but I have tentatively assigned it 5.25 meters, giving the palace a facade rising, in all, just over 12 meters. I have also tentatively assumed that the side chambers 21 and 22 supported a second storey (e.g., to shield the king from view when he ascended the stairs in 22), but this may be incorrect.

Fisher assumed that the window was a "Window of Appearance" (1917, 222), but there are objections to this view. First, it would have been unusually high, in that it was located in a second storey of court 19, onto which it faced; all the archaeologically attested "Windows of Appearance" are located in ground floor rooms and, although they are elevated so as to rise above floor level inside the hall and above ground level outside the hall, the elevation is not very great. For example, the sill of the "Window of Appearance" at Medinet Habu rose 3.37 meters above the floor of the court on which it opened in its first manifestation; and 2.59 meters above a low platform in front of it in its second (Hölscher 1941, 39, Figure 17 and Plate 3; Plate 4); and the situation with the "Window of Appearance" in the administrative palace ("King's House") at Amarna must have been similar (Kemp 1976, 81-82; Pendlebury 1951, 87 and Plate 46.4). Second, the known 'Windows of Appearance' faced *outwards* from the throne room in order to overlook a court in front of the palace; here, at Memphis, the window looks over an inner court, within the palace, and faces towards the throne room. More specifically, all known "Windows of Appearance" face north; this example faces south. It is, therefore, unlikely to have been a "Window of Appearance" in the usual sense; but it may have been similar in form. The balustrade and columns may have been set into the wall of the chamber above Room 20, in which case the roofed colonnade of court 19 may have been broken at this point (as in Figure 8). Or they may have formed part of a balcony extending as far as the edge of the colonnade roof.

Court 19 was a large stone-paved one, surrounded by a low platform bearing a colonnade and with a drain running north-south along its center. A ramp led down from room 20 to the platform, and other ramps rose from the platform to room 24 and the columned "vestibule" room 18. The roof line of the colonnade was placed by Fisher at 8.25 meters above the platform, but apparently (in one elevation) he envisaged that the east and west walls of the court continued to rise, forming a shielding wall about 2.75 meters high. This was evidently pure supposition, but I have included it in the reconstruction.

The "vestibule" (18) is an impressive hall with columns 7.75 meters high. Fisher was apparently undecided about the height of the roof line and does not show it, but since the columns were markedly higher than those of court 19 (6.25 meters), the roof of 18 was clearly higher than that of the colonnade. Tentatively, I have made it as high as that of the throne room, but it may have been lower, since the throne room (7) columns were 8.25 meters high.

With good reason (column heights and those of the main northern doorways), Fisher placed the roof line of the throne room at 9.62 meters and depicts the flanking chambers on its east, west, and south with a much lower roof line, never exceeding 6.5 meters high. In fact, he shows the lower roof as sloping down toward the exterior walls and the latter themselves with a steep batter, but I have not reproduced these details in my schematic reconstruction. The evidence for the lower roof line was good and was based on the heights of stone door frames within the subsidiary chambers themselves.

Fisher also assigned to the throne room six windows carved in stone, assuming four on each side between the column rows and two flanking the throne dais at the rear. In actuality, the remains of at least two windows, apparently from the throne room, were found, one outside the east, the other the west side of the palace (Fisher 1917, 218-220; cf. also 1921, 33; 1924, 97), but these were not the only window fragments found in the palace, and the subject requires further investigation. Fisher also published, without comment, a drawing of another "window" (1924, 99). There are, in fact, at least two actual examples of these "windows" in the University Museum, but the lower parts with their open slots are entirely restoration. The distinctive iconography in the upper part of these objects is, in fact, identical with that found, not on windows, but on true doors in the gate-towers (= a pseudo-palace?) of Medinet Habu (Hölscher 1951, 6 and Plate 20 (upper door) and on both real and false doors in the ritual or cult palace at the same temple (Hölscher 1941, 48 and Plates 36 and 37). Since these Memphis examples are small, they are likely to be false rather than real doors, although it is hard to envisage their location. There are at least three locations for false doors, i.e., niches balancing real doorways in the palace, namely, on the west wall of room 20, the west side of the facade of room 18, and on the south side of the west wall (inner face) of room 5, but in each case the width of the niche is too wide. Alternatively, each false door may have been set in a wall behind a throne (rooms 5, 7), as in the Medinet Habu palace (Hölscher 1941, 48-49 and Plate 7), but the appropriate niches are not recorded on the plan; perhaps they were too shallow to survive.

As to the interior of the palace, Fisher provides a good impression of the visual effect of the columns and door frames, with their scenes of the king smiting foreign enemies and making offerings to Ptah and their use of paint, colored faience inlay and gilding. Examples of the elaborate and simpler door frames are published in Fisher (1924; cf. also Müller 1981, with comparative data from other from other Ramesside palaces), but the variations in epithets, scenes, and other details -- and their probable correlation with the different functions of various parts of the palace -- require further study. The throne dais found *in situ* in the throne room (Figure 2) is deservedly famous as the best preserved example ever found (Kuhlmann 1977, 79-80; for a recent, but incomplete drawing, cf. Jeffreys, Malek, and Smith 1986, Figure 6). Fisher does not do justice in his published description (1917, 220) to the extraordinarily well preserved royal bathroom (rooms 8, 9) with its stone-lined walls covered with protective hieroglyphs topped by royal cartouches and a cornice. A stone screen of similar style was found in room 1, a latrine (Fisher 1917, 220).

A point of special interest is the extent that the walls, ceilings, and floors were painted with designs and scenes. The survival rate of frescoes on the mud plaster surfaces of palace interiors is, of course, very low, although Tell el Amarna has yielded some spectacular examples (Arnold 1976; Smith 1981, 328-330; on the floors cf. Petrie 1894, 12-14; von Bissing 1941), and less well preserved examples have been found in earlier palaces (Smith op. cit., 281, 285-295) but not, or as far as I know, in other Ramesside ones. Fisher was in no doubt that frescoes had been used extensively in Merenptah's palace, referring to evidence in court 19, area 26, vestibule (18) and throne room (7), and in rooms 11, 12 and 14, 10 and 5 (Fisher 1917; also 1921, 30 and 33; 1924, 93-96) and embellishing the scale model of the throne room with elaborate floor scenes modelled after the pools, vegetation, birds, animals, and bound prisoners found on Amarna floors and wall scenes depicting royal processions, boats, and other subjects. In fact, the wall and floor scenes are almost entirely reconstructions (cf. Fisher 1924, 93 and 95), for Fisher's detailed notes on the surviving frescoes show that typically it was the painted dadoes of heraldic plants and hieroglyphs that were best preserved. The floors *had* been painted, but only geometrical border designs survived, not the main subject matter (Figure 3), and there was evidence (very fragmentary) for frescoed scenes on the north wall of court 19 and the east door jamb of room 2. Fisher also suggested that the ceiling of the throne room had yellow stars on a blue ground (1924, 97) apparently an inference from the only evidence for ceiling decoration I have found in his notes, namely, the fallen "ceiling stucco" in room 20 which had traces of "blue and yellow paint" on it.

III

Merenptah's Palace: Utilitarian and Cosmological Aspects

The Basic Function of the Palace

Although it has been described as "the actual residential palace of Merenptah in Memphis" (Ricke 1932, 64), it is, in fact, clear that the palace is essentially a ceremonial one (Stadelmann 1973, 235 n. 81), for it lacks the suites for queens and other family members and storage and service areas, all of which can be seen in the only well documented residential palace we have (Figure 6) that of Amenhotep III at Malkata (Smith 1981, 283-286). Merenptah's palace (Figures 1, 5) is supplied with a private throne room (5), bedroom (10), latrine (1), dressing-room (2) and bathroom (8-9), evidently for the use of the pharaoh; but such apartments are standard in ritual and ceremonial palaces and were intended for the short-term comfort of the king while using the palace (perhaps sometimes for less than a day) for whatever purposes intended for it. The ceremonial nature of the palace is further indicated by its large scale and its emphasis upon courts and halls clearly intended for ceremonial use (Figure 4). The entire building, at 110.30 X 30 meters, is, in fact, comparable in scale to the impressive funerary temples of Ramesses II and III at Thebes. Excluding the first of their two courts in each case for comparative purposes (Merenptah's palace has only one court) as well as the surrounding, non-temple structures, the former measures 128 X 57.6 meters and the latter 100.83 X 47 meters. Yet, in Merenptah's palace this large area is occupied by only 17 halls and rooms and a court; moreover, the halls are on a much greater scale than any of the rooms - the largest (vestibule 18 and throne hall 7) combined occupy 55.66% of the total roofed floor space, and the four largest combined (20, 18, 7, and 5) occupy 72.60%.

What then were the functions of this non-residential ceremonial palace? Stadelmann (ibid.) suggested it was a "temple-palace," defined as "one attached to a temple and used occasionally by the pharaoh when taking part in festivals" (Badawy 1968, 35); but there are objections to this interpretation. Archaeologically, the only known examples of such temple-palaces (Figure 5) are those attached to the royal funerary temples at Thebes (Stadelmann 1973) and, probably, one attached to an Aten temple at Amarna unless, indeed, the "Aten-temple" in question is actually a royal funerary temple (Millet, quoted in Redford 1984, 146); on the Amarna example, cf. Kemp 1976, 91-92). Now, *all* of these have a facade dominated by a centrally placed "Window of Appearance," set at the ground floor level of the palace and in immediate conjunction to the principal throne room and (usually) its vestibule; this is not the case at Merenptah's palace (Stadelmann 1973, 235 n. 81, but without reference to the Amarna example, cf. Kemp 1976, 91-92). Moreover, if one takes it that Merenptah's palace was functionally connected to the great Ptah temple (as Stadelmann suggests, ibid.), then it is correctly oriented -- i.e., is at right angles to the processional axis of the temple -- but too far away. The other temple-palaces referred to are *within* the enclosure of the relevant temple; Merenptah's palace is not only outside the Ptah temple enclosure, it also stands *within* another enclosure which, in fact, separates it further from the processional approach which the other temple-palaces open directly upon. If however, one argues there is *another* temple immediately adjacent to Merenptah's palace and within the same enclosure (see above), then the problem of proximity is removed; but -- to judge from the location of this supposed temple's courtyard -- Merenptah's palace would either parallel it in orientation (north-south) or lie right across its processional axis, should the supposed temple have had an east-west axis. Neither situation is found with the other temple-palaces; and in any case, as seen above, the supposed "temple" may in fact be part of yet another palace.

If Merenptah's palace is not a temple-palace in the usual meaning of the term, neither does it appear to be an administrative palace (Figure 5). We have one reasonably sure example of the latter, from the possibly but not (in these regards) necessarily eccentric and atypical site of Tell el Amarna, the so-called, "King's House." This was a non-residential palace with a "Window of Appearance" opening up into a large court and was the setting for the ceremonial rewarding (and presumably appointment and promotion) of officials (Kemp 1976; on the ceremonies, cf. references in Arnold 1977) and probably for more mundane administrative activities also, for the chief offices of the bureaucracy were located immediately adjacent to the palace (O'Connor 1982, 21). In fact, the basic plan and arrangement is strongly reminiscent of the funerary temple-palaces described above and equally deviates from that of Merenptah's palace; the latter does *not* have, so far as we know, the "public" court or the ground floor level "Window of Appearance" in close conjunction with the throne room and other halls, all evident in the Amarna administrative palace.

Closer, sometimes much closer, parallels to Merenptah's palace are provided by the core of the "North Palace" at Amarna and the so-called "North Harem" -- adjacent to the "Great Palace" -- at the same site (Kemp 1985, 309-315). Both of these palaces (Figure 6) are like Merenptah's palace in having a strongly rectangular form, whereas the Amarna administrative palace and the temple-palaces of royal funerary temples tend to form square blocks facing onto approximately square courts.

More specifically, we find in the "North Palace" -- beyond a first court (not attested at Memphis, but possibly there) -- a high pylon-like feature roughly comparable to the two-storied facade of Merenptah's palace, an inner court containing a large pool, and then a square vestibule, followed by one oriented east-west, and then a throne room. A royal suite lay south of the square vestibule (Smith 1981, 317, Figure 304). The "water court" did not have a colonnade like Merenptah's court (19) but was flanked by single rows of trees (Newton 1924, 295 and Plates XXVIII, XXIX)
which were reminiscent of such a colonnade, and it has been suggested - on very dubious grounds -- that the pylon-like feature had a formal window set in it (Whittemore 1926, 4), which reminds us of the inward facing, second-storey window or balcony attested at Memphis. These various parallels between the "North Palace" and Merenptah's palace are certainly suggestive, although evidently they also differ in significant ways. Unfortunately, the function of the "North Palace" proper is unclear. It is flanked by cult-areas (first court), by animal quarters and non-royal residential and/or office units ("water court"), and by an aviary and banqueting hall (?) (rear section) and appears, therefore, to be a recreational palace (cf. Badawy 1962, 92). The "North Palace" is not directly associated with any other structure, but it stands close to a monumental ramp (or gateway?), beyond which lies the great residential palace-complex of Amarna (Kemp 1976, 96-98 and Figure 4); the "North-

179

Palace" therefore, as far as we can tell -- and much in its vicinity remains unexcavated -- is an adjunct to the residential palace, not to a temple. Merenptah's palace, on the other hand, certainly seems in some sense to be an adjunct to a temple (the Ptah temple); we do not know if there was a residential palace nearby and certainly there are no obvious recreational adjuncts associated with it.

With the "North Harem" (Figure 6), we have a palace which is more akin to that of Merenptah. Uphill has already noted some similarities -- both temples flank a larger complex, both have a flanking passage on one side, both are similar in width (Uphill 1970, 155) -- but I think the analogies can be pursued much further in the areas of plan, context, and possible function. Both palaces are similar in scale and both are ceremonial, not residential; moreover, their plans, while by no means identical, show some striking similarities. Due to a poor state of preservation, the actual means of access to the "North Harem" is not clear; Pendlebury, in his reconstruction (1951, 38 and Plates XIIIa and XIV) assigned it an entrance on the south only, ultimately providing a link with the route that linked the "Great Palace" and the "King's House" via a bridge; but it is possible there was also an entrance on the north, for another major gateway (C) lay a little north of the "North Harem" and might equally well have suggested a northern entrance as well. In any case, the orientation of the chief halls of the "North Harem" shows it is oriented towards the north. At the northern end, Pendlebury reconstructed "servants quarters" (ibid., 38), but these look too formal for that (ibid., Plate XIV). The extant remains might even be interpreted as casement walls (ibid., Plate XIIIA) intended to support an elevated facade, reminiscent of that of Merenptah's palace. Immediately south lie two halls with square piers (?) and a small court, none paralleled at Memphis; but these are succeeded by a court flanked on three sides by colonnades or, on the long sides, possibly multi-windowed walls that would have provided a colonnade effect (ibid., 38-39). This roughly parallels the Memphis court (19), although the "North Harem" court also has storerooms on each long side and is itself largely occupied by a sunken area supplied with flanking gardens, a pool (north end), and a "well" (south end). These features are not found at Memphis where, however, it is noticeable that the court is slightly sunken and is paved with stone -- uniquely so for the palace -- the floor sloping down to a shallow depression running along the central axis. Nevertheless, it seems most unlikely that this area served as a (very shallow) pool. Beyond the court of the "North Harem" one moves into a columned vestibule, oriented east-west, and then a multi-columned hall which, in view of its position on the central axis, was probably a throne room, although no dais was found. These would correspond to rooms 18 and 7 at Memphis. East of the throne room is another columned hall (also a throne room?), leading on southwards to a cluster of rooms that might be the remains of a royal suite; these then would roughly correspond to rooms 5 (private throne room) and the adjacent suite in Merenptah's palace.

The "North Harem" and Merenptah's palace are also very similar in context (Figure 7). Each lie within a large walled enclosure (both are adjacent to its east side), and the walled area occupies roughly the same or very similar amounts of space in both instances. Moreover, this walled space at Amarna was occupied by "the Great Palace" with its large ceremonial halls and courts on the south, a vast cental(???) court, and further monumental structures of uncertain character on the north. It has been persuasively argued that we do not have here some form of temple (as Uphill had argued, 1970) but rather a complex intended for royal ceremonies (Assman 1972). What these might have been is uncertain: Assman has suggested they might have been connected with the sed-festival (ibid., 150) -- a periodically enacted and very major festival of royal renewal -- being perhaps "the architectural stage for the common or joint sed-festival celebration of both god and king" (ibid., 151). Assman adds that these celebrations might also have been in part public and witnessed by a large segment of the city's population (ibid., 155) while Kemp has raised the possibility that the "Great Palace" was used for such semi-public ceremonies as the "reception of a foreign prince or envoy" (Kemp 1976, 99). In any event, it is important to recall that, as seen above, Merenptah's palace, like the "North Harem," was also possibly an adjunct to another, perhaps much grander palace, yet another point of similarity with the "North Harem."

The Amarna "Great Palace" and the Merenptah "Great Palace" (?) are also similar in that both are located near the corner of the enclosure of a great temple, and both front -- on the south -- the processional axis of that temple (Aten temple at Amarna, Ptah temple at Memphis; compare Pendlebury 1951, Plate I with Jeffreys 1985, Plate 63). This conjunction seems to emphasize that while the two "Great Palaces" are for the celebration of major royal festivals and ceremonies, these in turn are strongly linked to the god of the major temple of each city. Perhaps the roots of the relationship go back to the temple of Luxor in Thebes which (although at a much greater distance than at Amarna and Memphis) also lies south of the main processional approach to Karnak temple (cf. Nims 1965, 14). A great annual festival (the Opet festival) required the god Amun-Ra to leave his Karnak temple, travel south to the Luxor temple, and sojourn there for a period. More to the point, however, Bell has recently shown in a fascinating article that the Luxor temple, as developed by Amenhotep III, was essentially "the temple dedicated to the divine Egyptian ruler, or more precisely, to the cult of the royal ka" (1985, 251-252), wherein the king not only re-enacted his mythicized life-story and its culminating point, the coronation through which he became endowed with a divine personality, but also underwent a process of ritual identification with Amun-Ra, the creator of the universe, himself (ibid.). Luxor is definitely in the form of a temple, not the palace-like complexes ("Great Palaces") of Amarna and perhaps Memphis; nevertheless, the possibility of some underlying conceptual similarities between the three seems quite strong and is reinforced by the possibility that Luxor temple was fronted by a great court where the (re-)deified king exposed himself to a jubilant populace and received the tribute of the empire (ibid., 273-275).

What then might have been the precise function of the two subsidiary palaces -- "North Harem" and Merenptah's palace -- immediately adjacent to and connected with these two "Great Palaces"? Obviously, the answers can only be speculative; perhaps the most likely is that both provided secluded palaces wherein the king was prepared for the ceremonies he was to perform in the "Great Palace" and to which he could periodically retire for rest and refreshment during the long day (or days) involved in those ceremonies. Or perhaps, given their large scale and impressive elaboration, the two subsidiary palaces were more intimately linked to the ceremonies of the "Great Palaces" than we might think. It is worth recalling that the eastern half of the Luxor temple includes an area which, while not planned as a palace, conceptually implies one in that the subject matter on its walls include the conception, birth, and rearing of the future king, and his ultimate recognition as king (Bell 1985, 257, referring to Murnane's conclusions). This "palace" is an integral part of the temple and presumably, therefore, of its ritual; could the same be said of the two subsidiary palaces in relationship to the "Great Palaces" of Amarna and, perhaps, Memphis?

The Palace as Cosmos

The specific functions of Merenptah's palace are important, but so is the fact that this unusually well preserved palace provides rich information about cosmological attributes that were probably common to all New Kingdom palaces, irrespective of the particular functions of each. The Egyptian palace as a cosmos is, so far as I can discover, a subject that has received little attention. Uphill published an interesting discussion of the Egyptian palace as a "ruling machine" (1972), but discussed its propagandistic effects rather than its cosmological significance; moreover, he concentrates on the somewhat specialized temple-palaces and palace-like features of the Medinet Habu complex. Kuhlmann (1977) has published an excellent study of the royal throne (as well as of its dais and baldacchin), including consideration of its cosmological aspects; but this does not include the royal palace as a whole. Palace types varied so as to reflect the human nature of the king and to meet his human needs and responsibilities; palaces were variously residential, recreational, administrative, or ceremonial and ritual. But the ceremonial aspects of royal life and the rendering of probably every palace as a cosmos reflected pharaoh's divine nature, as the incarnated *ka* of primaevally created kingship, as Horus son of Osiris and as Amun-Ra, who created and perpetually renews the universe.

The first point to notice is that while the ground plans of palace and temple have long been recognized to be similar in important ways (cf. e.g., Steindorff 1896), the fact that we can render Merenptah's palace in three-dimensional form underlines even more strongly how analogous a royal palace could be to the basic New Kingdom temple type (cf. Hawkes 1974, 152; and also Figures 8 and 9). The approximate equivalences are: the strongly rectangular mode, reflecting processional temple rituals/palace ceremonies; the temple pylon/elevated palace facade (with a monumental window recalling the notch in the pylon?); a colonnaded court in both; a floor level rising gradually towards the rear of both temple and palace; and finally, a series of roofed columned halls and other chambers at the rear in both temple and palace. The architectural emphasis in the roofed section is upon temple offering hall, sanctuary and shrine, and palace vestibule, throne room and throne. As in the temple, the roof line of the more important palace halls is higher than that of the surrounding chambers. In part this is due to the need, in the palace, to create light and air for centrally located rooms (similarly in the private house; cf. Smith 1938, Plate LXVII), but the analogy to the temple -- given the other similarities noted -- is also significant. Such elevated roof lines for major halls occurred in other palaces, e.g., the second ritual palace of Ramesses III at Medinet Habu (Hölscher 1941, Plates 8 and 9) and perhaps the administrative palace at Amarna (Kemp 1976, 87). They recall, but are not identical with, the basilican halls that occur rarely in New Kingdom temples and may have a special connection with the cult of the king (Haeny 1970, especially 71-72).

The temple-like character of Merenptah's palace and presumably others is unmistakable in terms of architectural form. The latter would have evoked the same cosmological implications as the temple-form and directly stated that the resident of such palaces, i.e., the pharaoh, was a god. The frontal elevation evokes the rising sun and the creative and renewing power it brings; the rising floor level, culminating in the throne-dais, evokes the primaeval mound; and the throne and its dais approximate the shrine, the doors of which, when opened, reveal a sacred image shining in glory - the god in the temple, the king in the palace. This last impression would have been further strengthened if, as was apparently the case in the later palace at Medinet Habu (Hölscher 1941, 52 and Plate 8), the rear part of the throne room was shut off by wooden screens with, of course, a central set of doors.

Other elements of Merenptah's palace further strengthen its significance as a representation of the cosmos. Its ceilings may well have been painted with celestial iconography evoking the sky. The portico (room 20) apparently had a ceiling painted as a night sky (a patch of fallen plaster was recovered), while winged sun-disks -- originally blazing with gold sheeting, some of which survived -- were carved on several door lintels, hinting at similar or other celestial iconography on the ceilings above. Indeed, at the Malkata palace, the ceilings of two major halls and of the king's bedroom were painted with flying figures of the royal vulture goddess Nekhbet (Smith 1981, 291-292). The walls of Merenptah's palace were also once covered with paintings, although only the lower dadoes and a few traces of higher scenes survived. As in a temple, one might guess these wall scenes to some degree reflected the events habitually occurring within a given hall or chamber (cf. Arnold 1962) but were also of cosmological significance. The exterior facade may well have borne, like temple pylons, scenes of the king slaying and capturing foreign enemies (compare the facades of the Medinet Habu temple-palaces, Hölscher 1941, Plate 3; cf. also Uphill 1972, 730-731), motifs which may have continued around the inner walls of the court (19), although here scenes of the king in public procession (similar to those of the gods in the temple "Festival Courts") may have also occurred. Within the columned halls, scenes of the court and the enthroned king are likely, and traces of such were found at the Malkata palace (Smith 1981, 291-292).

The columns and doorways of the palace, built of stone and hence better preserved, make our sense of the palace decoration more concrete. The columns themselves are in the form of gigantic plants, evoking, like temple columns, the primaeval landscape of the sacred world and typically had upon their surfaces, as well as royal names and epithets, scenes of the king offering to Ptah and smiting foreign enemies, i.e., carrying out the primary functions of Egyptian kingship, of stimulating divine benevolence and extending order throughout the terrestrial realm. Around the base of some columns, are adorers representing different parts of Egypt and other regions and specifically "adoring the good god," i.e., the king, and venerating his various divine attributes -- yet another indication that the palace was indeed the temple of the king (for an extended version of such eulogistic praising recited or sung in the palace by courtiers, see Breasted 1906, III, 288; Kitchen 1976, 355.10-356.13). On the lintels of major doors, scenes of royal life were depicted (Figure 10) -- enthronement, escort by the gods -- and scenes of dominating foreigners occur also on some door jambs. The scenes of foreign victory had also, of course, an apotropaic function, warding off -- as in temple -- the forces of supernatural chaos and evil that would try to overwhelm this model of the orderly universe.

As noted earlier, the throne dais survived intact (Figure 2) and was richly embellished with bound foreigners; it represented the primaeval mound upon which the king took the form of the sun-god as the creator, bringing into being universal order or Maat (the hieroglyph for which the dais literally represents), while the foreigners conveyed the message that the pharaoh ruled the entire universe as king and overcame cosmic chaos as a creator-god (Kuhlmann 1977, 93-95). The kiosk, which the dais supported, was not so much cosmically significant as a collection of powerful, supernaturally protective devices for the safety of the royal person (ibid., 90-92); the cosmological themes, as we have seen, were actually picked up by the palace itself.

Finally, we come to the floors, made of mud-plastered brick as in other palaces. Those of Merenptah's palace had certainly been painted, and although only the decorative borders had survived, Fisher thought the main content would have been representations of pools filled with fish and fringed with aquatic and other plants from which birds flow upwards and through which young animals, such as calves, gambolled. Central avenues along these floors would be filled with representations of captive, prostrate and bound foreigners. This was a likely assumption on Fisher's part, for such floor paintings were found at Malkata and Amarna (Arnold 1976) and probably existed in Ramesside palaces also, for the same themes are picked up in tiles that once decorated walls in such palaces (Strauss 1978). While no doubt decorative, such floor designs (which are found specifically in throne rooms) had cosmological meaning also; that of the foreigners is evident, and continues the theme of the daises, to which such central avenues actually ran. But, what of the other motifs?

Many years ago Borchardt suggested that some of the motifs, together with the plant columns that rose from them, represented the inundated Egyptian landscape, and this was indeed perhaps one aspect of them, for audience-halls so decorated were sometimes called "Inundation Halls" (Borchardt 1902, 41-43, 48-49; Stadelmann 1975, 554). Borchardt also guessed they referred to the swamp where the infant Horus was raised, because the king *was* Horus, son of Osiris (ibid., 49). However, in their totality, these floor scenes evoke another concept, a connection which has not, I believe, been noted before. Hymns addressed to the sun-god -- Amun-Ra or Aten -- of both the Eighteenth Dynasty and the Ramesside Period -- describe the terrestrial universe bursting into life and hastening to adore the sun-god as he illuminates it with light at sunrise and re-awakens it from death-like darkness, in effect renewing the orderly universe that was brought into being in primaeval times. Men, upward-flying birds, bounding animals, and even the turning plants all adore the sun-god, and interwoven with these themes are frequent references to the orderly governance of Egypt and the cosmos and the overthrow of foreigners and supernatural chaos (Lichtheim 1976, 91-92, 96-97; Barucq and Daumas 1980, 212-213, 245-246 - both Ramesside). The analogy seems clear: the floor scenes are largely the visual equivalent of the hymns, and when the king appears on his throne as an embodiment of the sun-god, he "illuminates" a representation of the terrestrial universe (extending over the floor before his throne) which adores and submits to him just as it does to the sun-god.

Enough has been said, especially with reference to Merenptah's palace, to establish that the royal palace is indeed a cosmos and that its ceremonies, like temple rituals, parallel the divine processes that brought into being and perpetually maintain the cosmos as a whole. In this way royal government is raised to the level of divine governance, palace as much as temple is integrated into the cosmos, and the ceremonies and business of government are infused with the supernatural power that make them effective.

Palace cosmology does not precisely parallel that of the temple. Rather, the palace represents the cosmos as seen from the pharaoh's perspective with his particular focus on the terrestrial realm within the cosmos as a whole. In contrast, temple cosmology emphasizes more the sacred realm occupied by the gods themselves:
the terrestrial realm is indeed evoked but is confined iconographically principally to the exterior of the temple and to its front segments (pylons, first court). In the palace iconography depicting and evoking the terrestrial realm is a dominant theme throughout the entire structure. Royal ceremonies and processions perhaps covered the walls; dominated foreigners on columns, door jambs, and floors (and walls?) extend from the front into the throne room and up the throne dais; the floor paintings and some column and door decoration depict terrestrial creation and its creatures. Moreover, the cultic activity of the king -- offering to the gods -- is repeatedly depicted, and this was one of his chief earthly roles. However, despite this non-temple-like emphasis on the terrestrial realm, the broader cosmos is also evoked by the palace, placing the terrestrial realm in its wider context. Columns and ceilings represent the cosmos as a whole, including the sacred realm of the gods; the throne room is clearly signaled to be a representation of the place of creation and of the repeated renewal of cosmic order; and periodically depicted are rituals of kingship carried out for pharaoh by the gods, rituals that endowed the pharaoh with his divine, as distinct from his human, nature. In such a setting, the ceremonies of kingship became supernaturally effective rituals; the business of governing state and empire became identified with the processes that maintained the order of the universe.

As in the temple, image -- in this case the palace as image of the cosmos -- is combined with utterance. The form of the palace shows that royal eulogies, such as one we have for Merenptah himself (Barucq and Daumas 1980, 448-489), are to be taken literally. The royal palace can be called the "beloved of Maat" -- i.e., of the orderly universe -- and the "Horizon of Ra," because it is indeed conceived of as the place of creation, as the cosmic horizon where renewal occurs, and as a three-dimensional embodiment of the cosmos. As the eulogy indicates, when Merenptah turns his face towards his courtiers, the setting created by the palace renders him literally the rising sun illuminating a rejoicing Egypt. The palace setting, in parallel with the eulogies, show that in his divine aspect the pharaoh shares his nature with that of Ra; that pharaonic rule extends over all lands; that, seated in this simalcrum of the cosmos, Pharaoh sees further than the solar disk itself. Here, in the palace, the pharaoh becomes transformed into the creator god; as earthly ruler he attends to the business of governance but renders this effective by being simultaneously (to quote the eulogy again) the lord of beauty who infuses all his creatures and the cosmos itself with the breath of life.

BIBLIOGRAPHY

Anthes, R. 1965.   *Mitrahineh 1956.* Philadelphia.

Arnold, D. 1962.   *Wandrelief und Raumfunktion in ägyptischen Tempeln des Neuen Reiches.* Berlin.

Arnold, D. 1975.   Erscheinungsfenster. *Lexikon der Ägyptologie* II, 14.

Arnold, D. 1976.   Fussboden. *Lexikon der Ägyptologie* II, 367-368.

Arnold, D. 1982.   Palast. *Lexikon der Ägyptologie* IV, 644-646.

Assman, J. 1972.   Palast or Tempel? Uberlegungen zur Architektur und Topographie von Amarna. *Journal of Near East Studies* 31, 143-155.

Assman, J. 1984a.   *Ägypten-theologie und Frömmigkeit einer frühen Hochkultur.* Kohlhammer.

Assman, J. 1984b.   Schöpfung. *Lexikon der Ägyptologie* V, 677-690.

Badawy, A. 1962.   The Symbolism of the Temples at 'Amarna. *Zeitschrift für ägyptische Sprache und Altertumskunde* 87, 79-95.

Badawy, A. 1968.   *A History of Egyptian Architecture. The Empire (The New Kingdom).* Berkeley and Los Angeles.

Baines, J. 1976.   Temple Symbolism. *Royal Anthropological Institute Newsletter* 15, 10-15.

Barta, W. 1979.   Königsdogma. Lexikon der Ägyptologie III, 485-494.

Barucq, A. and Daumas, F. 1980.   *Hymnes et Prieres de l'Egypte ancienne.* Les editions du Cerf.

Bell, L. 1985.   Luxor Temple and the cult of the Royal Ka. *Journal of Near Eastern Studie* 44, 251-294.

Borchardt, L. 1902.   Die Cyperussäule. *Zeitschrift für ägyptische Sprache und Altertumskunde* XL, 36-49.

Breasted, J. 1906.   *Ancient Records of Egypt.* Chicago.

Fisher, C. 1917.   The Eckley B. Coxe Jr. Egyptian Expedition.

	The Museum Journal (Philadelphia) VIII, 211-237.
Fisher, C. 1921.	The Throne Room of Merenptah. *The Musuem Journal* (Philadelphia) XII, 30-34.
Fisher, C. 1924.	Merenptah's Throne Room. *The Museum Journal* (Philadelphia) XV, 93-100.
Gardiner, A. 1947.	*Ancient Egyptian Onomastica* II. Oxford.
Hawkes, J. 1974.	*Atlas of Ancient Archaeology.* McGraw-Hill.
Haeny, G. 1970.	*Basilikale Anlagen in der ägyptischen Baukunst des neuen Reiches.* Mainz.
Helck, W. 1958.	*Zur Verwaltung des mittleren und neuen Reichs.* Leiden-Cologne.
Hölscher, U. 1941.	*The Excavation of Medinet Habu III. The Mortuary Temple of Ramesses III*, Part III. Chicago.
Hölscher, U. 1951.	*The Excavation of Medinet Habu IV. The Mortuary Temple of Ramesses III*, Part III. Chicago.
Hornung, E. 1971.	*Conceptions of God in Ancient Egypt.* Translated by J. Baines. Cornell.
Jeffreys, D. G. 1985.	*The Survey of Memphis - Part One: The Archaeological Report.* London
Jeffreys, D. G., Malek, J. and Smith, H. S. 1986.	Memphis, 1984. *Journal of Egyptian Archaeology* 72, 1-14.
Kàkosy, L. 1977.	Heliopolis. *Lexikon der Ägyptologie* II, 1111-1113.
Kemp, B. 1976.	The Window of Appearance at el-Amarna, and the Basic Structure of This City. *Journal of Egyptian Archaeology* 62, 82-99.
Kemp, B. 1985.	Tell el-Amarna. *Lexikon der Ägyptologie* VI, 309-319.
Kitchen, K. 1973.	*The Third Intermediate Period in Egypt.* Warminster.
Kitchen, K. 1976.	*Ramesside Inscriptions. Historical and Biographical* II.7. Oxford.
Kitchen, K. 1982.	*Pharaoh Triumphant. The Life and Times*

of Ramesses II. Aris and Phillips, Boston.

Krauss, R. 1980.   Merenptah. *Lexikon der Ägyptologie* IV, 71-76.

Kuhlmann, K. 1977.   *Der Thron im alten Ägypten.* Glückstadt.

Lexikon der Ägyptologie. 1972.   Helck, W., Otto, E. and Westendorf W. (eds.). *Lexikon der Ägyptologie*, I-VI. Wiesbaden.

Lichtheim, M. 1976.   *Ancient Egyptian Literature II. The New Kingdom.* Berkeley, Los Angeles, London.

Moret, A. 1902.   *Le rituel du culte divin journalier en Égypte.* Paris.

Müller, M. W. 1981.   Bemerkungen zu den Kacheln mit Inschriften aus qantir und zu Rekonstruktionen gekachelter Palasttore. *Mitteilungen des deutschen archäologischen Instituts, Cairo* 37, 339-357.

Nelson, H. 1944.   The Egyptian Temple. *Biblical Archaeologist* VII, 44-53.

Newton, F. 1924.   Excavations at el-'Amarna, 1923-24. *Journal of Egyptian Archaeology* 10, 289-298.

Nims, C. 1965.   *Thebes of the Pharaohs.* New York.

O'Connor, D. 1982.   Cities and Towns in: *Egypt's Golden Age* 17-25. Boston.

Pendlebury, J. 1951.   *The City of Akhenaten*, Part III. London and Oxford.

Petrie, W. M. F. 1909a.   *Memphis I.* London.

Petrie, W. M. F. 1909b.   *The Palace of Apries (Memphis II).* London.

Porter, B., Moss, L. and Malek, J. 1981.   *Topographical Bibliography of Ancient Egyptian Hieroglyphic Texts, Reliefs and Paintings. III² Memphis, Part 2.* Oxford.

Redford, D. 1984.   *Akhenaten. The Heretic King.* Princeton.

Ricke, H. 1932.   *Der Grundriss des Amarna-Wohnhauses.* Leipzig.

Rochemonteix, M. de. 1887.   Le temple égyptien. *Revue interna-*

tionale de l'enseignement 15 July 1887.

Smith, E. B. 1938.　　*Egyptian Architecture as Cultural Expression.* New York, London.

Smith, H. S.
and Jeffreys, D. G. 1986.　　A Survey of Memphis, Egypt. *Antiquity* LX, 88-95.

Smith, W. S. 1981.　　*The Art and Architecture of Ancient Egypt.* Revised with additions by W. K. Simpson. Harmondsworth.

Stadèlmann, R. 1973.　　Tempelpalast und Erscheinungsfenster in den Thebanischen Totentempeln. *Mitteilungen des deutschen archäologischen Instituts, Cairo* 29, 221-242.

Stadelmann, R. 1973.　　Audienzhalle. *Lexikon der Ägyptologie* I, 554.

Stadelmann, R. 1979.　　Totentempel und Millionenjahrhaus in Theben. *Mitteilungen des deutschen archäologischen Instituts, Cairo,* 35, 304-321.

Steindorff, G. 1896.　　Haus und Tempel. *Zeitschrift für ägyptische Sprache und Altertumskunde* 34, 107-110.

Strauss, C. 1978.　　Kachel. *Lexikon der Ägyptologie* III, 287-288.

Uphill, E. 1970.　　The Per-Aten at Amarna. *Journal of Near Eastern Studies* 29, 151-166.

Uphill, E. 1972.　　The Concept of the Egyptian Palace as a "Ruling Machine." Ucko, P., Tringham, R. and Dimbleby, G. (eds.). *Man, Settlement and Urbanism,* 721-734. London.

Uphill, E. 1984.　　*The Temples of Per Ramesses.* Aris and Phillips.

Vandier, J. 1955.　　*Manuel d'archéologie egyptienne, II. Les grandes époques. L'architecture religieuse et civile.* Paris.

von Bissing, F. W. 1941.　　*Der Fussboden aus dem Palaste des Königs Amenophis IV zu El Hawata im Museum zu Kairo.* München.

Wente, E. 1982.　　Funerary Beliefs of the Ancient Egyptians. *Expedition* 24.2, 17-26.

Westendorf, W. 1983.   Die Geburt der Zeit aus dem Raum.
                           Göttinger Miszellen 63, 71-76.

Wheatley, P. 1971.   *The Pivot of the Four Quarters*. Chicago.

Whittemore, T. 1926.   The Excavations at el-'Amarnah. Season
                           1924-5. *Journal of Egyptian Archaeology*
                           XII, 3-12.

Wilson, J. 1969.   In Praise of the City Ramses: Pritchard,
                           J. (ed.): *Ancient Near Eastern Texts
                           Relating to the Old Testament*. Princeton.

CAPTIONS

Figure 1.   Plan of the palace of Merenptah, Memphis.

Figure 2.   The rear section of Merenptah's palace; throne room on left, royal suite on right.

Figure 3.   Stone bed platform, with access ramp, in bedroom of royal suite. In front of ramp, patch of painted floor stucco; such fragments were found in other rooms and halls.

Figure 4.   View of Merenptah's palace; foreground court 19, followed by vestibule (18) and throne room (20). The man standing in the doorway between 18 and 7 brings out the large scale of the architecture.

Figure 5.   Comparative, schematic plans (all at about the same scale) of various palaces. 1, columned hall or colonnade; 2, throne-hall or -room; 3, royal suite (B=bedroom, b=bathroom); 4 and 5, other or uncertain functions.

Figure 6.   Comparative, schematic plans (all at about the same scale) of various palaces. For the function codes 1-5, see Figure 5.

Figure 7.   The "Great Palace" of Amarna and the "Great Palace" (?) of Memphis compared; both approximately at the same scale.

Figure 8.   The palace of Merenptah in three-dimensional form; based on Fisher's elevations and sections.

Figure 9.   Three-dimensional drawing of the funerary temple of Ramesses III at Medinet Habu; Hölscher 1941, 7, Figure 3.

Figure 10.   Part of the lintel of a monumental doorway from Merenptah's palace.

Figure 1

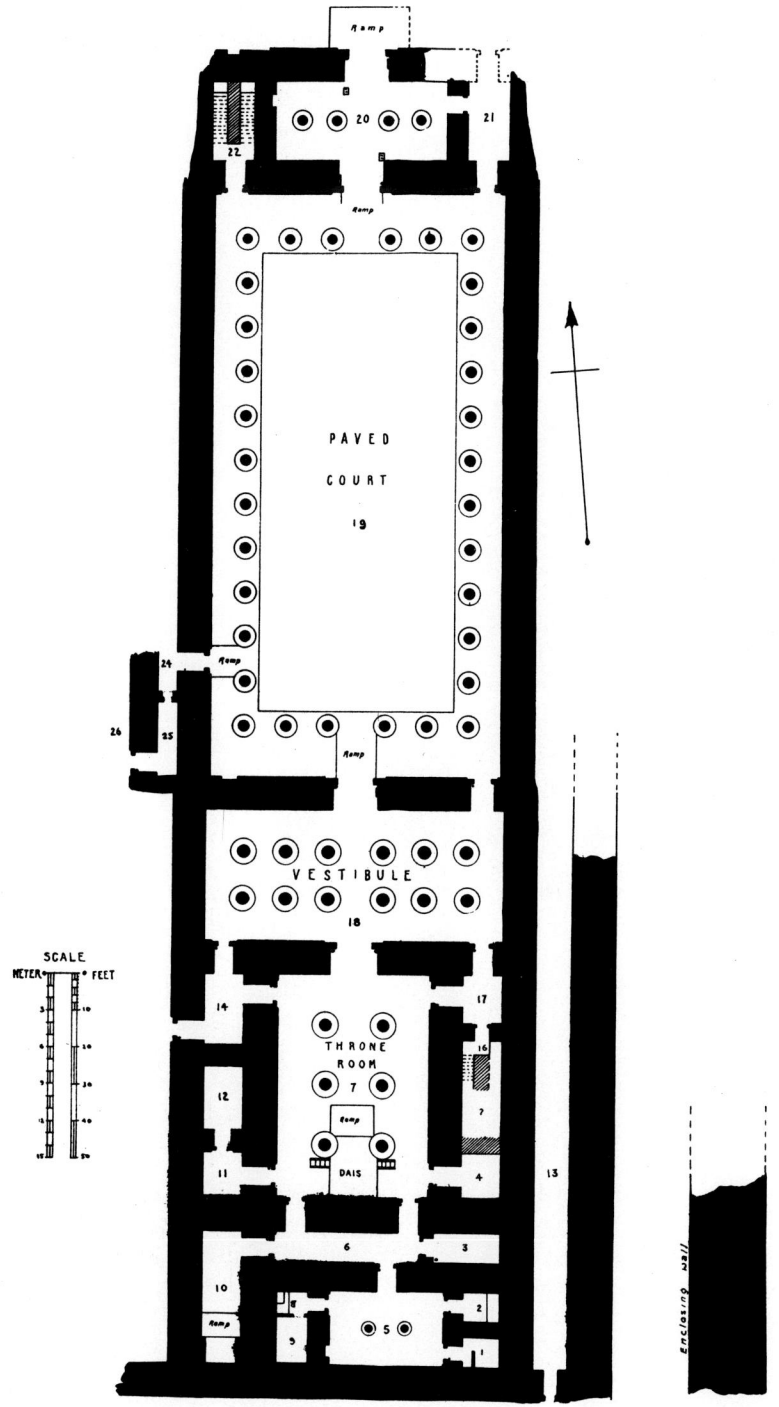

Figure 2

Figure 3

Figure 4

Figure 5

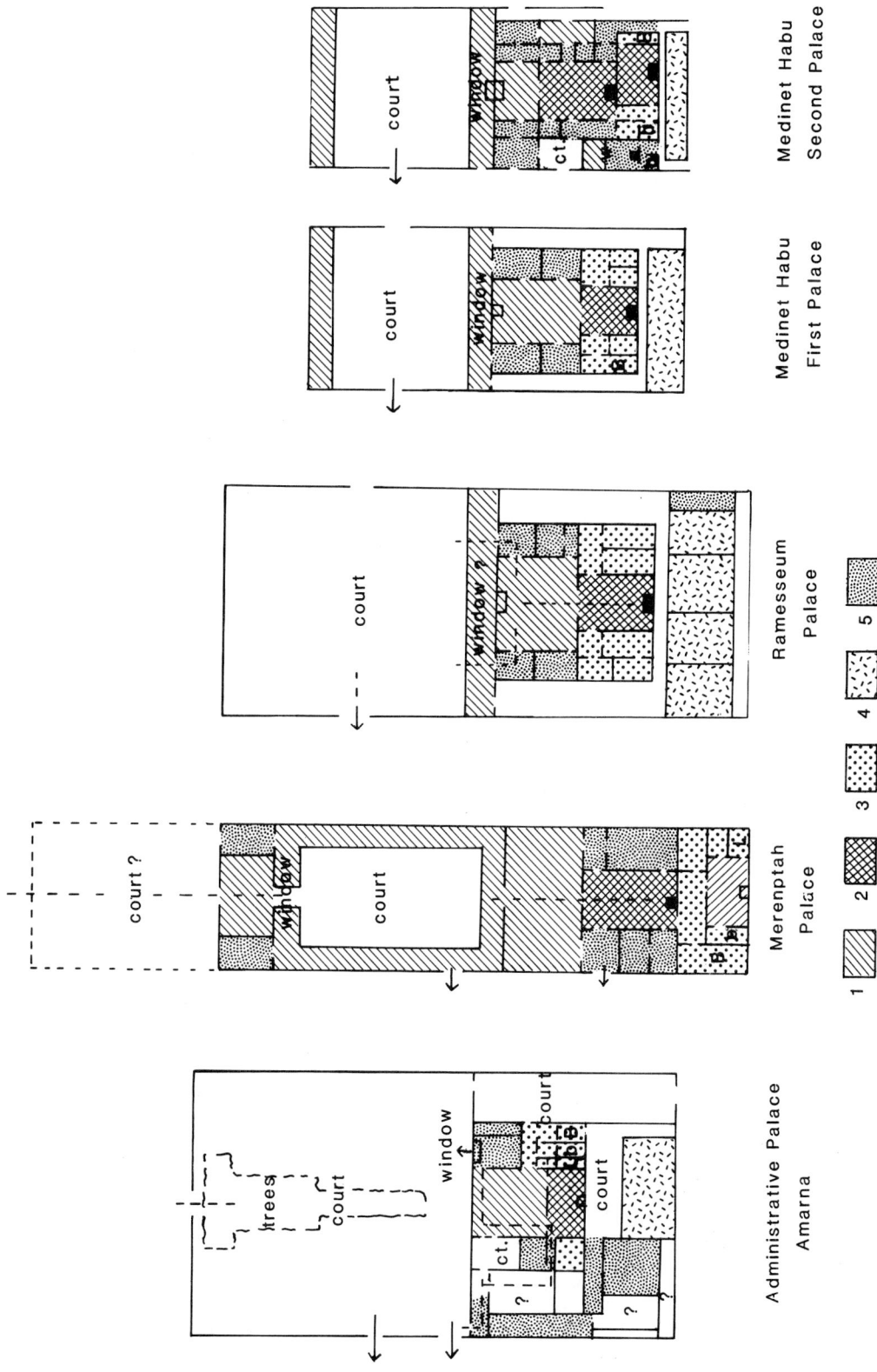

Administrative Palace
Amarna

Merenptah
Palace

Ramesseum
Palace

Medinet Habu
First Palace

Medinet Habu
Second Palace

1 2 3 4 5

195

Figure 6

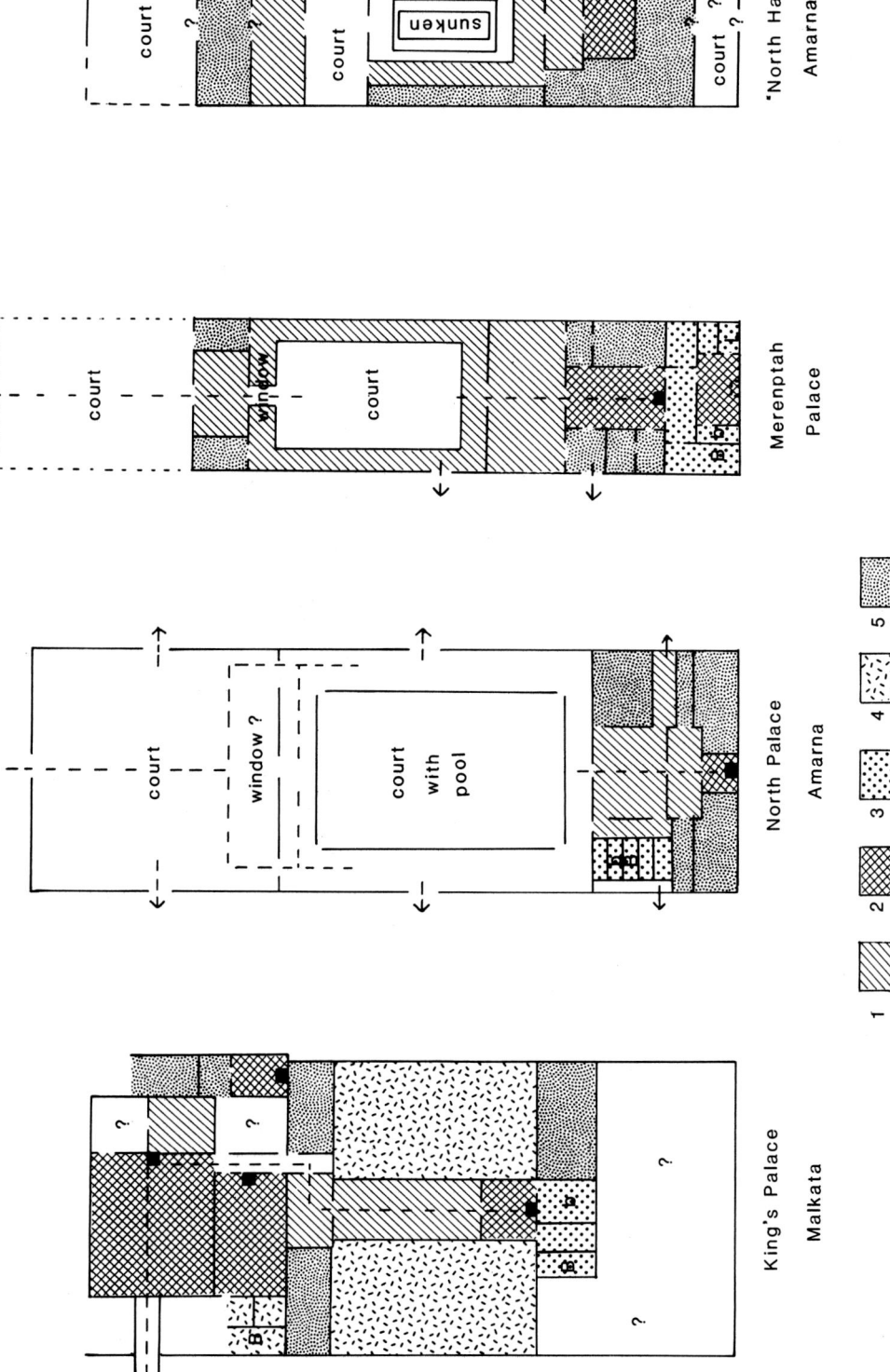

King's Palace

Malkata

North Palace

Amarna

Merenptah

Palace

"North Harem"

Amarna

court with pool

window ?

court

court

window

court

court

sunken

court ?

court ?

court ?

1   2   3   4   5

196

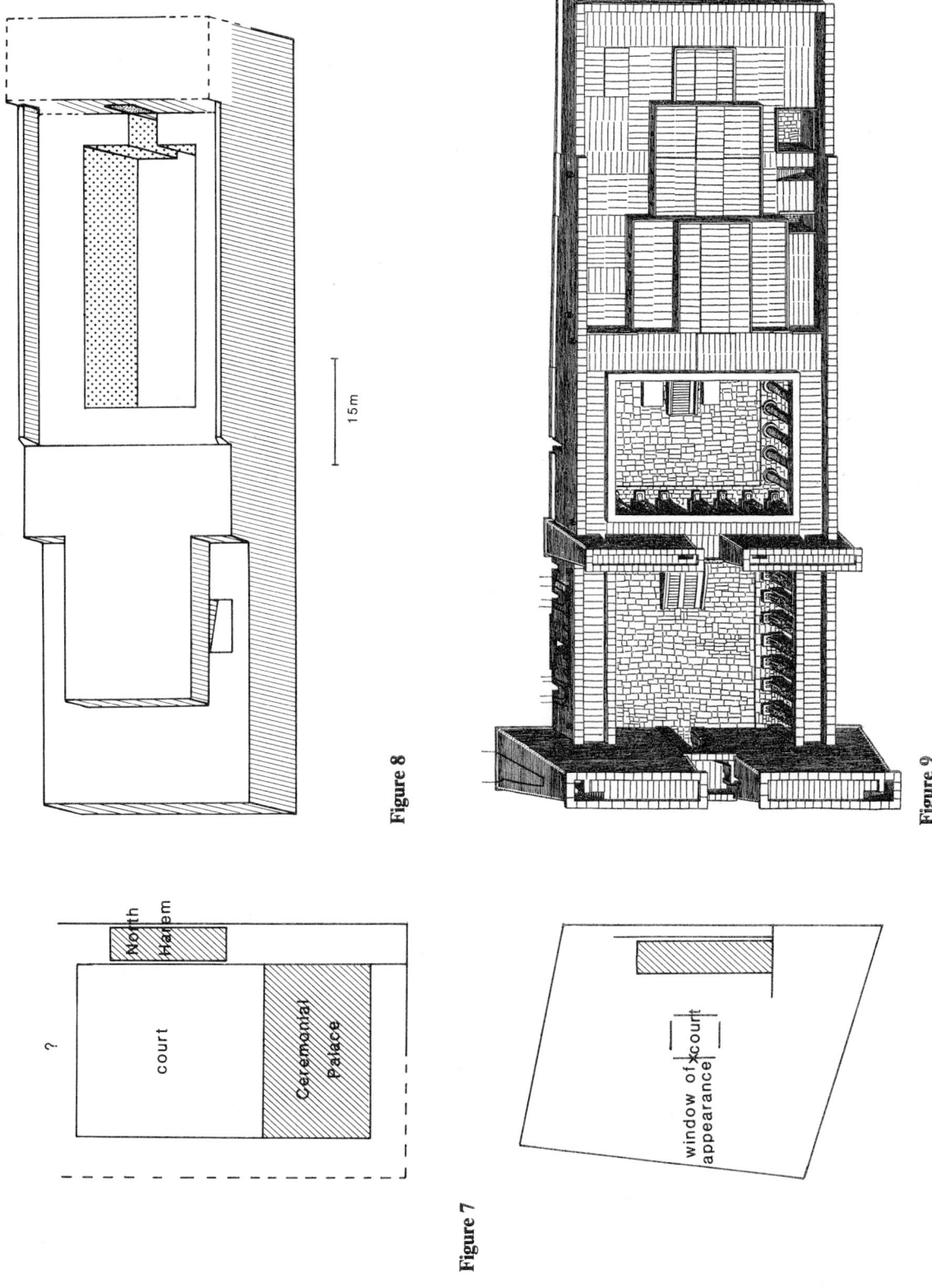

Figure 8

Figure 9

North
Harem

?

court

Ceremonial
Palace

window of
appearance

court

Figure 7

15m

197

Figure 10

RECENT WORK AT NORTHERN PIRAMESSE

Results of Excavations by the
Pelizaeus-Museum, Hildesheim, at Qantir

Edgar B. Pusch

1. Introduction

Since 1980 the Pelizaeus-Museum, Hildesheim, has worked jointly with the Austrian Archaeological Institute, Cairo, in the northern part of Piramesse within the area of Qantir village (Markaz Faqus, Muhafzah Sharkijah).[1] During one preliminary season and five excavation campaigns, an area of almost 15,000 square metres was worked. Parallel to the excavations themselves, we were able to do several soundings and surveys within the adjoining fields, which led to the identification and localization of excavations by Mahmoud Hamza,[2] Labib Habachi, and Ahmed Abdel-Salam Ahmed. The exact position of these excavations had not been known before.

The major goal of our project is to contribute to the knowledge of the history and settlement structure of Piramesse and to further our knowledge about settlement architecture in general. Therefore, we started our excavation in an area identified and reconstructed as the palace area by MANFRED BIETAK.[3] This excavation, which was named Q I and is nearly finished, includes parts of the above mentioned excavations of our Egyptian colleagues. The results of the work can be summarized as follows. The excavated area contains four stratigraphically distinct layers: 1) an extremely destroyed and disturbed 18th Dynasty layer (C/D_1); 2) a large-scale metal factory of the late 18th(?) to early 19th Dynasty (B_3); 3) a military comple dating to Ramesses II (B_2); and finally 4) a demolition level of this military installation (B_1).[4] All this military installation layers and levels are

---

1 The present article is a slightly enlarged version of a lecture intended to be read during the symposium on Ramesses the Great. It has been augmented by the results of the fifth excavation campaign at the site of Qantir. The results are subject to minor changes and further refinements with regard to stratigraphy and dating since only part of the documentation was evaluated. I am very grateful to Dr. DAVID ASTON for his kind assistance in the editing of my English text.

The excavation is kindly financed by the Deutsche Forschungsgemeinschaft, Bonn.
I am greatly indebted to Dr. ARNE EGGEBRECHT, Director of the Pelizaeus-Museum, Hildesheim, for entrusting me with the position of field director from the very beginning. I also want to express my sincere thanks to Dr. MANFRED BIETAK and Dr. JOSEPH DORNER, Austrian Arch. Inst., Cairo, for their constant cooperation and for our many discussions about our excavations and Tell el-Dab'a material. None of the results would have come to light without the kind support of the Egyptian Antiquities Organization, their officials, my many collaborators, and the excellently trained and highly specialized workmen from Quft. Fig. 1; compare BIETAK 1979, 227, fig. 1; BIETAK 1975, map 1 and 4; HAMZA 1930, fig. 1; and PUSCH 1987a, fig. 1.

2 HAMZA 1930.

3 See BIETAK 1975, 33 ff., fig. 1 (on p. 43) and fig. 44 (opposite p. 212); compare BIETAK 1984, s.v. "Ramsesstadt"; see also PUSCH 1987a-b, fig. 1 and FREED 1987, 34.

4 See fig. 2 on page 000.

stratigraphically equal to the Tell el-Dab'a strata B to C, and possibly even to D_1 of the early 18th Dynasty.[5] This view is strongly suggested by an evaluation of our contexts and finds. While there is little to be said about the earliest settlement (Stratum C/D_1), the other strata are distinct and can almost be called well preserved. All of them make valuable contributions to our knowledge of the Ramesside Period with respect to functional and historical details, especially during the reign of Ramesses II.

STRATUM	DATE	FUNCTION	CONTENTS
B1	post Ramesses II (Merenptah/ Ramesses III?)	unknown	material mainly of stratum B_2, namely inscribed octogonal pillars
B2	Sethi I/ Ramesses II	military area: chariotry/work-shops	pillared hall, multifunctional workshop-area, scribal bureau with sanctuary of *Dhwtj nb Hmnw*
B3	late 18th(?) to early 19th Dynasty	industrial bronze fab-rication/ workshops	smelting(?)-ovens melting-channels, multi-workshops and offices
C/D1	early 18th Dynasty Amenophis II(?)	unknown	pottery

Fig. 2 Stratigraphical grid of excavation area Q I.

2. Early 18th Dynasty Level

The remains are too scarce to determine the function of the early 18th Dynasty level (C/D_1). The disturbances by the upper levels are so serious that only a few bricks and a tiny "islands" of floors are preserved. This unfortunate situation also pertains to the finds. Their dating, based on the pottery, is not to be doubted,[6] especially since a scarab was found naming *ntr nfr nb t3wj '3-hprw-r' mrj Imn*: Amenophis II, although this came to light in a secondary position.[7] Regrettably, nothing has been observed thus far which would give a clue to its function.

---

5 These have recently been described by BIETAK 1985, 131; see also BIETAK 1968, 88 ff.; 1970, 17 f.; and 1979, 236 ff. The labeling of the layers as strata B1 to C/D1 has to be understood as a general stratigraphical comparison. The Qantir strata B1-3 are not necessarily identical with strata named thus in Tell el-Dab'a. Stratum B stands for "Ramesside Period" in both sites. The index numbers may denote layers of different date.

6 See D. ASTON 1987 (forthcoming).

7 See E. PUSCH 1989 b (forthcoming).

3. Metal Industry and Workshops

The next stratum (B$_3$) contains the metal factory and cuts deeply into the one just described. It comprises two distinct areas. South of an enclosure wall of 2 1/2 cubits thickness, there are rooms for processing organic and inorganic materials, such as wood and leather, metal and stone. North of the enclosure wall and within an unroofed area, we uncovered seven "melting channels." Each of them has a length of more than 15 metres. They were built from parallel rows of mudbricks about 20 cm. apart into which blast pipes were inserted.[8] These blast pipes were worked by foot bellows,[9] a construction almost identical to the scenes depicted in the tomb of Rekhmire.[10] Adhesive slag and embedded remains of bronze, as well as crucibles with similar materials preserved within them, enable us to define this area as a bronze workshop.[11] These constructions[12] are significant not only because of their rarity but most of all because of their huge size and intensity of use. We have several indications that these "channels" were in use practically at the same time. The closeness of the tyeres allows us to estimate that several hundred people were working the foot bellows simultaneously.[13] Taking into consideration that these constructions continued for more than 60 metres to the east, as well as more than 50 metres to the west of the described area, and that HAMZA 1930, 62 ff. described identical blast pipes which he found more than 200 metres northeast of our excavation, one can surely speak of a large scale metal industry. For what purpose these tremendous amounts of bronze had been melted, I cannot yet say. We did find apparent casting pits sunk into the sand between the "melting channels." These contained fragments of firebrick along with ashes, burnt clay, tyeres, crucibles, and bronze,[14] but we have not yet assembled these fragments in a way

8 See fig. 3; for blast pipes/tyeres, see TYLECOTE 1981, 107 ff., especially those from Tell Zeror, fig. 13 on p. 116 (3 upper objects).

9 For foot/pot bellows in general, see DAVEY 1979, 101 ff. Foot bellows have not yet been identified at Qantir but are very likely contained within the rich pottery finds which are now being studied by DAVID ASTON. The vast extension of the metal factory excludes, in my opinion, the possibility that the blast pipes were worked by skin bellows (see below).

10 See fig. 4, DAVIES 1973, pl. 52.

11 Several different kinds of crucibles have been identified and reconstructed by Dr. G. WEISGERBER, German Mining Museum, Bochum, to whom I am deeply grateful for providing me with specialised literature and a reconstruction of the melting channel technique. For comparable crucibles, see BEIT-ARIEH 1985, fig. 13, 5-7, 13 and DAVEY 1985, pl. 13, 2+4.

12 For the construction of the Qantir melting channels, see the very similar hypothetical reconstruction by TYLECOTE 1981, 117, fig. 14 and E. PUSCH 1987d.

13 This estimate is based on part of one of the best preserved melting channels which contained 39 tyeres spread over 7.00 m. on both sides. This would amount to more than 80 tyeres and more than 40 people per melting channel, equally distributed on both sides working the pot bellows only. To these, an uncertain number of further workmen must be added. They would have carried the crucibles to the casting pits, since it is not at all clear that this was done by the same people, not to mention supervisors and the like. The calculation is based exclusively on the excavated melting channels covering an area of about 240 square metres. Judging from identical layers to the east and the west of these, and adding the finds of HAMZA 1930 as well as the "cross furnaces," the metal industry may have covered an area of more than 30,000 square metres (see below).

14 For comparable casting pits with similar contents, see those of the Phidias workshop in

which could possibly tell us the objects which were once cast in this area.[15] Small casting moulds of limestone may well belong to the upper stratum B_2 (see below). It is clear, however, that not only ingots were melted down but also folded arrowheads and knives, proving an extensive and careful recycling of the precious metal.

In same stratum B_3 and on the same absolute height, is a series of at least three furnaces of a completely new and different type, lying north of the "melting channels." This "cross furnace," provisionally so named because of its cross-like structure, has an extension of 9.00 metres north-south and $x + 6.00 + y$ metres east-west (fig. 5). At least two of these were built on a common east-west axis. One was excavated exemplarily, while the others were left untouched as soon as their general similarity to the first had been proven. The highest temperature was effective from top to bottom and from the center to the outer regions of the "cross furnace," judging from the oxidation of the originally unburnt mudbricks. The whole structure is partitioned into several chambers by thin dividing walls, their floors paved with mudbrick slightly sloping to the center within the compartments but with a steep gradient from compartment to compartment. The lowest point was reached in a slag pit which still contained lumps of slag, including metal. In all compartments liquid could flow, as is proven by slag adhering to walls and floors. Since the adhering slag and the lumps of slag from the slag pit look quite similar, if not identical, by visual comparison, I tentatively suggest that the "cross furnace" was also used for metal processing in one way or the other.

The completely different structure of the "cross furnaces," in comparison to the "melting channels," may give rise to a different functional identification. While the "channels" are clearly structures for melting bronze in crucibles, the "cross furnaces" may possibly be interpreted as smelting devices. This would be a novelty regarding technique, size, and date, but as a hypothesis, it has to be proven by further studies and analyses.

Since the "cross furnaces" and the "melting channels" belong together stratigraphically, we have an obvious north-south distribution, provided the identification of the "cross furnace" as a smelting furnace is correct as follows: 1) smelting - "cross furnace"; 2) melting/casting - "melting channels/ casting pits" between them; 3) south of the enclosure wall: small multifunctional workshops for hot and cold metalworking, including other substances such as stone, bone, leather, and the like. Herewith, the whole production line from ore to final product could be archaeologically documented, including work places, raw materials, and tools. The dating of this level is based upon the dating of the previous one, the pottery contained within the layers (ashes, burnt clay, and floors), and on the inscribed objects of the following level.

4. The Chariotry and Adjoining Installations

While the multifunctional workshop south of the enclosure wall continued to function into the third level (B_2), the metal industry north of the enclosure was abandoned and leveled. This part was now turned into a vast courtyard lined with limestone columns, octagonal in

---

Olympia and at the Kerameikos in Athens (SCHNEIDER/ZIMMER 1986, 18-22, especially figs. 1 and 3).

15 The Rekhmire scenes show the casting of bronze doors for the temple of Amun (above n. 9 and fig. 4). These would call for rectangular or at least oblong pits. At Qantir, only circular pits have been identified so far.

section, and inscribed with the protocol of Ramesses II.[16] Their heights can be calculated to have been slightly more than 3.60 metres, equaling seven royal cubits. This is based upon more than 26 pieces, having a length of up to 2.60 metres. All of them were originally produced by Sethi I and re-used by Ramesses II after proportions and inscriptions had been changed. This courtyard and the adjoining southern workshops - now also containing a scribal office with a sanctuary for "Thoth of Hermopolis" - belonged to what once had been a chariotry. Within the floors, layers, and stratigraphically contemporary pits, we found more than 400 yokesaddle-knobs, yokeknobs, and decorative discs of calcite, marble, fayence, and bone belonging to the chariot body.[17] Additionally, we unearthed bronze fragments of horse-bits, one complete and undamaged set of horse-bits,[18] axlenails with a covering of gold-leaf-plated stucco,[19] and a completely unique object which may be called an ancient Egyptian hub-cap.[20] This last object is a conical bronze tube with a thickened edge, which was slipped over the nave of the wheel. Prints of horses' hooves (clearly identified by their shape) within mud floors and organic layers round off this functional designation.

An extraordinary feature, which is unique in Egypt and the ancient Near East, is that represented by seven limestone shield moulds, one of them still in situ. Two different shield types, or rather the metal applications of these shields, were produced from them by embossing out of bronze sheets special designs covering the edges and certain parts of the shield surface.[21] Probably, both types have to be attributed to Hittite culture. The first is the so-called figure-eight or pontic shield,[22] carried by the Hittites and their allies in the battle of Qadesh[23] and again represented in a relief of the ninth century B.C. from Sinjerli.[24] The second shield type is square to trapezoidal in contour, having a stylized bull's head in the center,[25] which reminds one of the Hittite storm and weather god, who was pictured and adored as a bull according to Anatolian representations[26] and Hittite

---

16 LECLANT 1982, fig. 11; FREED 1987, 35 top.

17 See E. PUSCH 1987 a-b (forthcoming).

18 Fig. 6; compare POTRATZ 1941, 7, fig. 5+7 and POTRATZ 1966, 103 ff., fig. 45e on p. 108 (No. 6) and fig. 108 on pl. XLVII (No. 8).

19 See U. HOFMANN 1987 (forthcoming).

20 For a similar device made of wood on the Florence chariot, see LITTAUER/CROUWEL 1985, 106. Its description has to be corrected insofar as the grain is not "running at right angles to that of the nave."

21 E. PUSCH 1987a, 1987c, and 1989a.

22 Fig. 7; photograph of one out of four designs, see LECLANT/ CLERC 1986, fig. 20, and PUSCH 1985, 1988a.

23 Fig. 8, WRESZINSKI 1936, 21; see also H. BORCHHARDT 1977, E6 ff., especially fig. 8 opposite E56.

24 See ORTHMANN 1971, pl. 58 f. (Zinçirli B/13a); ORTHMANN 1975, 357; BOSSERT 1942, No. 927.

25 Photograph of one out of three designs, see LECLANT/CLERC 1986, fig. 19; PUSCH 1989a.

26 See MACQUEEN 1986, fig. 136 (Alaca); BOSSERT 1942, No. 510.

descriptions of idols.[27] To these moulds one more has now to be added. This fragmentary piece shows parts of a rectangular shield framing a calf in "flying gallop" in the lower left corner. The style and finishing of the motif remind me of similar representations originating in the Aegean and later introduced into Near Eastern cultures.[28] Since more than half of the motif is lost, it may possibly be reconstructed as a hunting scene or as a "calf attacked by a lion." Limestone fragments in storage but as yet unstudied may yield further parts of this shield mould. I think of this surprising and singular object in the context of the other shield moulds, having reached Piramesse via the Anatolian and Syro-Palestinian regions. On one point I want to put special weight. None of these objects is an Anatolian shield, but, on the contrary, all of them are tools for producing applications with which Hittite, or generally speaking, Near Eastern types of shields were covered. Moreover, since one of these moulds still remained in situ in the workshop, and since most of the necessary equipment for the manufacture of shields, such as hammers and chisels, were found on the floors, I do not hesitate to conclude that these shields were produced by foreigners on the spot inside Piramesse. Since, furthermore, the Egyptians carried exclusively oblong shields rounded at the top, it must be concluded that Hittite workmen produced or repaired figure-eight shields for Hittite troops - chariotry and infantry - in Qantir.[29] To these weapons may be added rich finds of daggers, javelin heads, and arrowheads of unusual kind. These comprise specialized projectiles, such as crossbow-like bolts, heads with heliacal edges, arrowheads with movable barbs, and others. This picture is completed by bronze scales of different proveniences, one fayence scale with a so-far undeciphered cartouche, and a single scale of a cheek piece of a boar's tusk helmet.[30] Of minor importance are bronze knobs and nails covered with gold foil and similar objects which may have been applications to several devices including chariots and their outfit.

Altogether, a picture can be formed which enriches our historical knowledge of ancient Egyptian foreign relations at the time of Ramesses II, namely the peaceful presence of Hittites on Egyptian territory at a time when Hatti has to be called a world power. This covers the fields of craftsmanship as well as the military level. Therefore, we have at least two independent possibilities for dating this stratum: the inscribed octagonal pillars of Ramesses II from the courtyard and the tools described above. Since Egypt and Hatti still had hostile relations in Ramesses II's fifth year and since the famous treaty between this pharaoh and Hattusili III was not signed until Ramesses II's 21st year, there is no possibility to date this weapon production and the respective layers before then. More likely, I should think, the production of shields was started after the marriage of Hattusili's eldest daughter to Ramesses II. This would mean, as a *terminus ante quem non*, year 34 of Ramesses II. The Egyptian and Hittite texts which describe this event tell us that Maatnofrure was accompanied by a large retinue, a considerable part of which must have remained as her personal attendants in Piramesse. In addition to these dating factors, we have several finds embedded into floors: among others, a stela showing one of the divine statues of Ramesses II, most probably *Mnṯw-m-t3wj* and a scarab which seems to name this statue. This Ramesside dating is also supported by the pottery studies being undertaken by Dr. DAVID ASTON as well as archaeological criteria.

---

27 See generally BRANDENSTEIN 1943 and ROST 1963, especially the list, p. 204 f.

28 See SCHACHERMEYR 1967, 44 ff.

29 See E. PUSCH 1987a, 1987c, and 1989a (all forthcoming) and PUSCH 1985, 135.

30 J. BORCHHARDT 1972, 18 ff., pl. 1, 3+5 as most similar objects and E. PUSCH 1989a (forthcoming).

Huge buildings lie to the east of the chariotry area and on top of the workshop levels of stratum B₃.[31] Their roofs were carried by whitewashed mudbrick pillars. One of these buildings, not yet completely excavated, contained at least 70 pillars arranged in seven rows of ten running in an east-west direction. A similar building which lay to the north of it may have had the same dimensions. The layout and construction reminds one of the so-called "Coronation Hall" in Amarna, which is now interpreted as a monumental vineyard. Indications for such an interpretation at Qantir are not yet present, and further excavations - seriously hampered by modern cultivation - have to be awaited.

There is one more aspect which has to be mentioned but which is not represented architecturally. Finds of animal bones studied by JOACHIM BOESSNECK and ANGELA VON DEN DRIESCH, Munich, led to the conclusion that there may have been a menagerie at Piramesse.[32] There would have been present hyenas, boars, aurochs, giraffes, various antelopes and gazelles (some of them not native to Egypt), ibexes and dama deer.[33] Additionally, we do have clear evidence of the royal animals, lion and elephant. Some of the above, however, may not have lived in the menagerie, their bones simply being still attached to animal skins brought to the capital as trophies. For instance, of the giraffe there are only parts of the skull and the horns left but nothing of the post-cranial skeleton. The menagerie must have been in the near vicinity of Q I and is most probably contemporary with the chariotry.

5. The Destruction Level of the Chariotry

The fourth and last layer (B₁) comprises a destruction horizon, mainly in the area of the courtyard. Deep depressions and pits cutting into all described strata were filled with debris of the broken walls and octagonal pillars. All of these have been reworked, the proportions and the Ramesses II inscriptions having been changed again. Direct evidence, such as further inscriptions for dating this level to the late Ramesses II or one of his followers, was not found. This may have taken place, on the one hand, in the time of Merenptah, since AHMED ABDEL-SALAM AHMED unearthed a large limestone pedestal inscribed with his name, or on the other, during the 20th or 21st Dynasty, since we have a number of potsherds tentatively dated to this period.

6. Conclusion

The result of the excavations directed by me during the last six years may be summarized as follows: a continuous settlement starting in the early 18th Dynasty and lasting well beyond the time of Merenptah can be archaeologically documented at Qantir. These layers not only support the knowledge gained from texts but add interesting and considerable historical and technological details, such as the presence of Hittite workmen and troops and the unique metal industry featuring several different types of ovens and furnaces.

---

31 LECLANT/CLERC 1986, fig. 18.

32 BOESSNECK/V.D. DRIESCH 1982, 136 ff. and 1987 (forthcoming).

33 A list of all animals possibly belonging to the menagerie will be published within a complete study of all bones by BOESSNECK/ V.D. DRIESCH 1987.

The new excavation area, Q IV, which is now thought to be soldiers' quarters on the basis of MANFRED BIETAK's criteria,[34] likewise promises rich rewards in terms of its finds. During the last years, I collected from this latter site, among other things, two limestone blocks: one showing the goddess Astarte on a horse with a king offering in front of her[35] and one calling a king "Beloved of Reshef."[36] The drill soundings promise an extensive stratigraphy. Surface finds include a fragment of Ramesses II as *ntr hq3 Iwnw*,[37] a quartzite fragment naming Merneptah, and a fayence mould of Ramesses III. This gives great hope not only that we will have excellent stratigraphy but also that this stratigraphy may be dated and add once again to our knowledge of the Ramesside Period and to its relations with its foreign neighbours.

---

34 BIETAK 1975, p. 43, fig. 1, fig. 44 (opposite 212) and 1984, 137/38; FREED 1987, 34; see above fig. 1 at the co-ordinates x = 1650-1570/y = 1640-1670.

35 See LECLANT 1960, 1 ff., especially Doc. 5; STADELMANN 1967, 96 ff.; HELCK 1971, 456 ff.

36 HELCK 1971, 450 ff.; STADELMANN 1967, 47 ff., for the close relationship between Astarte and Reshef, see 101 f. and 103 f. including n. 3 on 105; and see pAnast. II 1/4-5 where Astarte is governing the East (!) of Piramesse as royal goddess.

37 According to this addition, the stela fragment is to be dated between the years 42 and 56; see EDEL 1976, 18-20 and 29 f.

LIST OF FIGURES

Fig. 1 Qantir 1984-1986: Position of excavation area Q I and earlier excavations in relation to site reconstruction by M. BIETAK 1984. The hatched areas of Q I are approximately identical with the extension of stratum B_3.

Fig. 2 Stratigraphical grid of excavation area Q I.

Fig. 3 Tyere with adhesive slag and bronze, Q I, FZ 84/545, stratum B_3 (drawing J. KLANG).

Fig. 4 Scenes from tomb of Rekhmire depicting constructions similar to the Qantir "melting channels."

Fig. 5 "Cross furnace," stratum B_3, late 18th(?) to early 19th Dynasty.

Fig. 6 Horse-bit, bronze, FZ 86/281A (+B), stratum B_2 (drawing J. KLANG).

Fig. 7 Mould for production of metal application of the Hittite figure-eight shield, obverse, FZ 84/1, stratum B_2, originally found in situ (drawing J. KLANG).

Fig. 8 Hittites and Hittite contingents carrying figure-eight and rectangular shields in the battle of Qadesh.

LIST OF PLATES

I. - Qantir, Stratum B$_3$: "Cross-furnace" for copper smelting (?), center part with oxydised mudbricks seen from north (square Q I-ax.a/3).

II. - Qantir, Stratum B$_3$: "Cross-furnace" for copper smelting (?), center part with chambers seen from west (square Q I-ax.a/3).

III. - Qantir, Stratum B$_3$: part of "melting channel" No. 2 for bronze production in square Q I-b/3 with layers of ashes and charcoal, tyeres before cleaning.

IV. - Qantir, Stratum B$_3$: part of "melting channel" No. 3 for bronze production in square Q I-b/4 destroyed by pit of stratum B$_{1-2}$, partly cleaned.

LITERATURE

ASTON, D.A. 1987   Bulletin de Liaison du Groupe international d'Etude de la Ceramique Egyptienne (forthcoming).

BEIT-ARIEH, I. 1985   Serabit el-Khadim: New Metallurgical and Chronological Aspects, in: Levant 17, 1985, 89ff.

BIETAK, M. 1968   Vorläufiger Bericht über die erste und zweite Kampagne der österreichischen Ausgrabungen auf Tell ed-Dab'a im Ostdelta Ägyptens 1966, 1967, in: *MDAIK* 23, 1968, 79ff.

1970   Vorläufiger Bericht über die dritte Kampagne der österreichischen Ausgrabungen auf Tell ed- Dab'a im Ostdelta Ägyptens 1968, in *MDAIK* 26, 1970, 15 ff.

1975   Tell el-Dab'a II, Wien 1975 (*ÖAWD* 4).

1979   Avaris and Piramesse, in: *Proc. of the Brit. Acad.* 65, London 1979, 225 ff.

1984   *Lexikon der Ägyptologie* V, Wiesbaden 1984.

1985   Tell el-Dab'a, in: *AfO* 32, 1985, 130ff.

BOESNNECK, J. and
A. V.D. DRIESCH 1982   Elefanten-, Löwen- und andere Tierknochen aus der Palastanlage der Ramessidenzeit bei Qantir im östlichen Nildelta, in: *Studien an subfossilen Tierknochen aus Ägypten*, München 1982, 136 ff. (*MÄS* 40).

1987   Weitere Tierknochenfunde aus der Palastanlage der Ramessidenzeit bei Qantir im östlichen Nildelta, in: *ÄAT* 10,2 (forthcoming).

BORCHHARDT, H. 1977   Frühe griechische Schildformen, in: *Archeologia Homerica* I, Kap.E, Teil 1, Göttingen 1977, E1 ff.

BORCHHARDT, J. 1972   *Homerische Helme*, Mainz 1972.

1977   Helme, in: *Archeologia Homerica* I, Kap.E, Teil 1, Gottingen 1977, E57 ff.

BOSSERT, H. TH. 1942   *Altanatolien*, Berlin 1942 (Die Ältesten Kulturen des Mittelmeer-kreises Vol. 2).

v. BRANDENSTEIN,
C.G. 1943   Hethitische Götter nach Bildbe-schreibungen in Keilschrifttexten, in: *MIO* 46, 1943, 1ff.

DAVEY, C.J. 1979   Some Ancient Near Eastern Pot Bel-lows, in: *Levant* 9, 1979, 101ff.

1985   Crucibles in the Petrie Collection and Hieroglyphic Ideograms for Metal, in: *JEA* 71, 1985, 142ff.

DAVIES, N.d.G. 1973   *The Tomb of Rekh-mi-Re' at Thebes*, New York 1973 (repr.).

EDEL, E. 1976   *Ägyptische Ärzte und ägyptische Medizin am hethitischen Königshof*, Düsseldorf 1976.

FREED, R. 1987   *Ramesses the Great, An Exhibition in the City of Memphis*, Memphis, Tennessee 1987.

HAMZA, M. 1930   Excavations of the Department of Antiquities at Qantir (Faqus Dis-trict), in: *ASAE* 30, 1930, 31ff.

HELCK, W. 1971   *Die Beziehungen Ägyptens zu Vorder-asien im 3. und 2. Jahrtausend v. Chr.*, Wiesbaden 1971, 2nd revised edition (ÄgAbh. 5).

HOFMANN, U. 1987   Ein ramessidischer Achsnagel aus Qantir (FZ 84/115), in: *ÄAT* 10,2 (forthcoming).

LECLANT, J. 1960   Astarté a Cheval d'après le repré-sentations Egyptiennes, in: *Syria* 37, 160, 1ff.

1982   Fouilles et travaux en Egypte et au Soudan, 1980-1981, in: *Orient.* 51, 1982, 411 ff.

1984   Fouilles et travaux en Egypte et au Soudan, 1982-1983, in: *Orient.* 53, 1984, 350 ff.

LECLANT, J. and
CLERC, G. 1986   Fouilles et travaux en Egypte et au

Soudan, 1984-1985, in: Orient. 55, 1986, 236 ff.

LITTAUER, M.A. and
CROUWEL, J.H. 1985   *Chariots and related Equipment from the Tomb of Tut'ankhamun*, Oxford 1985 (TTS 8).

MACQUEEN, J.G. 1986   *The Hittites and their contemporaries in Asia Minor*, London 1986, revised edition of 1975.

ORTHMANN, W. 1971   *Untersuchungen zur späthetitischen Kunst*, Bonn 1971.

1975   (ed.) *Der Alte Orient, Propyläen Kunstgeschichte* 14, Berlin 1975.

POTRATZ, J.H.A. 1941   Die Pferdegebisse des zweistromländischen Raumes, in: *AfO* 14, 1941-44, 1 ff.

1966   *Die Pferdetrensen des Alten Orient*, Rome 1966 (Anal. Or. 41)

PUSCH, E.B. 1985   Qantir, in: *AfO* 32, 1985, 135 f.

1987a   Erster Bericht über die vom Pelizäeus-Museum Hildesheim in Qantir unternommenen Arbeiten 1980, 1982, 1983, in: *ÄAT* 10,1, Bamberg 1987 (forthcoming).

1987b   Streitwagentruppen in Qantir, in: *ÄAT* 10,2, Bamberg 1987 (forthcoming).

1987c   Geräte zur Herstellung von Metallbeschlägen fur hethitische Schilde, in: *ÄAT* 10,2, Bamberg 1987 (forthcoming).

1987d   Industrielle Metallverarbeitung der Späten Bronzezeit in Qantir-Piramesse, in: *Ägypten und Levante* 1 (ed. M. BIETAK), Wien (forthcoming).

1989a   Ausländisches Kulturgut in Qantir-Piramesse, in: Beihefte zu *SAK 3* (Acts of the 4th Intern. Congr. of Egyptology, Munich 1985, forthcoming).

1989b   *Dritter Bericht uber die vom Pelizäeus-Museum Hildesheim in Qantir unternommenen Arbeiten* 1987 (forthcoming).

211

ROST, L. 1963   Zu den hethitischen Bildbeschrei-
bungen, in: *MIO* 8, 1963, 161 f.

SCHACHERMEYR 1967   *Ägais und Orient*, Wien 1967 (DAWW
93).

SCHNEIDER, G. and
ZIMMER, G. 1986   Technische Keramik aus antiken
Bronzegusswerkstätten in Olympia
und Athen, in: *Berliner Beiträge zur
Archäometrie* (BBA) 9/1984, 1986, 17 ff.

STADELMANN, R. 1967   *Syrisch-palästinensische Gottheiten
in Ägypten*, Leiden 1967.

TYLECOTE, R.F. 1981   From Pot Bellows to Tyeres, in:
Levant 13, 1981, 107ff.

WRESZINSKY, W. 1936   *Atlas zur altägyptischen Kulturge-
schichte Bd. 2, Leipzig 1936.

Figure 1

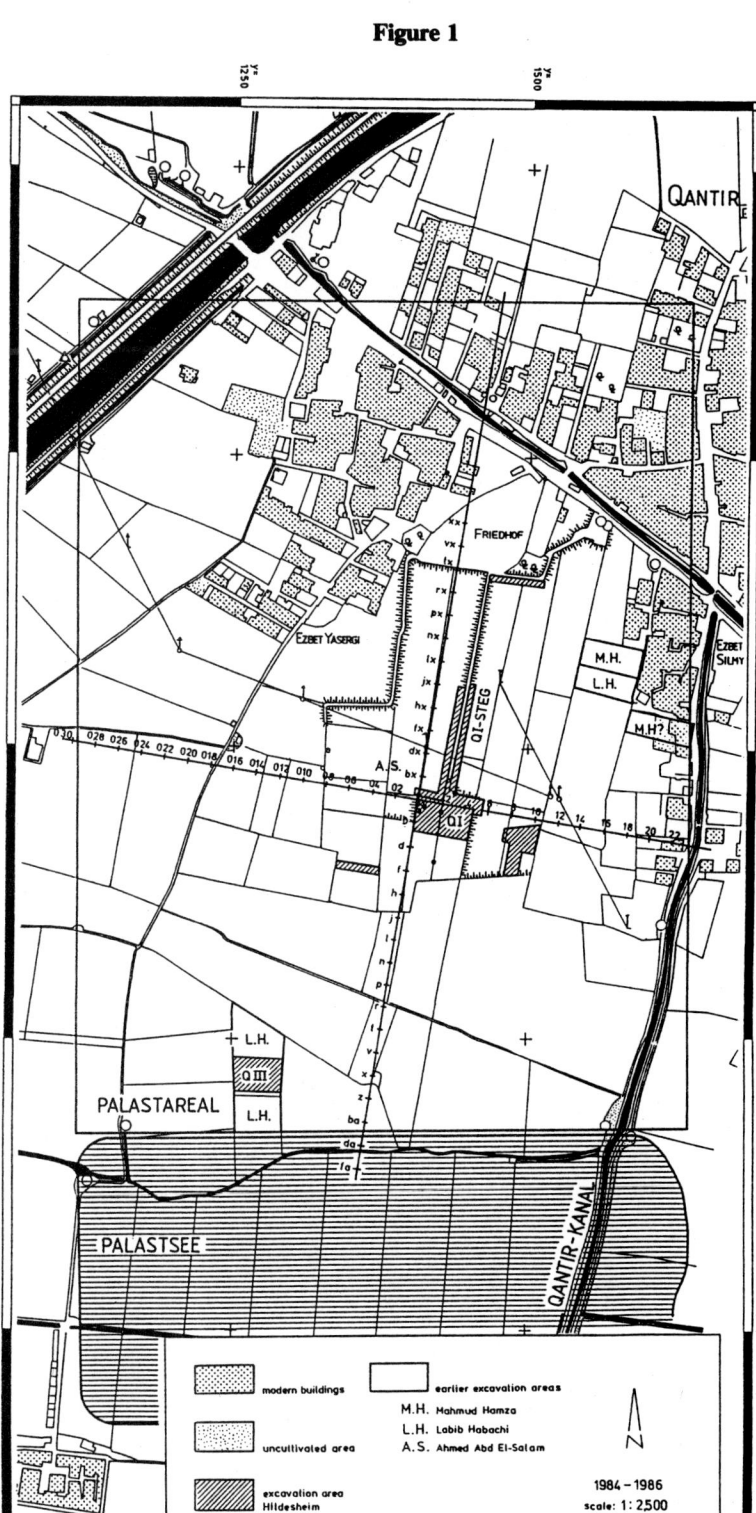

213

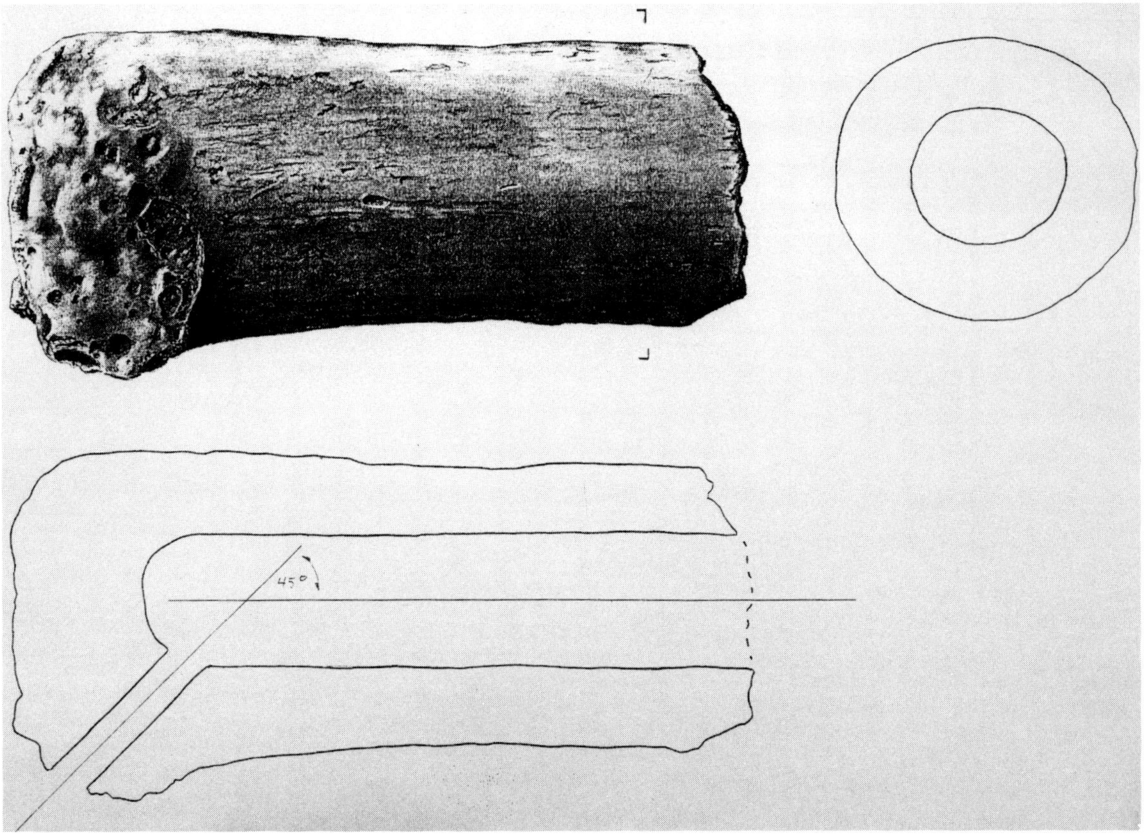

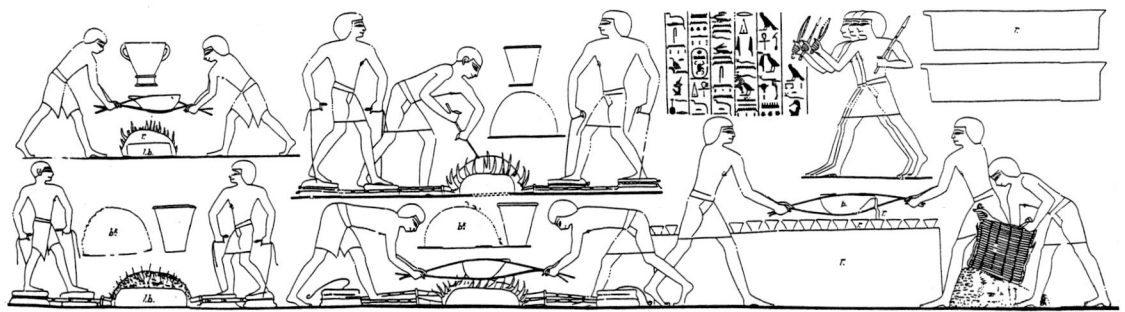

Figure 3

Figure 4

Figure 5

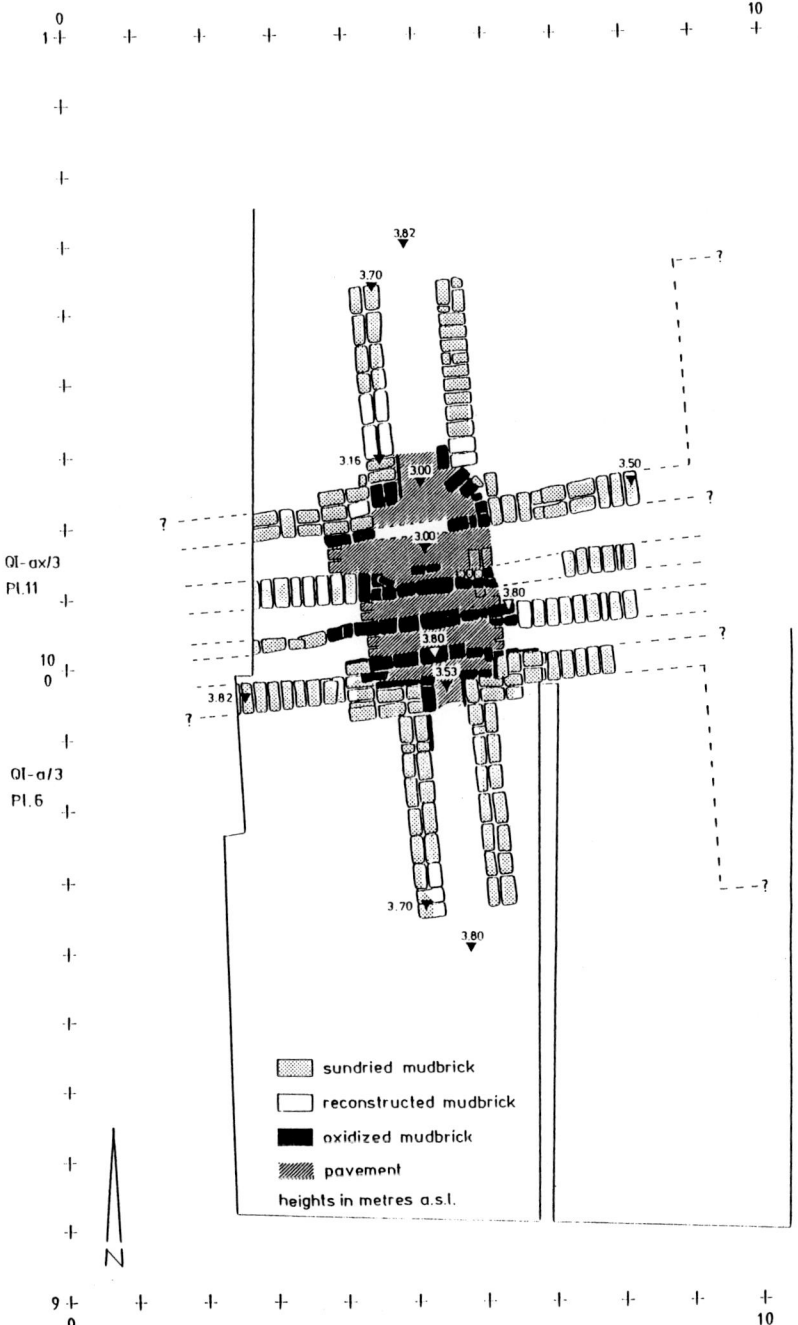

sundried mudbrick

reconstructed mudbrick

oxidized mudbrick

pavement

heights in metres a.s.l.

215

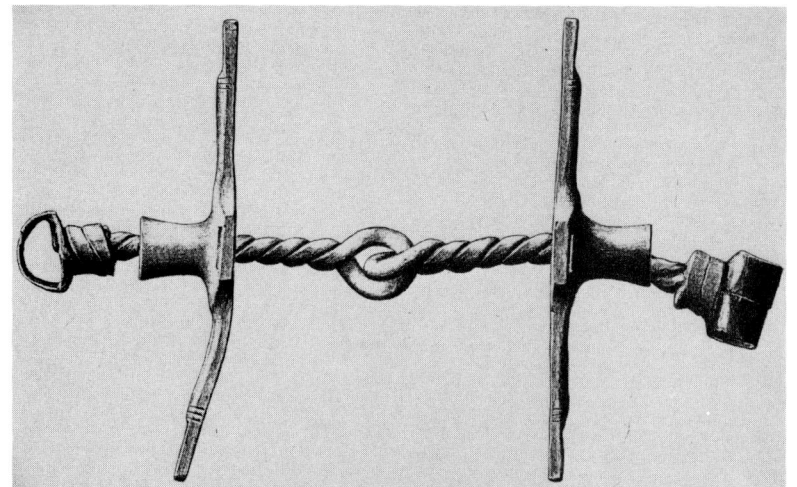

Figure 6

Figure 7

Figure 8

216

Plate I

Qantir, Stratum B3: "Cross-furnace" for copper-smelting (?),
center-part with oxydised mudbricks seen from north (square
QI-ax.a/3)

Plate II

Qantir, Stratum B3: "Cross-furnace" for copper-smelting (?),
center-part with chambers seen from west (square QI-ax.a/3)

Plate III

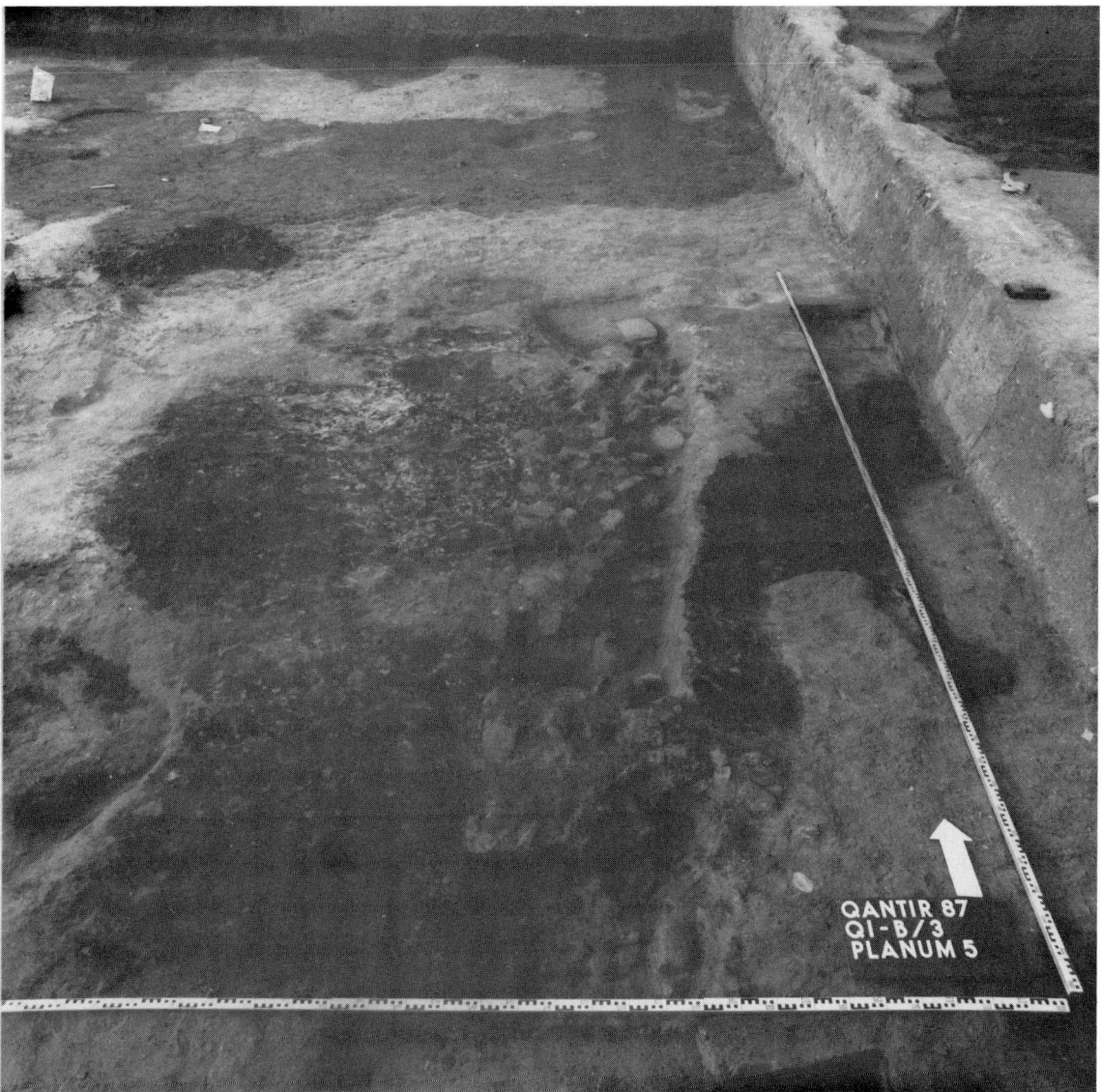

QANTIR 87
QI-B/3
PLANUM 5

Qantir, Stratum B3: part of "melting channel" No. 2 for
bronze production in square QI-b/3 with layers of ashes
and charcoal, tyeres before cleaning

Plate IV

QANTIR 87
QI-B/4
PLANUM 4-5

Qantir, Stratum B3: part of "melting channel" No. 3 for
bronze production in square QI-b/4 destroyed by pit of
stratum B1-2, partly cleaned

RAMESSES II AS MEDIATOR

Ali Radwan

The role of the king as the only and traditional link between his subjects and the deities is without doubt one of the most important aspects of the divine kingship in ancient Egypt.[1] It is quite reasonable that the closest approach of men to their deities can only be achieved through the sole successor of gods on earth, namely the king, with whom alone they can be in direct connection. According to Egyptian belief, the mediation of the king is essential to the achievement of good fortune in the afterlife. It is, therefore, understandable that every human being tried to express (or represent) in every possible way his constant loyalty to his monarch.[2] Such religious concepts can easily be confirmed and attested not only by means of the literary sources but also in a more obvious manner in the available pictorial renderings which can be cited throughout the history of pharaonic Egypt.[3] In this respect we have to refer to the importance of the formula of offerings for the cult of the dead and how it reveals in a clear way the same intermediate role of the Egyptian king.[4]

It is well known that the most celebrated mediator during all periods of pharaonic Egypt was Akhenaten. After the dogmatic rules of the Amarna religion, this only son of the Aten had the only right to perform every kind of ceremony which belonged to this deity.[5] Even the owners of the private tombs in Amarna could not directly worship the Aten without the mediation of their king, who is always depicted together with the queen and one or more of her daughters. Although there is no exact parallel to these extreme views during the Amarna Period, one is inclined to find some forerunners of them in a small number of representations which show kings (Sesostris I, Amenemhat II, Sesostris III, Anyotef V,

1 For some aspects of the divinity of the reigning or dead king, see most recently,
L. Bell, in *Mélanges Gamal E. Mohktar* (1985), 31 ff.; L. Bell, in *JNES* 44 (1985), 251 ff.;
A. Radwan, in *Ägypten, Dauer und Wandel* (Symposium in *DAIK*) 1985, 53 ff. For the
king as mediator, see e.g., A. Radwan, *Darstellungen des Königs, MÄS* 21 (1969), 41 ff.;
D. Wildung, in *OLZ* 68 (1973), 564; H. te Velde, in *LÄ* IV (1982), 161 f.; A. Radwan,
"Zum Erscheinen des Veziers Paser in der Begleitung Ramses II" (ICE-Munich, 1985),
in *SAK* (forthcoming).

2 J. Assmann, "König als Sonnenpriester," Abh. *DAI Kairo* (1970), 64, n. 2.

3 Cf. e.g., W. Westendorf, *Darstellungen des Sonnenlaufes, MÄS* 10 (1966), 22 ff., pl. 8
(the name of the king fills the space between heaven and earth); A. Radwan, in *Ägypten,
Dauer und Wandel* (1985), 60 ff., figs. 12-16 (king in the attitude of the god Shu);
see further the interesting remarks of D. Kurth, *Den Himmel stutzen* (1975), passim,
especially 103 f., 139 ff., 145 f.; H. te Velde, "The Theme of the Separation of
Heaven and Earth in Egyptian Mythology," in *Studia Aegyptiaca* 3, Budapest (1977), 161 ff.,
especially 167.

4 W. Barta, in *LÄ* IV (1982), 584 f.; G. Lapp, *Opferformel des Alten Reiches* (1986),
passim; G. Lanczkowski, "Königtum im MR," in *Neumen Sacral Kingship*, Leiden
(1959), 280; A. Radwan, *MÄS* 21 (1969), 2, 41 ff.; A.M. Moussa - H. Altenmüller, in
MDIK 31 (1975), 93 ff.; A. Radwan, "Concerning the Identification of the King with the God,"
in *Bull. of the Fac. of Arch., Cairo University* I (1976), 24 ff.

5 G. Fecht, in *ZÄS* 85 (1960), 99, n. 3; J. Assmann, in *JNES* 31 (1972), 155, n. 83;
Trigger, Kemp, O'Connor, and Lloyd, *Ancient Egypt* (1983), 221; U. Rössler-Köhler, in
Fs Westendorf (1984), 936; L. Bell, in *JNES* 44 (1985), 291.

Rahotep, Thutmosis I, Hatshepsut, Thutmosis III, Amenophis II, Thutmosis IV, and Amenophis III) who are standing in different positions of adoring and offering in front of the deity while the private person (or persons) comes behind them or in the lower part of the scene.[6] From all the periods after Akhenaten, it is only in the reign of Ramesses II that we meet again with this kind of representations in plenty.[7] The majority of them come from private stelae. Our few select examples may serve to demonstrate and stress the same concept of mediation for Ramesses II, similar to the way it had been in the reign of Akhenaten.[8]

In fact, the intermediate role of Ramesses II could be indicated briefly in the following manner:

1 - The invocation of Ramesses II (or his royal *ka*) in the formula of offerings or at prayer.

It is quite significant that the frequent invoking of Ramesses II (or rather his royal *ka*) beside the complete deities in the offering formula[9] could be taken simply as another feature of the deification of this king. It would seem, however, that the king is playing here in a clear way the traditional role of mediation as he is always the last mentioned of the invoked deities. In one instance a very curious wording of the formula of funerary offerings

---

6 See A. Radwan, "Paser" (ICE-Munich, 1985) in *SAK* (forthcoming), n. 8; A. Nibbi, in *JEA* 62 (1976), 45 ff.; 9 = A. Nibbi, *Ancient Egypt* (1981), pl. 9 = H.G. Fischer, *The Orientation of Hieroglyphs* I. *Reversals* (1977), 105, fig. 106 (Amenemhat II); Fl. Petrie, *Memphis* I (1909), 7, pl. VII, 46 (Thutmosis I); E. Brunner-Traut, *Die alten Ägypter* (1974), fig. 43 (Thutmosis III); W. Kaiser, *Ägyptisches Mus. Berlin* (Cat. 1967), 59, 641; A. Radwan, *MÄS* 21 (1969), 42 f., pl. V (Amenophis II); J. Vandier, *Manuel* II (1954), 512, fig. 303; S. Hassan, *Great Sphinx* (1953), 81, fig. 66 (Thutmosis IV); D. Wildung, *Staatl. Sammlung ägyptischer Kunst* (Cat. 1976), 82 f. (Amenophis III).

7 For some examples from the period after Akhenaten and before Ramesses II, cf. H.M. Stewart, *Egypt. Stelae, Reliefs and Paintings* I (1976), 50 f., pl. 41, 1 (Tutankhamun); A. Radwan, *MÄS* 21 (1969), 49 f. (Horemheb); A. Radwan, in *Orientalia* 43 (1974), 393 ff., pl. 42 (Horemheb); M. Tosi - A. Roccati, *Stele* (1972), No. 50090 (Sethos I); S. Hassan, op. cit., 263, fig. 199 (Sethos I); L. Limme, *Stèles Egyptiénnes* (Brussels 1979), 28 f. (Sethos I accompanied by his son, the crown prince Ramesses, who is acting as a fan-bearer).

8 For the survival of some aspects and elements of the Eighteenth Dynasty (especially the Amarna period) in the reign of Ramesses II, cf., e.g., M. Cramer, in *ZÄS* 72 (1936), 96, n. 9; G. Fecht, in *ZÄS* 85 (1960), 117; H. Brunner, in *ZÄS* 97 (1971) 16 f.; A. Radwan, in *Bull. of the Fac. of Arch., Cairo University* I (1976) 26, n. 2; Trigger, Kemp, O'Connor, and Lloyd, op. cit., 220 f. Remarkable enough is the fact that both of the two kings had the title of the high priest of a god: S. Wenig, in *LÄ* I (1975), 212, n. 28 (Akhenaten as the high priest of Re-Harakhty-Aton); G. Legrain, in *BIFAO* 13 (1916), 37, pl. III, 4 = K. Sethe, in *ZÄS* 58 (1923), 54 (Ramesses II as the high priest of Amun).

9 W. Barta, *Operformel* (1968), 141, n. 4; L. Bell, in *JNES* 44 (1985), n. 216; A. Moret, *Cat du Musée Guimet*, Galerie Egyptiénne (1909), pl. 52 (65); O. Koefoed-Petersen, in *Miscellanea Gregoriana* (1941), 126, fig. 6; E. Brunner-Traut - H. Brunner, *Ägyptische Sammlung der Universität Tübingen* (1981), 102 (471)= the same authors, in *Osiris, Kreuz und Halbmond, Cat. Stuttgart-Hannover* (1984), 78 f. 64); see also G. Roeder, *Ägypt. Inschriften* II, *Berlin* (1924), 307 (Ramesses II who is assimilated with Amun).

on the lap of a private statue[10] is quite interesting as the word *'nsw'* is replaced by the name of Ramesses II (*nsw-bit: Wsr-M3^ct-R^c-stp-n-R^c*). Here the king is acting according to the funerary rules as the only giver of all kinds of offerings on which the gods and afterwards every justified deceased could live.[11]

Furthermore, the same concept of mediating by means of the royal *ka* is evidently attested on some private stelae from Deir El-Medineh on which the royal *ka* (with the epithet ^c*nh-m-M3^ct*)[12] of Ramesses II is praised (beside the deity) by the private person (or persons) on the lower part of those stelae.[13]

2 - Ramesses II as the only offerer on some private stelae.

The clearest pictorial renderings of Ramesses II in his function as mediator are doubtless those on some private stelae which show him in the upper part offering to one or more deities while the owner (or owners) of every stela is depicted in the lower part in the attitude of worshipping (sometimes with a short inscribed hymn).[14] The offering king is acting here for the benefit of the private man. It is, therefore, quite reasonable for us to consider this kind of representation as a practical explanation of the literal translation of the funerary formula *htp-di-nsw* "a boon (or offering) which the king grants (or gives)."

3 - The mediation of Ramesses II who is represented by his cartouches (or cartouche).

The peculiar appearance of the cartouches of this king on some private statues, stelae, etc.,[15] has also its significance and can only be considered as a substitute for the figure of

---

10 M.L. Bierbrier, *Hieroglyphic Texts...Brit. Mus.* 10 (1982), 22, pl. 49.

11 For some parallels of the invoking of the royal *ka* (i.e. the deified king) in the Eighteenth Dynasty, cf. E. Otto, *Topographie* (1952), 65, n. 8; *Hieroglyphic Texts...Brit. Mus.* V, 11, pl. 37; v. Bissing, in *Archiv für Orientforschung* 8 (1932-33), 123 ff., pl. on p. 125; H. Ricke, *Totentempel Thutmoses' III* (1939), 30 f.; *Urk.* IV 1201 f.; E. Drioton, *Médamoud 1926, Inscriptions* (1927), 50.

12 Cf. B. Bruyère, *Deir El-Médineh 1935-1940* (1952), 65 ff.; A. Radwan, in *MDIK* 29 (1973), 74, n. 15.

13 B. Bruyère, op. cit., 37 (63), pl. 10; 116 (273) fig. 197; 116 (274), fig. 198; 117 (276); fig. 199; Berlin 2093: A. Radwan, in *MDIK* 29 (1973), 74(6). For the royal *ka* and the intermediate function of the king, cf. most recently L. Bell, in *JNES* 44 (1985) 251 ff.; see further, e.g., H. Frankfort, *Kingship and the Gods* (1948), 78.

14 Cairo Museum: Special Register 14296: small stela of limestone (62 cm - 37 cm) - from Deir El-Medineh - now in Port Said Museum; S. Bosticco, *Museo di Firenze* (1965) 54; J. Cerny, *Bankes Collection* (1958), 9; M. Tosi - A. Roccati, *Stele* (1972), 61 f. (50030); L. Habachi, in *BIFAO* 80 (1980), 18, pl. 6 (B); L. Habachi, in *Mélanges J. Vercoutter* (1985), 137 ff., pl. 1 and 2; L. Habachi, in *Sixteen Studies on Lower Nubia* (1981), 54, fig. 19; G. A. Gaballa, in *BIFAO* 71 (1972), 129 ff., fig. 1, pl. 23; cf. further, H. Altenmüller, "Amenophis I als Mittler," in *MDIK* 37 (1981), 1 ff., pl. 1.

15 J. C. Goyon - C. Trauecker, *Cahiers de Karnak* VI (1980), 129 ff., pl. 34, 35 = K. A. Kitchen, *Ram. Inscriptions* VII, 4 (1987), 109; W. C. Hayes, *Scepter* II (1978), 349, fig. 218; O. Koefoed-Petersen, *Cat. des Statues et Statuettes Egyptiénnes*

the mediator himself. The intentional reproduction of this kind of cartouche leaves the impression that they were inscribed on purpose.[16]

4 - The cult-statues of Ramesses II.

A group of cult-statues of Ramesses II can also be explained as having the same intermediate function. We mean those statues of the king "who hears the prayers"[17] or petitions of his subjects in order to speak in favour of them while conveying their best wishes to the deities.[18] The lower part of a private stela in the British Museum[19] shows one of these cult-statues of Ramesses II (with the epithet R^c-n-hk3w) with the owner of the stela kneeling and doing his worship in front of it, while the Theban triad with Thoth are depicted alone in the upper part. All such statues stood in front of (or within) the temples of the gods. In the case of the so-called ram-headed sphinxes of Amun with the small Osirian figure of Ramesses II between its front legs,[20] we can presume the same concept of mediating. A scene in a Theban private tomb shows Ramesses II under the head of the Hathor-cow.[21] The king is called here p3 ntr ^{c}3 ("The Great God"). He deserved, therefore, his own worship beside the mighty goddess. The same meaning could be accepted easily in the case of the cult-statue of the deified Ramesses II (as a squatting

(1950), 35 f., pl. 70; B. Bruyère, *Deir El-Médineh 1948-1951* (1951), 31 f.,
fig. 2; F. Smekens, *Oudheidkundige Musea-Antwerpen, Cat.* VIII, 26, 8; E. Brunner-Traut
- H. Brunner, *Ägyptische Sammlung der Universität Tübingen* (1981), 102 (471);
J. Cerny and others, *Graffiti de la Montagne Thébaine* I, 2 (1971), pls. 130,
131; cf. also J. Broekhuis, *De Godin Renenwetet* (1971),
25 (32), pl. 6; *PM* II , 734; B. Bruyère, *Deir El-Médineh 1935-1940* (1952), 38
(79), pls. 12, 38; D. Wildung, in *Münchner Jahrbuch der bildenden Kunst* 36 (1985),
27 f., fig. 17; for parallels from other periods, cf., e.g. B. Von Bothmer,
Das Museum für Altägyptische Kunst in Luxor (1981), 94 (Amenophis III); W. M. van Haarlem
- R. A. Lunsingh Scheurleer, *Gids voor de afdeling Egypte, Allard Pierson Museum
- Amsterdam* (1986), 24 f. (Ramesses IV).

16 Cf. A. Radwan, *MÄS* 21 (1969), 41, n. 5, 6.

17 L. Habachi in *BIFAO* 71 (1972), 83, n. 6.

18 L. Bell, in *JNES* 44 (1985), 259 f., 271, n. 97; for this subject cf. further
L. Bell, in *Mélanges G. E. Mokhtar* I (1985) 58, n. 204; A. Radwan, in
Ägypten, Dauer und Wandel (1985), 58 ff.; R. El-Sayed, in *BIFAO* 79 (1979), 155 ff.;
L. Kàkosy, in *Acta Antiqua Academiae Scientiarum Hungaricae* 15 (1967), 369 ff.; P. Derchain,
"Le Rolé du roi," in *Le Pouvoir et le sacré*, Brussels (1962), 72, n. 32; C. Leblanc, in
Mélanges G.E. Mokhtar II (1985), 76 f.; A. Moret, in *Rev. Égyptologique* I, 1
(1919), 5, pl. 3 (priest of a cult-statue of Thutmosis III).

19 M. L. Bierbrier, *Hieroglyphic Texts...Brit. Mus.* 10 (1982), 25 f., pl. 61.

20 See, e.g., R. E. Freed, *Ramesses the Great - An Exhibition in the City of Memphis* (1987),
58 pl. on p. 60 f.; for some forerunners of this form, cf. J. Vanier, *Manuel* III,
Album (1958), pl. 102, 5 (Amenophis II); S. Curto, *Museo Egizio di
Torino* (1984) 118 (Thutmosos IV); S. Wenig, *Führer durch das Berliner Ägyptische
Museum* (1961), 71, Abb. 31 (Amenophis III).

21 *LD* III, 199, h; see further, C. Desroches-Noblecourt - J. Vercoutter, *Un Siècle
de fouilles Françaises en Égypte 1880-1980* (1981), 255 (273).

child) and the god Hauron.[22] There is no need to agree with the common interpretation of protection for those specific figures of this god-king (Ramesses II) who had done his best to maintain his deified forms in every possible way.

---

22 R. E. Freed, op. cit., 130 f.; M. Saleh - H. Sourouzian, *Hauptwerke im Ägyptischen Museum - Kairo* (1986), 203; U. Rössler-Köhler, "König als Kind," in *Fs. W. Westendorf* (1984), 932 f.; for the king of Egypt as a child, cf., e.g. P. Munro, in *SAK* 6 (1978), 131 ff.; E. Feucht, in *LÄ* III (1980) 425, n. 14.

THE STATUES OF KING MERENPTAH

Hourig Sourouzian

The fourth king of the 19th Dynasty, Merenptah, succeeded his father, Ramesses II, about 1224 B.C. Merenptah was the thirteenth son of Ramesses II and the fourth child of the second Great Royal Consort Iset Nofret. He had assumed high military functions during his father's reign, and after the death of his elder brothers, he had become heir to the throne, some time after the fifty-fifth regnal year of Ramesses the Great. Merenptah was middle-aged when he succeeded to the throne and was to reign for about ten years.

This was a time when the great temples of Egypt had been rebuilt or restored by his predecessors, and new temples had been erected all over Egypt by Ramesses II, whose omnipresent colossi dominated the temple courts and the high pylons. In fact, there was not much left to build except for the compulsory mortuary temple on the West Bank in Thebes and, of course, the preparation of the royal tomb in the Kings' Valley.

It seems, then, that Merenptah's reign was destined to be the pious prolongation of that of his father, with the maintenance of the cults in the existing temples by means of dedications, renewal texts, or what we call usurpations. Indeed, the reign was disturbed by the invasion of the Sea Peoples and the Libyans, a coalition of foes whom Merenptah successfully repelled in his fifth regnal year.

Thus, the great inscription in Karnak and the victory stelae were carved after his victory, and even the construction of a temple and a palace in Memphis, whose gates Merenptah had "reopened" after having protected it from the foreign invasion, may also be the consequence of the victory.

A ten-year reign might seem short compared to the 67 year reign of Ramesses II, but if we consider the tremendous number of new foundations during the 14 years of Seti I, a ten-year reign could have been more fruitful, if it were necessary. But it was not, as we have seen, and it seems really that there was little left to do except dedicate statues to the temples.

The statues of Merenptah are certainly not as numerous as those of his father, but they include most of the types representative of royal statuary, and they even introduce some new types.

We will not consider the statues usurped by Merenptah from the kings of the Middle Kingdom in Pi-Ramesses, Memphis, or Armant. Nor will we consider the ones usurped from Amenophis III and Ramesses II in Luxor, or other temples of Egypt. They will be mentioned only if they bear important inscriptions or representations of Merenptah's family.

A. The Seated Statues

Although practically all the statues representing Merenptah seated are either usurped or very fragmentary, we shall start the list with the only remaining bust of a seated statue, because it is the only one clearly bearing the features of the king (Plate Ia).

Bust of Merenptah in painted grey granite, now in Cairo, CG 607, found by Petrie in 1896, in the second court of Merenptah's mortuary temple in Thebes, H. 91 cm., lower part lost. [102][1]

This was part of a seated statue of the king, as is shown by the low back pillar and the movement of the left arm, which is slightly advanced.

The king wears the nemes with a uraeus, a beard, and a broad collar. The nemes is relatively low on the top and roughly sculpted with regular striations to suggest the pleated cloth. Its rounded lappets cover the broad collar, which is also roughly carved. Behind the ears, the nemes does not form a right angle with the face but is incurved. The head of the uraeus extends above the top of the nemes, and its two loops, almost parallel, are slightly asymmetrical and placed directly above the large band on the forehead; the band is perceptibly recessed. Two straps, delineated by incised lines, join the beard to the headdress. The beard is broken, and two lines are engraved on the neck.

The portrait is that of a rather young ruler; the face is oval-shaped, rather long, and the cheeks are not bulging as on other statues of Merenptah. The ears are big and vertical but not protruding. Small incisions suggest that they are pierced. The eyes are narrow and elongated by cosmetic lines, which are in slightly raised relief and framed with incised lines. The eyebrows, also in relief and delineated by incised lines, follow the curve of the eyes. The nose is straight, narrow, and long. The mouth is horizontal with lips relatively large but not bulging.

The torso, with its naturalistic modelling of the muscles and the chest, is narrow and expresses youth and strength. On the shoulders of the king are engraved his cartouches. The back pillar bears the beginning of his titulary.

Although it has been said that this statue may be usurped from Amenophis III, the complete recarving of the head gives us a true portrait of Merenptah. It has been noted by Vandier that the features of this portrait strongly resemble those of a statuette of Ramesses II in Baltimore, but the majority of the well known portraits of Ramesses are so different from this representation, that we may count it as an original likeness of Merenptah.

A fragment of the throne of another seated statue of the king was seen by Naville in Bubastis. On the side of the back-rest was engraved the name of the crown prince Sety Merenptah. [23]*

B. The Standing Statues

a) The mummiform type

Statuette in limestone, New York, MMA 26.7.1451, found in the Valley of the Kings, H. 19 cm. (Plate Ib). [110]*

It bears the same features as the bust from the funerary temple: large ears, narrow eyes, roughly pleated nemes. Here the uraeus has no loops.

---

1 For Bibliography, see: Hourig Sourouzian, *Les Monuments du roi Merenptah*, SAAIK 22, Mainz 1989. The numbers written in [] by each statue here correspond to those of Merenptah's monuments in that publication.

All other known Osiride statues of Merenptah from Armant represent reuses from the Middle Kingdom, and the mummiform type is otherwise only represented in high relief on the lid of the second granite sarcophagus of Merenptah, now in his tomb, and in an Osiride figure of the King carved on the lid of his third sarcophagus, which was usruped by Psusenes (Cairo Museum, JE87297B). On both representations the characteristic features found on the face of the royal bust from the funerary temple are repeated. [106, 107]*

b) The classical striding type

There are from the reign of Merenptah very few statues of the classical type in which the king is represented striding and holding the *mks* (container of documents) in each hand, wearing a crown, and the *shendyt* kilt.

1) Statue of Merenptah in black granite, Cairo CG 42148, found by Legrain in 1904 in the "cour de la cachette" of Karnak, H. 1 m. 35, headless (Plate II). [85]*

Striding, holding the two *mks*, the king wears the *shendyt* (pleated short kilt), held by a large belt decorated with chevrons, as well as a broad collar and a beard, now broken. The headdress was not the nemes but rather a crown. In the oval of the belt is engraved his prenomen, Baenre Meryamon. In addition, there are two cartouches on the chest, and his name is also on the shoulders and on the upper side of the base, as well as on the two rolls. Two cartouches again are engraved in the place of the bracelets.

On the left side of the statue is the following inscription: Year II, His Majesty has come to see his father Amon-Re, King of Gods, King of Upper and Lower Egypt Baenre Meryamon, Son of Re, Merenptah, beloved Amon-Re. The back pillar is decorated on three sides with inscriptions of praise.

It is clear that the king has dedicated this statue to the Temple of Amon during his visit to Thebes in the second regnal year, perhaps during the festival of Opet. Found in the cachette, it stood perhaps in the same court with the great historical inscriptions of Merenptah. No trace of usurpation is to be seen on this statue. The loss of the head is, of course regrettable, because we have here a sculpture of excellent workmanship which is admirably polished. Although it is very conventional work, we find some features characteristic of other statues of Merenptah: the rather long torso, compared to those of Ramesses II; the vertical median line above the navel. Two similar statues, in grey granite were found in the Luxor Temple. They were usurped from Amenophis III. One wears the nemes and bears on the left side the effigy of the King's Daughter, King's Great Wife, and King's Sister, Bentanta. It is now in the Luxor Museum (Cat. no 129). The second statue, headless, wearing a crown, and bearing the effigy of the Great Royal Consort, Iset Nofret, is still in the forecourt of the Luxor Temple. The fragments of a third similar statue are lying to the west of the pylon of the Luxor Temple. [99]*

2) Colossal statue of Merenptah in pink granite, Cairo Museum JE 35126, found by Chaban in Ashmunein (Hermopolis) in front of a temple of Amon started by Ramesses II, finished by Merenptah, and decorated by Sety II, H. 4 m. 85 (Plate III). [65]*

The statue was found in front of the pylon on which Merenptah had carved a great dedication text. The king, striding, stands on a high base which is carved in the form of the jubilee sign. The statue's back slab is in the shape of an obelisk. The whole was placed on a high pedestal of limestone decorated with the titulary of Merenptah, Beloved of Thot.

The king wears the nemes and the double crown. A uraeus is placed right over the large band, as on the bust of Merenptah from his mortuary temple. Its tail is raised over the Red

Crown. A large beard, left undecorated, adorns the chin; there are no creases on the neck. The king wears two bracelets.

The pleated kilt has a central apron. It is inscribed with the names of the king, decorated with a leopard head, flanked by three streamers on each side, and terminated by a border of seven uraei crowned with solar disks. There is a ribbon loop on its right side, from which hangs the loose end of a belt. Around the hips is a large belt decorated by chevrons. An animal tail hangs between the legs.

The two cartouches of Merenptah flanked by two uraei form a pendant on the chest; they are also found symmetrically, one on each shoulder and on the concave outer face of each roll. In the oval of the belt is his name Merenptah Hotephermaat, the Great God; on the kilt are his two cartouches.

On the left side is a representation of the King's Son, Sety Merenptah, the future Sety II. Standing, holding the fan with the left hand, he raises his right hand to touch the leg of the colossus. The prince wears a long dress and sandals; on his wig hangs the side lock of youth with curled end, and a uraeus is raised on the forehead. His titles: Hereditary Prince, Chief of the Two Lands, Royal Scribe, General, Eldest King's Son, Sety Merenptah.

The statue bears simultaneously features of Ramesses II and Merenptah. It was recut from an architrave of Thutmosis III, which explains the narrowness of the body and the rather unfortunate proportions. Under the base was the name of Ramesses II, which means that Merenptah has either usurped or finished decorating a statue of his father. Nevertheless, the decoration has some peculiarities worth noting. The base in the form of a Heb-sign is rare and is attested on very few royal statues. The inscriptions mention, after the royal names, the epithets, "Beloved of Shepsy, Residing in Hermopolis," and "Beloved of Thot, Lord of Hermopolis." The inscriptions of the pedestal on which the statue stood mention the king as beloved of Thot and of Harmakhis on the front, and beloved of Thot and of Amon on the sides. One of the Horus names of the king on the front is formed with the epithet, "Lord of Jubilees like Tatenen," which reminds us of the Horus name of Ramesses II. The other is the usual Horus name: The Strong Bull Who Rejoices with Maat. Finally, on the back pillar, the two forms of the coronation name of the king are given in parallel: Baenre Meryamon and Baenre Meryneteru. It seems that Merenptah has tried to assemble in this one statue all aspects of his kingship.

C. The Standard-Bearer Statues

The standard-bearer statue, attested since Thutmosis IV, flourished in the Ramesside Period. Five are known from the reign of Merenptah.

1) Merenptah holding two standards in pink granite, Cairo Museum JE 37483, found in Tanis in 1906, H. 2M 68 (Plate IVa). [38]*

The king holds two standards, rectangular in section, each topped with a standing statuette of a god. The king wears a round wig with small curls on which the frontal uraeus is attached without the usual fillet; this may be a difference from the statues of Ramesses II. On top of this wig, a circular base surrounded by a frieze of uraei wearing sun disks holds the Atef crown with ribbed central element, the disk, two ostrich feathers, and two twisted horns. The beard is broken, and no creases are marked on the neck. On the preserved left arm, the king wears a bracelet, and on the right shoulder the deltoid is indicated by an engraved pattern resembling the *ms* sign.

The ceremonial pleated kilt is the same as on the last statue. On the staves, the statuettes of the gods are destroyed, but according to the inscription on the back slab of the royal statue where the king is "Beloved of Ptah-Tatenen" on one hand and "of Amun" on the other, the statuettes may have been representations of these gods.

On the left side of the statue, the prince Sety Merenptah, wearing the same long dress with large sleeves and holding the fan vertically, has the same medium length wig as on the preceding statue, but the side lock is uncurled, and there is no uraeus.

His titles are Hereditary, or in this case, Crown Prince on the Seat of Geb, Controller of the Two Lands for his Father, King's Eldest Son [Sety] Merenptah. The titles "Crown Prince on the Seat of Geb" and "Controller for his Father" show, as M. Eaton-Krauss has stated, that the prince has assumed a position of deputy. The last title is also attested for another son of Merenptah, called also Merenptah, on a statue from Tanis of the Middle Kingdom usurped by King Merenptah, now in East Berlin (1265).

2) Second statue of Merenptah holding two standards in pink mottled granite, Cairo Museum, CG 37481, from Tanis, H. 1 m. 96 (Plate IVb). [39]*

The king holds two standards, rectangular in section, and topped by seated statuettes of gods. Here the king is wearing a long wig composed of parallel strands which form a visor over the brow and fall in long locks to the collar bones, which are marked clearly in relief. Here again the uraeus, now broken, is attached to the coiffure without a fillet. The king is beardless (all royal statues wearing this wig have no beard); two lines are engraved on the neck. There are no bracelets, at least on the preserved left arm. He wears the same ceremonial kilt as on the two preceding statues. On his left shoulder is the engraved deltoid in the form of a *ms* sign. On the right staff, is preserved a seated statuette of an anthropomorphic god with a beard, perhaps to be identified with Amon-Re, Lord of the Thrones of the Two Lands; the last three signs of this epithet are preserved on the side of the throne. On the left staff probably sat the god Ptah-Tatenen, considering the inscription on the corresponding staff.

Again, we find the representation of the crown prince on the left side of the statue. Similarly dressed and wearing sandals, he holds the fan obliquely over his left shoulder and wears the same medium length wig without a uraeus, but adorned with the uncurled side lock. His titles are "Praised and Beloved by Him (i.e. the king), His Son, the Hereditary Prince, the [King's] Son [Sety] Merenptah, true of voice."

These two statues from Tanis show the king with a round face but very mild features. The torso is young and athletic; on the sides of the legs is found an accentuated sinew. In comparison, statues of Ramesses II, such as those from Kom el-Hisn and Abukir, show a much shorter torso, more stylized muscles, and more accentuated features. (Cairo RT 21/11/14/18 and CG 574).

3) The third standard-bearer statue of Merenptah in pink granite, Cairo Museum JE 66571, found in Kom Medinet Madi by Vogliano in 1936, H. 1 m. 96, represents him with only one staff, rectangular in section, held along his side. (Plate V). [61]*

This statue is the same type as the last with these differences: the face is much rounder, with bulging eyes; a fillet holds the uraeus which has asymmetrical loops; a rectangular pendant once adorned the chest; traces of a collar may be seen around the neck; and finally, the single staff is topped by the head of a falcon god in the form of an aegis with the broad collar. The god wears the tri-partite wig and what seems to have been the double crown. (The god Horus?) Since the feet are preserved, we may notice that the king is wearing sandals. This statue is closer in style to those of Ramesses II.

The statue has a back pillar with rounded top. On its left side, the crown prince is again depicted in the same long dress and wig with uncurled side lock, and without uraeus. He holds a ḥk3t scepter horizontally and the ꜥnḫ sign. His titles are Hereditary Prince, Royal Scribe, General, King's Eldest Son, Sety Merenptah.

4) A similar statue in pink granite, Copenhagen National Museum 345, registered provenance Alexandria, H. 1 m 50, headless. [40]*

M. Eaton-Krauss first brought this statue to my attention and sent me a slide and the copy of its inscriptions published by Schmidt. In Satzinger's list of royal standard bearers, it is Dok. A33. Later, M.-L. Buhl kindly sent me photographs of the sides and the back of this statue. Recently, while consulting Rifaud's *Voyage en Égypte, en Nubie et lieux circonvoisins*, edited in 1830, I realized that this statue is the same as the one seen by Rifaud in Tanis and reproduced on his plate 125. Rifaud's statue (Plate VIb) is mentioned by Porter-Moss and appears in the list of C. Chadefaud's, *Les Statues porte-enseignes de l'Egypte ancienne*, Paris. 1882, under PE MN p2, (*Tanis, statue disparue*). This traveler of the last century has given the statue a head belonging to another, which is reminiscent of that of the seated statue of Ramesses II in Turin. On the drawing we can also see the lower part and the base of a statue (which perhaps belong to it). It must have been left *in situ* when the headless body was transported to Alexandria.

The inscriptions on Rifaud's statue correspond exactly to those of the Copenhagen sculpture. On the side, we find, instead of the crown prince, the King's Wife and the King's Mother Iset Nofret, that is Merenptah's mother and Ramesses II's consort. Only the upper part of Iset Nofret is preserved. The queen wears the usual headdress with horns, and two high feathers, common to Ramesside queens.

5) A standard-bearer statue in alabaster, Louvre E 25474, provenance unknown, H. 25 cm. (Plate VII). [127]*

The king is holding one staff on his left side; the lower part is lost. The king is wearing an undecorated round wig, a beard, and a pleated ceremonial kilt with ornamented apron. The cartouche of Merenptah is engraved on the right shoulder and the back pillar bears a part of his protocol.

The forehead and the wig are perforated by two holes. According to Vandier, they are perhaps due to the later reuse of the statue.

The face is much rounder than on any other statue of Merenptah, but the individual features are reminiscent of the bust of Merenptah found in his mortuary temple.

D. The Smiting Pose

With the representation of the king smiting a foe, a completely new type of statue is invented.

Merenptah smiting a foe in pink granite, Cairo Museum, CG 1240, found in Medinet Habu, but most probably originates from the mortuary temple of Merenptah in Thebes, H. 2 m. 60 (Plate VIII). [103]*

The king, striding, holds with his left hand the hair of a bound Libyan prisoner. With the right hand, he holds a sickle with which he strikes the head of the foe. The king wears the long wig with parallel strands adorned with the uraeus and the fillet. He is beardless and barefoot. He wears the pleated kilt with an ornamented apron. It is bordered by six uraei, instead of the usual seven found on all other statues of Merenptah represented with this kilt.

On the left side, as usual, the prince Sety Merenptah, in the long costume and holding the fan obliquely over his left shoulder, wears no uraeus but has the side lock of youth with curled end. His titles are Hereditary Prince, Chief of the Two Lands, King's Son of his Body, Whom He Loves, Sety Merenptah, true of voice.

The back pillar has a rounded top, and the irregular base is roughly inscribed with the protocol of the king.

Although the quality of the sculpture is poor, this is the first time in royal statuary that the theme of smiting the enemy, otherwise richly illustrated in relief or painted representations, appears in the round. The other known examples of this type date from the 20th Dynasty.

E. The Kneeling Statues

1) Theophorus statue in red granite, Cairo Museum CG 562, found in Thebes, exact provenance unknown but most probably the Temple of Ptah in Karnak, H. 1 m. 45 cm. [89]*

The king is kneeling, holding a seated headless figure of the god Ptah in front of him. The king wears the nemes with the usual large pleats and low top. The uraeus here is slightly lower than usual. The beard is attached to the chin with straps marked in relief. He wears the *shendyt* with particularly regular pleats, a large belt with very regular chevrons, two bracelets, and no sandals. On the shoulders are *ms*-like signs. On the side of the legs is again this very salient sinew. The face is round, the eyes bulging, and the nose has been added.

The back slab with rounded top is inscribed with names of Merenptah, Beloved of Ptah, Beloved of Sakhmet. On the plinth linking the statue of Ptah to the chest of the King, the two cartouches of Merenptah are followed by the epithet "Beloved of Ptah of Merenptah." Two cartouches are on the throne of the god, and one is on each shoulder of the king.

2) Naophorus statue in limestone, Cairo Museum JE 59679, found by Mahmoud Hamza in 1929 in Athar en-Naby, ancient Khery-Aha, near Heliopolis, H. 99 cm., head and torso of the king destroyed (Plate IX). [18]*

This statue represents the king kneeling and holding in front of him a naos with a standing statue of a god. The costume is the usual *shendyt* with regular pleats; the belt is remarkably decorated with chevrons forming in the middle a row of lozenges in raised relief. The sandals have ribbed soles and are also admirably rendered. The whole sculpture, with the graceful movement of the feet, is of great quality.

The god in the naos wears a tri-partite wig crowned by the sun disk, two feathers, and two horns. There are traces of a collar. He wears a short, vertically pleated kilt with belt and lower border. He holds an $^{c}nḫ$ sign in his right hand. The left is destroyed. On the top of the naos is a scarab in high relief.

The inscriptions all mention the epithet of Merenptah, Beloved of Hapy, Father of Gods. From all of the solar symbols, M. Hamza has deduced that the statue was dedicated to a sun temple in the domain of Hapy at Khery-Aha, where we know there was a temple of Ramesses II.

This statue also is a rare type in royal statuary. However, it is more frequent in private sculpture.

3) Kneeling statue of the king, protected by a falcon in pink granite. Cairo Museum R.T. 22/11/14/3, from Nebesheh. (Plate X). [58]*

Here again we have a new type in that the statue group is on top of a pillar. The fasciculated pillar is a reuse in the upper part of which Merenptah has had recut a kneeling royal statue under the protection of a falcon. The two statues are headless.

We know of the existence of a commemorative column of Merenptah found recently by S.H. Bakry in Heliopolis. A round column is topped with an abacus, much like the staves which the king holds on the standard-bearing statues. A hollow on top of the Heliopolis column indicates that it supported an emblem or a statue, now lost. Here we have an illustration of it. This column, supporting a statue of Merenptah, may have an earlier parallel in the "obelisk" of Abguig in the Fayoum, dating from Sesostris I. This so-called obelisk has, in reality, a rounded top and a deep hollow, suggesting that it supported an emblem or a statue. However, in the form of a monolith, Merenptah's is the first known example. This type will later spread throughout the Roman world and is recalled in the commemorative column of Napoleon in the Place Vendome, Paris.

F. Dyads

In the middle of the Delta village called Kafr Matboul, two groups representing Merenptah with a deity were seen and recorded in 1893 by A. Kamal. In 1922 these groups were seen again and partly published by H. Gauthier in 1923, but without any illustrations. Since then, they have been lying in the village. In 1982, trying to complete the illustrations for my dissertaton on the monuments of Merenptah which I had just defended in the Louvre, I went to Kafr Matboul with colleagues from the German Institute of Archaeology, accompanied by Mr. Sayed Hegazi. The groups were still lying in the village, face up, but had sunk in the mud after a recent rain. The E.A.O., which kindly gave me permission to study and publish these statues, intends to transport them to the Cairo Museum.

1) Dyad in red granite, Kafr Matboul, found by A. Kamal in 1893, published by H. Gauthier in 1923, H. 2 m. 75 (Plate XIa). [33]*

This dyad, one of the most original in royal sculpture, represents the king and the god Re. It illustrates a scene otherwise known only in relief or painted representations where the king receives from a god the staff for millions of years. This is, to my knowledge, unique in sculpture in the round. From much later, at the end of the Ramesside Period, there is a small wax group with the representation of a corollary scene, found in the Valley of the Kings and now in the Luxor Museum.

The king is on the right side of the group. He holds the staff of years with his left hand, and his right arm is crossed over his chest, holding a scepter, perhaps the crook. He wears the nemes surmounted by a huge sun disk, at the center of which is a uraeus in high relief. He has the ceremonial beard and wears a long pleated dress with a starched projecting sporran. The falcon-headed god to his left offers the king the staff for millions of years with his left hand, and his right is posed on the right shoulder of the king. Crowned also by the sun disk, he wears a tri-partite wig and a short kilt. The staff bears the remains of a damaged inscription where a "Heb-Sed, eternally and in peace" is mentioned. The back slab is inscribed with six columns of text, each giving the protocol of the king. Among these, in two of his Horus names, the usual "Rejoicing with Maat" is replaced by *3ḫ n Rˁ* and *3ḫ n Tm*.

2) Second Dyad in red granite, Kafr Matboul, found by A. Kamal 1893, published by H. Gauthier in 1923, H. 2m 75 (Plate XIb). [34]*

The second, more conventional dyad, shows the king and the god standing side by side and hand in hand. The king, on the left side of the group, wears a round wig surmounted by two high feathers and two horns. He has a beard and probably wears a short kilt. The god, on his right, seems to be crowned by a flat cap with two high feathers, i.e. Amon's crown. He is bearded and wears a short kilt.

The back slab bears similar inscriptions to those of the first group, but in Gauthier's copy none of the god's names are preserved.

3) Dyad in green slate, Cairo Museum CG 1092, from Upper Egypt, H. 65 cm (Plate XII) [128]*

A third group of Merenptah, much smaller in size, is now in the magazines of the Cairo Museum. By courtesy of Dr. Saleh, I have obtained a slide of this much damaged group. The king and a goddess stand and embrace each other. Their heads and feet are lost. The goddess wears the archaic, tight-fitting dress and a tri-partite, striated wig. The king wears the pleated kilt; a part of a belt, decorated with the rhomboid pattern, is still preserved. We find Merenptah's cartouche on the chest, at left, and in the inscription on back slab. The smooth modeling of this sculpture and the type of the royal belt are closer to the Eighteenth Dynasty royal statuary than to the representations of Merenptah. Thus, the dyad may well be a reuse.

4) Dyad in pink granite, present location unknown, from Tell el Yehudiyah, H. unknown. [20]*

A fourth group representing Merenptah with Seth, much damaged, is mentioned by Griffith, without any further description. The statue is no longer *in situ*, and I could not trace its position.

G. Triads

We now come to the triads of which we have three examples.

1) Osiris, Merenptah, and Isis in alabaster, now in the second court of the Temple of Ramesses II at Abydos, from the Temple of Osiris at Abydos, published by A. Zayed, H. 1m 23 (Plate XIIIa). [72]*

The triad is in high relief and the back slab is in the form of a stela. It was found in the Temple of Osiris at Abydos. It shows Osiris flanked by Merenptah and Isis. This group, also damaged, has been published by A. Zayed. The slab, much thicker than usual, is inscribed on both sides, on the top, and the back, where Merenptah addresses Osiris.

234

2) Hathor, Merenptah, and Mut or Horus in limestone, located in el-Babein near es-Siririyeh, H. 2m 80 (Plate XIIIb). [64]*

The second triad is a rock cut group in the rock chapel of Merenptah in el-Babein, near es-Siririyeh. Here the king stands between Hathor (to his left) and a deity wearing the double crown, whether Mut or Horus, it is difficult to identify.

3) Merenptah, Ptah, and a Goddess in red granite, left in situ in Tanis by Montet. [41]*

Of the third triad, only the lower part has been seen and described. It was left *in situ* by Montet in Tanis. The group represented Merenptah between Ptah and a goddess.

H. Sphinxes

All sphinxes of Merenptah are usurpations except two small headless examples found by Mariette in the Serapeum. One was damaged and left *in situ*. The other is in the Louvre (No. 393). Two additional sphinxes, also headless, are found near the great portal of the Montu temple at Karnak. [13, 90]*

CONCLUSION

We have seen that not only the common types are represented in Merenptah's statuary, but also new types, some of them unique, have made their appearance.

In conclusion, the private statues of Merenptah's reign also have some very original and new types: for example, a limestone group dedicated by a fan-bearer Ramesses-Userpehty who has represented Osiris seated and flanked by Ramesses II and Merenptah (CG 1208); and the kneeling statue of the Vizier Panehsy, holding in front of him two statues of Merenptah and his consort Iset-Nofret, found in Deir el Medineh.

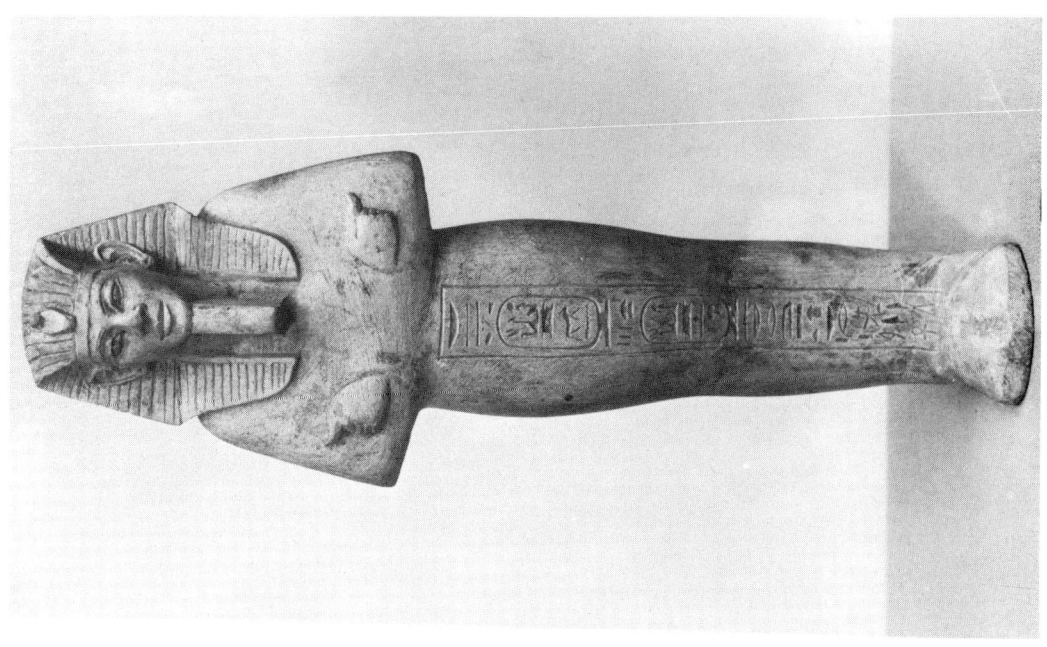

Plate I

b.

a.

c.

Plate II

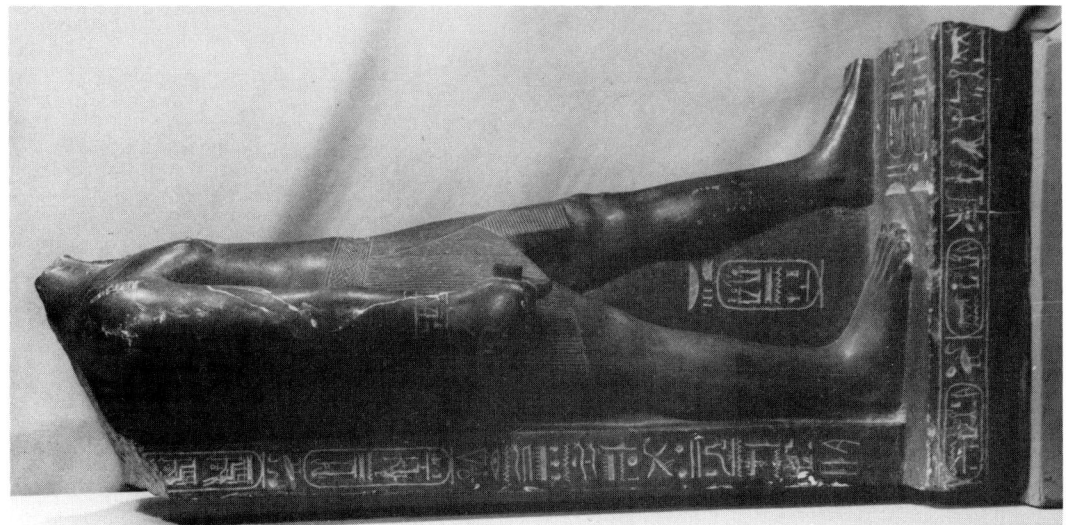

b.

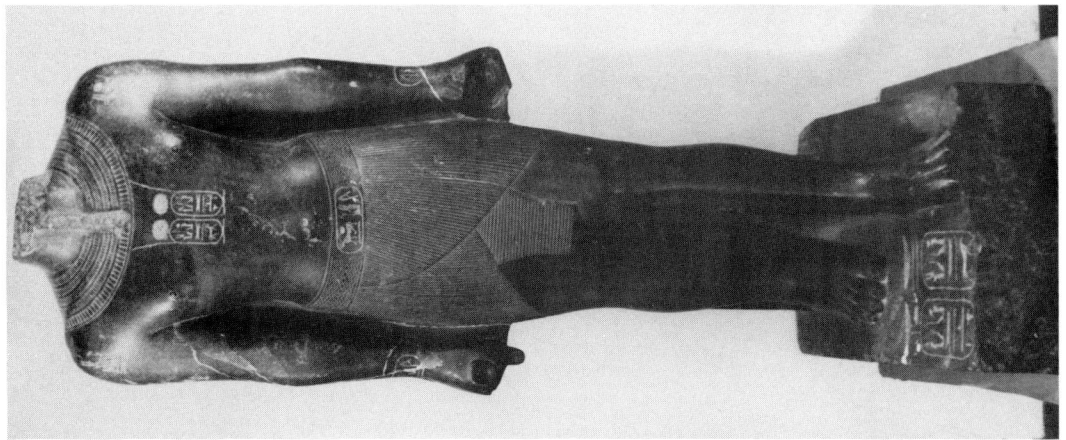

a.

238

Plate III

Plate IV

a.

b.

Plate V

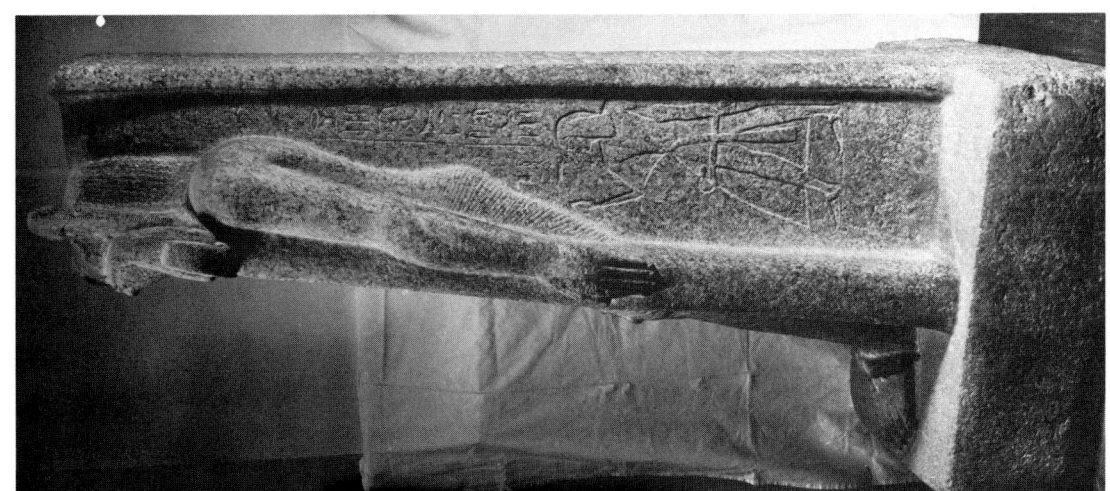

b.

a.

Plate VI

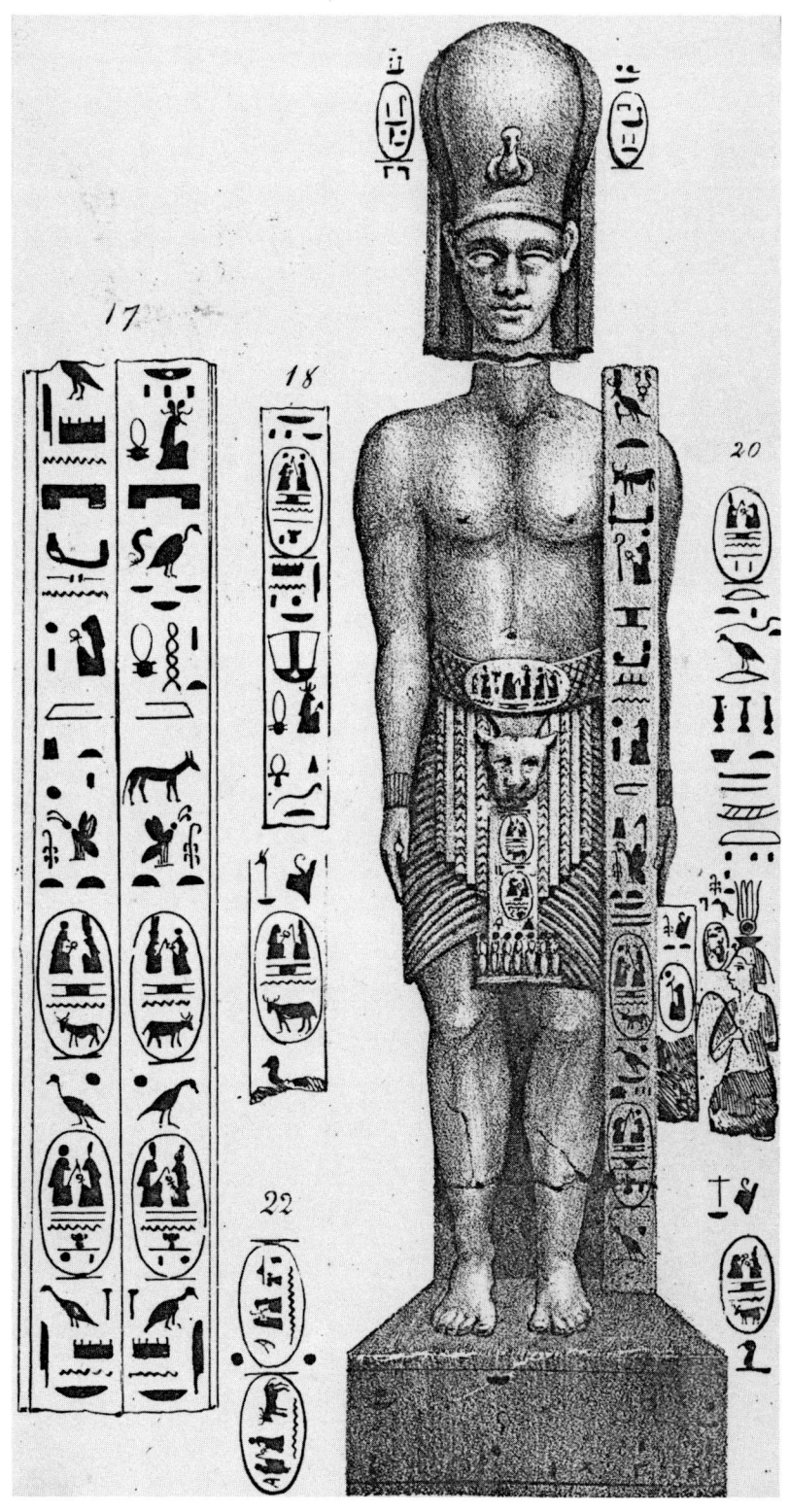

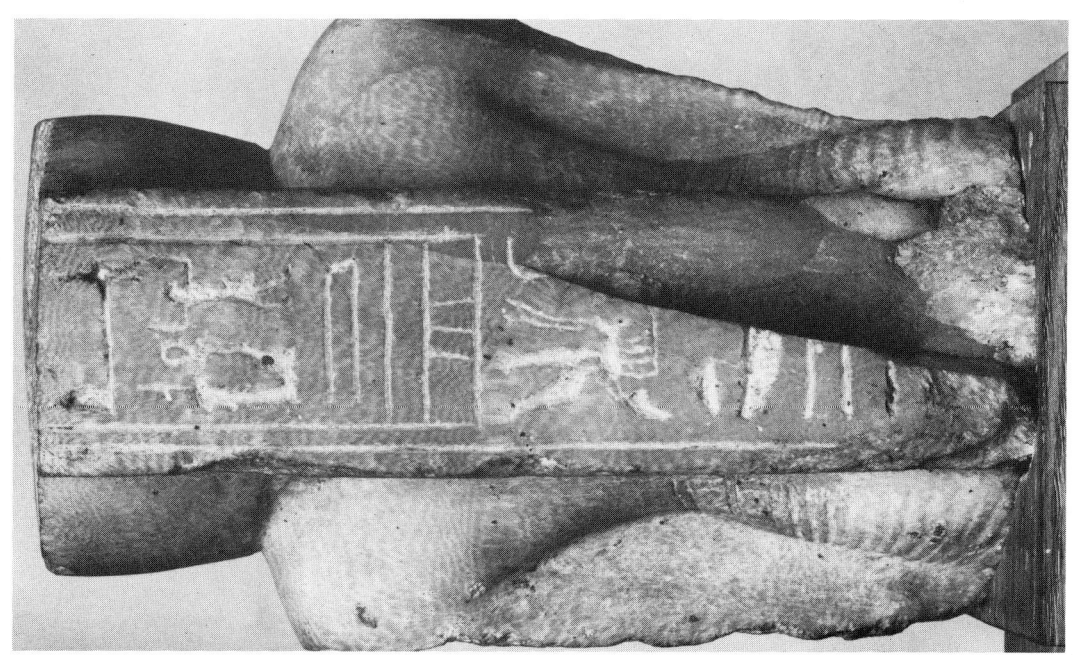

b.

Plate VII

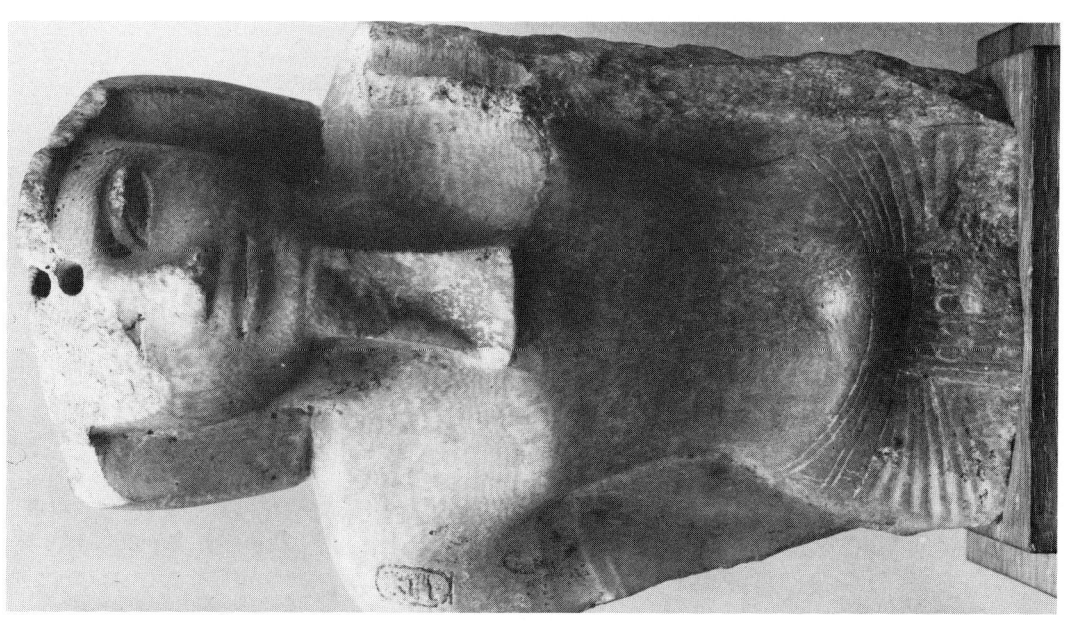

a.

Plate VIII

244

Plate IX

b.

a.

Plate X

Plate XI

b.

a.

247

Plate XII

248

Plate XIII

a.

b.

THE MORTUARY TEMPLE OF SETI I AT GURNA:
EXCAVATION AND RESTORATION

Rainer Stadelmann

The long reign of Ramesses II completely dominates the second half of the New Empire, and his tremendous building activity impressed his name on nearly every monument in the valley of the Nile.[1] Consequently, the two centuries of the 19th and 20th Dynasties are called the Ramesside Period, and with the gorgeous exhibition of his work and records in our time, he was indisputably bestowed with the epithet, "the Great." The existence of his inscriptions and royal titulary in every place and even on monuments of his predecessors has nearly overshadowed the glory and the greatness of his noble father, Seti I, second king and virtual founder of the 19th Dynasty. Yet, it was Seti I who laid the foundations for the recovery of Egypt after the decline of the Amarna Period. Seti was the first king after Akhenaton to follow his father, Ramesses I, in the traditional and legal father-son succession to the throne, inaugurating a renaissance of kingship, as his name, "Repeating the Births" declares. The renaissance was not only in politics and religion, but also a true renaissance in architecture and art. The architecture of the Post-Amarna Period in Thebes is confined to the construction of pylons for the processional roads between Karnak and Luxor on the east side and Karnak and the mortuary temples on the west side, where the temple of Haremhab had not less than three brick pylons in front of the temple house proper, which is a mere remake of the temples of the Mid-Eighteenth Dynasty. The art of this period, including the short reign of Ramesses I, is nothing but beautiful and expressive, yet mellow, and finally without further possible development.

With the beginning of the reign of Seti I, there occurred a concerted return to the traditions of the 18th Dynasty, the time of Thothmosis II to Amenophis III. The art displays a serene beauty, elegance, and perfection; the relief sculpture returns to purity of line, even to a certain academic coolness which deliberately denies the exaggeration and motion of the immediately previous period. The devotion of the king, clearly shown in the position of his body slightly bent forward in a sign of reverence toward the gods, and the victorious battle scenes against the enemies of Egypt in the North, East, and West are now the main subjects; they cover the walls of the gigantic pylons, the temple walls, and the columns of the hypostyle hall.

When Seti[2] came to the throne, the cults and temples, abandoned during the reign of Akhenaton, had already been reinstated, but many of the sanctuaries were still devastated, the pictures of the gods mutilated, and the holy names hacked out. Seti started an extensive restoration programme, recutting the figures and rewriting the inscriptions. His building activity was extraordinary. I will only mention the centers of Heliopolis/Memphis, Abydos, and Thebes. In Abydos, Seti came out with the idea of constructing a mortuary temple for all the gods of Egypt at the most holy place near the tomb of Osiris. But it was at Thebes where he undertook the most ambitious building programme with the gigantic hypostyle hall at Karnak (later regarded as a wonder of the world), the magnificent royal tomb, and his own mortuary temple in Western Thebes.

---

1. Rainer Stadelmann, "Die lange Regierung Ramesses' II.," in *Mitteilungen des Deutschen Archäologischen Instituts Kairo (MDAIK)* 37, 1981, 457-463.

2. On Seti I, see *Lexikon der Ägyptologie* V 911-917.

This mortuary temple is situated in the northern part of the Theban necropolis, on the ridge of the desert and just opposite the temples of Karnak, on the direct processional road which led from the Temple of Amun in Karnak to the Valley of Deir el-Bahari (Fig. 1). Besides the mortuary temples of Mentuhotpe and Hatschepsut at Deir el-Bahari, the Ramesseum, and the temple of Ramesses III at Medinet Habu, it is the best preserved temple in Western Thebes. It is the only one with the temple house proper still standing, displaying on its walls, reliefs and inscriptions which are missing in other mortuary temples. The elegant colonnade of its facade is formed of ten lotiform columns, strongly reminiscent of those of the 18th Dynasty (Pl. 1). The nearly complete roofs are still in place after an earlier restoration done by Barsanti on behalf of the Antiquities Department in 1910 to 1913. Nevertheless, this temple had been more or less neglected in previous research, which is as follows: the French Expedition designed a plan and reconstructed the facade in classical style, considering the temple as a royal palace; Wilkinson and Lepsius, later, in the middle of the last century depicted the still standing houses of the Late Roman and Coptic Periods, as well as sphinxes and parts of the pylons, the magazines, and the enclosure wall, which had all disappeared at the beginning of our century, when the temple court was covered with high, growing briar and camel thorn (Pl. 2a).

The outstanding state of preservation of the temple house and the importance of the whole precinct in the development of temple architecture and worship were the main reasons why the German Institute of Archaeology in 1970 came to choose this mortuary temple for excavation, study, and publication. After a short survey, excavation started in 1971 and has continued for ten seasons which combined digging, recording, and restoring. Several preliminary excavation reports,[3] one volume of relief and inscriptions,[4] and a second volume on the ceramics and the finds[5] have appeared; a third volume about the excavation and the architecture is in preparation.[6]

The splendid facade of the mortuary temple of Seti with its three main gates displays better than any other temple the classical tri-partite division of the well developed pattern of Theban funerary temples (Fig. 2 and Pl. 1). A building inscription on the architrave declares that Ramesses II found the temple of Seti after the death of his father in an unfinished state, and he decided to complete the work,[7] an explicit statement against all theories of coregency based on supposed contemporary building activity of Seti and Ramesses in the Gurna temple.

On both sides of the main portal, we find the specific name of the temple: *Hwt-ntr Akh-Seti-mrj-n-Ptah* or *Akh-Seti-mrj-n-Jmn m pr-Jmn*, "The Temple, Glorious is Seti Merenptah or Seti Merienamun in the House of Amun." It is the same name which designates the Great Hypostyle Hall of the Temple of Amun in Karnak. There is, in addition to or by

3. Rainer Stadelmann, "Der Tempel Sethos' I. in Gurna," in *MDAIK* 28, 1972, 293 ff.; *MDAIK* 33, 1977, 125 ff.; *MDAIK* 38, 1982, 395 ff.

4. Jürgen Osing, *Der Tempel Sethos' I. in Gurna, Die Reliefs und Inschriften*, Bd. 1. *Archäologisches Veröffentlichungen, Deutsches Archäologisches Institut*, Bd. 20, Mainz 1977.

5. Karol Mysliwiec, *Der Tempel Sethos' I. in Gurna. Die Funde. Archäologische Veröffentlichungen. Deutsches Archäologisches Institut*, Bd. 57, Mainz 1987.

6. Rainer Stadelmann, *Der Tempel Sethos' I. in Gurna. Architektur und Deutung. Archäologisches Veröffentlichungen. Deutsches Archäologisches Institut*, Bd. 30, Mainz 1988.

7. *KRI* II 534-637.

virtue of this designation, an actual relation between these two temples, which is well attested during the Feast of the Valley.

Like all Egyptian temples, the mortuary temple of Seti had a high enclosure wall made of sun-dried bricks which were approximately 3.15 meters thick (6 Egyptian cubits). Parts of it, or at least the foundations, we unearthed in the north, west, and east. It was completely covered by heaps of modern excavation debris. When searching for the northwest corner of this enclosure wall, we realized that this corner was built as a massive tower 5 x 5 ms (10 Egyptian cubits). Following the foundations of the wall westwards and northwards, we found a sequence of towers or buttresses at intervals of approximately 17, 30 ms or 33 Egyptian cubits (Pl. 2b). No other of the older mortuary temples of the 18th Dynasty had this kind of enclosure wall, which, therefore, was one of the new features that Seti introduced in Thebes. Otherwise, this kind of enclosure wall is not unknown in religious architecture: in the Early Dynastic Period, temples and funerary palaces of the kings were surrounded by paneled enclosure walls constructed of sun-dried bricks; in the 3rd Dynasty, Djoser had, for the first time, assigned this typical brick construction to stone architecture in his magnificent funeral monument in Sakkara. Paneled walls maintain a certain religious significance in the funerary architecture until the temples of Hatschepsut at Deir el-Bahari, but it is only in the monument of Seti I in Gurna that a funerary temple is enclosed by a paneled wall, reflecting the idea of a fortress of the gods. We encounter here, and further in the structure of the temple, a conscious renaissance of traditional features revived from Old Kingdom funerary architecture to guarantee the king's afterlife.

Excavated brickwork is quickly endangered by weather and environment and must be protected at once either by covering it again with debris or by building over it again. We considered the remains of the structures found in the temple area too important to be covered again and decided, therefore, to reconstruct them to a certain height in order to present a general impression of the funerary monument (Pl. 3). The ancient bricks were covered with a handsome layer of mud mortar over which we started the reconstruction with the same sun-dried bricks as the ancient Egyptians, but we used a much smaller size brick in order to distinguish ancient bricks from new ones. Bricks and mortar were mainly produced from our own excavation debris. This debris consisted of inundation mud mixed with the brick material of the ancient dwellings which were still standing in the temple courts until the last century. Of course, we did not rebuild the massive walls of the Ramesside Period but used a kind of frame construction, refilling the interior of the wall with the debris of the old enclosure. But we kept the original inclination of the walls, which we had observed on higher standing parts. At present, the northern wall and a great part of the western wall are completed and can already be used as a tourist walk-a-round for taking photographs. We reconstructed two of the towers as magazines for the abundant mass of ceramics and small finds, the last tower (the northeast) as a guard house beside the gate which serves as the modern entrance.

The first pylon was built of bricks, as all pylons in Western Thebes before the time of Ramesses II, whereas the gate was constructed of limestone and sandstone. It completely collapsed, probably during an earthquake - perhaps the same earthquake which ruined the Ramesseum and so many temples in Thebes - because we found blocks of the gateway dispersed over a large area. Modern houses nearly encircle the picturesque ruins. During the excavation season in the spring of 1987, we removed, with the help of the well trained gang of stone workers from Deir el-Bahari under Reis Ali, the enormous architraves and discovered some new sculpted blocks from the gate in the mounds of debris. In the future the limestone walls of the gate will be strengthened. As for the decorated blocks and architraves, we plan to put them on an embankment in front of the gate, thereby avoiding a too artificial reconstruction and guarding the picturesque view of the gate and the village behind.

A processional road linked the First and Second Pylon. This dromos was paved with sandstone slabs, some of which were still in place. In Roman times the Second Pylon was reused as an entrance to the little village which had been established between the walls of the first court. One of the slabs of the pavement proved to be a stela of a great general, Heqamaatrenakht, who came and visited Thebes during the reign of Ramesses V together with all his family to adore the gods of our temple.

The first court of a Ramesside funerary temple may be called the Court of the King. Colossal statues of the king dominated the courts of the Ramesseum and Medinet Habu; in Seti's temple court, two giant sphinxes are lying beside the entrance to the court. The south side of the courts of the Ramesseum and Medinet Habu temples was faced by royal cult-palaces. When we began our excavation, we were especially eager to know whether there was also a palace in Seti's temple area. Our expectations were not high regarding the very disturbed ground used for a long time as garden land by the villagers. But to our great delight, walls, foundations, and even architectural structures appeared rather undisturbed under a layer of large houses from the Ptolemaic and Roman periods (Pl. 4a).

From these houses only some traces of walls and the caves or cellars full of ceramics remained, confronting us with the surprising fact that the latest ceramics of the 4th and 5th centuries A.D. were collected in the deepest layers (Pl. 4b). These houses over the palace area were, as I said, rather large buildings of wealthy people who had a great quantity of wine jars in their cellars and even imported, nicely polished, Greek ceramic and glass fragments, some of which we found elsewhere.

Better preserved were the foundations of the palace, completely built in sun-dried bricks, except the facade which was of limestone. The structure and the dimensions are exactly the same as those of the palace of the Ramesseum and the first palace of Medinet Habu, from which we can study Hölscher's reconstruction of the twelve-columned hall. The facade and the portico of Seti's palace were still free-standing, whereas in the later temples, it was bounded by the two pylons of the temple (Fig. 2). The entrances are on both sides of the window of appearance, under which the wall decoration, in fine relief, shows offering bearers who are clearly foreigners, according to their clothes. The discovery of a palace within the temple precinct of Seti, which proves by its measurements to be a model palace and the standard prototype of all the later temple palaces, indicates and underlines strongly that these palaces were never meant as residential palaces. They were only ritual temple palaces for the dead king,[8] whose statue may have been placed on the throne in front of the window of appearances. Indeed, we found no trace of a royal statue, probably because it was fashioned in wood, since it had to be portable and thus has perished. Yet, we found in the Ptolemaic layers a marvelous limestone head of Queen Tuja,[9] wife of Seti I and mother of Ramesses II, sadly reused as a door socket (Pl. 9).

Another surprise was awaiting us on the north side of this court. At first, there seemed to be no buildings except a plain wall closing the court with a gateway opening into the courts of the magazines. While cleaning these courts, we found two limestone slabs, badly eroded, which at first looked like door sills. After a deeper excavation, they appeared to be two sphinxes (Pl. 5a). Their heads are lost, and their bodies were never smoothed. Seti may have ordered them just before his death, which explains why they remained unfinished and had not even been placed symmetrically. They stood in front of a side entrance and on

---

8. Stadelmann,"Tempelpalast und Erscheinungsfenster in den thebanischen Totentempeln," in *MDAIK* 29, 1973, 221 ff.

9. Hourig Sourouzian, "Une tête de la reine Touy à Gurna," in *MDAIK* 37, 1981, 445 ff.

both sides of a passage leading to the northern gate of the enclosure wall. They may well have been two of the many sphinxes which Lepsius saw standing in the court with their heads still preserved and are perhaps also those reported by Wilkinson. The passage was paved with bricks and was still in use in later periods. We found traces of successive repairs in brick, and we restored again the ancient pavement with modern bricks (Pl. 5b). Shops and factories for the production of alabaster dishes and installations for copper smelting, well known from reliefs of the Old Kingdom onwards but observed here for the first time archaeologically,* were grouped on both sides of the passage, perhaps an early prototype of the modern alabaster factories of our day.

Seti's mortuary temple is, likewise, the first in Thebes to have its own complex of magazines planned with the construction of the temple on its northern side (Fig. 2). The previous mortuary temples of the 18th Dynasty had, rather, received the deliveries directly from the central storehouse of the Temple of Amun, as we have no trace of magazines before Seti I. Unfortunately, our magazines were demolished and covered by later habitations (Pl. 6a). The last interesting evidence of the use of the Ramesside storage area vanished when Petrie, in a three-day excavation, removed all the remains of these magazines. Yet, from a later habitation in these magazines, comes a very worn, but still picturesque, model bed, some rare examples of which have been found earlier in Thebes. On it is depicted a lovely genre scene with the nude goddess Qadesh standing on a papyrus boat in the swamp. Beside her, we recognize two dancing Bes figures.

The use of fire in the magazines has burnt parts of the walls and baked the bricks. They have thus preserved the ancient brick stamps of Seti I (Pl. 6b). The fact that the magazines were built with bricks of Seti means that they were completed during his reign and not later by Ramesses II, as it was supposed before, according to Ramesses' inscriptions. This is an important indication concerning the sequence of construction and regarding the economy of mortuary temples in general in the Ramesside Period.

During the excavation of the magazines, we simultaneously protected the brick walls in the same way as described before. In a future restoration, we intend to reconstruct at least a part of the vaults of one of the magazines.

From the walls of the Second Court, the festival court, nothing remains. On the walls of the temple facades, we can recognize the badly mutilated figures of the bark-procession which passed through this court, namely, the bark of Amun, that of King Seti, and the deified queen, Ahmes Nefertari. Like no other temple in Thebes, that of Seti shows the clear tri-partite structure. To the south we find the actual funerary complex, to the north the sun court, and in the middle, occupying the main part, the sanctuary of Amun, the resting place of the Great God during his procession of the Beautiful Feast of the Valley.

In the southern part of the temple and in front of his own funerary complex, Seti incorporated a small mortuary temple for his father, Ramesses I, who had not completed a mortuary temple for himself during his short reign (Fig. 2). It comprises a small hypostyle hall, the decoration of which was only partly executed at the death of Seti and was completed during the reign of Ramesses II. Therefore, it is Ramesses II who acts as royal priest and who is crowned in front of the Theban Triad and in the presence of his father, Seti, who is depicted as a god. These scenes are often referred to as evidence for a coregency between Seti and Ramesses. In reality, they are purely religious and part of the ritual of a temple coronation. The main sanctuary of this small temple is a large bark sanctuary serving also as the mortuary chapel of Ramesses I; it has a magnificent, large,

---

* Editor's note, see also Edgar Pusch, "Recent Work at Northern Piramesse," pp. 197, for another example of copper smelting.

double false door depicting Ramesses I as Osiris. This false door has been recently restored by the skillful restorer of the EAO, who are cooperating with us and supporting our efforts in the salvage of the endangered parts of the temple house.

The fact that Seti had planned this mortuary chapel for his father from the beginning is proved by a set of foundation deposits for Ramesses I. They were placed near those of Seti and contained, besides vessels and model offerings, beautiful model bricks of limestone with the name of Ramesses I.

The funerary apartments of Seti I suffered badly during he destruction of the southwest part of the temple in the late Ramesside Period. Only the antechamber is preserved. The visible foundations of three rooms differ from the plan of the royal mortuary cult rooms, which we find, for example, better preserved in Medinet Habu; however, the mortuary cult rooms of the Ramesseum may not have been so different from those of Seti.

A rich set of foundation deposits had been put in a pit near the southwest corner (Pl. 7a-d). They underline the importance of the mortuary cult rooms within the temple. Originally, they were placed on a large inscribed fayence plate surrounded by a great number of funerary vessels. Four nicely coloured name stones with the names of Seti, small cartouches of fayence, and model tools of copper are the main objects, apart from a large number of model offerings in fayence with thick gold covers. It is foreseen that these objects will one day be exhibited in the Luxor Museum.

The northern part of the temple included a large open court consecrated to the cult of the sun god. In the middle of the court, stands the offering altar. Niches in the walls around the court served as naoi for royal statues which shared the offerings and the cult depicted on the walls.

The procession of the barks on the facade leads to the central gate of the temple and, through it, into a splendid hypostyle hall with six columns. On the walls offering scenes from the Feast of the Valley alternate with representations of introduction to the gods, temple coronation, and rituals of consecration of offerings.

Only parts of the wall relief were finished during the reign of Seti; it was completed by his son Ramesses. The fine, beautiful, and elegant, but somewhat academic relief of Seti (Pl. 8) contrasts with the hasty style of Ramesses' sunken relief (Pl. 9).

For our recording and photographing, we preferred artificial light in the evenings as it gives a much better contrast. Sometimes, the light attracted unbidden guests like the snake which intrigued and worried tremendously our photographic staff. Photogrammetry was mainly applied for a complete and uninterrupted presentation of a whole wall.

In several inscriptions the hypostyle hall is called *pr-wrw*, which may mean sanctuary but reminds one also of the Old Kingdom *pr-wrw* reception hall of the royal pyramid temples, a function which fits well with the hypostyle hall. On both sides of the hall, we find three chapels. Two of them are connecting rooms to the northern and southern wings of the temple.

Chapels II and III are consecrated to the royal bark and the deified king, who receives offerings, while his mortuary temple, personified as a goddess, stands behind him. The most interesting scenes, however, are found in Chapel V, which has been completely misunderstood until now. On the north wall, we recognize the king and Amun standing side by side and being purified or baptized by the gods Thot and Horus. By this joint baptism, the god is assimilated to the king, who becomes the specific Amun of the temple,

"Glorious is Seti." As divine king, he is depicted on the west wall receiving the offerings consecrated by the *Jun-mutef* priest; on the east wall, the king becomes Amun-Min-Kamutef, the regenerative manifestation of Amun, standing in front of the offering list.

Reborn and purified, the king mounts some steps into a transverse corridor, where he is received and suckled by the goddesses, Mut and Hathor. Here again, we have parallels in Old Kingdom pyramid temples (the temples of Sahure and Neuserre) and also from the temple of Seti at Abydos. The corridor leads to five chapels, as in the pyramid temples. The southern belongs to Ptah and the northern to Osiris, whereas the three central chapels are those of the Theban Triad. The central chapel is the bark sanctuary of Amun; the walls are decorated with the holy bark of Amun. The socle which is standing in this room belonged, perhaps, to one of the smaller chapels, as it is not decorated as is the one we see in the relief on the wall. After the offerings to the bark, the shrine was opened and the statue of the god brought into the next room, the roof of which is supported by four pillars. These pillars are decorated with offering scenes showing the four main manifestations of Amun: Amun-Re, and Amun-Min-Kamutef, Amun-Reharachte, Atum and Osiris. Four chapels, two in the south and two in the north, can be assigned to these manifestations. On the wall of the northwestern chapel, we recognize a rare representation of the Osiris myth. The dead Osiris is lying on a bed, Isis and the Nephthis as mourners lament on both sides, while Isis as a bird, sitting on Osiris, receives from the dead Osiris her son, Horus.

A large false door was inserted in the back wall of the temple. Through this door the dead king, coming from his tomb in the remote valley behind the mountains, was able to enter his temple. Also, the god Amun may be thought to pass through this gate in the evening to enter the mountains of the west on his nocturnal journey through the netherworld.

A few more tasks to be accomplished by our mission are left for future years. The sacred lake with its small Osiride island to the south of the temple must be restored. The excavation of the gate of the First Pylon has to be completed, and a final restoration of this gate will be undertaken.

The brick walls of the palace are, for the moment, well protected but will be built up to the higher level of the brick walls of the courts. In the magazine area, we intend to rebuild parts of the well preserved tracts and indicate, at least in one or two of the long magazines, the vaulted roofing.

PLATES

Plate 1

Plate 2

a.

b.

Plate 3

Plate 4

a.

b.

Plate 5

a.

b.

Plate 6

a.

b.

Plate 7

a.

b.

c.

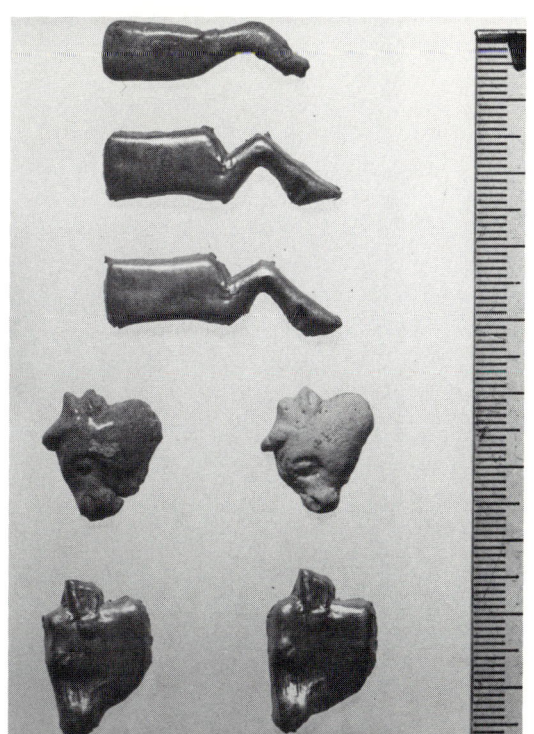

d.

Plate 8

b.

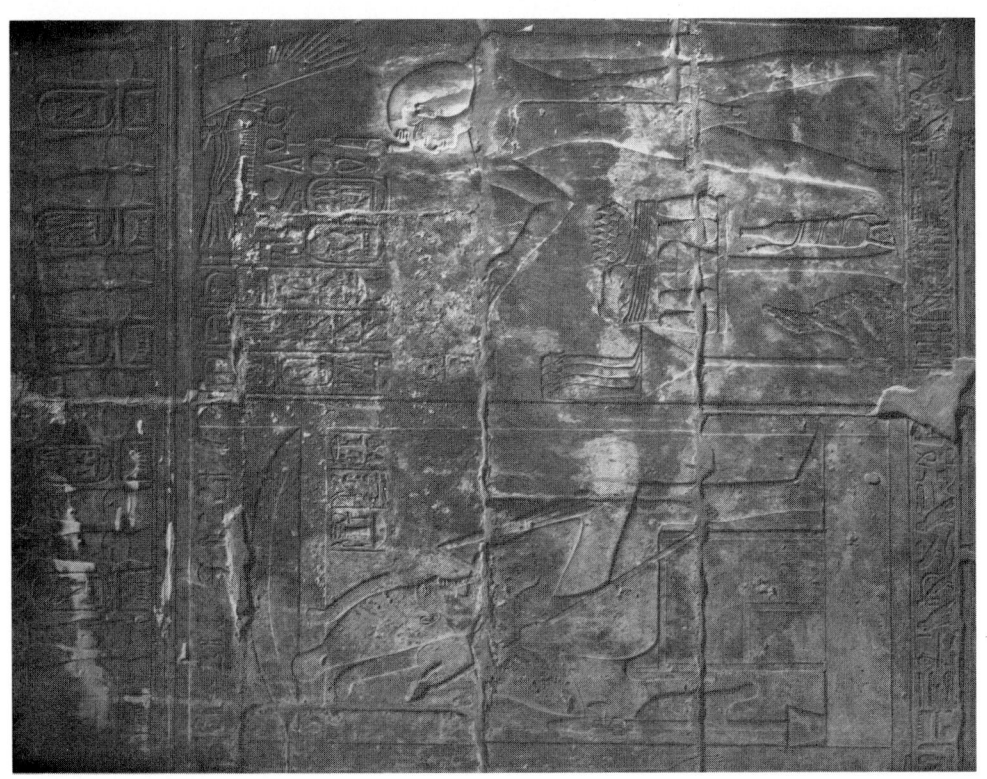

a.

Plate 9

Figure 1

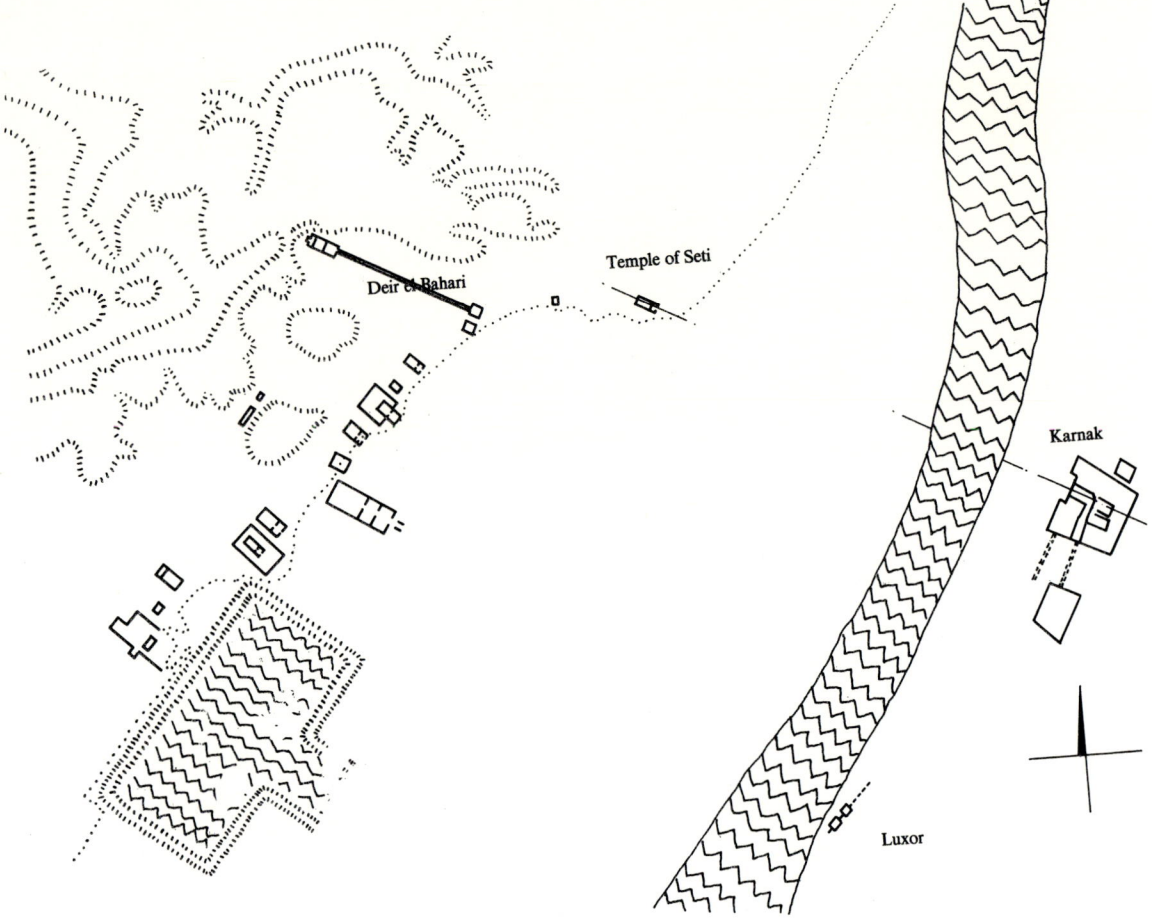

Deir el Bahari

Temple of Seti

Karnak

Luxor

Figure 2

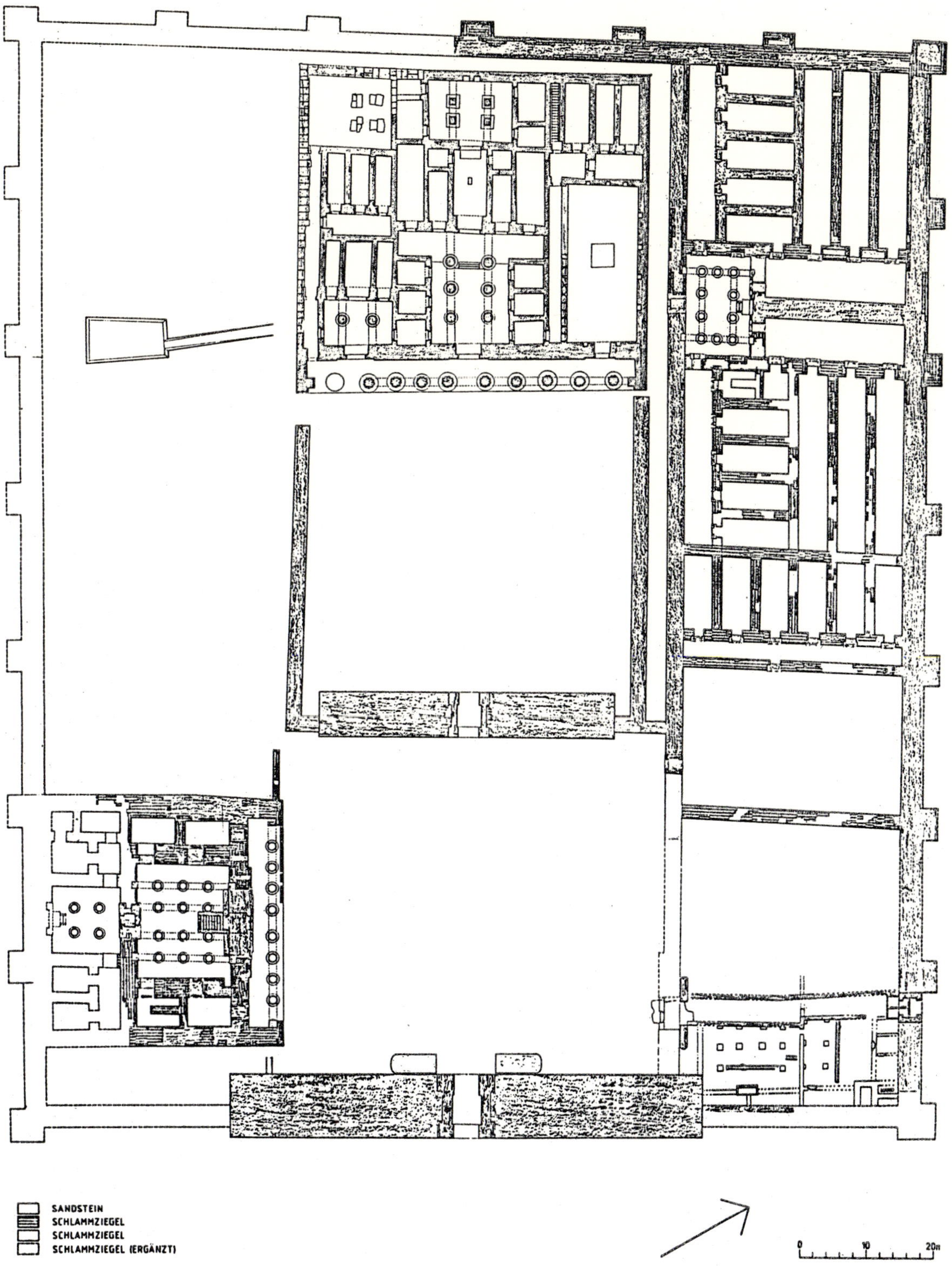

SANDSTEIN
SCHLAMMZIEGEL
SCHLAMMZIEGEL
SCHLAMMZIEGEL (ERGÄNZT)

0   10   20m